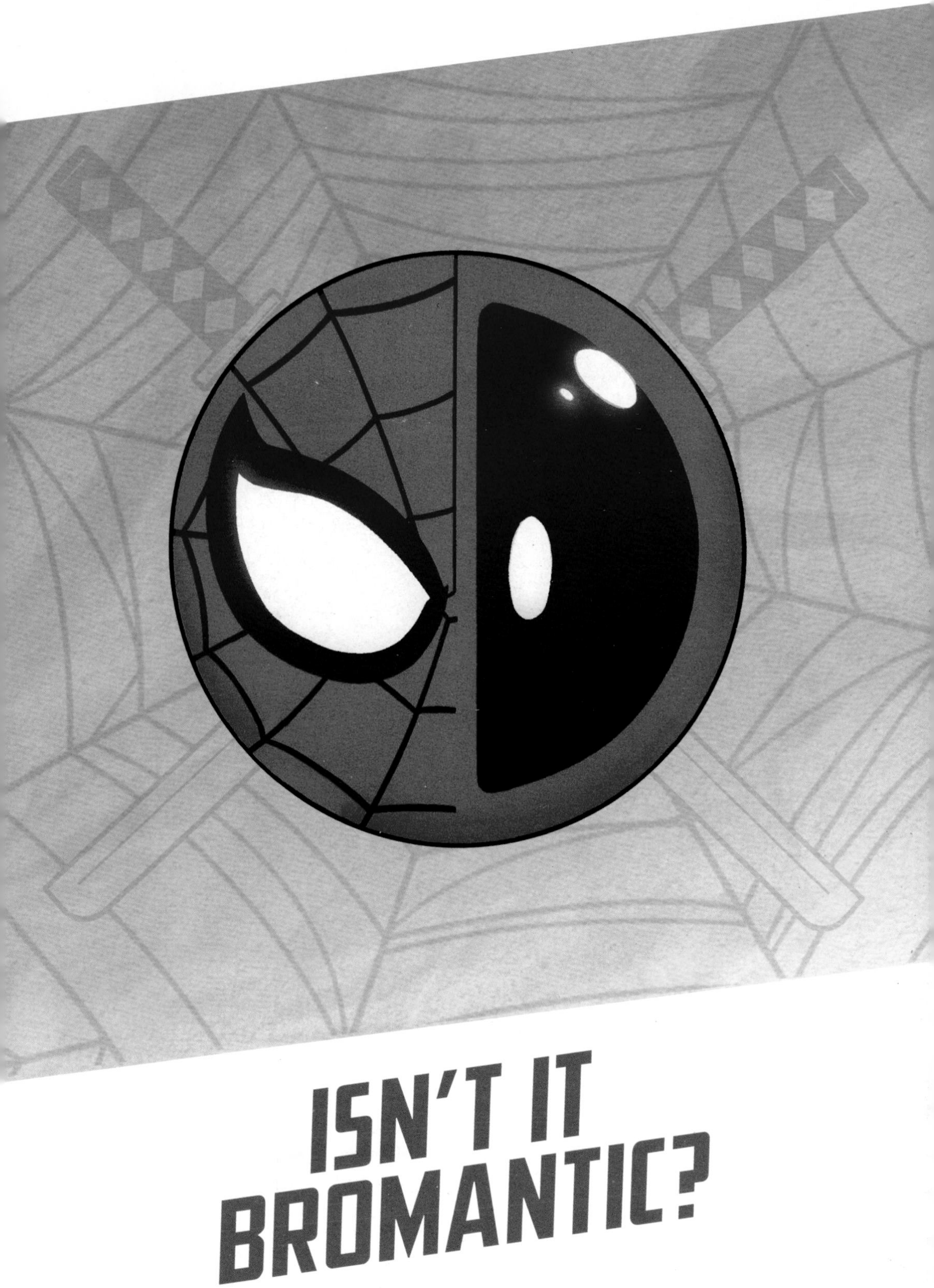

ISN'T IT BROMANTIC?

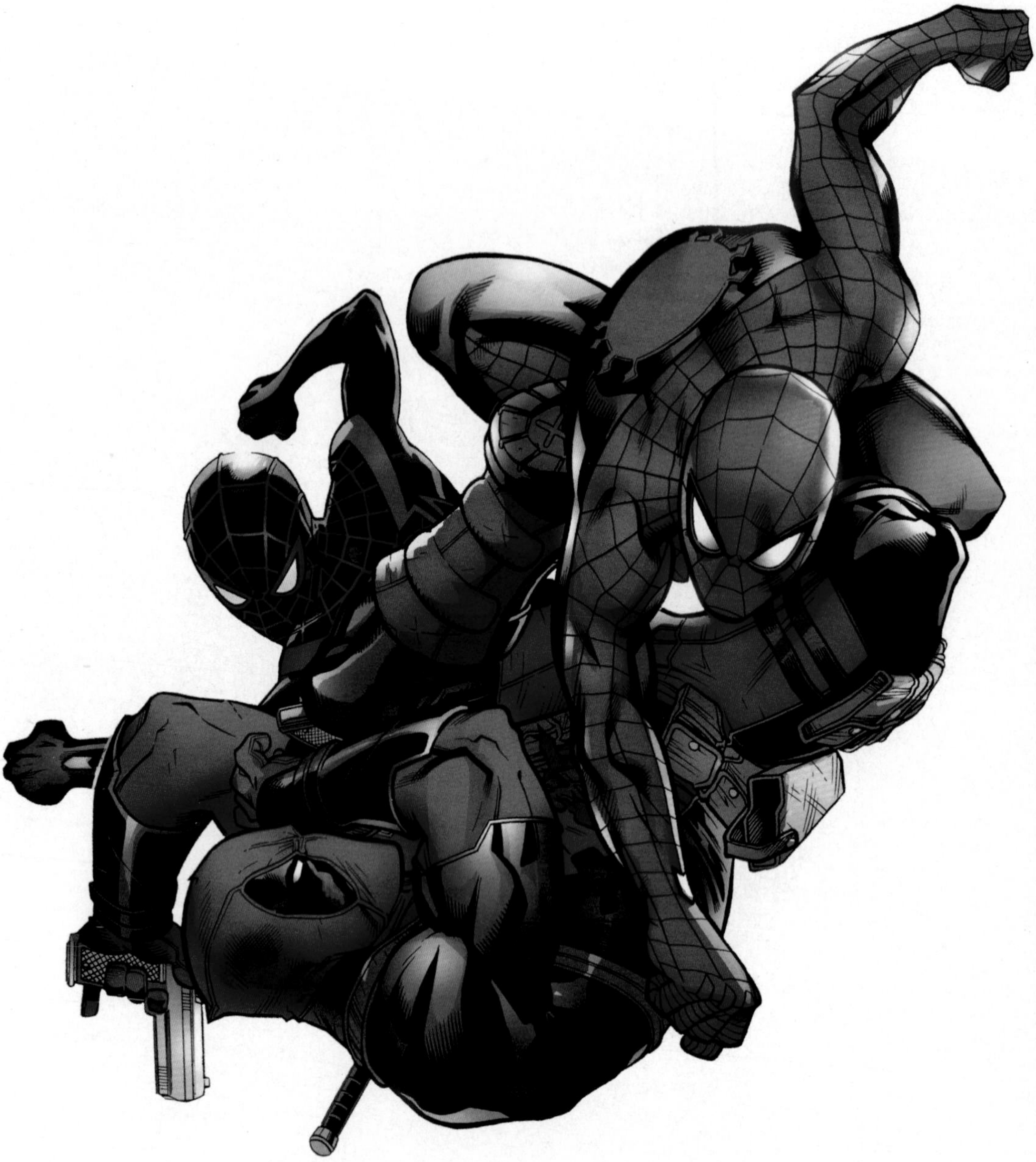

Collection Editor **JENNIFER GRÜNWALD**
Associate Editor **SARAH BRUNSTAD**
Editor, Special Projects **MARK D. BEAZLEY**
VP, Production & Special Projects **JEFF YOUNGQUIST**
SVP Print, Sales & Marketing **DAVID GABRIEL**
Book Designer **ADAM DEL RE**

Editor In Chief **AXEL ALONSO**
Chief Creative Officer **JOE QUESADA**
Publisher **DAN BUCKLEY**
Executive Producer **ALAN FINE**

SPIDER-MAN CREATED BY
STAN LEE & **STEVE DITKO**

DEADPOOL CREATED BY
ROB LIEFELD & **FABIAN NICIEZA**

SPIDER-MAN/DEADPOOL VOL. 1: ISN'T IT BROMANTIC. Contains material originally published in magazine form as SPIDER-MAN/DEADPOOL #1-5 and #8. First printing 2016. ISBN# 978-0-7851-9786-7. Published by MARVEL WORLDWIDE, INC., a subsidiary of MARVEL ENTERTAINMENT, LLC. OFFICE OF PUBLICATION: 135 West 50th Street, New York, NY 10020. **Printed in Canada.** ALAN FINE, President, Marvel Entertainment; DAN BUCKLEY, President, TV, Publishing & Brand Management; JOE QUESADA, Chief Creative Officer; TOM BREVOORT, SVP of Publishing; DAVID BOGART, SVP of Business Affairs & Operations, Publishing & Partnership; C.B. CEBULSKI, VP of Brand Management & Development, Asia; DAVID GABRIEL, SVP of Sales & Marketing, Publishing; JEFF YOUNGQUIST, VP of Production & Special Projects; DAN CARR, Executive Director of Publishing Technology; ALEX MORALES, Director of Publishing Operations; SUSAN CRESPI, Production Manager; STAN LEE, Chairman Emeritus. For information regarding advertising in Marvel Comics or on Marvel.com, please contact Vit DeBellis, Integrated Sales Manager, at vdebellis@marvel.com. For Marvel subscription inquiries, please call 888-511-5480. **Manufactured between 6/17/2016 and 7/25/2016 by SOLISCO PRINTERS, SCOTT, QC, CANADA.**

10 9 8 7 6 5 4 3 2 1

MARVEL COMICS
BEGRUDGINGLY PRESENTS...

PETER PARKER WAS BITTEN BY AN IRRADIATED SPIDER, GRANTING HIM AMAZING ABILITIES, INCLUDING THE PROPORTIONAL SPEED, STRENGTH AND AGILITY OF A SPIDER, AS WELL AS ADHESIVE FINGERTIPS AND TOES. AFTER LEARNING THAT WITH GREAT POWER, THERE MUST ALSO COME GREAT RESPONSIBILITY, HE BECAME THE WORLD'S GREATEST SUPER HERO! HE'S...

THE WORLD'S GREATEST SUPER HERO!
The AMAZING SPIDER-MAN

AVENGER...ASSASSIN...SUPERSTAR! WADE WILSON WAS CHOSEN FOR A TOP-SECRET GOVERNMENT PROGRAM THAT GAVE HIM A HEALING FACTOR THAT ALLOWS HIM TO HEAL FROM ANY WOUND. DESPITE EARNING A SMALL FORTUNE AS A GUN FOR HIRE, WADE HAS BECOME THE WORLD'S MOST BELOVED HERO. AND IS THE STAR OF THE WORLD'S GREATEST COMICS MAGAZINE (NO MATTER WHAT THAT JERK IN THE WEBS MAY THINK). CALL HIM THE MERC WITH THE MOUTH...CALL HIM THE REGENERATIN' DEGENERATE...CALL HIM...

DEADPOOL

JOE KELLY
Writer

ED McGUINNESS
Penciler

MARK MORALES WITH **LIVESAY** (#8)
Inkers

JASON KEITH
Colorist

VC's JOE SABINO
Letterer

ED McGUINNESS WITH **MARK MORALES** (#1, #8), **MARTE GRACIA** (#1-2) & **JASON KEITH** (#3-5, #8)
Cover Art

DEVIN LEWIS
Assistant Editor

JORDAN D. WHITE & **NICK LOWE**
Editors

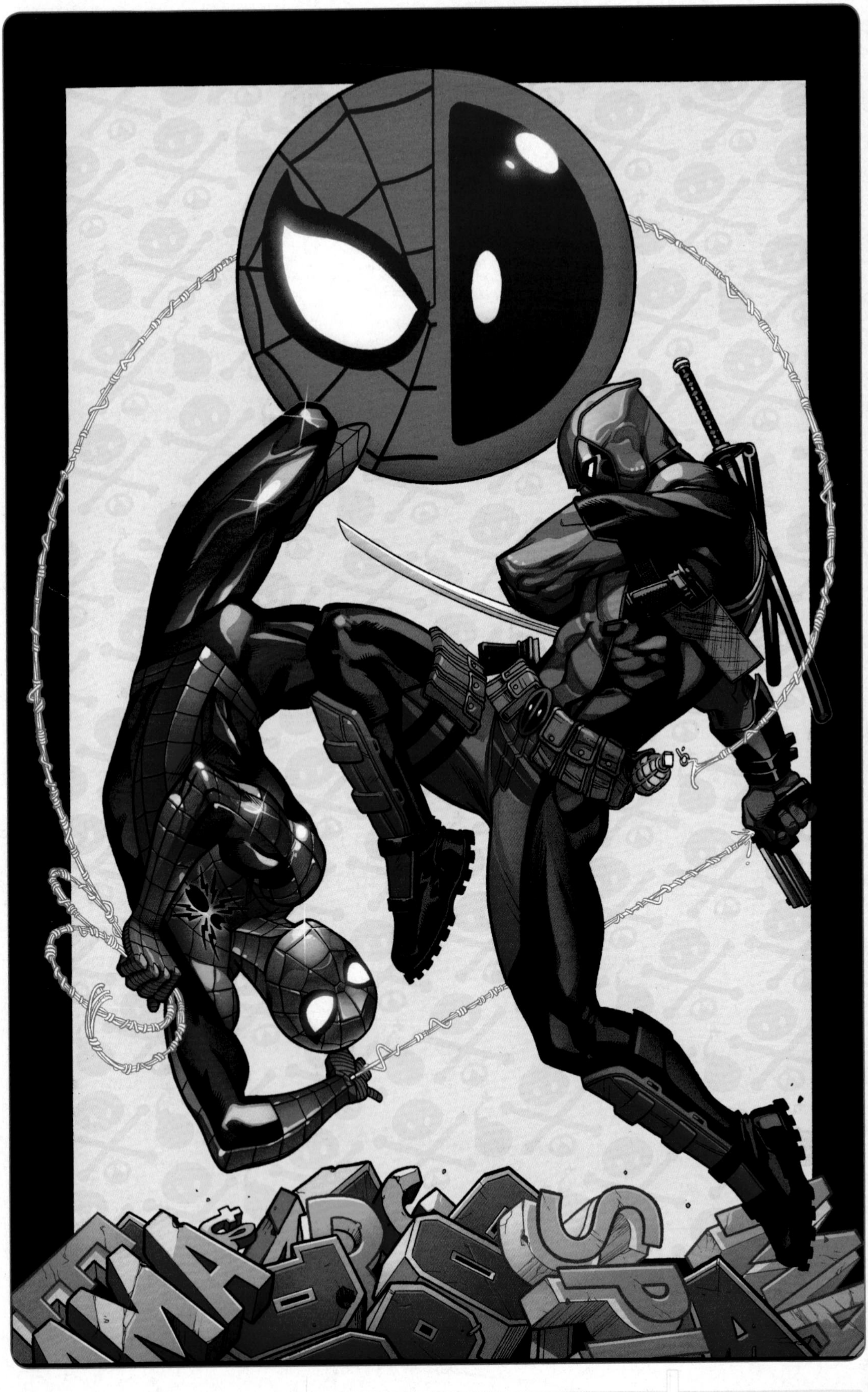

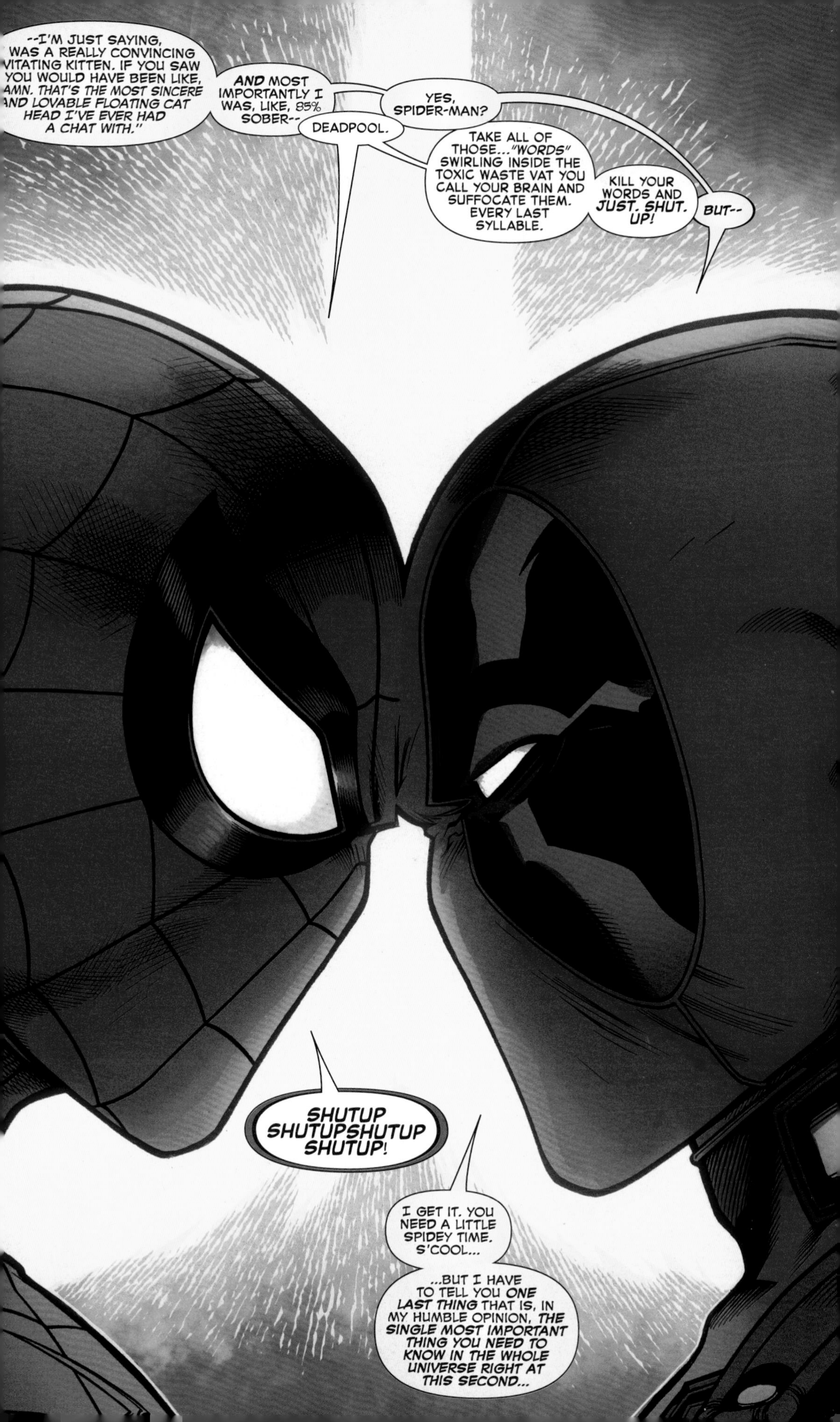
--I'M JUST SAYING, WAS A REALLY CONVINCING VITATING KITTEN. IF YOU SAW YOU WOULD HAVE BEEN LIKE, AMN. THAT'S THE MOST SINCERE AND LOVABLE FLOATING CAT HEAD I'VE EVER HAD A CHAT WITH."
AND MOST IMPORTANTLY I WAS, LIKE, 85% SOBER--
DEADPOOL.
YES, SPIDER-MAN?
TAKE ALL OF THOSE..."WORDS" SWIRLING INSIDE THE TOXIC WASTE VAT YOU CALL YOUR BRAIN AND SUFFOCATE THEM. EVERY LAST SYLLABLE.
KILL YOUR WORDS AND JUST. SHUT. UP!
BUT--
SHUTUP SHUTUPSHUTUP SHUTUP!
I GET IT. YOU NEED A LITTLE SPIDEY TIME. S'COOL...
...BUT I HAVE TO TELL YOU ONE LAST THING THAT IS, IN MY HUMBLE OPINION, THE SINGLE MOST IMPORTANT THING YOU NEED TO KNOW IN THE WHOLE UNIVERSE RIGHT AT THIS SECOND...

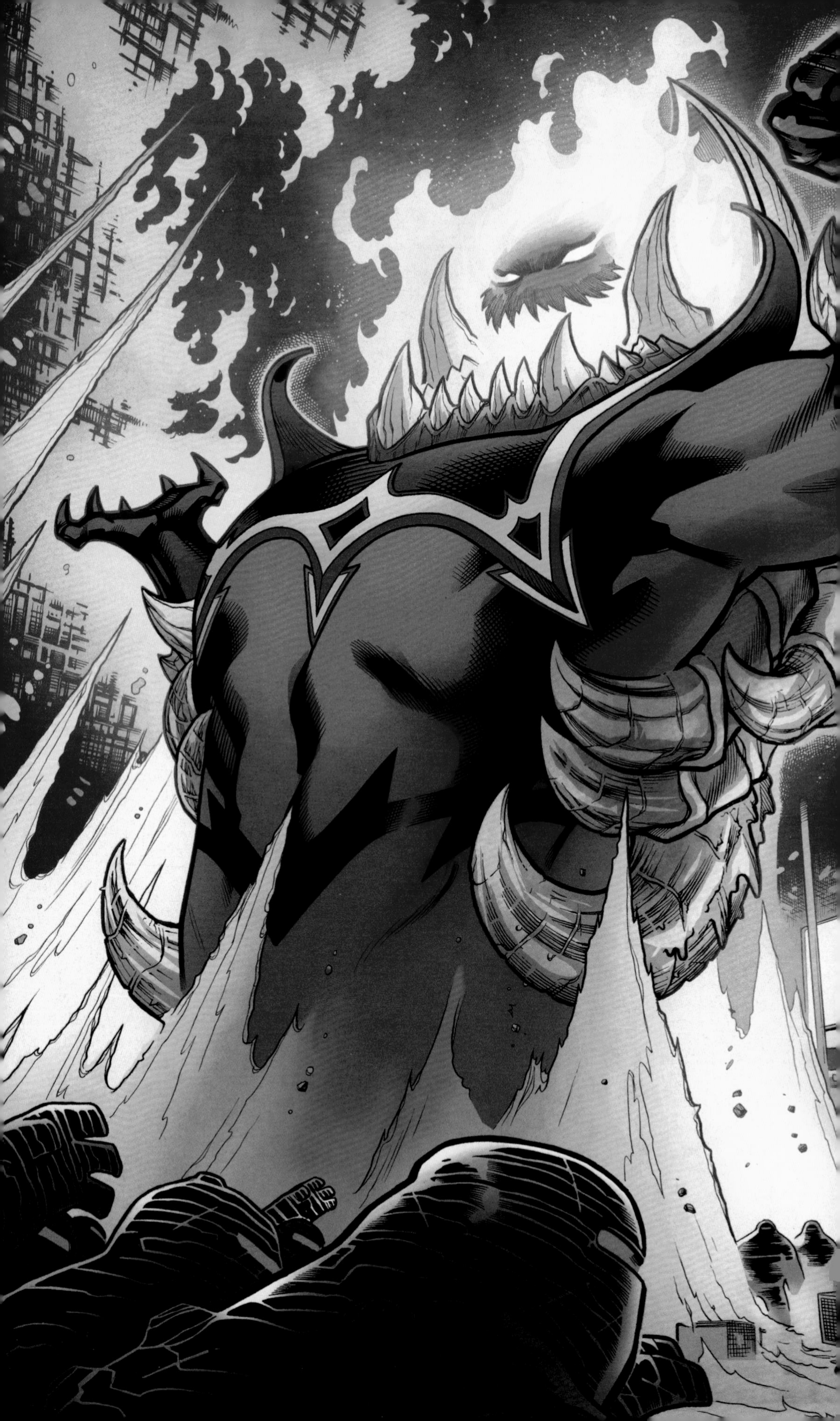

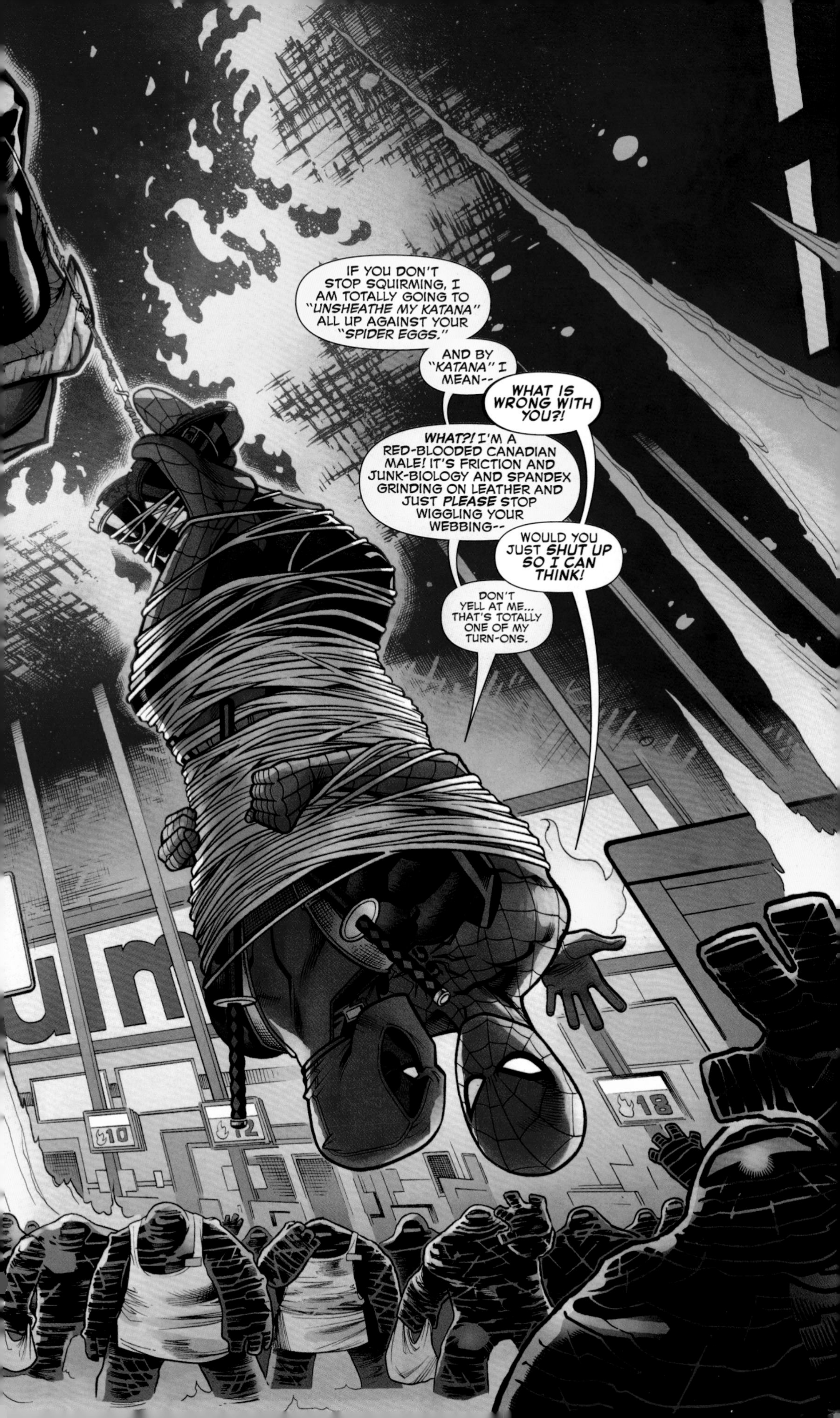
IF YOU DON'T STOP SQUIRMING, I AM TOTALLY GOING TO "UNSHEATHE MY KATANA" ALL UP AGAINST YOUR "SPIDER EGGS."
AND BY "KATANA" I MEAN--
WHAT IS WRONG WITH YOU?!
WHAT?! I'M A RED-BLOODED CANADIAN MALE! IT'S FRICTION AND JUNK-BIOLOGY AND SPANDEX GRINDING ON LEATHER AND JUST PLEASE STOP WIGGLING YOUR WEBBING--
WOULD YOU JUST SHUT UP SO I CAN THINK!
DON'T YELL AT ME... THAT'S TOTALLY ONE OF MY TURN-ONS.
10
12
18

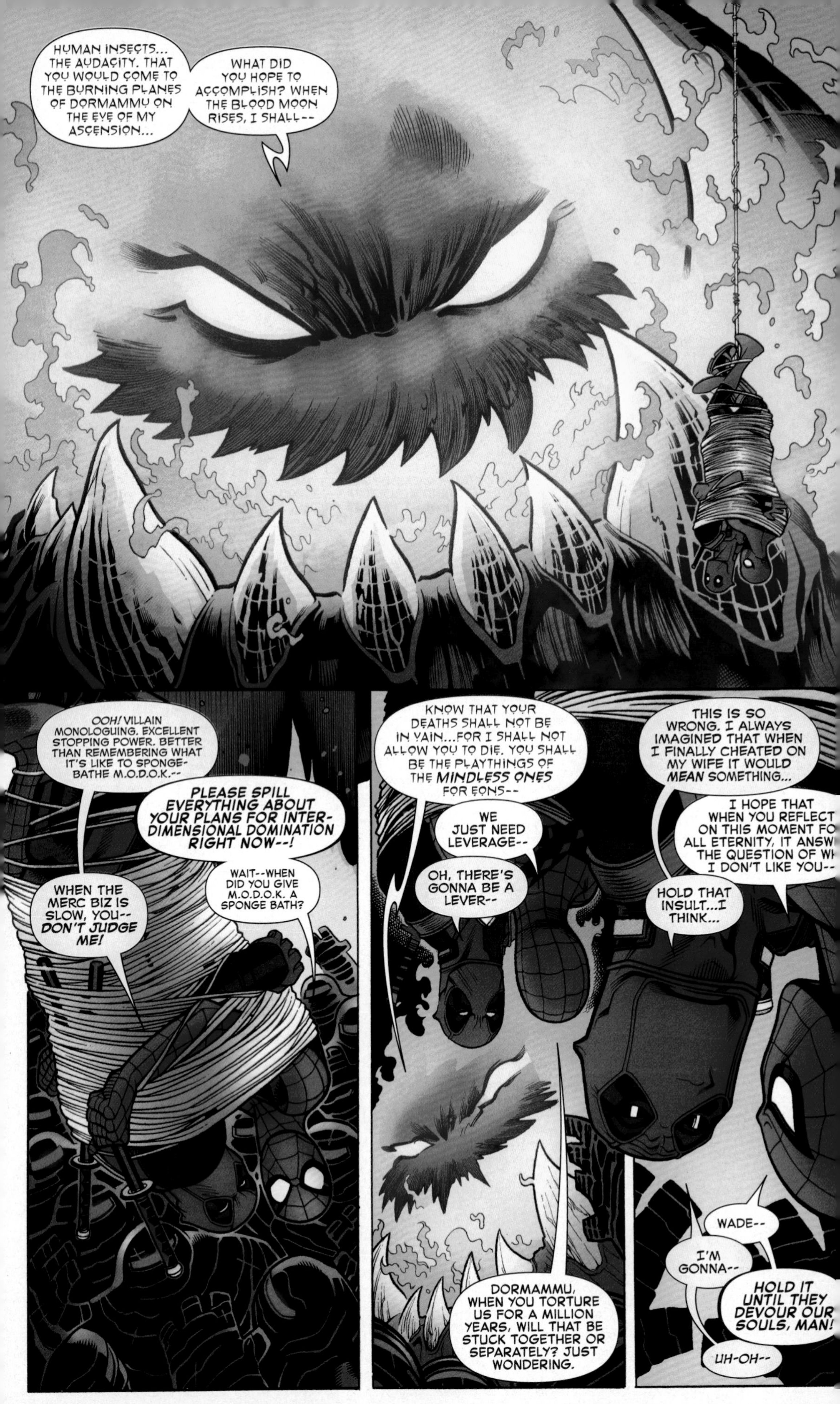
HUMAN INSECTS... THE AUDACITY. THAT YOU WOULD COME TO THE BURNING PLANES OF DORMAMMU ON THE EVE OF MY ASCENSION...
WHAT DID YOU HOPE TO ACCOMPLISH? WHEN THE BLOOD MOON RISES, I SHALL--
OOH! VILLAIN MONOLOGUING. EXCELLENT STOPPING POWER. BETTER THAN REMEMBERING WHAT IT'S LIKE TO SPONGE-BATHE M.O.D.O.K.--
PLEASE SPILL EVERYTHING ABOUT YOUR PLANS FOR INTER-DIMENSIONAL DOMINATION RIGHT NOW--!
WAIT--WHEN DID YOU GIVE M.O.D.O.K. A SPONGE BATH?
WHEN THE MERC BIZ IS SLOW, YOU-- DON'T JUDGE ME!
KNOW THAT YOUR DEATHS SHALL NOT BE IN VAIN...FOR I SHALL NOT ALLOW YOU TO DIE. YOU SHALL BE THE PLAYTHINGS OF THE MINDLESS ONES FOR EONS--
WE JUST NEED LEVERAGE--
OH, THERE'S GONNA BE A LEVER--
THIS IS SO WRONG. I ALWAYS IMAGINED THAT WHEN I FINALLY CHEATED ON MY WIFE IT WOULD MEAN SOMETHING...
I HOPE THAT WHEN YOU REFLECT ON THIS MOMENT FO ALL ETERNITY, IT ANSW THE QUESTION OF WH I DON'T LIKE YOU--
HOLD THAT INSULT...I THINK...
DORMAMMU, WHEN YOU TORTURE US FOR A MILLION YEARS, WILL THAT BE STUCK TOGETHER OR SEPARATELY? JUST WONDERING.
WADE--
I'M GONNA--
HOLD IT UNTIL THEY DEVOUR OUR SOULS, MAN!
UH-OH--

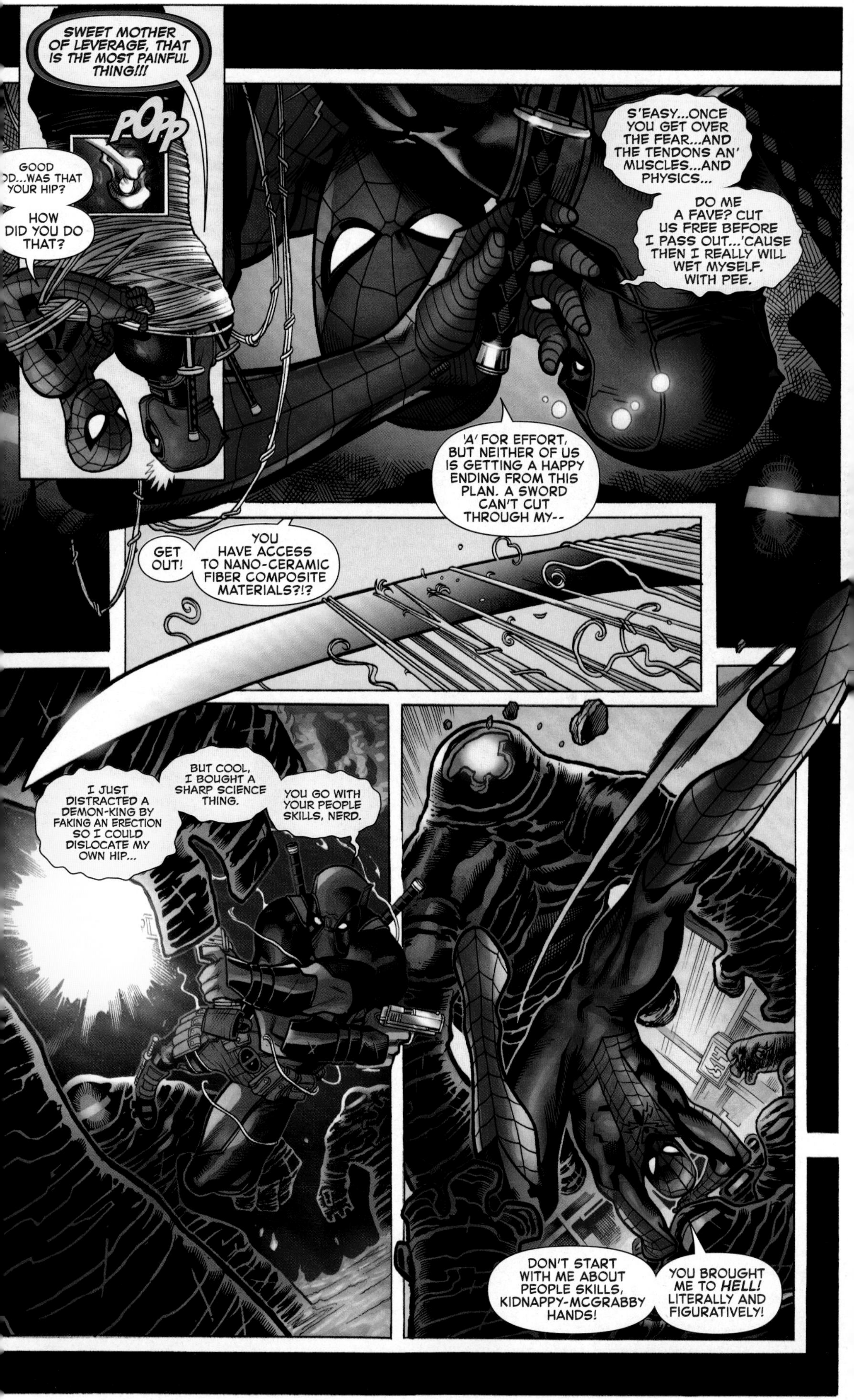
SWEET MOTHER OF LEVERAGE, THAT IS THE MOST PAINFUL THING!!!
POPP
GOOD ...D...WAS THAT YOUR HIP?
HOW DID YOU DO THAT?
S'EASY...ONCE YOU GET OVER THE FEAR...AND THE TENDONS AN' MUSCLES...AND PHYSICS...
DO ME A FAVE? CUT US FREE BEFORE I PASS OUT...'CAUSE THEN I REALLY WILL WET MYSELF. WITH PEE.
'A' FOR EFFORT, BUT NEITHER OF US IS GETTING A HAPPY ENDING FROM THIS PLAN. A SWORD CAN'T CUT THROUGH MY--
YOU HAVE ACCESS TO NANO-CERAMIC FIBER COMPOSITE MATERIALS?!?
GET OUT!
I JUST DISTRACTED A DEMON-KING BY FAKING AN ERECTION SO I COULD DISLOCATE MY OWN HIP...
BUT COOL, I BOUGHT A SHARP SCIENCE THING.
YOU GO WITH YOUR PEOPLE SKILLS, NERD.
DON'T START WITH ME ABOUT PEOPLE SKILLS, KIDNAPPY-McGRABBY HANDS!
YOU BROUGHT ME TO HELL! LITERALLY AND FIGURATIVELY!

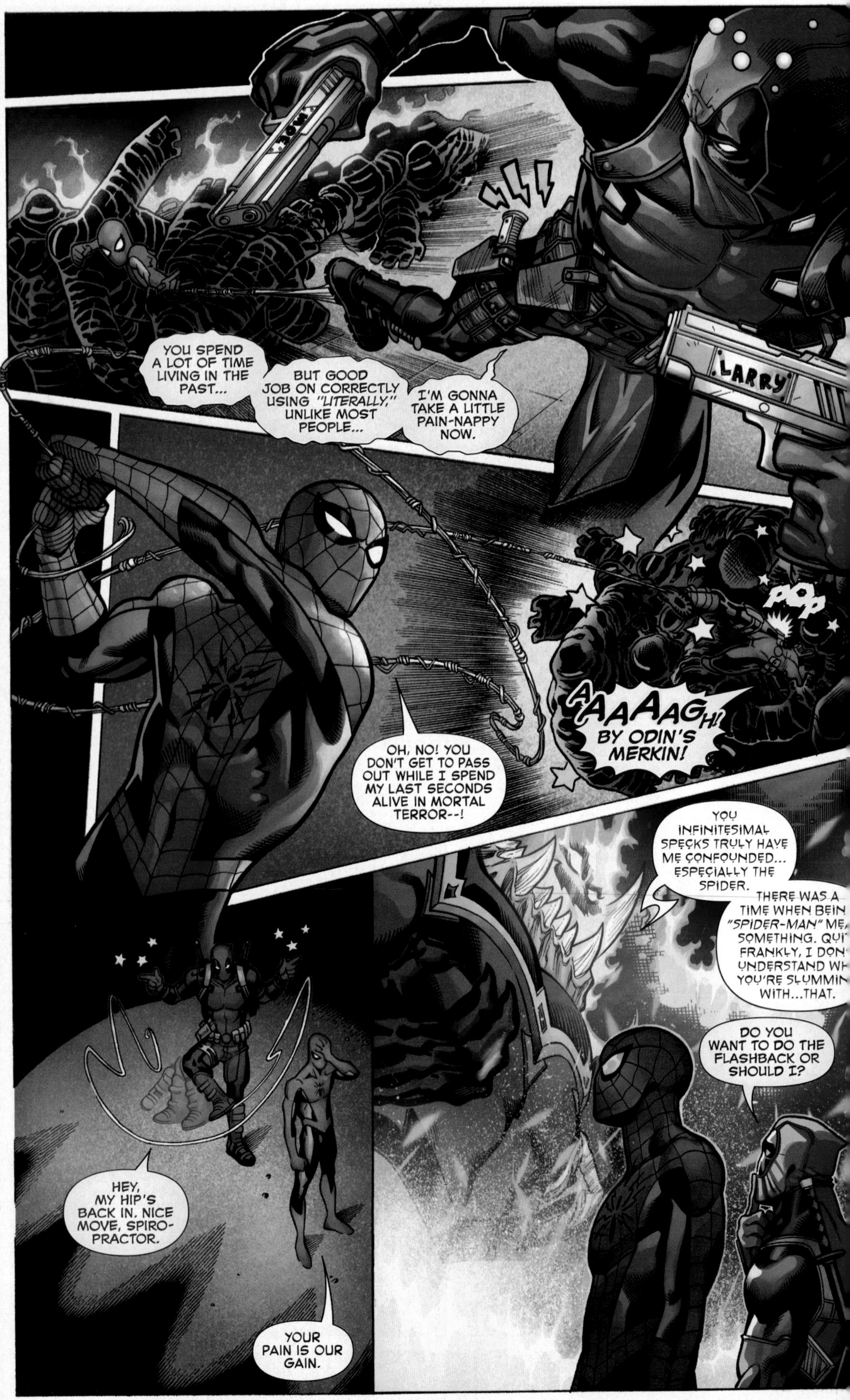
LARRY
YOU SPEND A LOT OF TIME LIVING IN THE PAST...
BUT GOOD JOB ON CORRECTLY USING "LITERALLY," UNLIKE MOST PEOPLE...
I'M GONNA TAKE A LITTLE PAIN-NAPPY NOW.
POP
AAAAAGH! BY ODIN'S MERKIN!
OH, NO! YOU DON'T GET TO PASS OUT WHILE I SPEND MY LAST SECONDS ALIVE IN MORTAL TERROR--!
HEY, MY HIP'S BACK IN. NICE MOVE, SPIRO-PRACTOR.
YOUR PAIN IS OUR GAIN.
YOU INFINITESIMAL SPECKS TRULY HAVE ME CONFOUNDED... ESPECIALLY THE SPIDER.
THERE WAS A TIME WHEN BEIN "SPIDER-MAN" ME SOMETHING. QUI FRANKLY, I DON UNDERSTAND WH YOU'RE SLUMMIN WITH...THAT.
DO YOU WANT TO DO THE FLASHBACK OR SHOULD I?

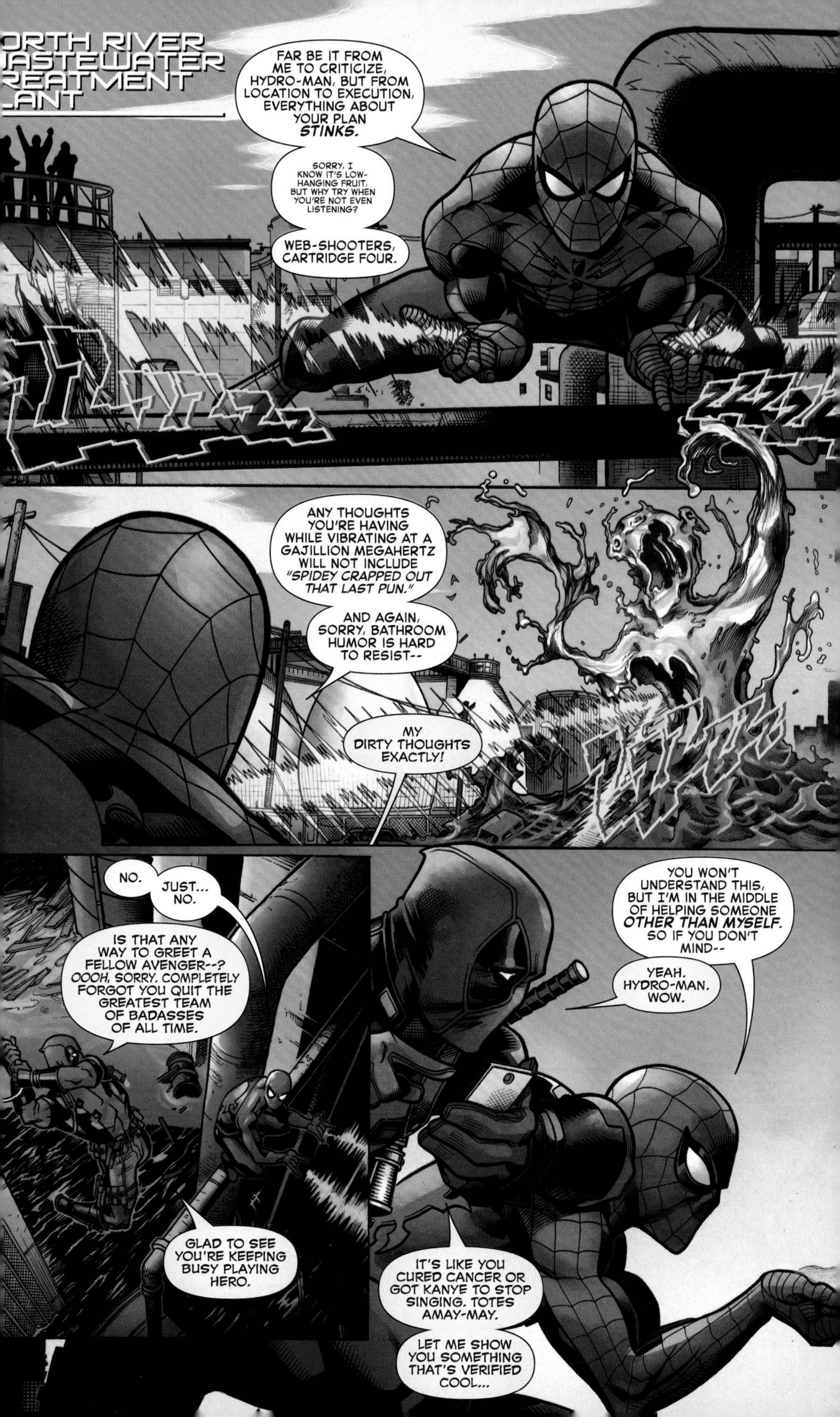
ORTH RIVER
ASTEWATER
REATMENT
LANT
FAR BE IT FROM ME TO CRITICIZE, HYDRO-MAN, BUT FROM LOCATION TO EXECUTION, EVERYTHING ABOUT YOUR PLAN STINKS.
SORRY, I KNOW IT'S LOW-HANGING FRUIT, BUT WHY TRY WHEN YOU'RE NOT EVEN LISTENING?
WEB-SHOOTERS, CARTRIDGE FOUR.
ANY THOUGHTS YOU'RE HAVING WHILE VIBRATING AT A GAJILLION MEGAHERTZ WILL NOT INCLUDE "SPIDEY CRAPPED OUT THAT LAST PUN."
AND AGAIN, SORRY, BATHROOM HUMOR IS HARD TO RESIST--
MY DIRTY THOUGHTS EXACTLY!
NO.
JUST... NO.
IS THAT ANY WAY TO GREET A FELLOW AVENGER--? OOOH, SORRY. COMPLETELY FORGOT YOU QUIT THE GREATEST TEAM OF BADASSES OF ALL TIME.
GLAD TO SEE YOU'RE KEEPING BUSY PLAYING HERO.
YOU WON'T UNDERSTAND THIS, BUT I'M IN THE MIDDLE OF HELPING SOMEONE OTHER THAN MYSELF. SO IF YOU DON'T MIND--
YEAH. HYDRO-MAN. WOW.
IT'S LIKE YOU CURED CANCER OR GOT KANYE TO STOP SINGING. TOTES AMAY-MAY.
LET ME SHOW YOU SOMETHING THAT'S VERIFIED COOL...

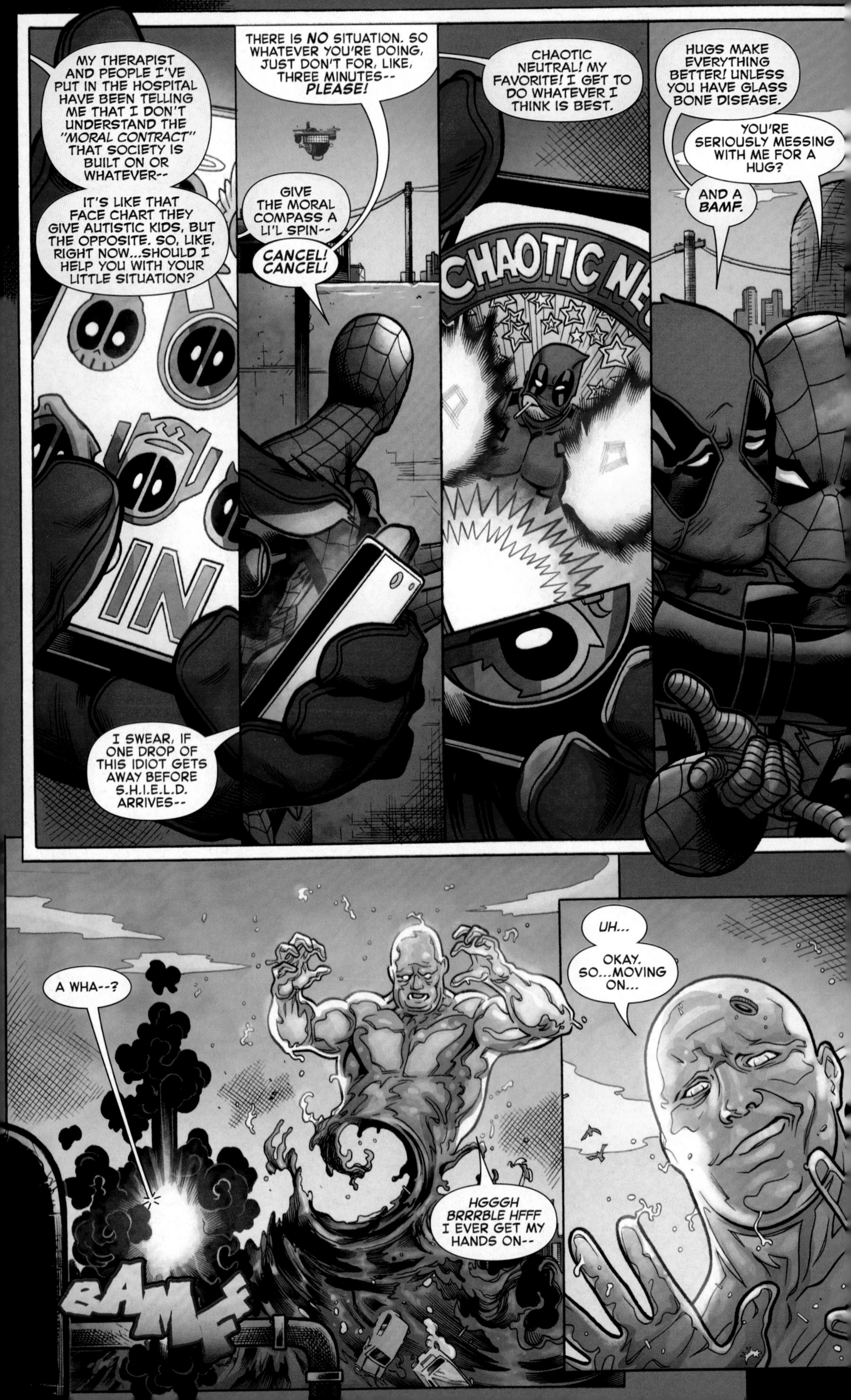

MY THERAPIST AND PEOPLE I'VE PUT IN THE HOSPITAL HAVE BEEN TELLING ME THAT I DON'T UNDERSTAND THE "MORAL CONTRACT" THAT SOCIETY IS BUILT ON OR WHATEVER--
IT'S LIKE THAT FACE CHART THEY GIVE AUTISTIC KIDS, BUT THE OPPOSITE. SO, LIKE, RIGHT NOW...SHOULD I HELP YOU WITH YOUR LITTLE SITUATION?
IN
I SWEAR, IF ONE DROP OF THIS IDIOT GETS AWAY BEFORE S.H.I.E.L.D. ARRIVES--
THERE IS NO SITUATION. SO WHATEVER YOU'RE DOING, JUST DON'T FOR, LIKE, THREE MINUTES-- PLEASE!
GIVE THE MORAL COMPASS A LI'L SPIN--
CANCEL! CANCEL!
CHAOTIC NEUTRAL! MY FAVORITE! I GET TO DO WHATEVER I THINK IS BEST.
CHAOTIC NE
HUGS MAKE EVERYTHING BETTER! UNLESS YOU HAVE GLASS BONE DISEASE.
YOU'RE SERIOUSLY MESSING WITH ME FOR A HUG?
AND A BAMF.
A WHA--?
BAMF
HGGGH BRRRBLE HFFF I EVER GET MY HANDS ON--
UH...
OKAY. SO...MOVING ON...

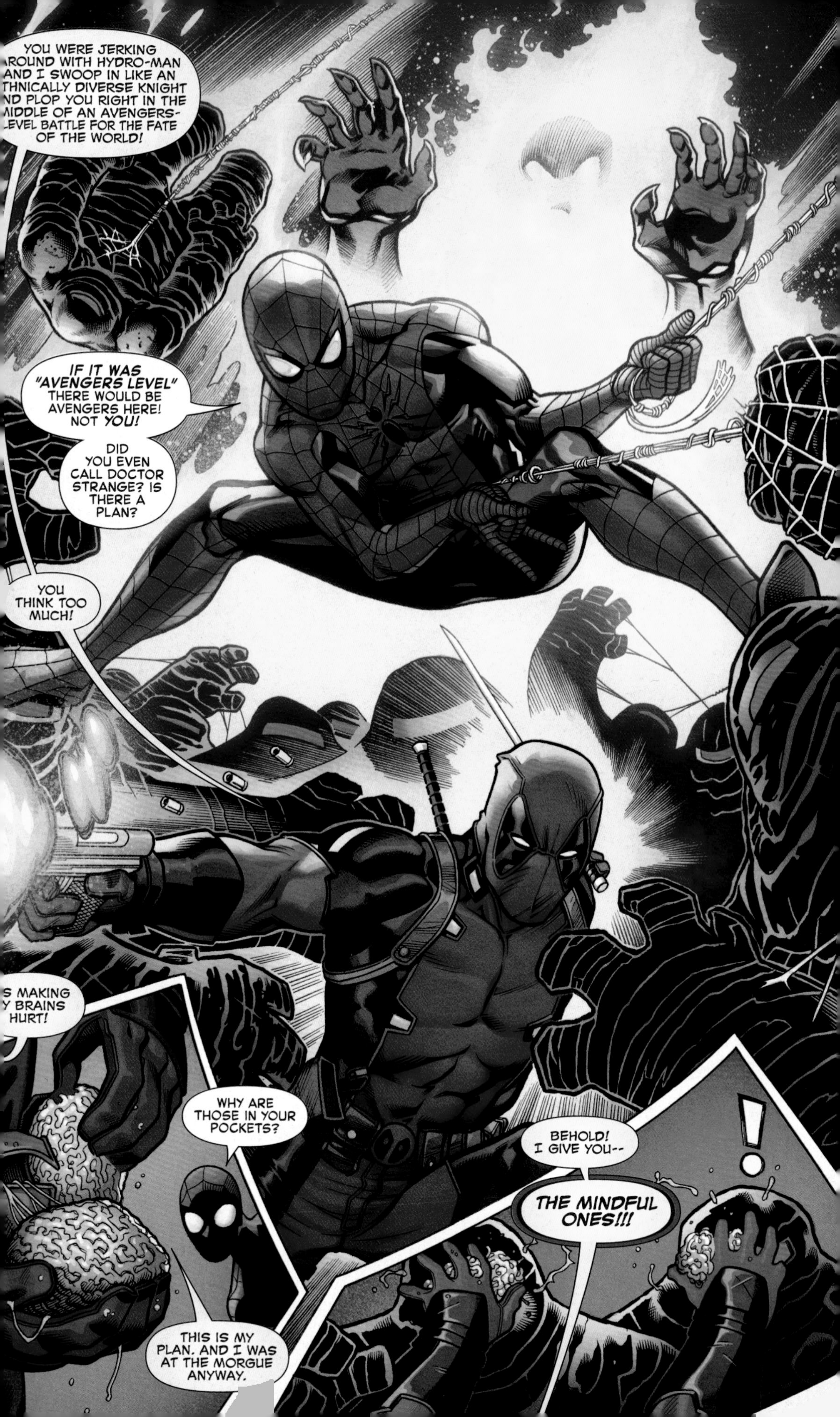
YOU WERE JERKING AROUND WITH HYDRO-MAN AND I SWOOP IN LIKE AN THNICALLY DIVERSE KNIGHT ND PLOP YOU RIGHT IN THE MIDDLE OF AN AVENGERS-LEVEL BATTLE FOR THE FATE OF THE WORLD!
IF IT WAS "AVENGERS LEVEL" THERE WOULD BE AVENGERS HERE! NOT YOU!
DID YOU EVEN CALL DOCTOR STRANGE? IS THERE A PLAN?
YOU THINK TOO MUCH!
S MAKING Y BRAINS HURT!
WHY ARE THOSE IN YOUR POCKETS?
THIS IS MY PLAN. AND I WAS AT THE MORGUE ANYWAY.
BEHOLD! I GIVE YOU--
THE MINDFUL ONES!!!
!

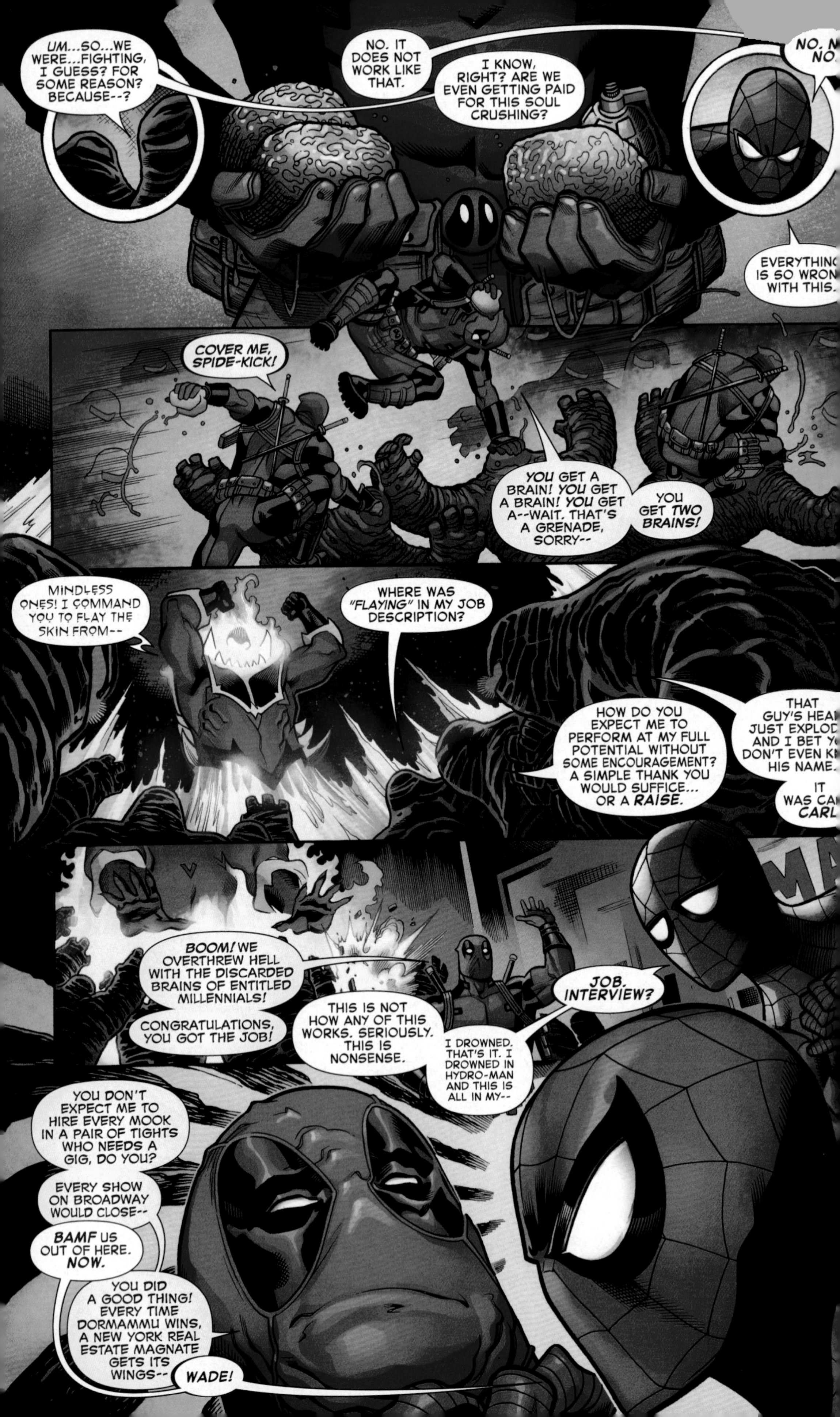
UM...SO...WE WERE...FIGHTING, I GUESS? FOR SOME REASON? BECAUSE--?
NO. IT DOES NOT WORK LIKE THAT.
I KNOW, RIGHT? ARE WE EVEN GETTING PAID FOR THIS SOUL CRUSHING?
NO. N NO.
EVERYTHIN IS SO WRON WITH THIS.
COVER ME, SPIDE-KICK!
YOU GET A BRAIN! YOU GET A BRAIN! YOU GET A--WAIT. THAT'S A GRENADE, SORRY--
YOU GET TWO BRAINS!
MINDLESS ONES! I COMMAND YOU TO FLAY THE SKIN FROM--
WHERE WAS "FLAYING" IN MY JOB DESCRIPTION?
HOW DO YOU EXPECT ME TO PERFORM AT MY FULL POTENTIAL WITHOUT SOME ENCOURAGEMENT? A SIMPLE THANK YOU WOULD SUFFICE... OR A RAISE.
THAT GUY'S HEA JUST EXPLOD AND I BET Y DON'T EVEN K HIS NAME.
IT WAS CA CARL
BOOM! WE OVERTHREW HELL WITH THE DISCARDED BRAINS OF ENTITLED MILLENNIALS!
CONGRATULATIONS, YOU GOT THE JOB!
THIS IS NOT HOW ANY OF THIS WORKS. SERIOUSLY. THIS IS NONSENSE.
JOB. INTERVIEW?
I DROWNED. THAT'S IT. I DROWNED IN HYDRO-MAN AND THIS IS ALL IN MY--
YOU DON'T EXPECT ME TO HIRE EVERY MOOK IN A PAIR OF TIGHTS WHO NEEDS A GIG, DO YOU?
EVERY SHOW ON BROADWAY WOULD CLOSE--
BAMF US OUT OF HERE. NOW.
YOU DID A GOOD THING! EVERY TIME DORMAMMU WINS, A NEW YORK REAL ESTATE MAGNATE GETS ITS WINGS--
WADE!

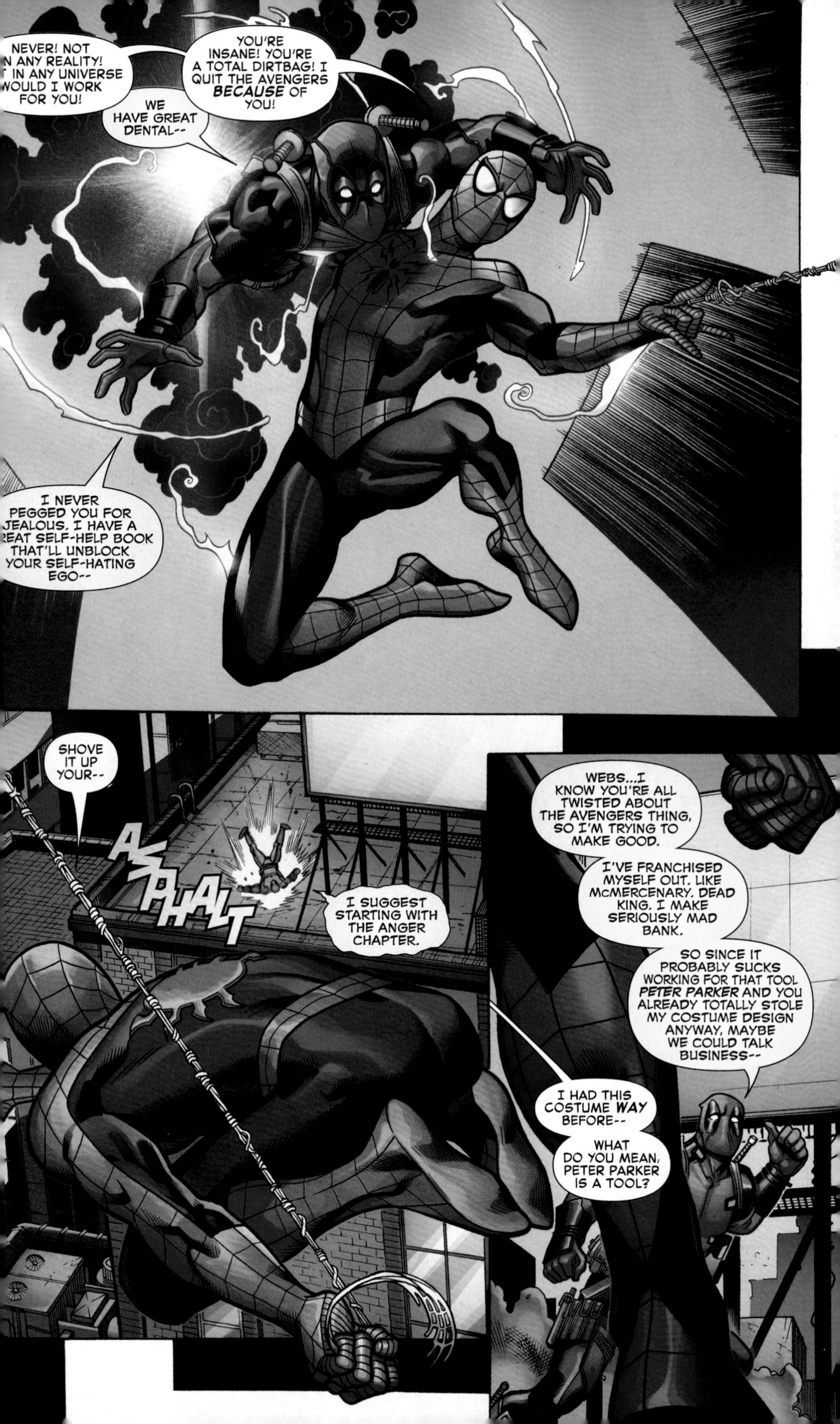

NEVER! NOT N ANY REALITY! T IN ANY UNIVERSE WOULD I WORK FOR YOU!
YOU'RE INSANE! YOU'RE A TOTAL DIRTBAG! I QUIT THE AVENGERS BECAUSE OF YOU!
WE HAVE GREAT DENTAL--
I NEVER PEGGED YOU FOR JEALOUS. I HAVE A REAT SELF-HELP BOOK THAT'LL UNBLOCK YOUR SELF-HATING EGO--
SHOVE IT UP YOUR--
ASPHALT
I SUGGEST STARTING WITH THE ANGER CHAPTER.
WEBS...I KNOW YOU'RE ALL TWISTED ABOUT THE AVENGERS THING, SO I'M TRYING TO MAKE GOOD.
I'VE FRANCHISED MYSELF OUT. LIKE McMERCENARY. DEAD KING. I MAKE SERIOUSLY MAD BANK.
SO SINCE IT PROBABLY SUCKS WORKING FOR THAT TOOL PETER PARKER AND YOU ALREADY TOTALLY STOLE MY COSTUME DESIGN ANYWAY, MAYBE WE COULD TALK BUSINESS--
I HAD THIS COSTUME WAY BEFORE--
WHAT DO YOU MEAN, PETER PARKER IS A TOOL?

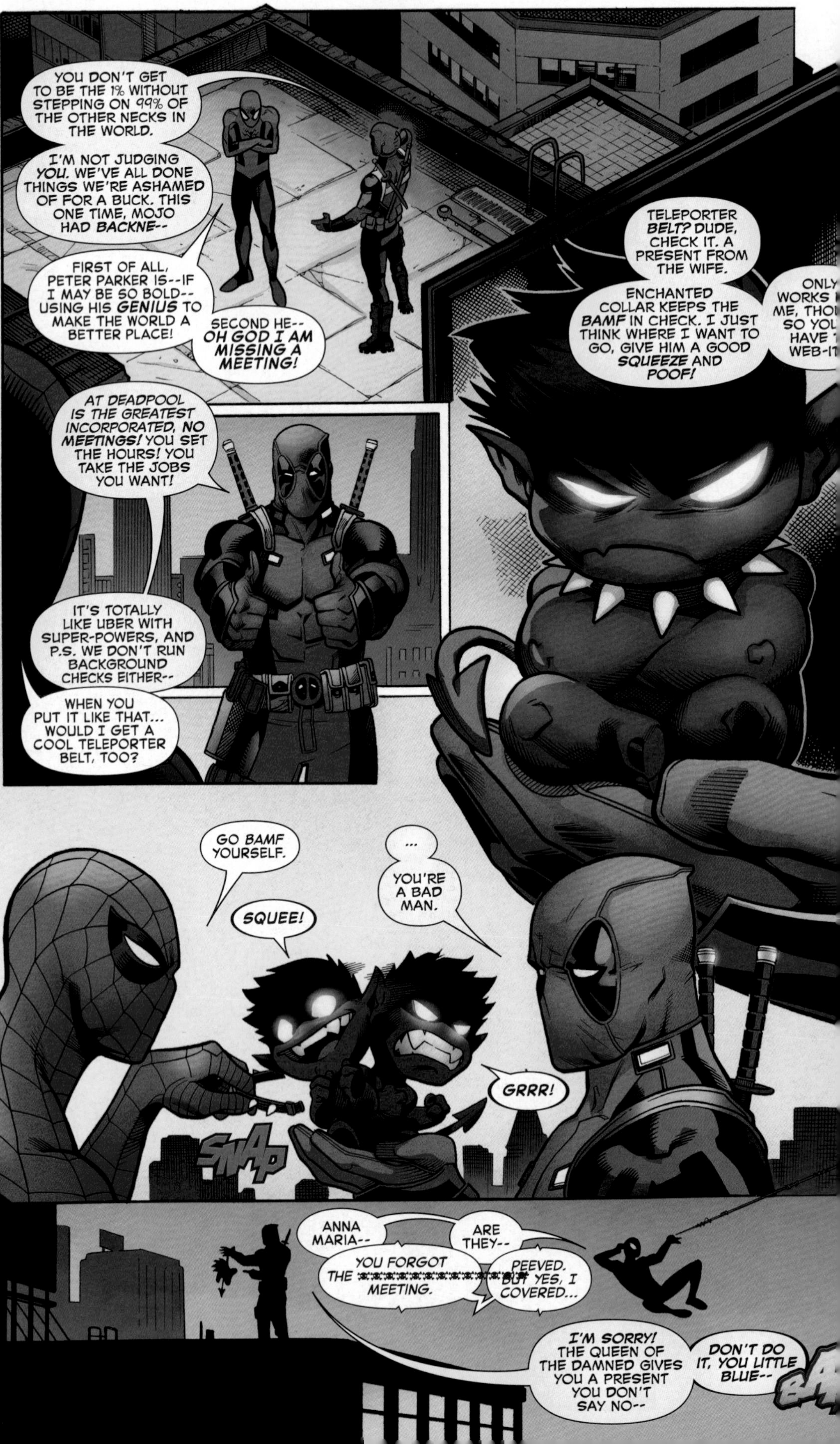

YOU DON'T GET TO BE THE 1% WITHOUT STEPPING ON 99% OF THE OTHER NECKS IN THE WORLD.
I'M NOT JUDGING YOU. WE'VE ALL DONE THINGS WE'RE ASHAMED OF FOR A BUCK. THIS ONE TIME, MOJO HAD BACKNE--
FIRST OF ALL, PETER PARKER IS--IF I MAY BE SO BOLD--USING HIS GENIUS TO MAKE THE WORLD A BETTER PLACE!
SECOND HE-- OH GOD I AM MISSING A MEETING!
AT DEADPOOL IS THE GREATEST INCORPORATED, NO MEETINGS! YOU SET THE HOURS! YOU TAKE THE JOBS YOU WANT!
IT'S TOTALLY LIKE UBER WITH SUPER-POWERS, AND P.S. WE DON'T RUN BACKGROUND CHECKS EITHER--
WHEN YOU PUT IT LIKE THAT... WOULD I GET A COOL TELEPORTER BELT, TOO?
TELEPORTER BELT? DUDE, CHECK IT. A PRESENT FROM THE WIFE.
ENCHANTED COLLAR KEEPS THE BAMF IN CHECK. I JUST THINK WHERE I WANT TO GO, GIVE HIM A GOOD SQUEEZE AND POOF!
GO BAMF YOURSELF.
SQUEE!
...
YOU'RE A BAD MAN.
SNAP
GRRR!
ANNA MARIA--
YOU FORGOT THE ☠☠☠☠☠☠☠☠☠☠☠☠☠ MEETING.
ARE THEY--
PEEVED. BUT YES, I COVERED...
I'M SORRY! THE QUEEN OF THE DAMNED GIVES YOU A PRESENT YOU DON'T SAY NO--
DON'T DO IT, YOU LITTLE BLUE--

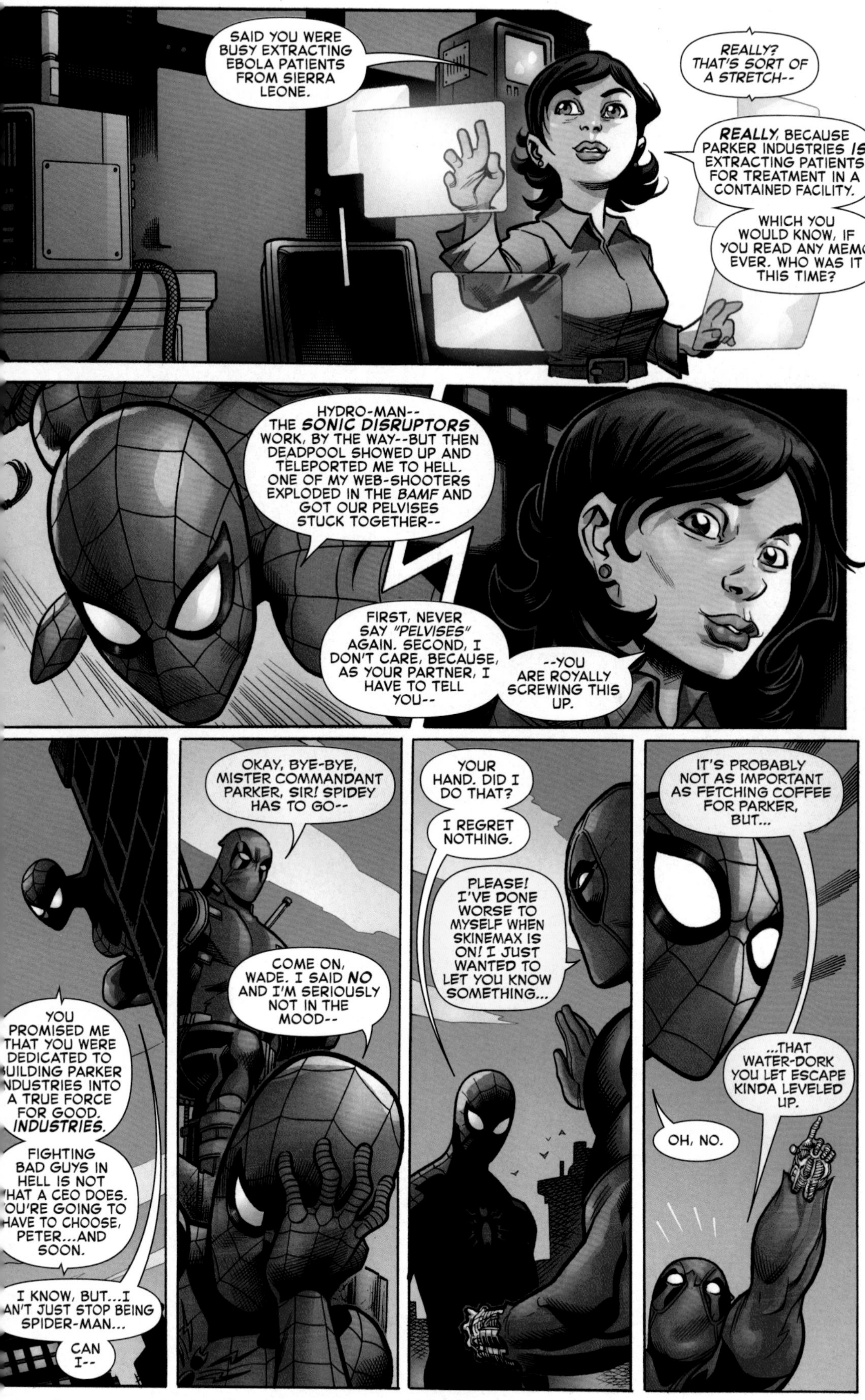

SAID YOU WERE BUSY EXTRACTING EBOLA PATIENTS FROM SIERRA LEONE.
REALLY? THAT'S SORT OF A STRETCH--
REALLY, BECAUSE PARKER INDUSTRIES IS EXTRACTING PATIENTS FOR TREATMENT IN A CONTAINED FACILITY.
WHICH YOU WOULD KNOW, IF YOU READ ANY MEMO EVER. WHO WAS IT THIS TIME?
HYDRO-MAN-- THE SONIC DISRUPTORS WORK, BY THE WAY--BUT THEN DEADPOOL SHOWED UP AND TELEPORTED ME TO HELL. ONE OF MY WEB-SHOOTERS EXPLODED IN THE BAMF AND GOT OUR PELVISES STUCK TOGETHER--
FIRST, NEVER SAY "PELVISES" AGAIN. SECOND, I DON'T CARE, BECAUSE, AS YOUR PARTNER, I HAVE TO TELL YOU--
--YOU ARE ROYALLY SCREWING THIS UP.
YOU PROMISED ME THAT YOU WERE DEDICATED TO UILDING PARKER NDUSTRIES INTO A TRUE FORCE FOR GOOD. INDUSTRIES.
FIGHTING BAD GUYS IN HELL IS NOT HAT A CEO DOES. OU'RE GOING TO HAVE TO CHOOSE, PETER...AND SOON.
I KNOW, BUT...I AN'T JUST STOP BEING SPIDER-MAN...
CAN I--
OKAY, BYE-BYE, MISTER COMMANDANT PARKER, SIR! SPIDEY HAS TO GO--
COME ON, WADE. I SAID NO AND I'M SERIOUSLY NOT IN THE MOOD--
YOUR HAND. DID I DO THAT?
I REGRET NOTHING.
PLEASE! I'VE DONE WORSE TO MYSELF WHEN SKINEMAX IS ON! I JUST WANTED TO LET YOU KNOW SOMETHING...
IT'S PROBABLY NOT AS IMPORTANT AS FETCHING COFFEE FOR PARKER, BUT...
...THAT WATER-DORK YOU LET ESCAPE KINDA LEVELED UP.
OH, NO.

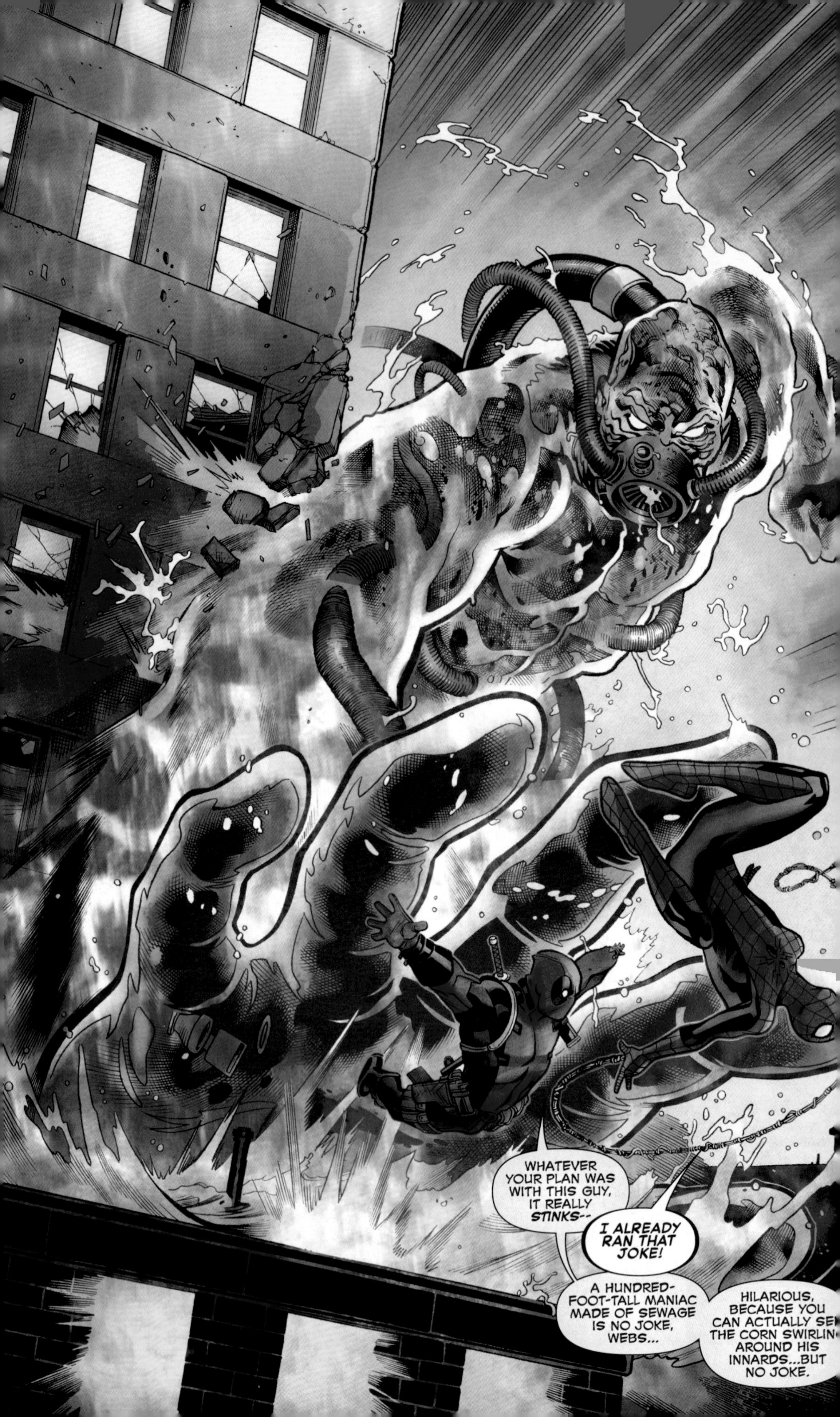
WHATEVER YOUR PLAN WAS WITH THIS GUY, IT REALLY STINKS--
I ALREADY RAN THAT JOKE!
A HUNDRED-FOOT-TALL MANIAC MADE OF SEWAGE IS NO JOKE, WEBS...
HILARIOUS, BECAUSE YOU CAN ACTUALLY SE THE CORN SWIRLIN AROUND HIS INNARDS...BUT NO JOKE.

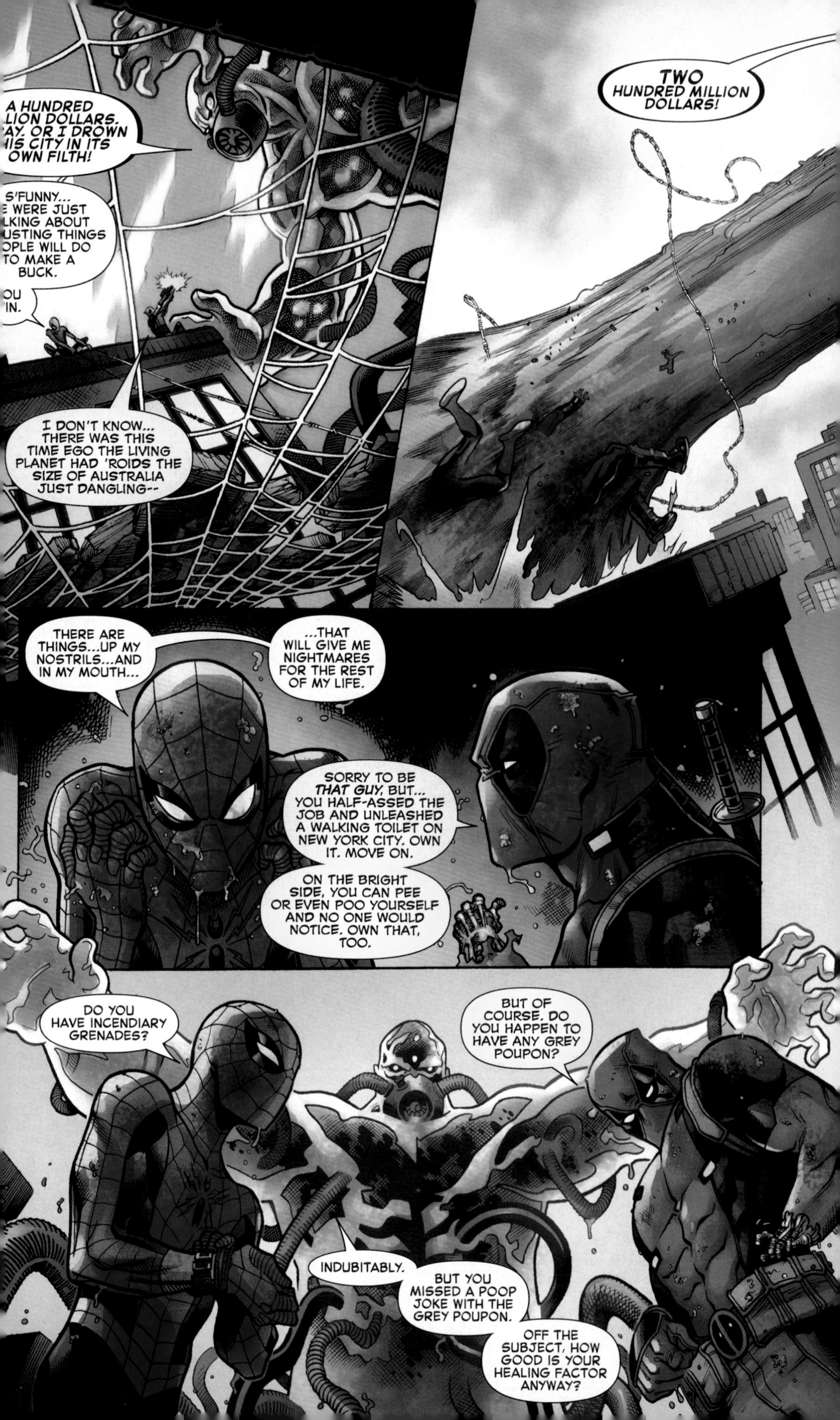
A HUNDRED
LION DOLLARS.
AY. OR I DROWN
IS CITY IN ITS
OWN FILTH!
S'FUNNY... E WERE JUST LKING ABOUT USTING THINGS OPLE WILL DO TO MAKE A BUCK.
OU IN.
I DON'T KNOW... THERE WAS THIS TIME EGO THE LIVING PLANET HAD 'ROIDS THE SIZE OF AUSTRALIA JUST DANGLING--
TWO HUNDRED MILLION DOLLARS!
THERE ARE THINGS...UP MY NOSTRILS...AND IN MY MOUTH...
...THAT WILL GIVE ME NIGHTMARES FOR THE REST OF MY LIFE.
SORRY TO BE *THAT GUY*, BUT... YOU HALF-ASSED THE JOB AND UNLEASHED A WALKING TOILET ON NEW YORK CITY. OWN IT. MOVE ON.
ON THE BRIGHT SIDE, YOU CAN PEE OR EVEN POO YOURSELF AND NO ONE WOULD NOTICE. OWN THAT, TOO.
DO YOU HAVE INCENDIARY GRENADES?
BUT OF COURSE. DO YOU HAPPEN TO HAVE ANY GREY POUPON?
INDUBITABLY.
BUT YOU MISSED A POOP JOKE WITH THE GREY POUPON.
OFF THE SUBJECT, HOW GOOD IS YOUR HEALING FACTOR ANYWAY?

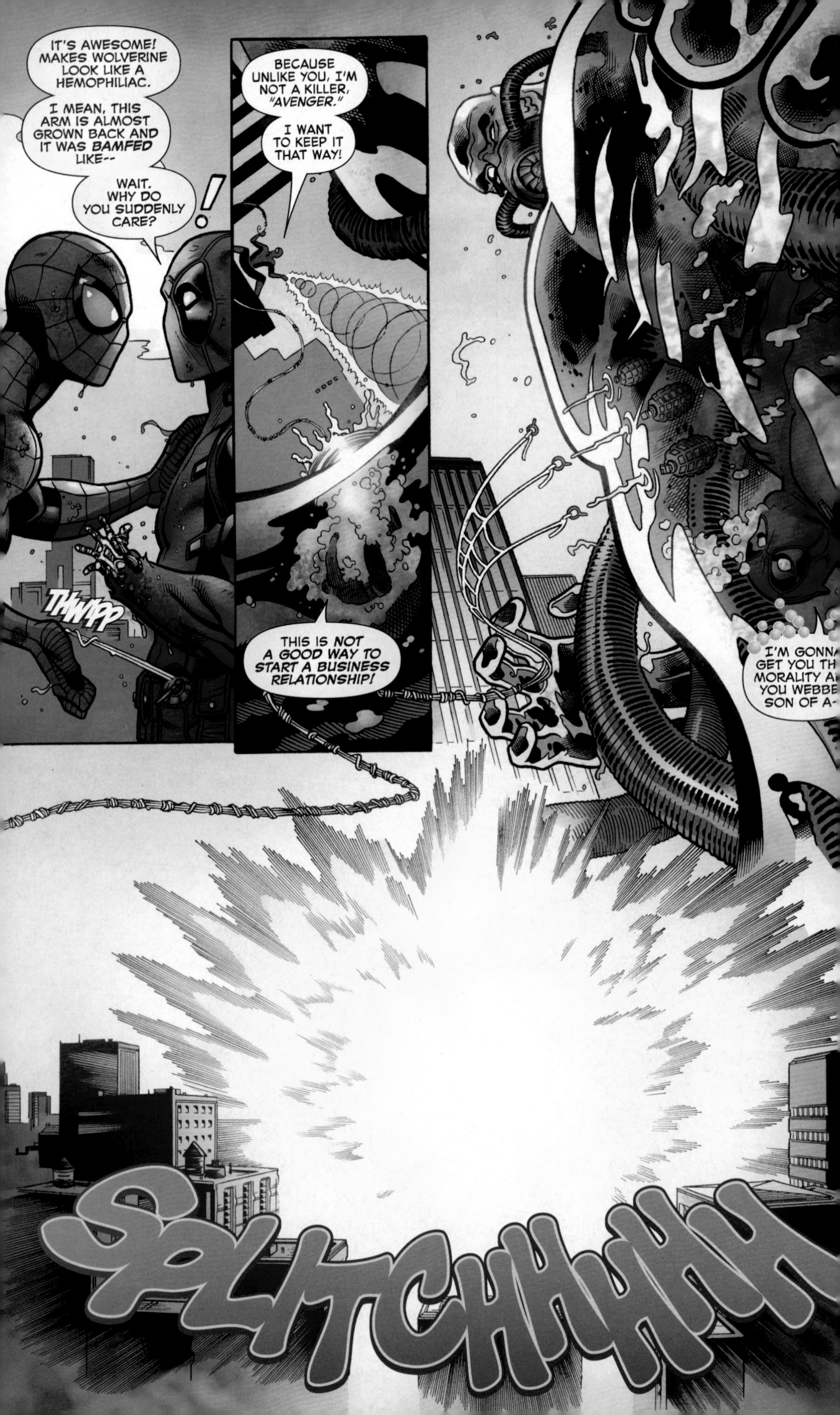
IT'S AWESOME! MAKES WOLVERINE LOOK LIKE A HEMOPHILIAC.
I MEAN, THIS ARM IS ALMOST GROWN BACK AND IT WAS BAMFED LIKE--
WAIT. WHY DO YOU SUDDENLY CARE?
!
THWIPP
BECAUSE UNLIKE YOU, I'M NOT A KILLER, "AVENGER."
I WANT TO KEEP IT THAT WAY!
THIS IS NOT A GOOD WAY TO START A BUSINESS RELATIONSHIP!
I'M GONNA GET YOU TH MORALITY A YOU WEBBE SON OF A-
SPLTCHHHH

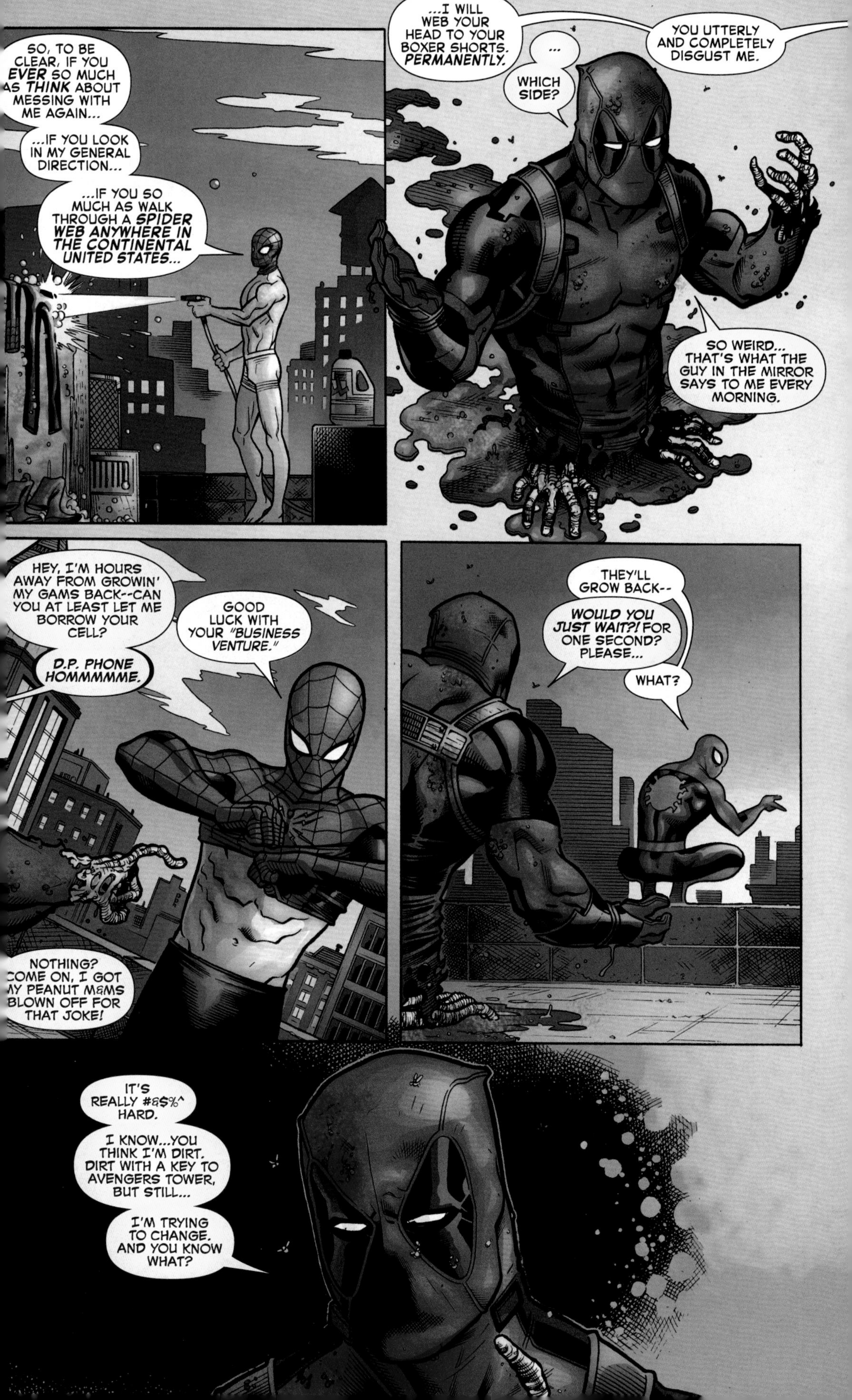
SO, TO BE CLEAR, IF YOU EVER SO MUCH AS THINK ABOUT MESSING WITH ME AGAIN...
...IF YOU LOOK IN MY GENERAL DIRECTION...
...IF YOU SO MUCH AS WALK THROUGH A SPIDER WEB ANYWHERE IN THE CONTINENTAL UNITED STATES...
...I WILL WEB YOUR HEAD TO YOUR BOXER SHORTS. PERMANENTLY.
...
WHICH SIDE?
YOU UTTERLY AND COMPLETELY DISGUST ME.
SO WEIRD... THAT'S WHAT THE GUY IN THE MIRROR SAYS TO ME EVERY MORNING.
HEY, I'M HOURS AWAY FROM GROWIN' MY GAMS BACK--CAN YOU AT LEAST LET ME BORROW YOUR CELL?
D.P. PHONE HOMMMMME.
GOOD LUCK WITH YOUR "BUSINESS VENTURE."
NOTHING? COME ON, I GOT MY PEANUT M&MS BLOWN OFF FOR THAT JOKE!
THEY'LL GROW BACK--
WOULD YOU JUST WAIT?! FOR ONE SECOND? PLEASE...
WHAT?
IT'S REALLY #&$%^ HARD.
I KNOW...YOU THINK I'M DIRT. DIRT WITH A KEY TO AVENGERS TOWER, BUT STILL...
I'M TRYING TO CHANGE. AND YOU KNOW WHAT?

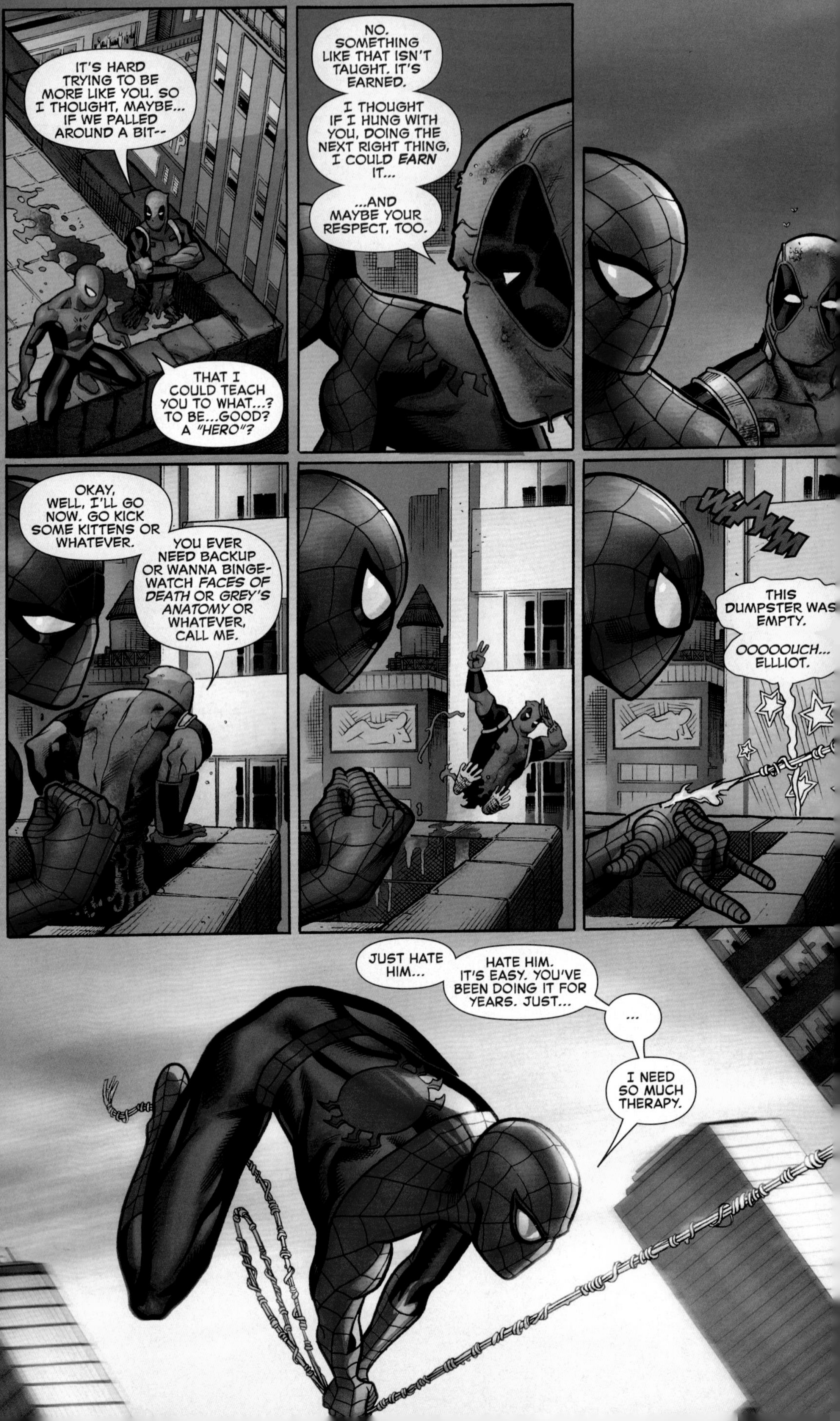
IT'S HARD TRYING TO BE MORE LIKE YOU. SO I THOUGHT, MAYBE... IF WE PALLED AROUND A BIT--
THAT I COULD TEACH YOU TO WHAT...? TO BE...GOOD? A "HERO"?
NO. SOMETHING LIKE THAT ISN'T TAUGHT. IT'S EARNED.
I THOUGHT IF I HUNG WITH YOU, DOING THE NEXT RIGHT THING, I COULD EARN IT...
...AND MAYBE YOUR RESPECT, TOO.
OKAY, WELL, I'LL GO NOW. GO KICK SOME KITTENS OR WHATEVER.
YOU EVER NEED BACKUP OR WANNA BINGE-WATCH FACES OF DEATH OR GREY'S ANATOMY OR WHATEVER, CALL ME.
WHAMM
THIS DUMPSTER WAS EMPTY.
OOOOOUCH... ELLIOT.
JUST HATE HIM...
HATE HIM. IT'S EASY. YOU'VE BEEN DOING IT FOR YEARS. JUST...
...
I NEED SO MUCH THERAPY.

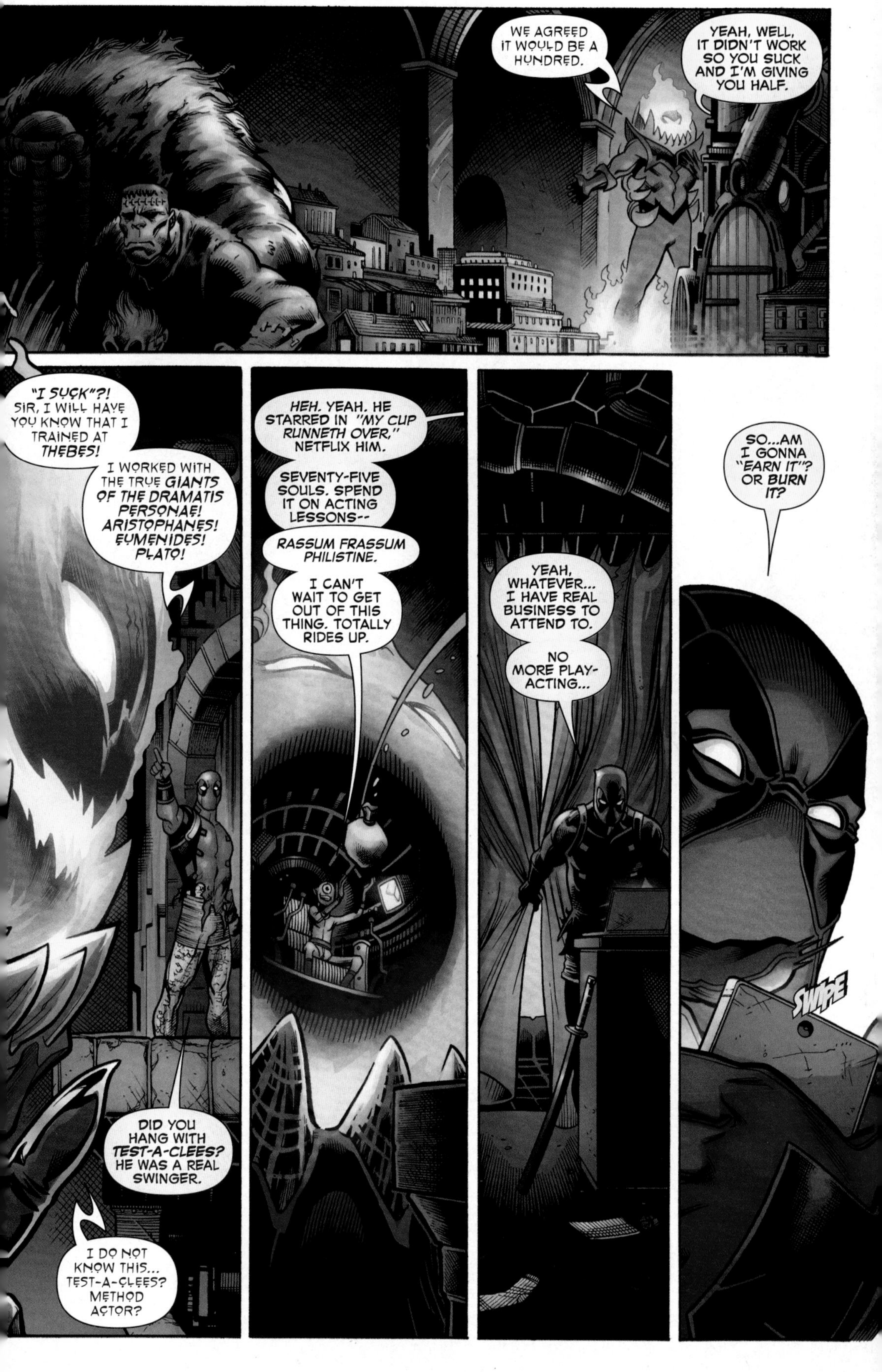
WE AGREED IT WOULD BE A HUNDRED.
YEAH, WELL, IT DIDN'T WORK SO YOU SUCK AND I'M GIVING YOU HALF.
"I SUCK"?! SIR, I WILL HAVE YOU KNOW THAT I TRAINED AT THEBES!
I WORKED WITH THE TRUE GIANTS OF THE DRAMATIS PERSONAE! ARISTOPHANES! EUMENIDES! PLATO!
DID YOU HANG WITH TEST-A-CLEES? HE WAS A REAL SWINGER.
I DO NOT KNOW THIS... TEST-A-CLEES? METHOD ACTOR?
HEH. YEAH. HE STARRED IN "MY CUP RUNNETH OVER," NETFLIX HIM.
SEVENTY-FIVE SOULS. SPEND IT ON ACTING LESSONS--
RASSUM FRASSUM PHILISTINE.
I CAN'T WAIT TO GET OUT OF THIS THING. TOTALLY RIDES UP.
YEAH, WHATEVER... I HAVE REAL BUSINESS TO ATTEND TO.
NO MORE PLAY-ACTING...
SO...AM I GONNA "EARN IT"? OR BURN IT?
SWIPE

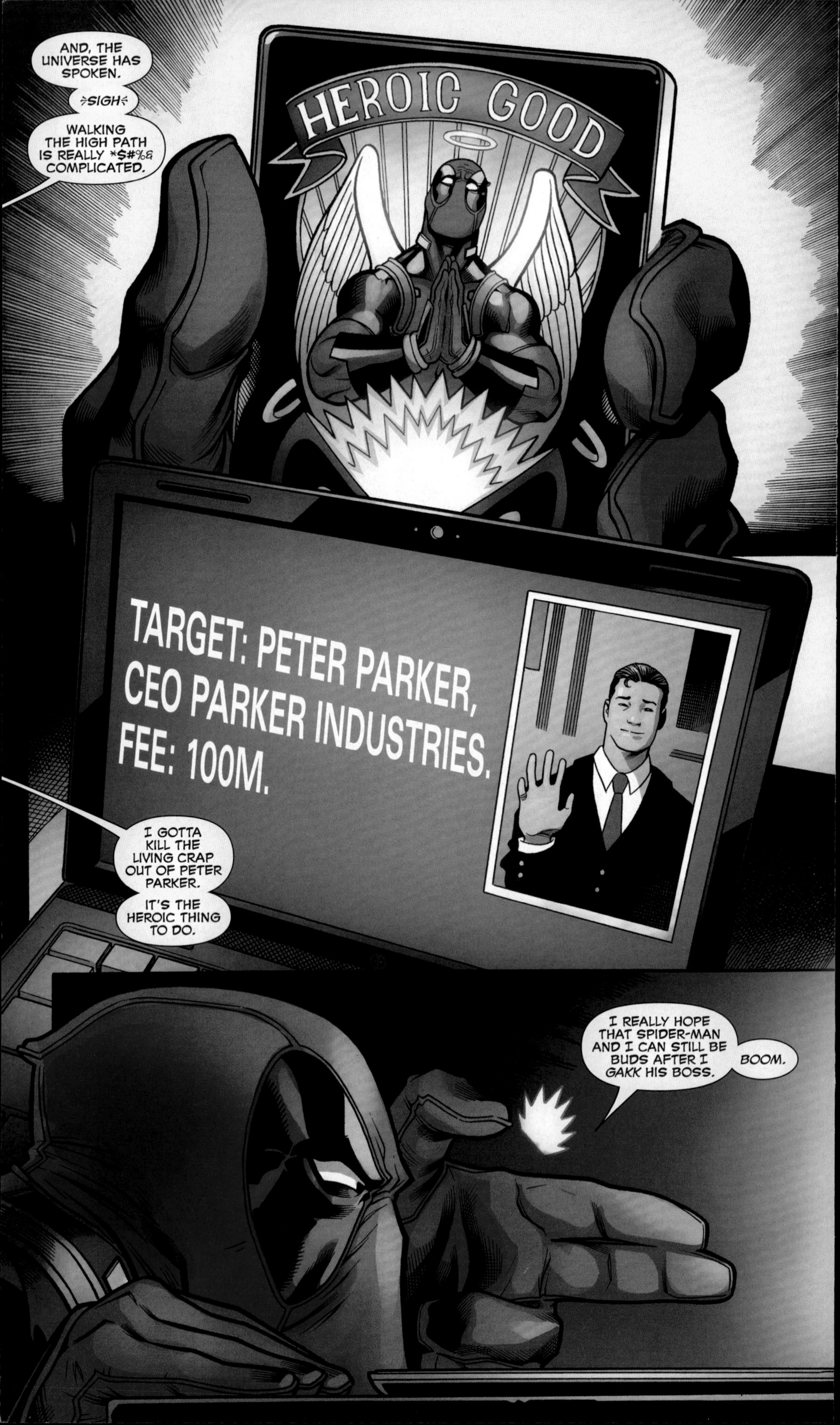
AND, THE UNIVERSE HAS SPOKEN.
SIGH
WALKING THE HIGH PATH IS REALLY *$#%& COMPLICATED.
HEROIC GOOD
TARGET: PETER PARKER, CEO PARKER INDUSTRIES. FEE: 100M.
I GOTTA KILL THE LIVING CRAP OUT OF PETER PARKER.
IT'S THE HEROIC THING TO DO.
I REALLY HOPE THAT SPIDER-MAN AND I CAN STILL BE BUDS AFTER I GAKK HIS BOSS.
BOOM.

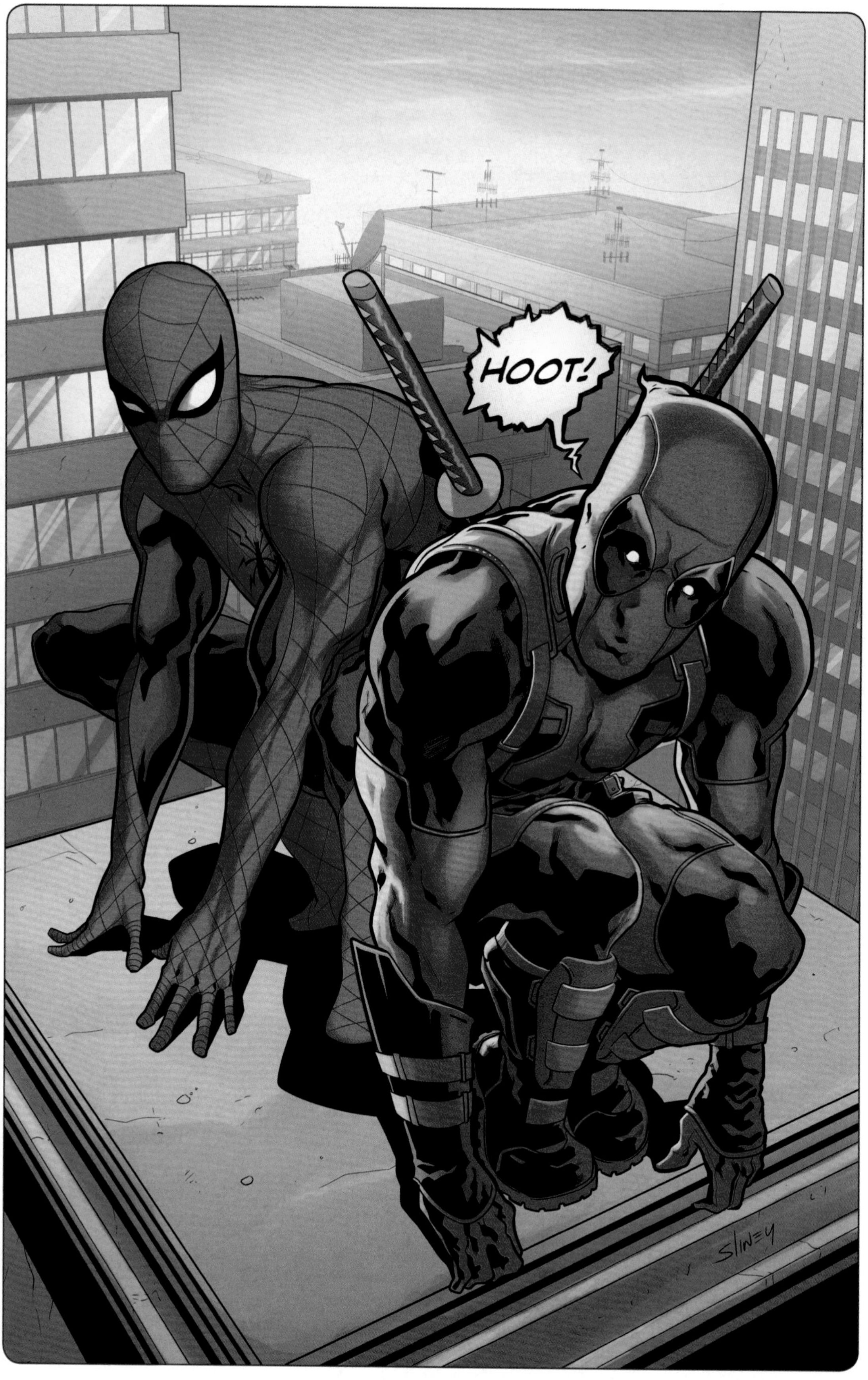
HOOT!
SLINEY

1 VARIANT BY
WILL SLINEY & FRANK MARTIN

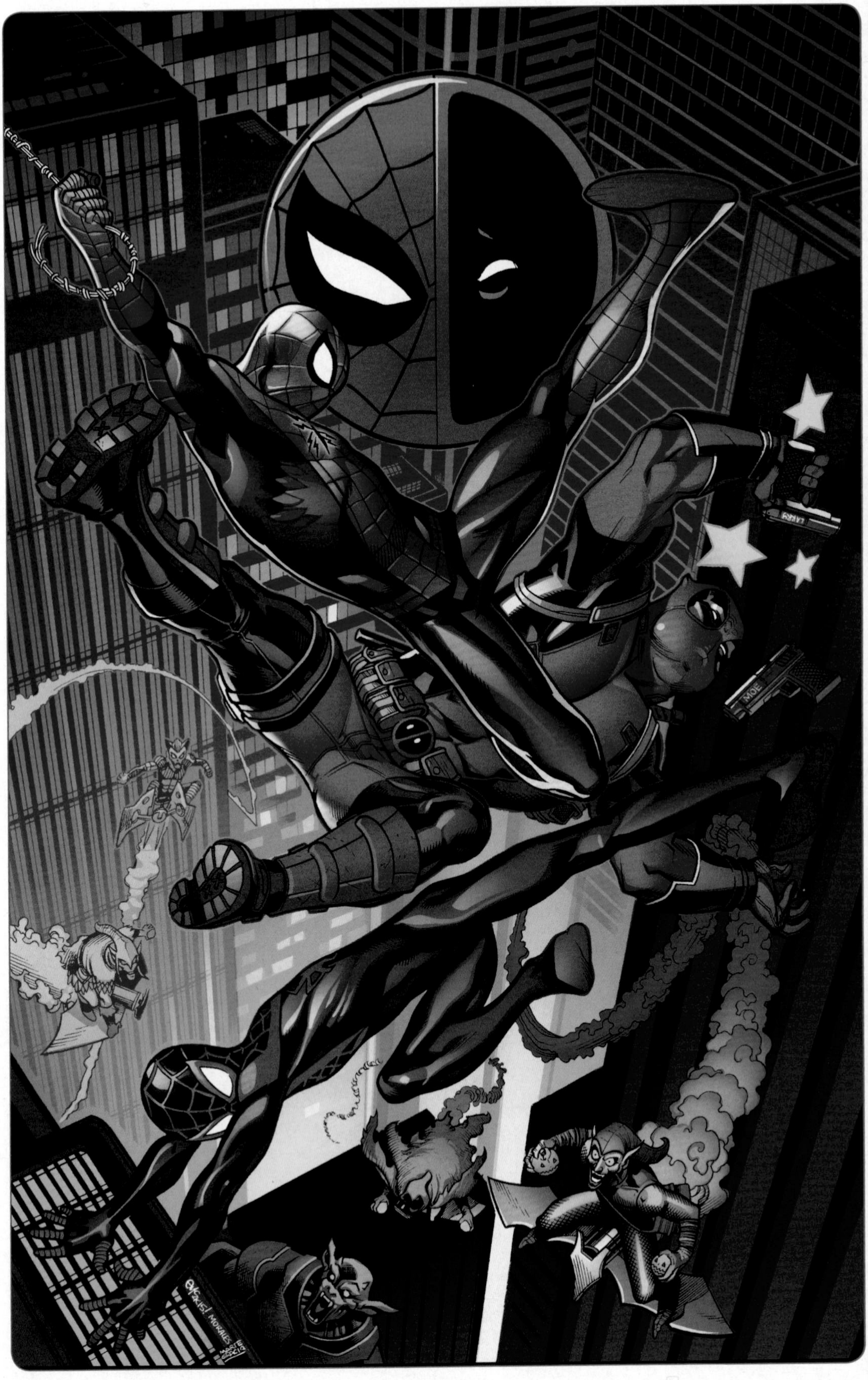
LARRY
MOE

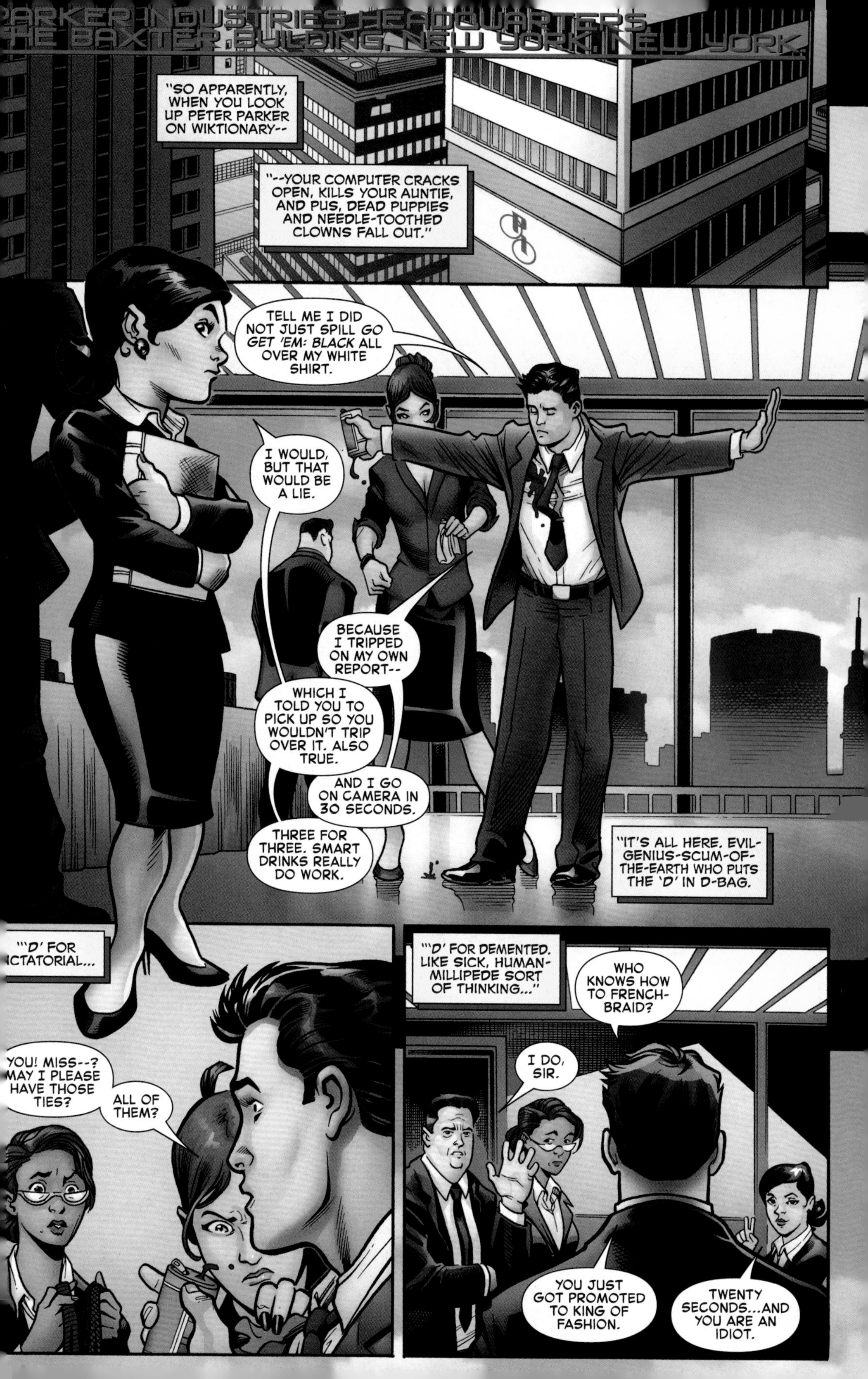
PARKER INDUSTRIES HEADQUARTERS
THE BAXTER BUILDING, NEW YORK, NEW YORK.
"SO APPARENTLY, WHEN YOU LOOK UP PETER PARKER ON WIKTIONARY--
"--YOUR COMPUTER CRACKS OPEN, KILLS YOUR AUNTIE, AND PUS, DEAD PUPPIES AND NEEDLE-TOOTHED CLOWNS FALL OUT."
TELL ME I DID NOT JUST SPILL GO GET 'EM: BLACK ALL OVER MY WHITE SHIRT.
I WOULD, BUT THAT WOULD BE A LIE.
BECAUSE I TRIPPED ON MY OWN REPORT--
WHICH I TOLD YOU TO PICK UP SO YOU WOULDN'T TRIP OVER IT. ALSO TRUE.
AND I GO ON CAMERA IN 30 SECONDS.
THREE FOR THREE. SMART DRINKS REALLY DO WORK.
"IT'S ALL HERE. EVIL-GENIUS-SCUM-OF-THE-EARTH WHO PUTS THE 'D' IN D-BAG.
"'D' FOR ICTATORIAL...
YOU! MISS--? MAY I PLEASE HAVE THOSE TIES?
ALL OF THEM?
"'D' FOR DEMENTED. LIKE SICK, HUMAN-MILLIPEDE SORT OF THINKING..."
WHO KNOWS HOW TO FRENCH-BRAID?
I DO, SIR.
YOU JUST GOT PROMOTED TO KING OF FASHION.
TWENTY SECONDS...AND YOU ARE AN IDIOT.

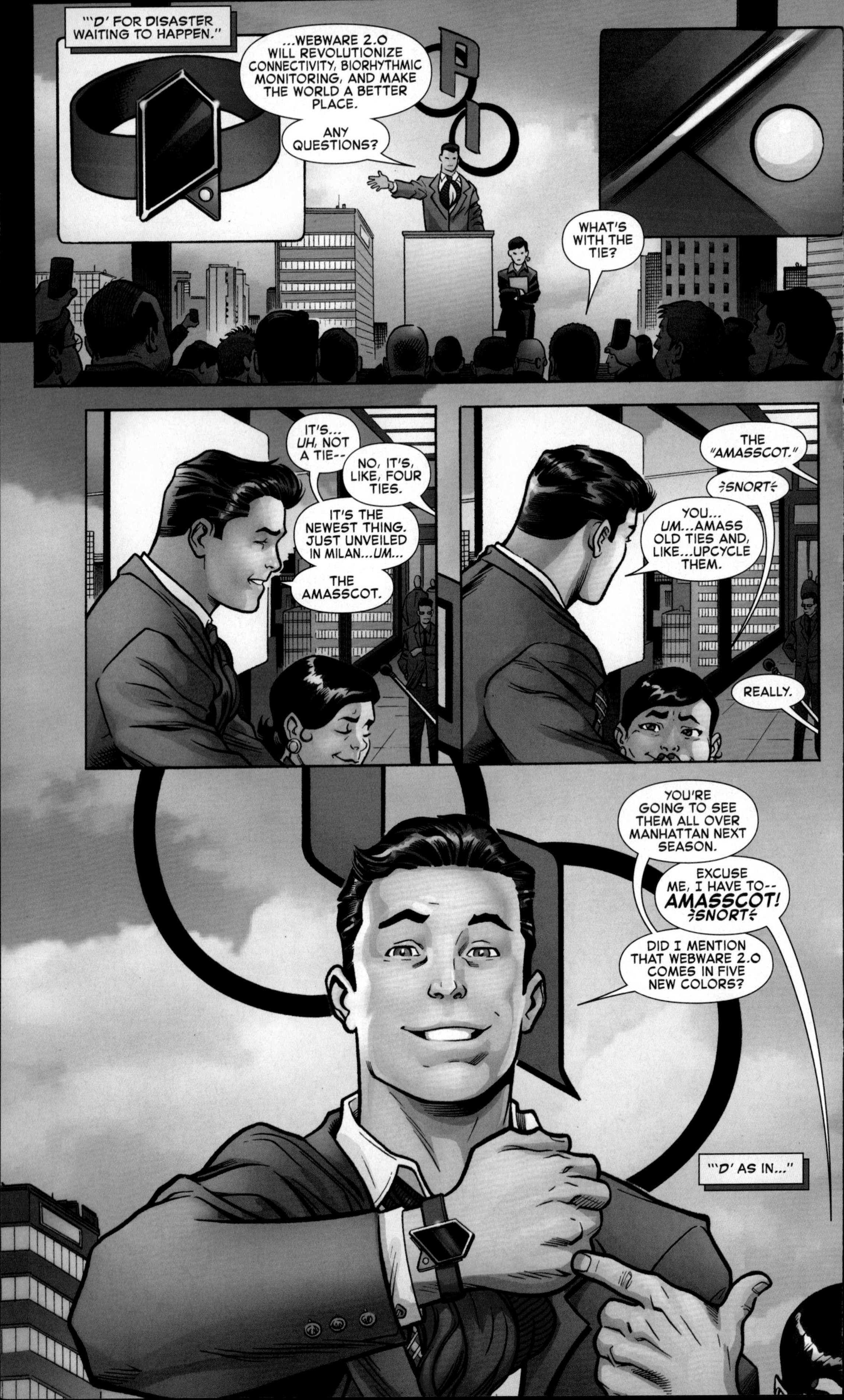
"'D' FOR DISASTER WAITING TO HAPPEN."
...WEBWARE 2.0 WILL REVOLUTIONIZE CONNECTIVITY, BIORHYTHMIC MONITORING, AND MAKE THE WORLD A BETTER PLACE.
ANY QUESTIONS?
WHAT'S WITH THE TIE?
IT'S... UH, NOT A TIE--
NO, IT'S, LIKE, FOUR TIES.
IT'S THE NEWEST THING. JUST UNVEILED IN MILAN...UM...
THE AMASSCOT.
THE "AMASSCOT."
SNORT
YOU... UM...AMASS OLD TIES AND, LIKE...UPCYCLE THEM.
REALLY.
YOU'RE GOING TO SEE THEM ALL OVER MANHATTAN NEXT SEASON.
EXCUSE ME, I HAVE TO-- AMASSCOT! SNORT
DID I MENTION THAT WEBWARE 2.0 COMES IN FIVE NEW COLORS?
"'D' AS IN..."

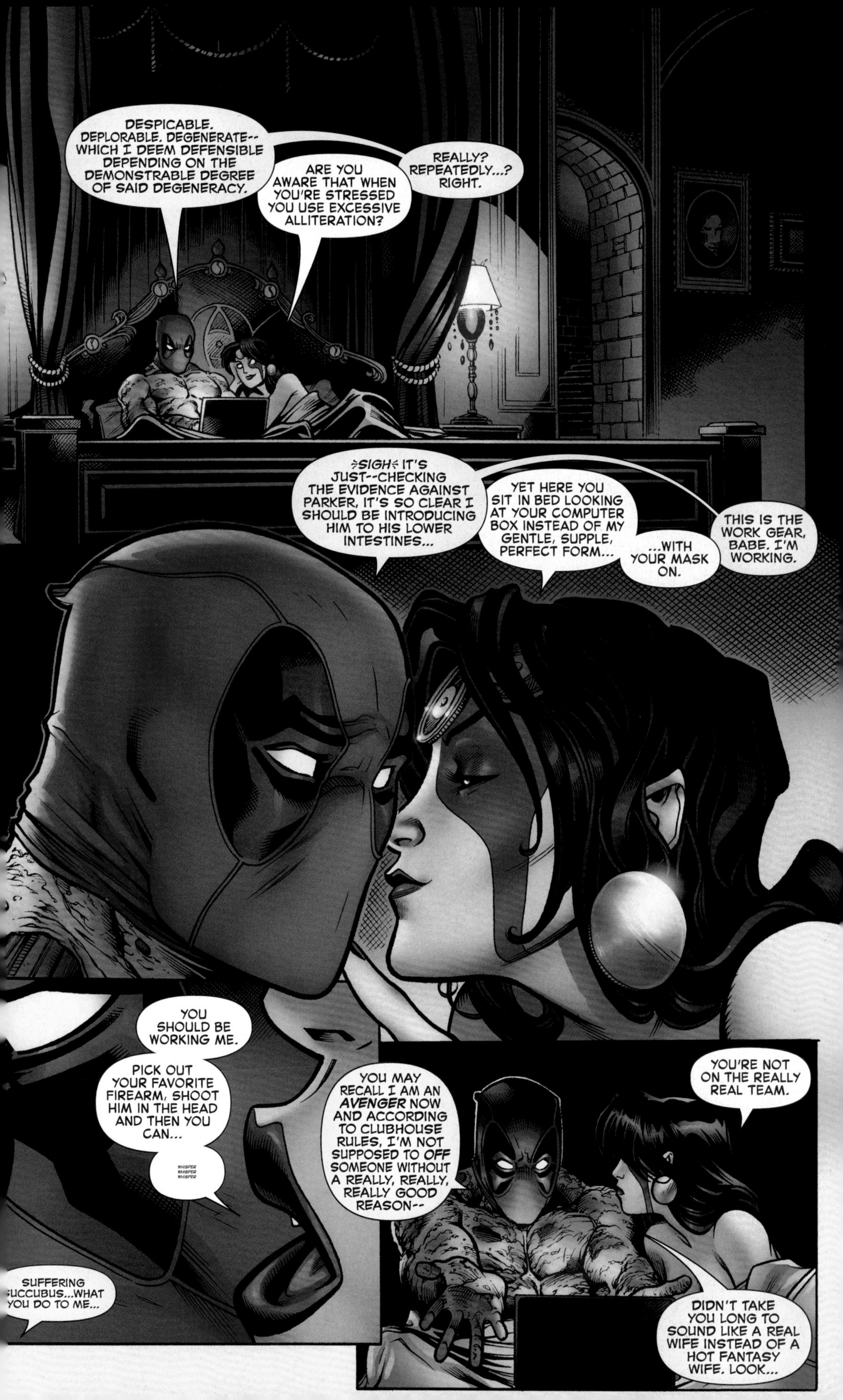
DESPICABLE. DEPLORABLE. DEGENERATE-- WHICH I DEEM DEFENSIBLE DEPENDING ON THE DEMONSTRABLE DEGREE OF SAID DEGENERACY.
ARE YOU AWARE THAT WHEN YOU'RE STRESSED YOU USE EXCESSIVE ALLITERATION?
REALLY? REPEATEDLY...? RIGHT.
SIGH IT'S JUST--CHECKING THE EVIDENCE AGAINST PARKER, IT'S SO CLEAR I SHOULD BE INTRODUCING HIM TO HIS LOWER INTESTINES...
YET HERE YOU SIT IN BED LOOKING AT YOUR COMPUTER BOX INSTEAD OF MY GENTLE, SUPPLE, PERFECT FORM...
...WITH YOUR MASK ON.
THIS IS THE WORK GEAR, BABE. I'M WORKING.
YOU SHOULD BE WORKING ME.
PICK OUT YOUR FAVORITE FIREARM, SHOOT HIM IN THE HEAD AND THEN YOU CAN...
WHISPER WHISPER WHISPER
SUFFERING SUCCUBUS...WHAT YOU DO TO ME...
YOU MAY RECALL I AM AN AVENGER NOW AND ACCORDING TO CLUBHOUSE RULES, I'M NOT SUPPOSED TO OFF SOMEONE WITHOUT A REALLY, REALLY, REALLY GOOD REASON--
YOU'RE NOT ON THE REALLY REAL TEAM.
DIDN'T TAKE YOU LONG TO SOUND LIKE A REAL WIFE INSTEAD OF A HOT FANTASY WIFE. LOOK...

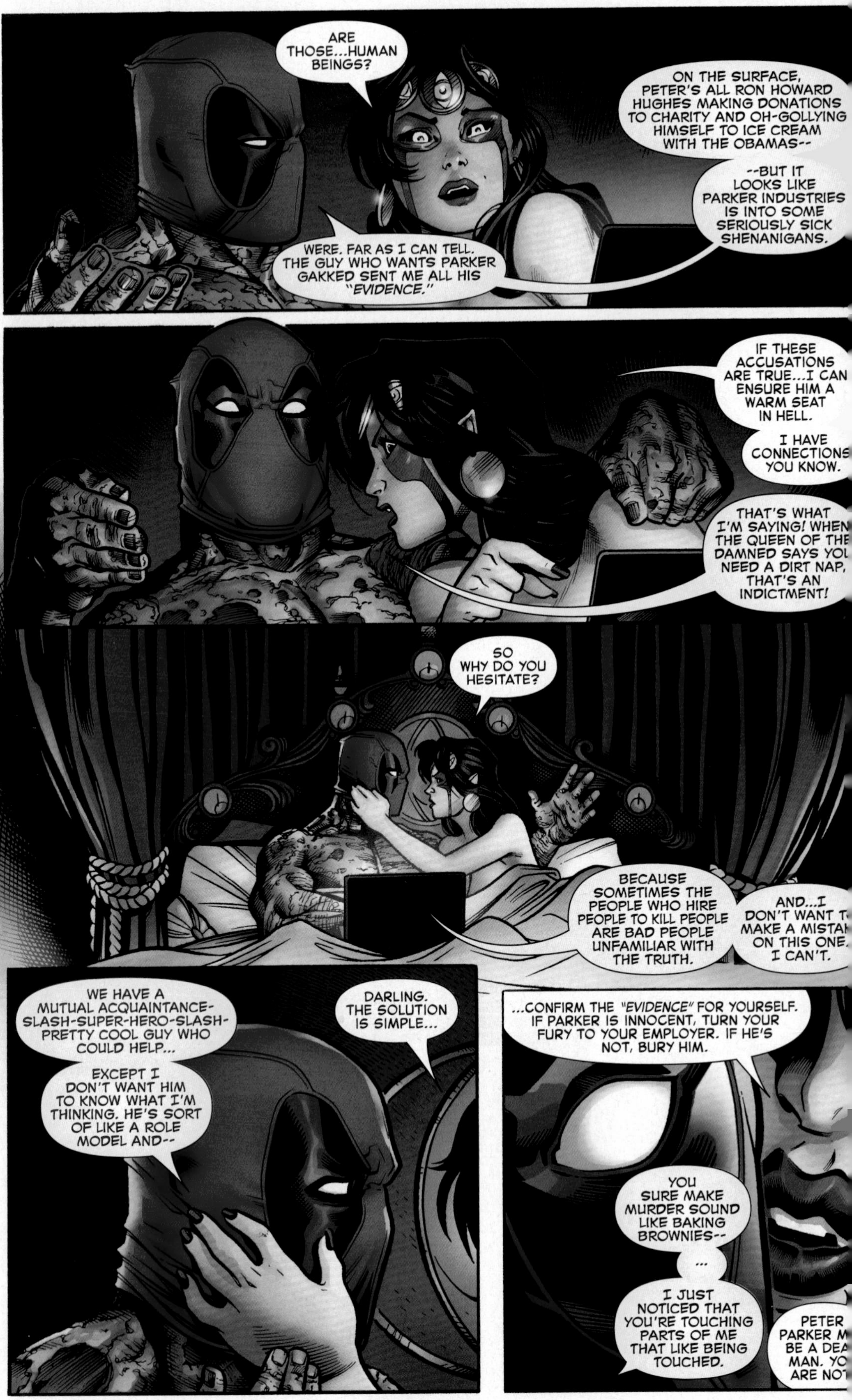
ARE THOSE...HUMAN BEINGS?
WERE. FAR AS I CAN TELL. THE GUY WHO WANTS PARKER GAKKED SENT ME ALL HIS "EVIDENCE."
ON THE SURFACE, PETER'S ALL RON HOWARD HUGHES MAKING DONATIONS TO CHARITY AND OH-GOLLYING HIMSELF TO ICE CREAM WITH THE OBAMAS--
--BUT IT LOOKS LIKE PARKER INDUSTRIES IS INTO SOME SERIOUSLY SICK SHENANIGANS.
IF THESE ACCUSATIONS ARE TRUE...I CAN ENSURE HIM A WARM SEAT IN HELL.
I HAVE CONNECTIONS YOU KNOW.
THAT'S WHAT I'M SAYING! WHEN THE QUEEN OF THE DAMNED SAYS YOU NEED A DIRT NAP, THAT'S AN INDICTMENT!
SO WHY DO YOU HESITATE?
BECAUSE SOMETIMES THE PEOPLE WHO HIRE PEOPLE TO KILL PEOPLE ARE BAD PEOPLE UNFAMILIAR WITH THE TRUTH.
AND...I DON'T WANT TO MAKE A MISTAKE ON THIS ONE. I CAN'T.
WE HAVE A MUTUAL ACQUAINTANCE-SLASH-SUPER-HERO-SLASH-PRETTY COOL GUY WHO COULD HELP...
EXCEPT I DON'T WANT HIM TO KNOW WHAT I'M THINKING. HE'S SORT OF LIKE A ROLE MODEL AND--
DARLING. THE SOLUTION IS SIMPLE...
...CONFIRM THE "EVIDENCE" FOR YOURSELF. IF PARKER IS INNOCENT, TURN YOUR FURY TO YOUR EMPLOYER. IF HE'S NOT, BURY HIM.
YOU SURE MAKE MURDER SOUND LIKE BAKING BROWNIES--
...
I JUST NOTICED THAT YOU'RE TOUCHING PARTS OF ME THAT LIKE BEING TOUCHED.

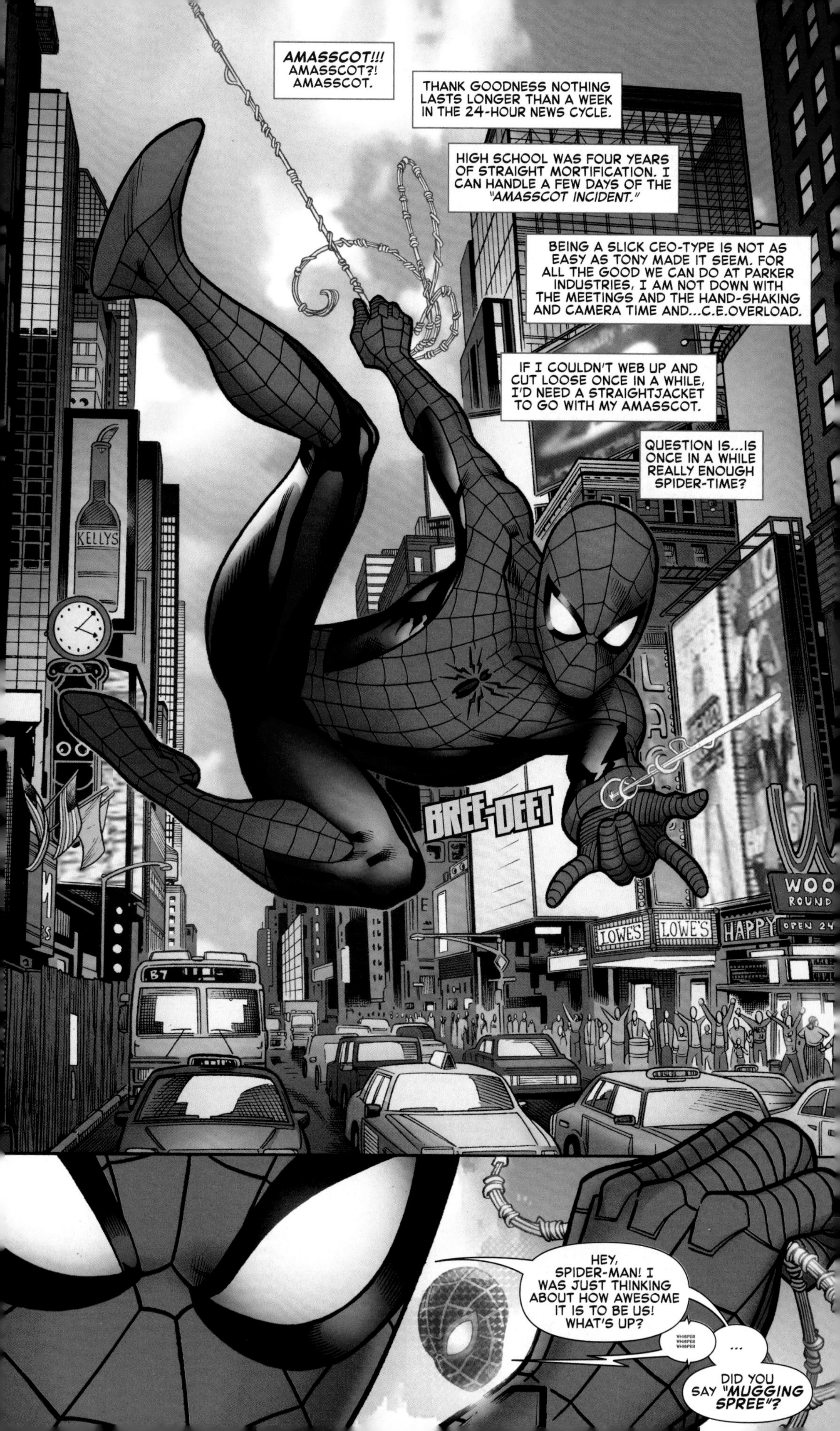

AMASSCOT!!! AMASSCOT?! AMASSCOT.
THANK GOODNESS NOTHING LASTS LONGER THAN A WEEK IN THE 24-HOUR NEWS CYCLE.
HIGH SCHOOL WAS FOUR YEARS OF STRAIGHT MORTIFICATION. I CAN HANDLE A FEW DAYS OF THE *"AMASSCOT INCIDENT."*
BEING A SLICK CEO-TYPE IS NOT AS EASY AS TONY MADE IT SEEM. FOR ALL THE GOOD WE CAN DO AT PARKER INDUSTRIES, I AM NOT DOWN WITH THE MEETINGS AND THE HAND-SHAKING AND CAMERA TIME AND...C.E.OVERLOAD.
IF I COULDN'T WEB UP AND CUT LOOSE ONCE IN A WHILE, I'D NEED A STRAIGHTJACKET TO GO WITH MY AMASSCOT.
QUESTION IS...IS ONCE IN A WHILE REALLY ENOUGH SPIDER-TIME?
KELLYS
BREE-DEET
B7
LOWE'S
LOWE'S
HAPPY
WOO
ROUND
OPEN 24
HEY, SPIDER-MAN! I WAS JUST THINKING ABOUT HOW AWESOME IT IS TO BE US! WHAT'S UP?
WHISPER WHISPER WHISPER
...
DID YOU SAY *"MUGGING SPREE"?*

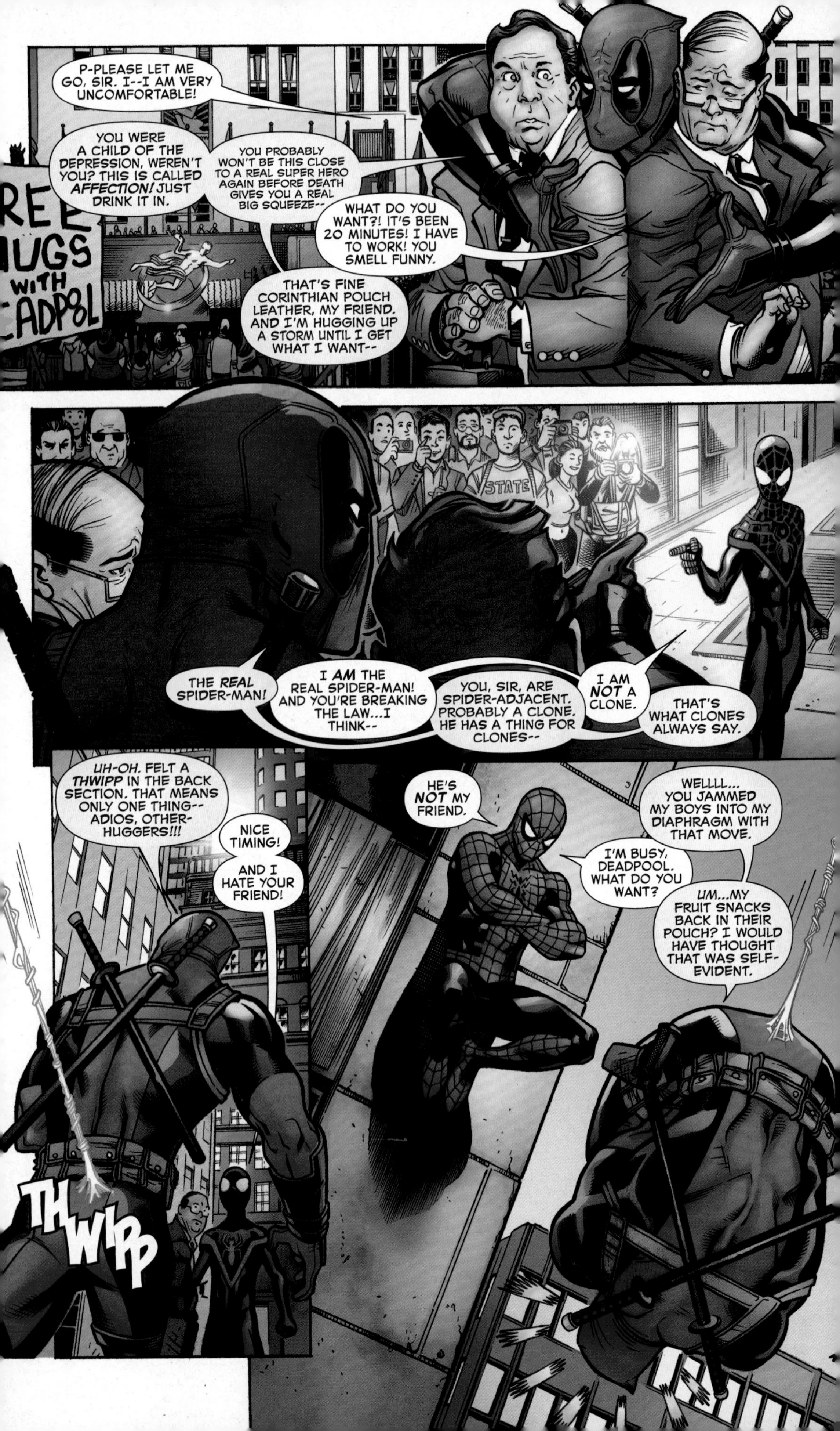
REE HUGS WITH EADP8L
P-PLEASE LET ME GO, SIR. I--I AM VERY UNCOMFORTABLE!
YOU WERE A CHILD OF THE DEPRESSION, WEREN'T YOU? THIS IS CALLED AFFECTION! JUST DRINK IT IN.
YOU PROBABLY WON'T BE THIS CLOSE TO A REAL SUPER HERO AGAIN BEFORE DEATH GIVES YOU A REAL BIG SQUEEZE--
WHAT DO YOU WANT?! IT'S BEEN 20 MINUTES! I HAVE TO WORK! YOU SMELL FUNNY.
THAT'S FINE CORINTHIAN POUCH LEATHER, MY FRIEND. AND I'M HUGGING UP A STORM UNTIL I GET WHAT I WANT--
STATE
THE REAL SPIDER-MAN!
I AM THE REAL SPIDER-MAN! AND YOU'RE BREAKING THE LAW...I THINK--
YOU, SIR, ARE SPIDER-ADJACENT. PROBABLY A CLONE. HE HAS A THING FOR CLONES--
I AM NOT A CLONE.
THAT'S WHAT CLONES ALWAYS SAY.
UH-OH. FELT A THWIPP IN THE BACK SECTION. THAT MEANS ONLY ONE THING-- ADIOS, OTHER-HUGGERS!!!
NICE TIMING!
AND I HATE YOUR FRIEND!
THWIPP
HE'S NOT MY FRIEND.
WELLLL... YOU JAMMED MY BOYS INTO MY DIAPHRAGM WITH THAT MOVE.
I'M BUSY, DEADPOOL. WHAT DO YOU WANT?
UM...MY FRUIT SNACKS BACK IN THEIR POUCH? I WOULD HAVE THOUGHT THAT WAS SELF-EVIDENT.

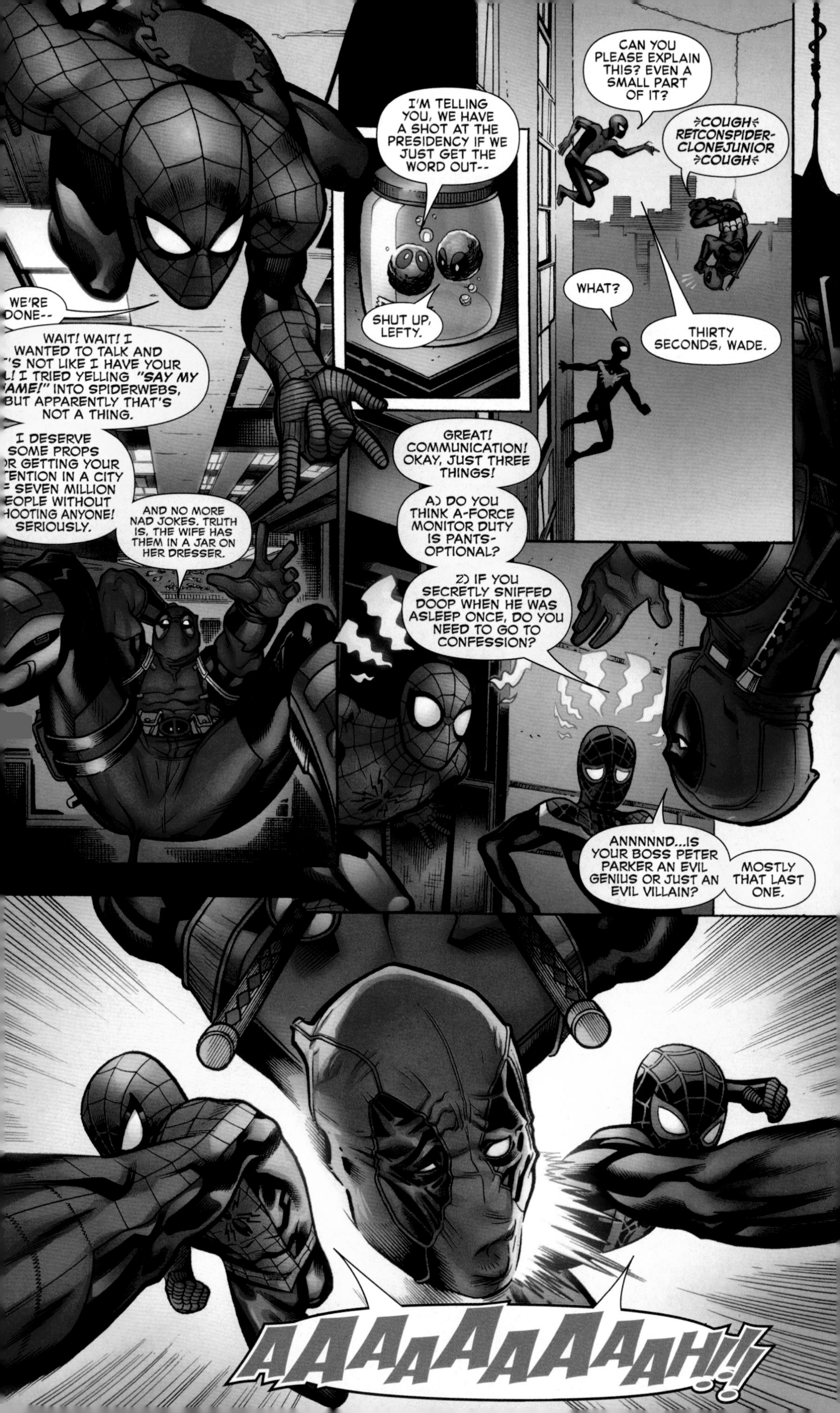

WE'RE DONE--
WAIT! WAIT! I WANTED TO TALK AND 'S NOT LIKE I HAVE YOUR L! I TRIED YELLING "SAY MY AME!" INTO SPIDERWEBS, BUT APPARENTLY THAT'S NOT A THING.
I DESERVE SOME PROPS R GETTING YOUR TENTION IN A CITY F SEVEN MILLION EOPLE WITHOUT HOOTING ANYONE! SERIOUSLY.
AND NO MORE NAD JOKES. TRUTH IS, THE WIFE HAS THEM IN A JAR ON HER DRESSER.
I'M TELLING YOU, WE HAVE A SHOT AT THE PRESIDENCY IF WE JUST GET THE WORD OUT--
SHUT UP, LEFTY.
CAN YOU PLEASE EXPLAIN THIS? EVEN A SMALL PART OF IT?
COUGH RETCONSPIDER-CLONEJUNIOR *COUGH*
WHAT?
THIRTY SECONDS, WADE.
GREAT! COMMUNICATION! OKAY, JUST THREE THINGS!
A) DO YOU THINK A-FORCE MONITOR DUTY IS PANTS-OPTIONAL?
Z) IF YOU SECRETLY SNIFFED DOOP WHEN HE WAS ASLEEP ONCE, DO YOU NEED TO GO TO CONFESSION?
ANNNNND...IS YOUR BOSS PETER PARKER AN EVIL GENIUS OR JUST AN EVIL VILLAIN?
MOSTLY THAT LAST ONE.
AAAAAAAAAAH!!!

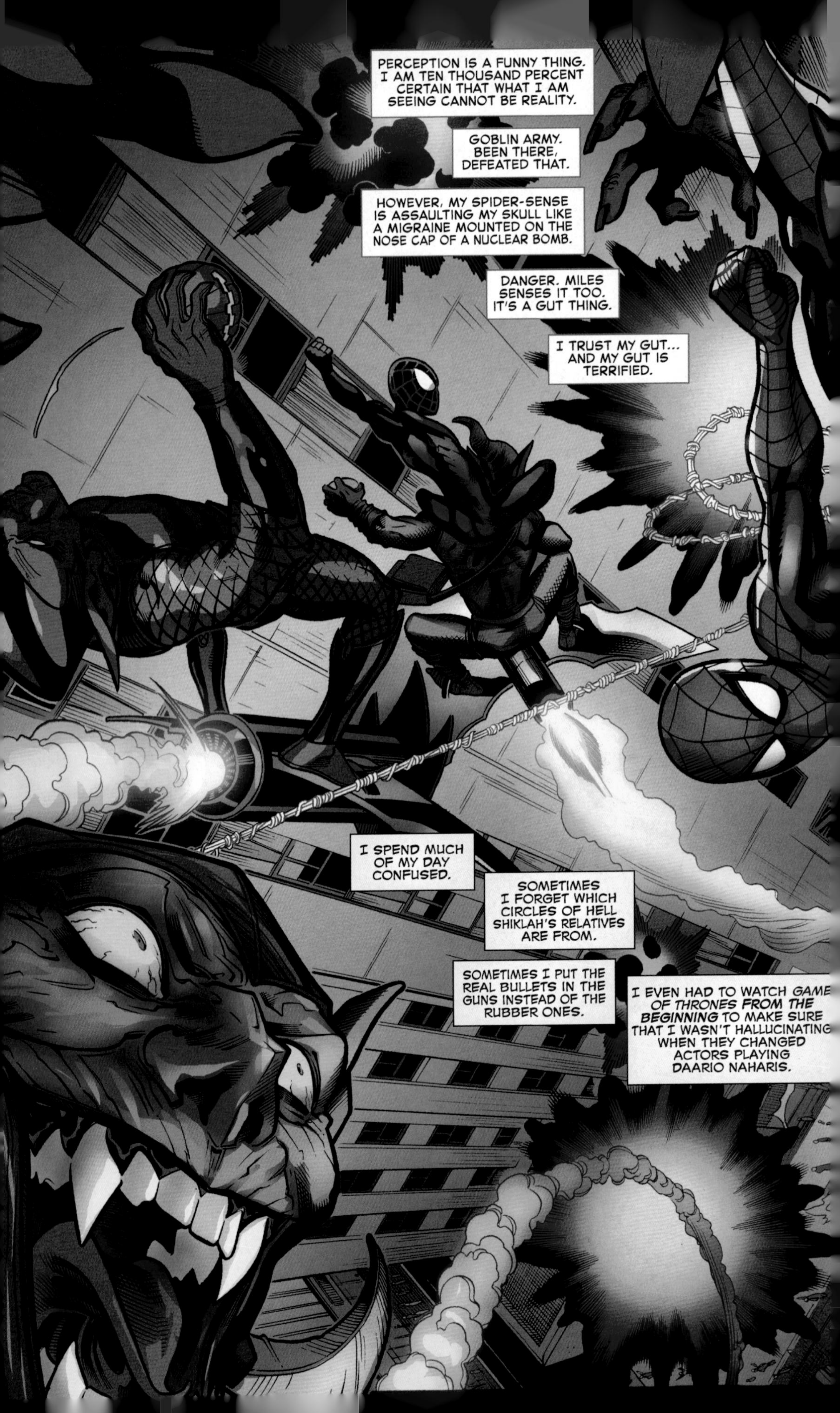
PERCEPTION IS A FUNNY THING. I AM TEN THOUSAND PERCENT CERTAIN THAT WHAT I AM SEEING CANNOT BE REALITY.
GOBLIN ARMY. BEEN THERE, DEFEATED THAT.
HOWEVER, MY SPIDER-SENSE IS ASSAULTING MY SKULL LIKE A MIGRAINE MOUNTED ON THE NOSE CAP OF A NUCLEAR BOMB.
DANGER. MILES SENSES IT TOO. IT'S A GUT THING.
I TRUST MY GUT... AND MY GUT IS TERRIFIED.
I SPEND MUCH OF MY DAY CONFUSED.
SOMETIMES I FORGET WHICH CIRCLES OF HELL SHIKLAH'S RELATIVES ARE FROM.
SOMETIMES I PUT THE REAL BULLETS IN THE GUNS INSTEAD OF THE RUBBER ONES.
I EVEN HAD TO WATCH *GAME OF THRONES **FROM THE BEGINNING*** TO MAKE SURE THAT I WASN'T HALLUCINATING WHEN THEY CHANGED ACTORS PLAYING DAARIO NAHARIS.

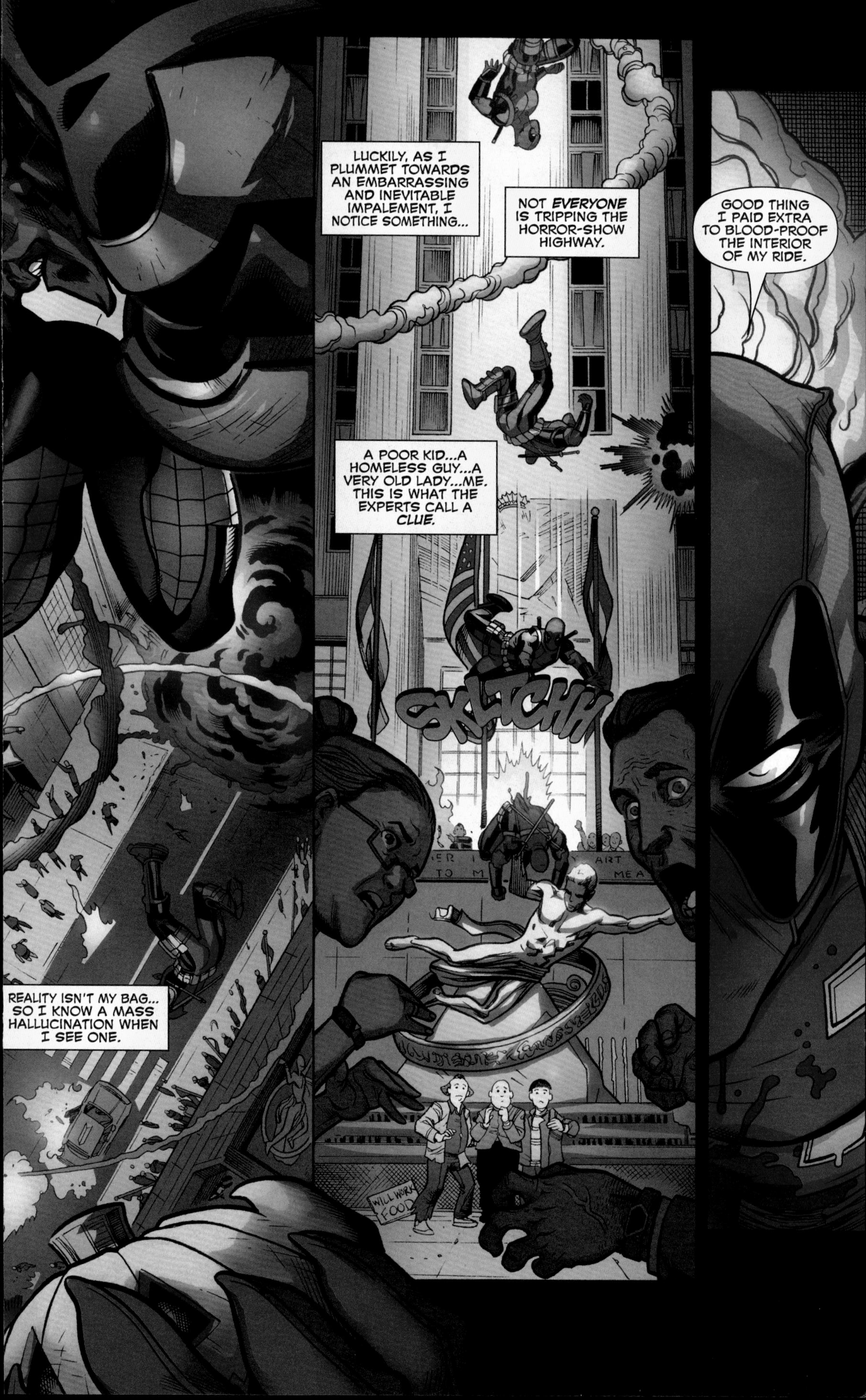
REALITY ISN'T MY BAG... SO I KNOW A MASS HALLUCINATION WHEN I SEE ONE.
LUCKILY, AS I PLUMMET TOWARDS AN EMBARRASSING AND INEVITABLE IMPALEMENT, I NOTICE SOMETHING...
NOT *EVERYONE* IS TRIPPING THE HORROR-SHOW HIGHWAY.
A POOR KID...A HOMELESS GUY...A VERY OLD LADY...ME. THIS IS WHAT THE EXPERTS CALL A *CLUE*.
SKLTCHH
WILL WORK FOOD
GOOD THING I PAID EXTRA TO BLOOD-PROOF THE INTERIOR OF MY RIDE.

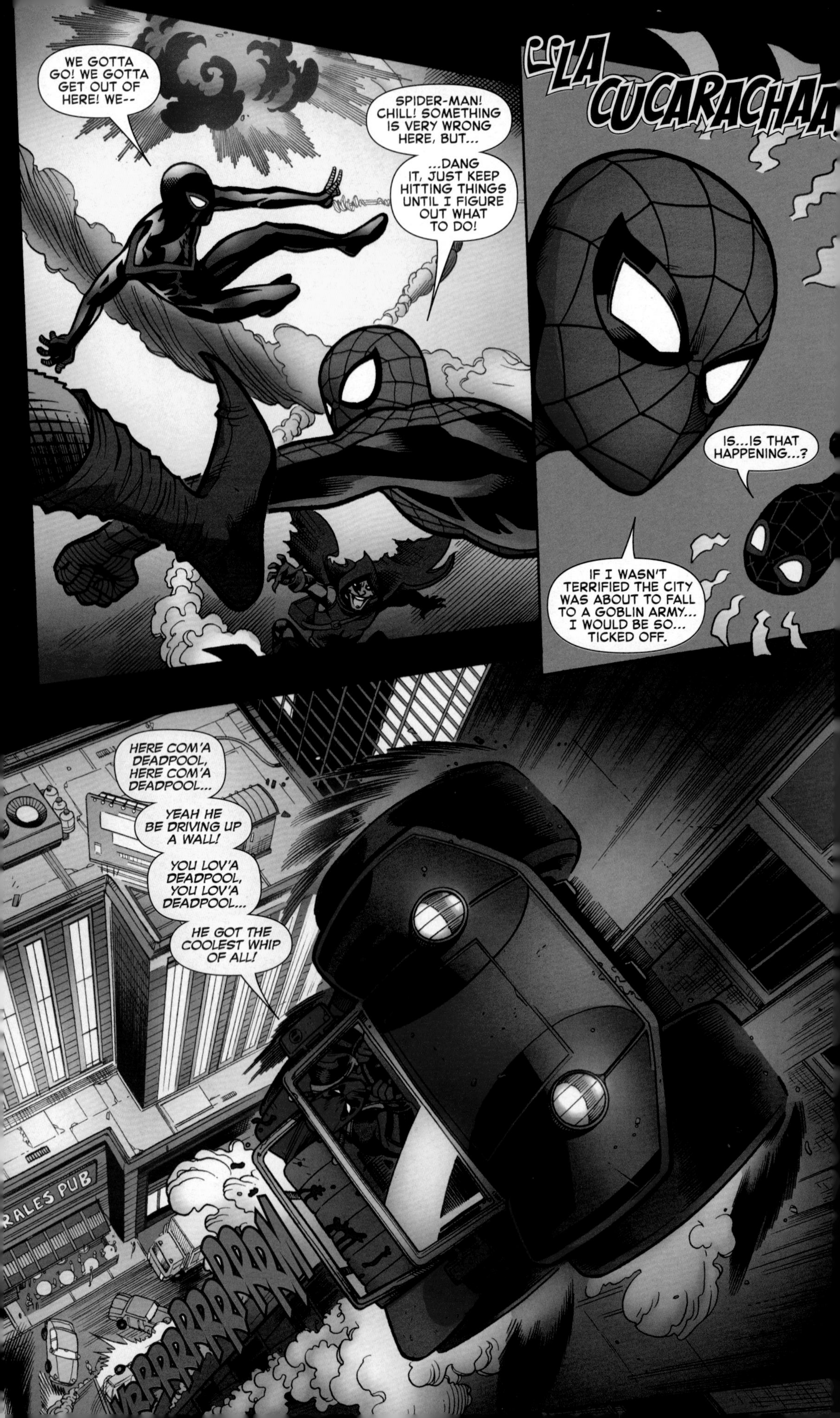

WE GOTTA GO! WE GOTTA GET OUT OF HERE! WE--
SPIDER-MAN! CHILL! SOMETHING IS VERY WRONG HERE, BUT...
...DANG IT, JUST KEEP HITTING THINGS UNTIL I FIGURE OUT WHAT TO DO!
¡¡LA CUCARACHAA
IS...IS THAT HAPPENING...?
IF I WASN'T TERRIFIED THE CITY WAS ABOUT TO FALL TO A GOBLIN ARMY... I WOULD BE SO... TICKED OFF.
HERE COM'A DEADPOOL, HERE COM'A DEADPOOL...
YEAH HE BE DRIVING UP A WALL!
YOU LOV'A DEADPOOL, YOU LOV'A DEADPOOL...
HE GOT THE COOLEST WHIP OF ALL!
RALES PUB
VRRRRRRRM

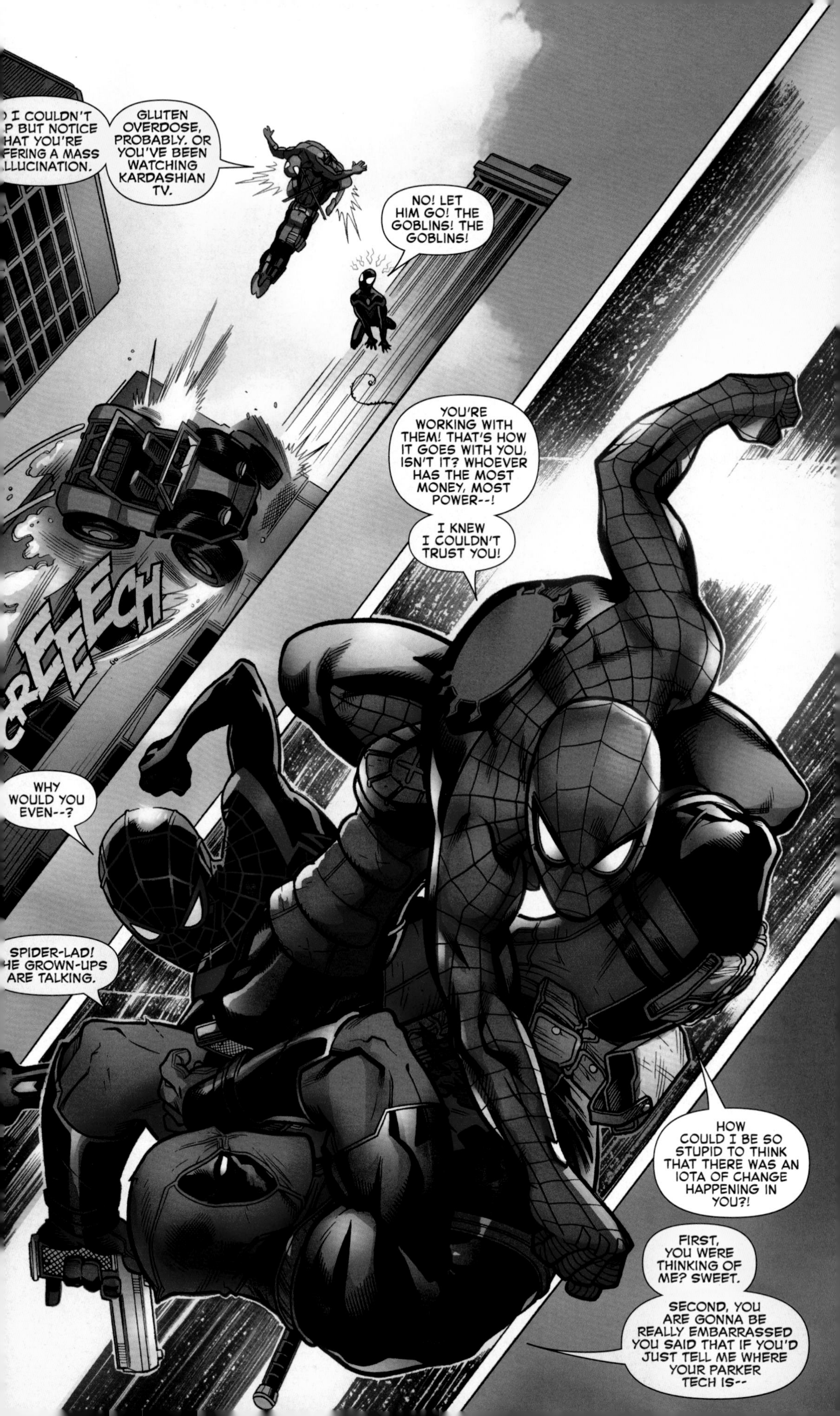

I COULDN'T
P BUT NOTICE
HAT YOU'RE
FERING A MASS
LLUCINATION.
GLUTEN OVERDOSE, PROBABLY. OR YOU'VE BEEN WATCHING KARDASHIAN TV.
NO! LET HIM GO! THE GOBLINS! THE GOBLINS!
SCREEECH
YOU'RE WORKING WITH THEM! THAT'S HOW IT GOES WITH YOU, ISN'T IT? WHOEVER HAS THE MOST MONEY, MOST POWER--!
I KNEW I COULDN'T TRUST YOU!
WHY WOULD YOU EVEN--?
SPIDER-LAD!
HE GROWN-UPS
ARE TALKING.
HOW COULD I BE SO STUPID TO THINK THAT THERE WAS AN IOTA OF CHANGE HAPPENING IN YOU?!
FIRST, YOU WERE THINKING OF ME? SWEET.
SECOND, YOU ARE GONNA BE REALLY EMBARRASSED YOU SAID THAT IF YOU'D JUST TELL ME WHERE YOUR PARKER TECH IS--

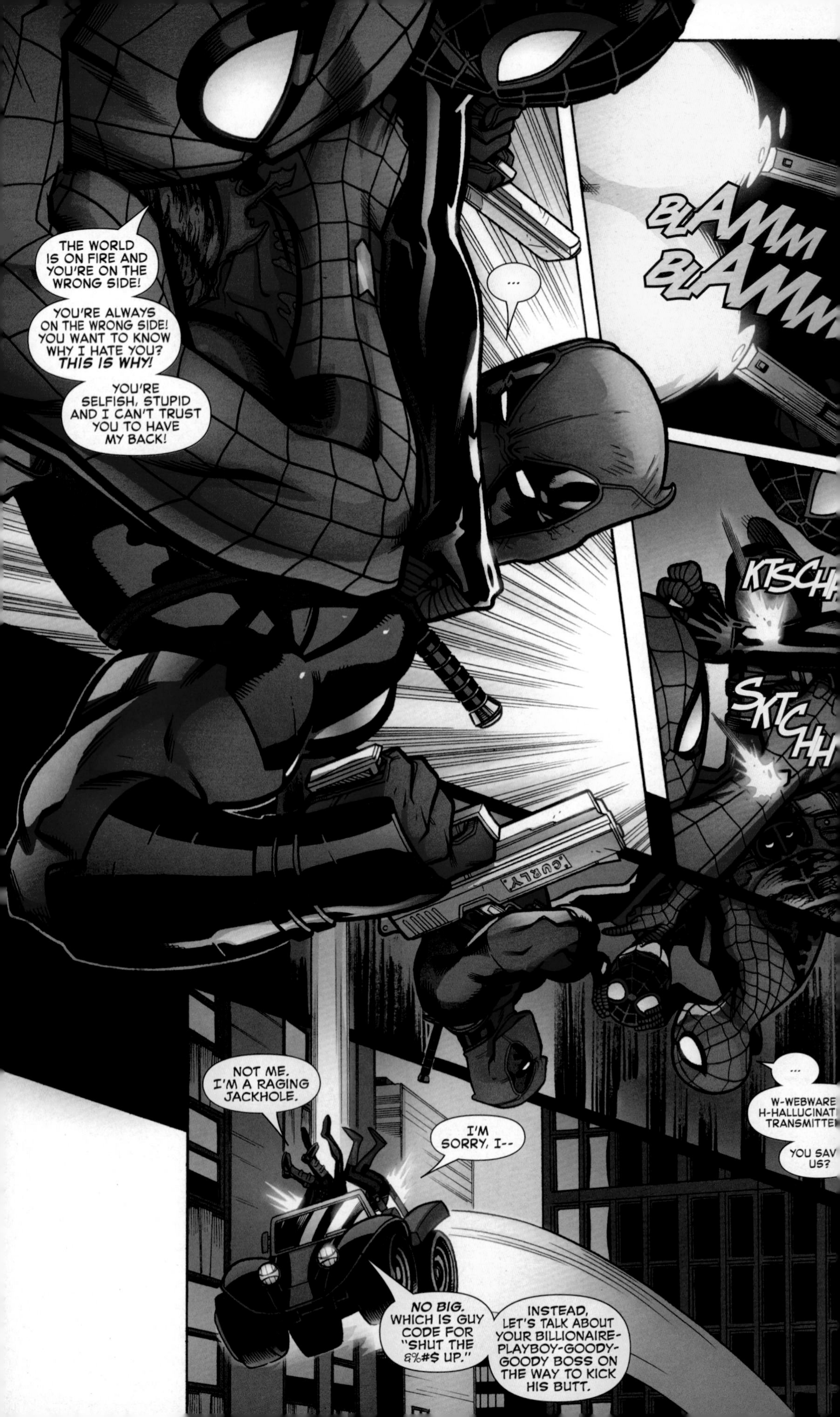
THE WORLD IS ON FIRE AND YOU'RE ON THE WRONG SIDE!
YOU'RE ALWAYS ON THE WRONG SIDE! YOU WANT TO KNOW WHY I HATE YOU? THIS IS WHY!
YOU'RE SELFISH, STUPID AND I CAN'T TRUST YOU TO HAVE MY BACK!
...
BLAMM
BLAMM
KTSCHH
SKTCHH
CURLY
...
NOT ME. I'M A RAGING JACKHOLE.
I'M SORRY, I--
NO BIG. WHICH IS GUY CODE FOR "SHUT THE &%#$ UP."
INSTEAD, LET'S TALK ABOUT YOUR BILLIONAIRE-PLAYBOY-GOODY-GOODY BOSS ON THE WAY TO KICK HIS BUTT.

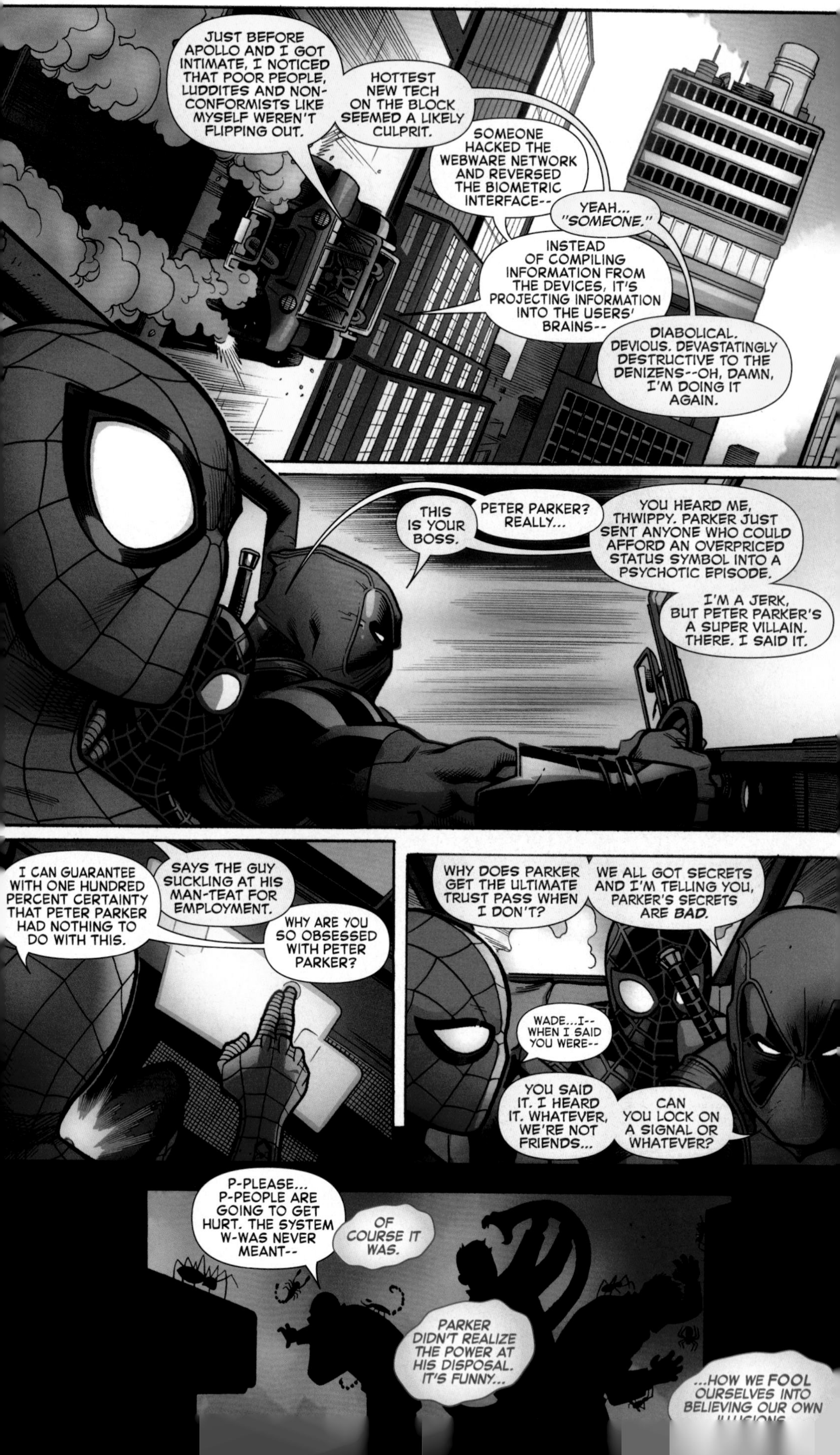

JUST BEFORE APOLLO AND I GOT INTIMATE, I NOTICED THAT POOR PEOPLE, LUDDITES AND NON-CONFORMISTS LIKE MYSELF WEREN'T FLIPPING OUT.
HOTTEST NEW TECH ON THE BLOCK SEEMED A LIKELY CULPRIT.
SOMEONE HACKED THE WEBWARE NETWORK AND REVERSED THE BIOMETRIC INTERFACE--
YEAH... "SOMEONE."
INSTEAD OF COMPILING INFORMATION FROM THE DEVICES, IT'S PROJECTING INFORMATION INTO THE USERS' BRAINS--
DIABOLICAL. DEVIOUS. DEVASTATINGLY DESTRUCTIVE TO THE DENIZENS--OH, DAMN, I'M DOING IT AGAIN.
THIS IS YOUR BOSS.
PETER PARKER? REALLY...
YOU HEARD ME, THWIPPY. PARKER JUST SENT ANYONE WHO COULD AFFORD AN OVERPRICED STATUS SYMBOL INTO A PSYCHOTIC EPISODE.
I'M A JERK, BUT PETER PARKER'S A SUPER VILLAIN. THERE. I SAID IT.
I CAN GUARANTEE WITH ONE HUNDRED PERCENT CERTAINTY THAT PETER PARKER HAD NOTHING TO DO WITH THIS.
SAYS THE GUY SUCKLING AT HIS MAN-TEAT FOR EMPLOYMENT.
WHY ARE YOU SO OBSESSED WITH PETER PARKER?
WHY DOES PARKER GET THE ULTIMATE TRUST PASS WHEN I DON'T?
WE ALL GOT SECRETS AND I'M TELLING YOU, PARKER'S SECRETS ARE BAD.
WADE...I-- WHEN I SAID YOU WERE--
YOU SAID IT. I HEARD IT. WHATEVER, WE'RE NOT FRIENDS...
CAN YOU LOCK ON A SIGNAL OR WHATEVER?
P-PLEASE... P-PEOPLE ARE GOING TO GET HURT. THE SYSTEM W-WAS NEVER MEANT--
OF COURSE IT WAS.
PARKER DIDN'T REALIZE THE POWER AT HIS DISPOSAL. IT'S FUNNY...
...HOW WE FOOL OURSELVES INTO BELIEVING OUR OWN

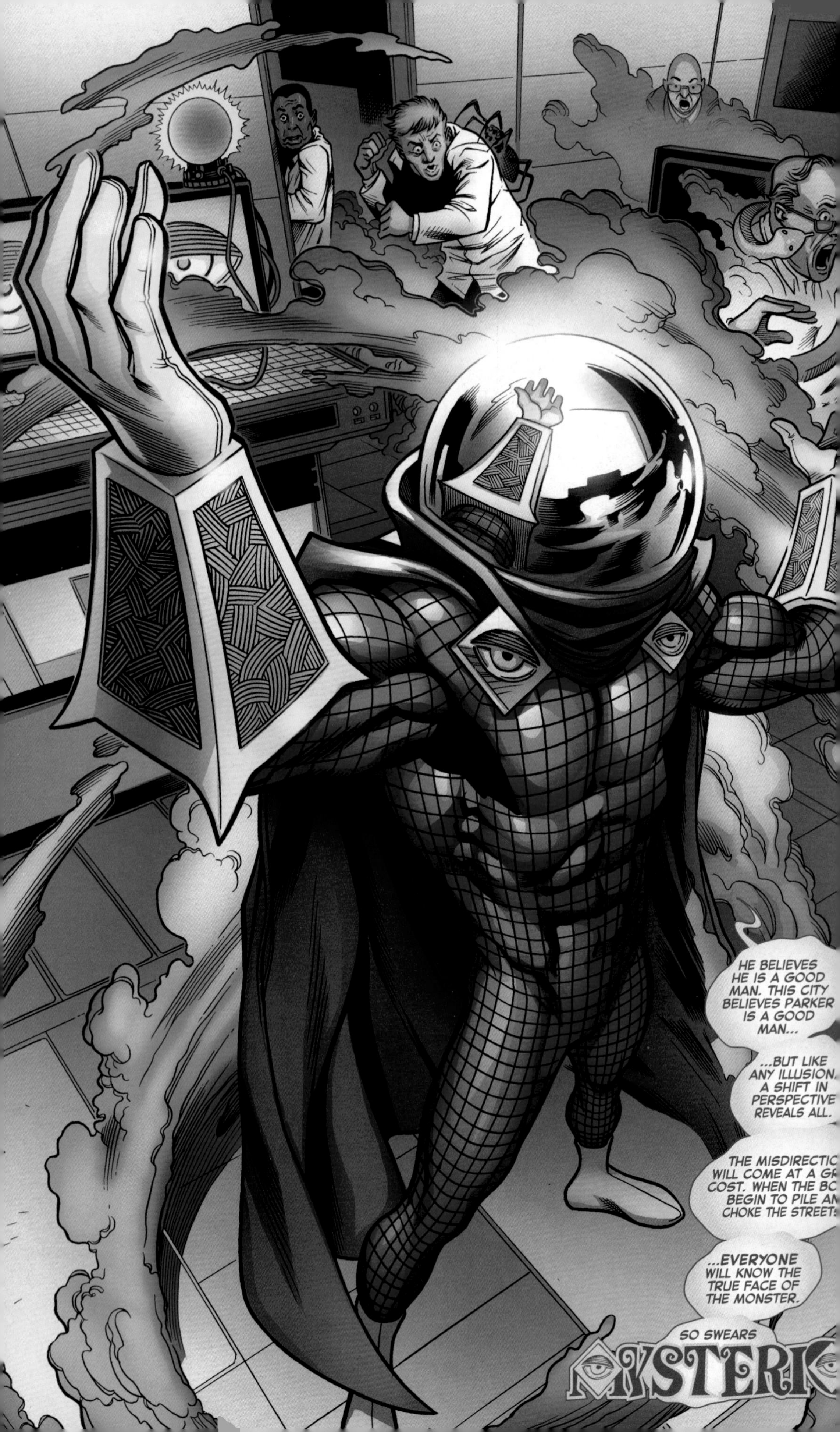
HE BELIEVES HE IS A GOOD MAN. THIS CITY BELIEVES PARKER IS A GOOD MAN...
...BUT LIKE ANY ILLUSION, A SHIFT IN PERSPECTIVE REVEALS ALL.
...EVERYONE WILL KNOW THE TRUE FACE OF THE MONSTER.
SO SWEARS

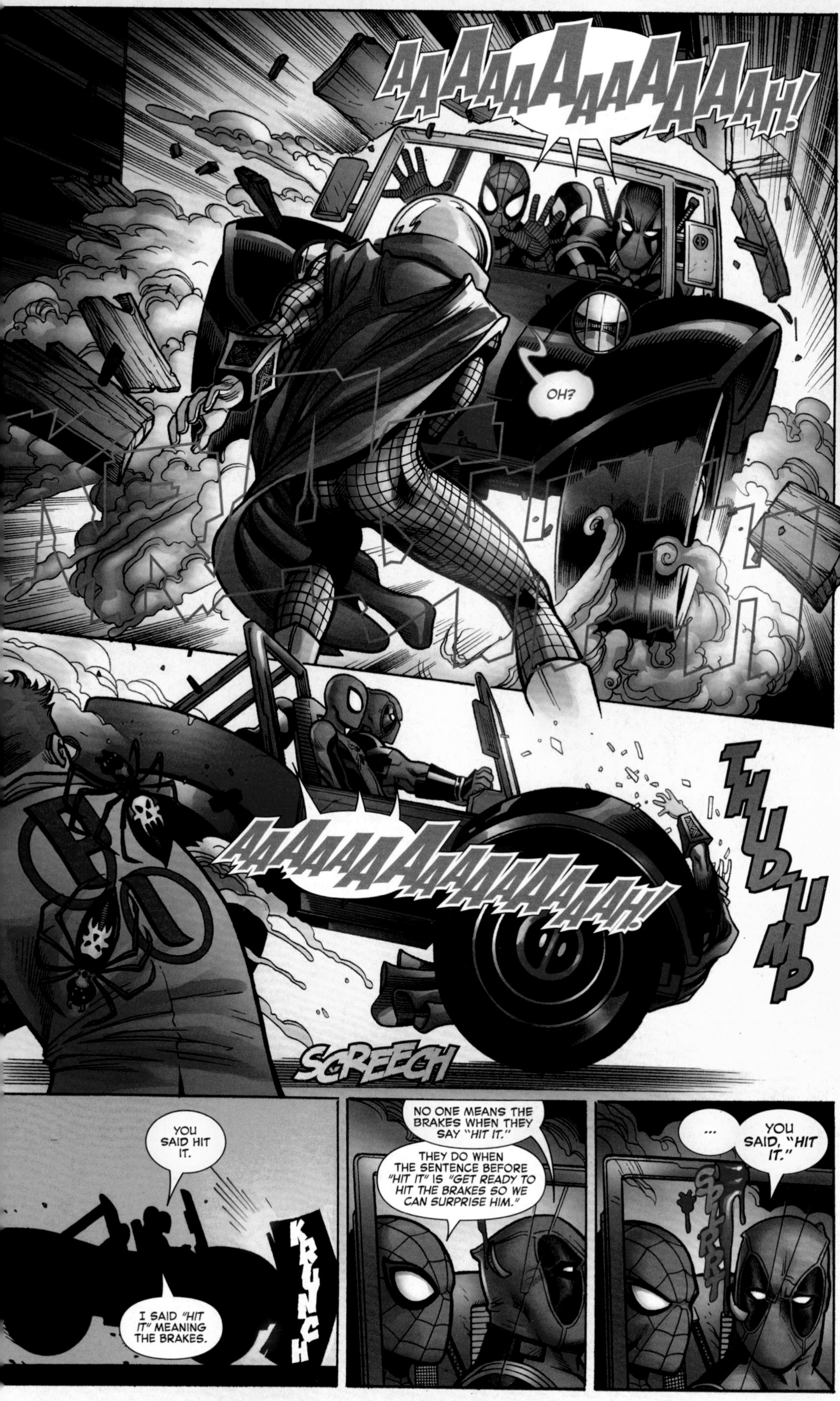
AAAAAAAAAAAAAH!
OH?
AAAAAAAAAAAAAAAAAH!
THUDUMP
SCREECH
YOU SAID HIT IT.
KRUNCH
I SAID "HIT IT" MEANING THE BRAKES.
NO ONE MEANS THE BRAKES WHEN THEY SAY "HIT IT."
THEY DO WHEN THE SENTENCE BEFORE "HIT IT" IS "GET READY TO HIT THE BRAKES SO WE CAN SURPRISE HIM."
...
YOU SAID, "HIT IT."

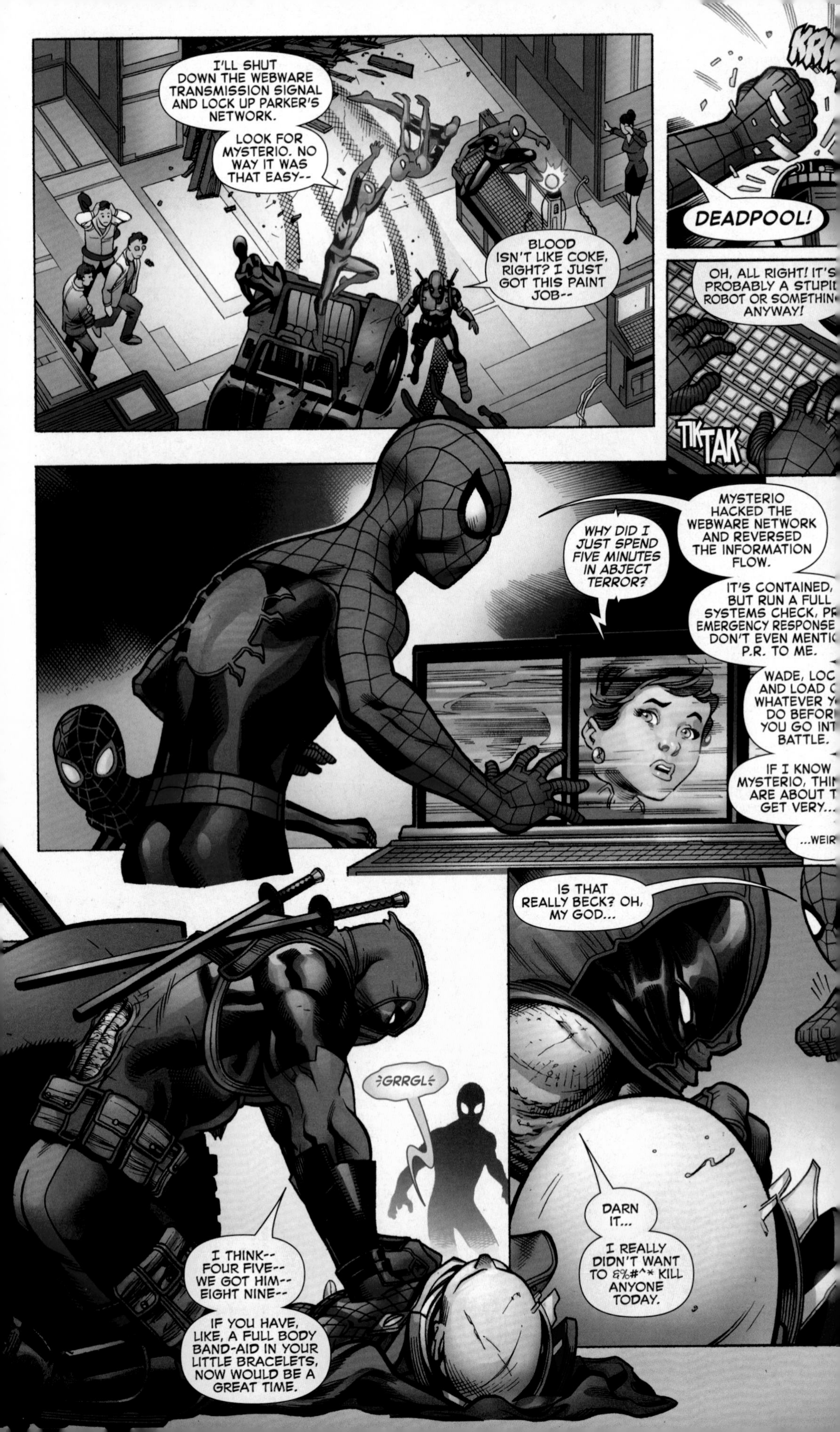

I'LL SHUT DOWN THE WEBWARE TRANSMISSION SIGNAL AND LOCK UP PARKER'S NETWORK.
LOOK FOR MYSTERIO. NO WAY IT WAS THAT EASY--
BLOOD ISN'T LIKE COKE, RIGHT? I JUST GOT THIS PAINT JOB--
DEADPOOL!
OH, ALL RIGHT! IT'S PROBABLY A STUPID ROBOT OR SOMETHING ANYWAY!
TIK TAK
MYSTERIO HACKED THE WEBWARE NETWORK AND REVERSED THE INFORMATION FLOW.
WHY DID I JUST SPEND FIVE MINUTES IN ABJECT TERROR?
IT'S CONTAINED, BUT RUN A FULL SYSTEMS CHECK, EMERGENCY RESPONSE DON'T EVEN MENTI P.R. TO ME.
WADE, LOC AND LOAD WHATEVER DO BEFOR YOU GO INT BATTLE.
IF I KNOW MYSTERIO, THI ARE ABOUT GET VERY...
...WEIR
IS THAT REALLY BECK? OH, MY GOD...
GRRGL
I THINK-- FOUR FIVE-- WE GOT HIM-- EIGHT NINE--
IF YOU HAVE, LIKE, A FULL BODY BAND-AID IN YOUR LITTLE BRACELETS, NOW WOULD BE A GREAT TIME.
DARN IT...
I REALLY DIDN'T WANT TO &%#^* KILL ANYONE TODAY.

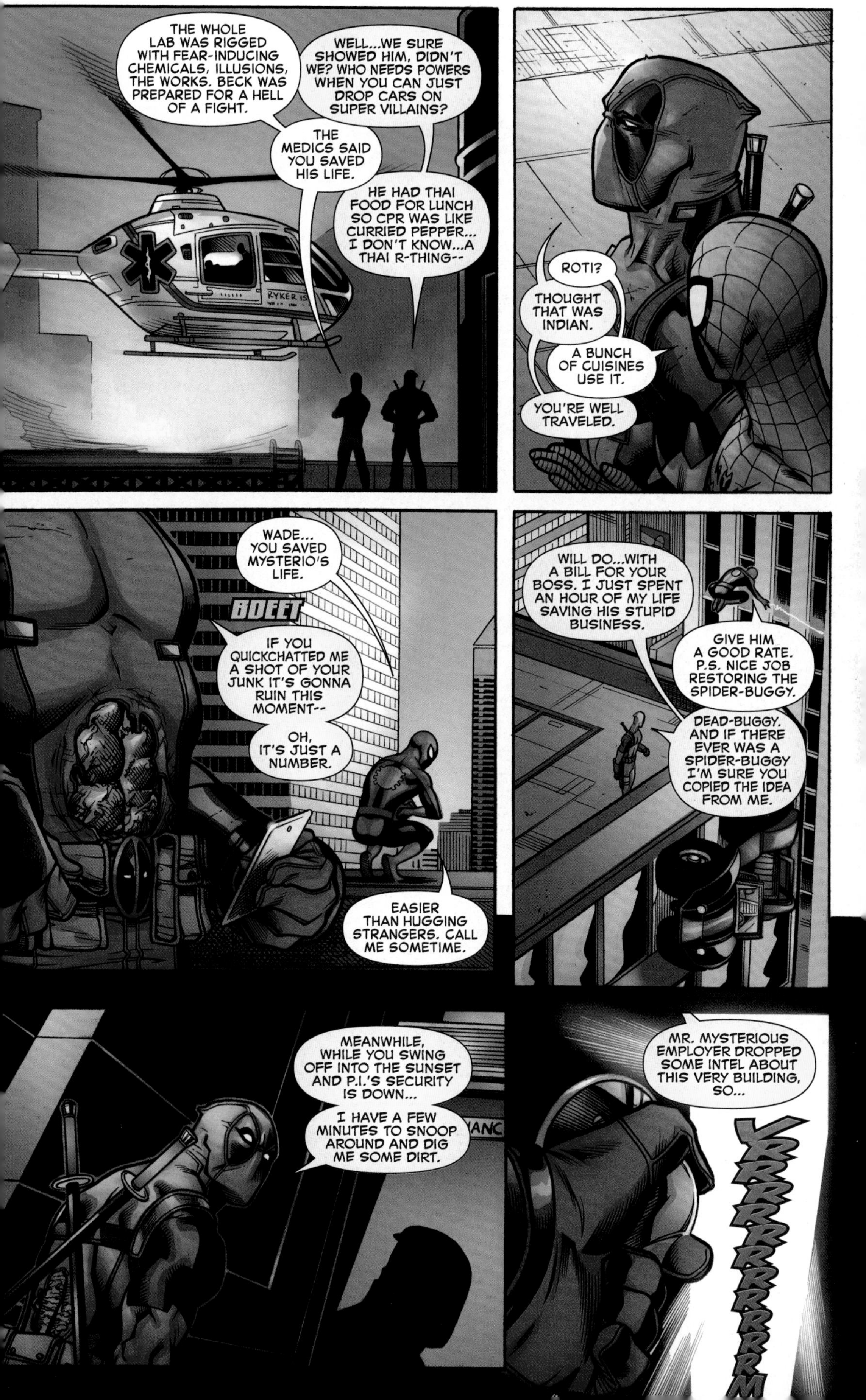
THE WHOLE LAB WAS RIGGED WITH FEAR-INDUCING CHEMICALS, ILLUSIONS, THE WORKS. BECK WAS PREPARED FOR A HELL OF A FIGHT.
WELL...WE SURE SHOWED HIM, DIDN'T WE? WHO NEEDS POWERS WHEN YOU CAN JUST DROP CARS ON SUPER VILLAINS?
THE MEDICS SAID YOU SAVED HIS LIFE.
HE HAD THAI FOOD FOR LUNCH SO CPR WAS LIKE CURRIED PEPPER... I DON'T KNOW...A THAI R-THING--
RYKER IS
ROTI?
THOUGHT THAT WAS INDIAN.
A BUNCH OF CUISINES USE IT.
YOU'RE WELL TRAVELED.
WADE... YOU SAVED MYSTERIO'S LIFE.
BDEET
IF YOU QUICKCHATTED ME A SHOT OF YOUR JUNK IT'S GONNA RUIN THIS MOMENT--
OH, IT'S JUST A NUMBER.
EASIER THAN HUGGING STRANGERS. CALL ME SOMETIME.
WILL DO...WITH A BILL FOR YOUR BOSS. I JUST SPENT AN HOUR OF MY LIFE SAVING HIS STUPID BUSINESS.
GIVE HIM A GOOD RATE. P.S. NICE JOB RESTORING THE SPIDER-BUGGY.
DEAD-BUGGY. AND IF THERE EVER WAS A SPIDER-BUGGY I'M SURE YOU COPIED THE IDEA FROM ME.
MEANWHILE, WHILE YOU SWING OFF INTO THE SUNSET AND P.I.'S SECURITY IS DOWN...
I HAVE A FEW MINUTES TO SNOOP AROUND AND DIG ME SOME DIRT.
MR. MYSTERIOUS EMPLOYER DROPPED SOME INTEL ABOUT THIS VERY BUILDING, SO...
YRRRRRRRRRRRM

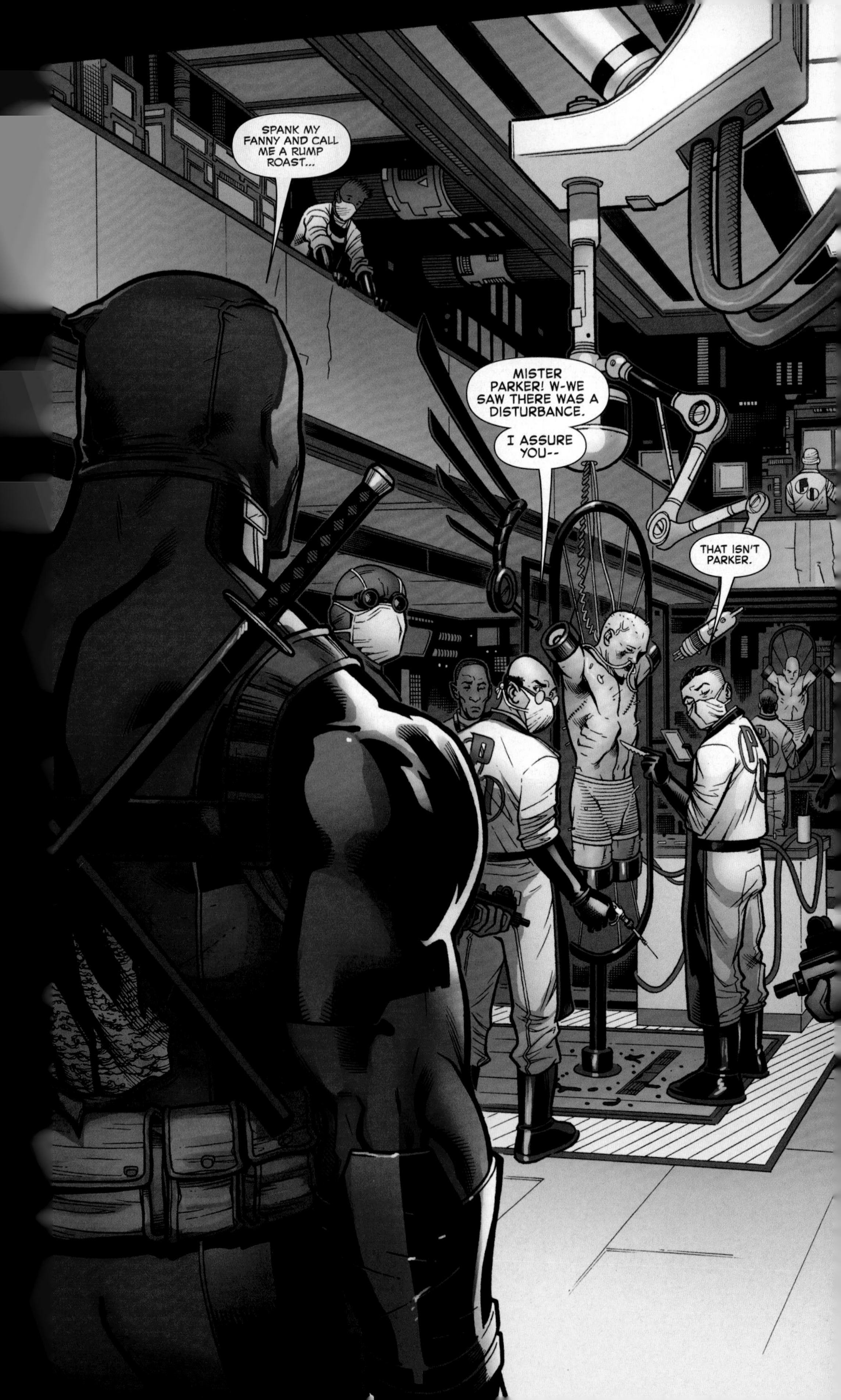
SPANK MY FANNY AND CALL ME A RUMP ROAST...
MISTER PARKER! W-WE SAW THERE WAS A DISTURBANCE.
I ASSURE YOU--
THAT ISN'T PARKER.

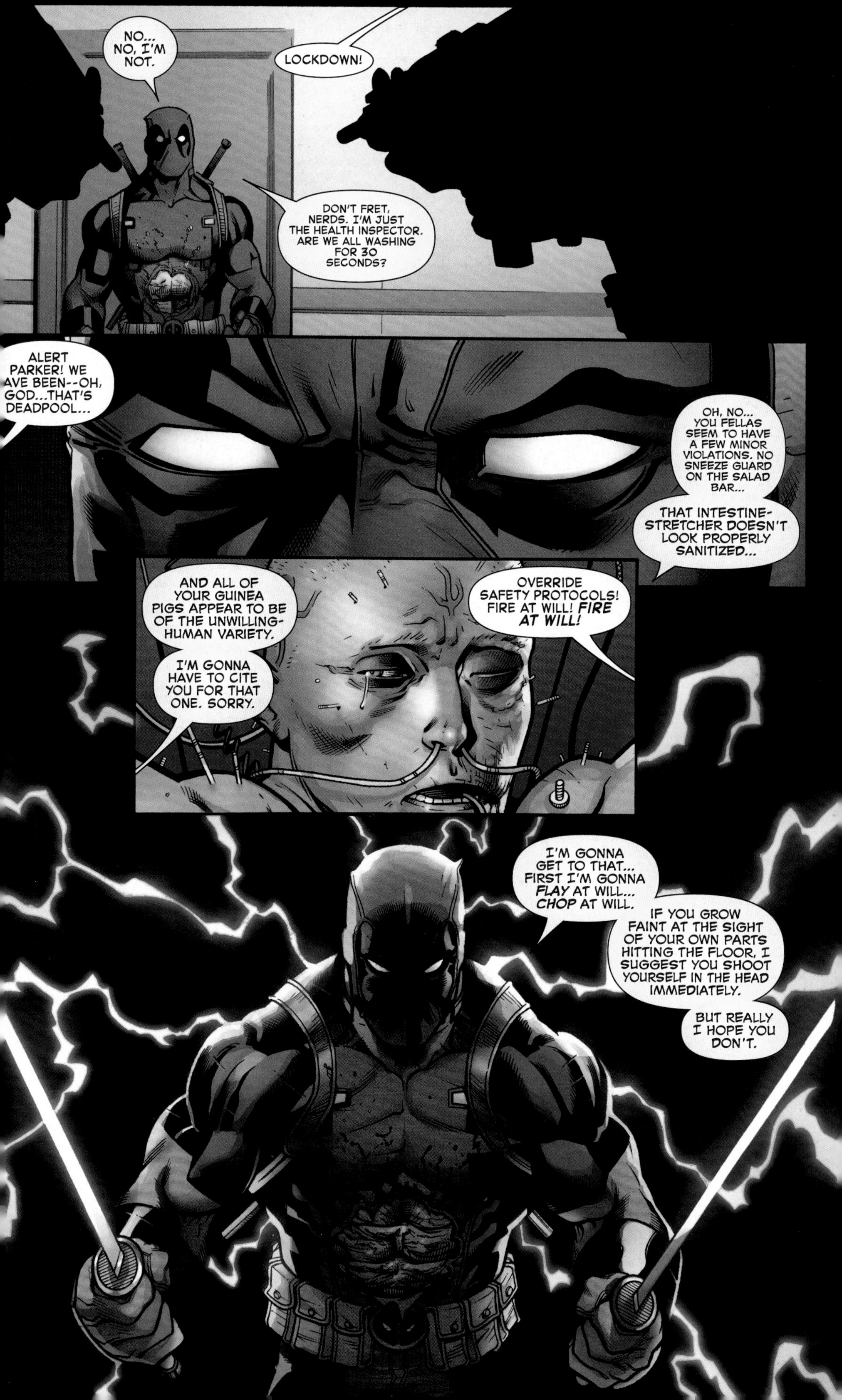
NO... NO, I'M NOT.
LOCKDOWN!
DON'T FRET, NERDS. I'M JUST THE HEALTH INSPECTOR. ARE WE ALL WASHING FOR 30 SECONDS?
ALERT PARKER! WE AVE BEEN--OH, GOD...THAT'S DEADPOOL...
OH, NO... YOU FELLAS SEEM TO HAVE A FEW MINOR VIOLATIONS. NO SNEEZE GUARD ON THE SALAD BAR...
THAT INTESTINE-STRETCHER DOESN'T LOOK PROPERLY SANITIZED...
AND ALL OF YOUR GUINEA PIGS APPEAR TO BE OF THE UNWILLING-HUMAN VARIETY.
I'M GONNA HAVE TO CITE YOU FOR THAT ONE. SORRY.
OVERRIDE SAFETY PROTOCOLS! FIRE AT WILL! FIRE AT WILL!
I'M GONNA GET TO THAT... FIRST I'M GONNA FLAY AT WILL... CHOP AT WILL.
IF YOU GROW FAINT AT THE SIGHT OF YOUR OWN PARTS HITTING THE FLOOR, I SUGGEST YOU SHOOT YOURSELF IN THE HEAD IMMEDIATELY.
BUT REALLY I HOPE YOU DON'T.

YEAAAAAAGH!
YEAH, SORRY. NORMALLY I MAKE MORE JOKES BEFORE THE AMPUTATIONS START. I'LL MAKE IT UP TO YOU...
...GOTTA MAKE A CALL FIRST. VOICE DIAL...
"CLIENT PATIENT ZERO."
BDEET
"SPEAK."
"YEAH, HI...DEADPOOL. SORRY FOR THE NOISE. I'M MAKING A LOT OF GUYS WISH THEY'D NEVER BEEN BORN."
"I DID NOT EXPECT TO HEAR FROM YOU. HAVE YOU CONSIDERED MY REQUEST...?"
YEAH. I'M IN. ALL IN.
THANK YOU...I CAN'T-- THANK YOU.
SERIOUSLY? IT'LL BE MY PLEASURE PUTT PARKER IN TH GROUND.
HAVE A NICE DAY.

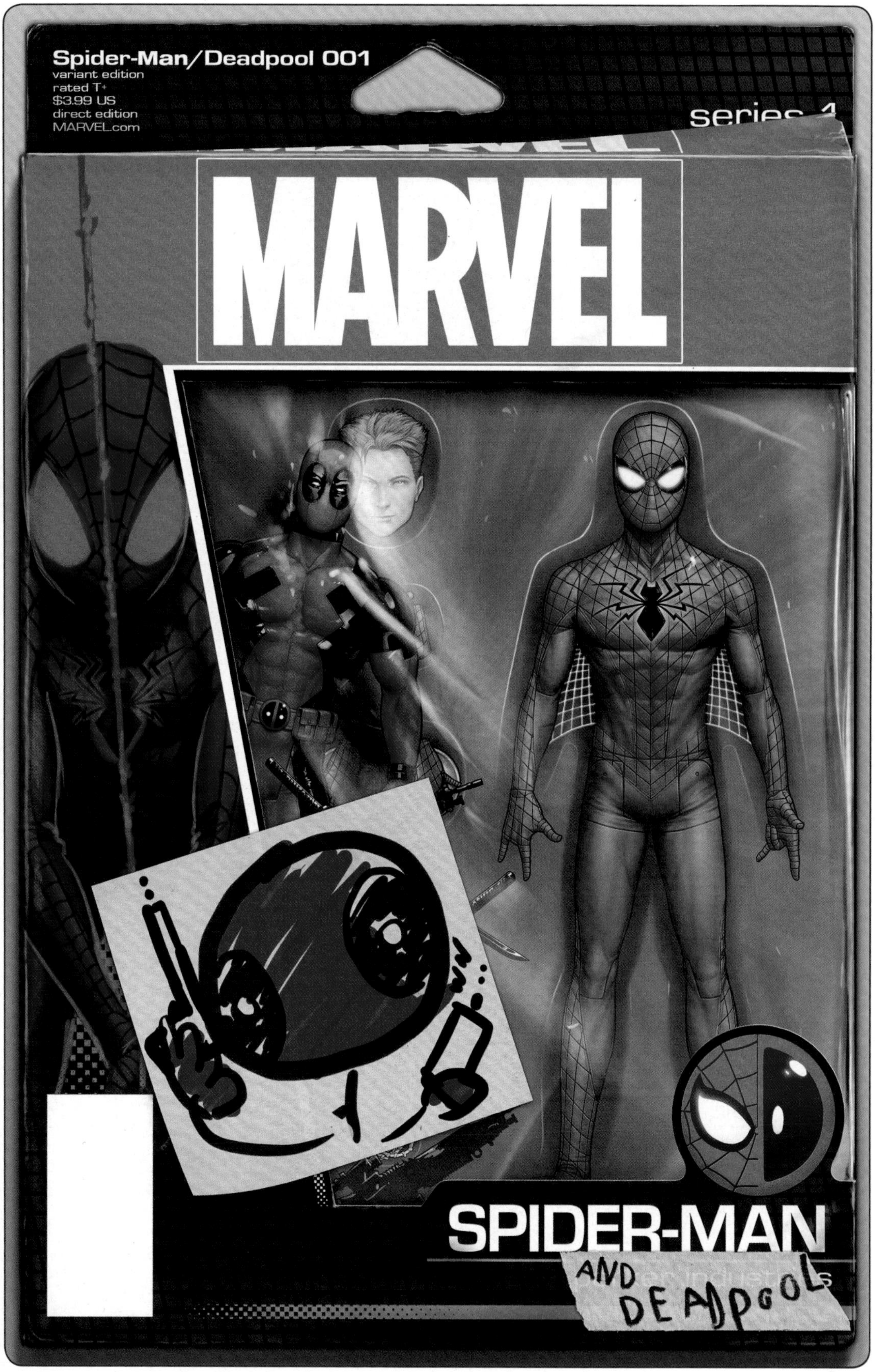
Spider-Man/Deadpool 001
variant edition
rated T+
$3.99 US
direct edition
MARVEL.com
MARVEL
SPIDER-MAN
AND DEADPOOL

1 ACTION FIGURE VARIANT BY
JOHN TYLER CHRISTOPHER

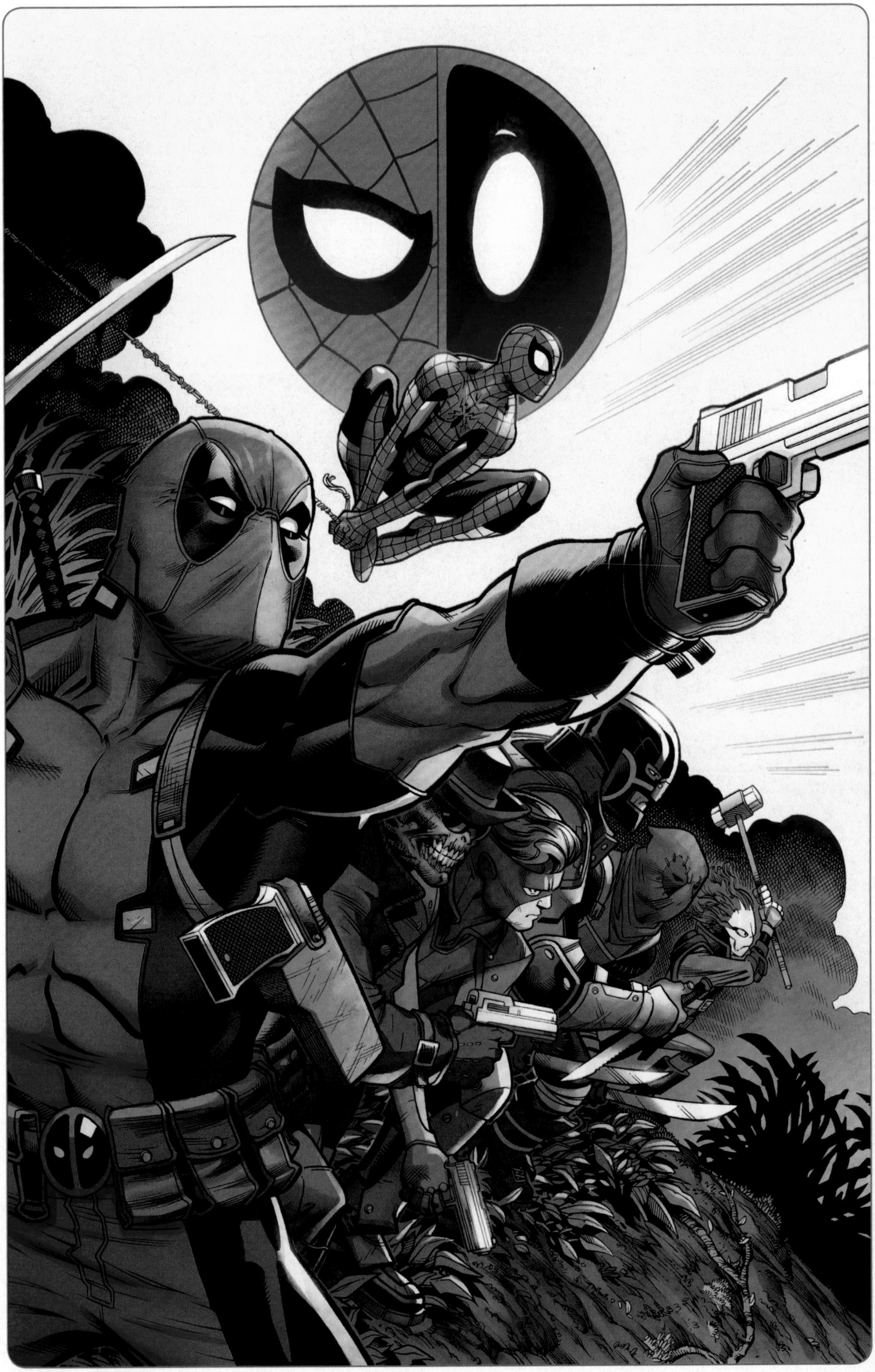

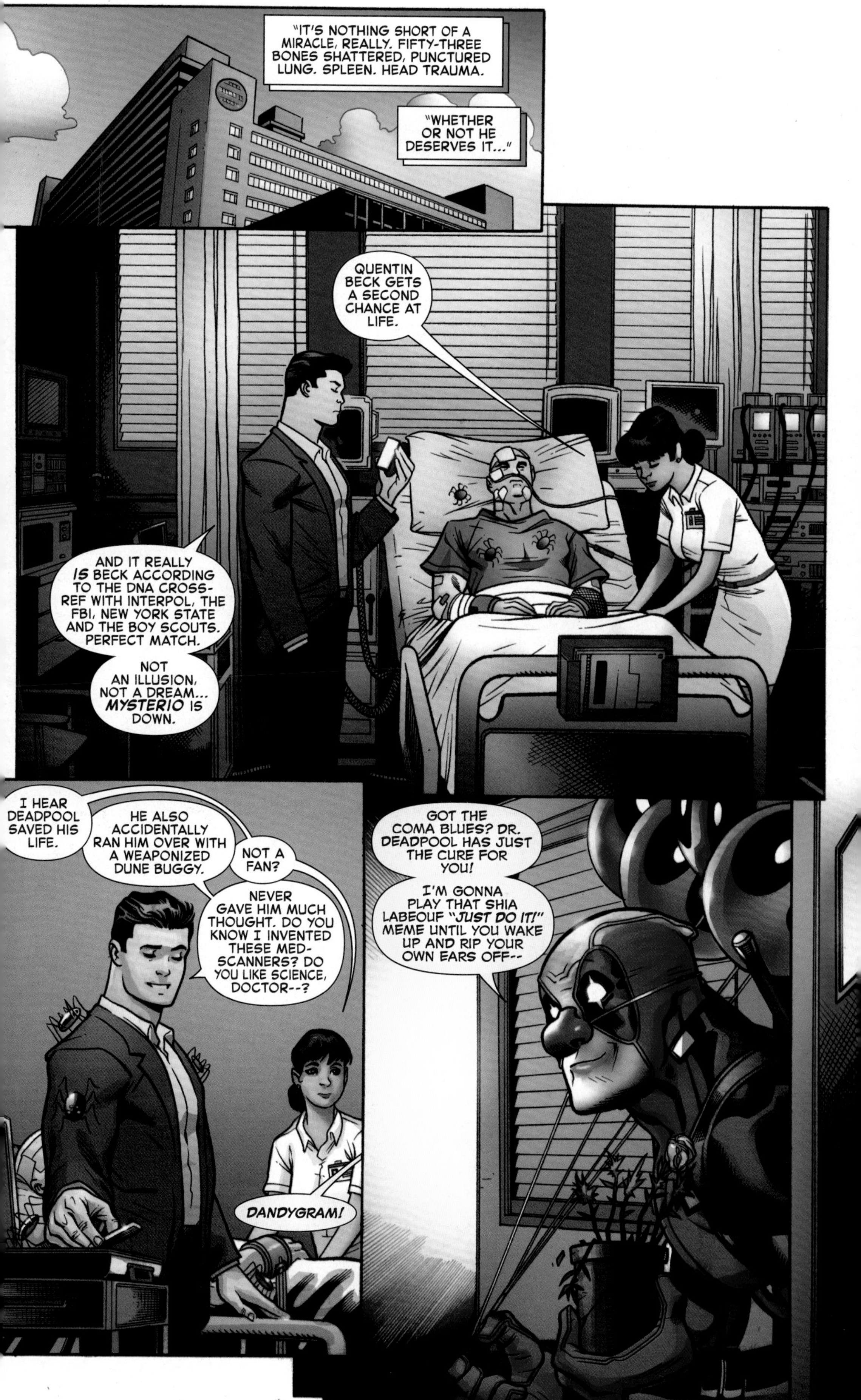
"IT'S NOTHING SHORT OF A MIRACLE, REALLY. FIFTY-THREE BONES SHATTERED, PUNCTURED LUNG. SPLEEN. HEAD TRAUMA.
"WHETHER OR NOT HE DESERVES IT..."
QUENTIN BECK GETS A SECOND CHANCE AT LIFE.
AND IT REALLY IS BECK ACCORDING TO THE DNA CROSS-REF WITH INTERPOL, THE FBI, NEW YORK STATE AND THE BOY SCOUTS. PERFECT MATCH.
NOT AN ILLUSION, NOT A DREAM... MYSTERIO IS DOWN.
I HEAR DEADPOOL SAVED HIS LIFE.
HE ALSO ACCIDENTALLY RAN HIM OVER WITH A WEAPONIZED DUNE BUGGY.
NOT A FAN?
NEVER GAVE HIM MUCH THOUGHT. DO YOU KNOW I INVENTED THESE MED-SCANNERS? DO YOU LIKE SCIENCE, DOCTOR--?
DANDYGRAM!
GOT THE COMA BLUES? DR. DEADPOOL HAS JUST THE CURE FOR YOU!
I'M GONNA PLAY THAT SHIA LABEOUF "JUST DO IT!" MEME UNTIL YOU WAKE UP AND RIP YOUR OWN EARS OFF--

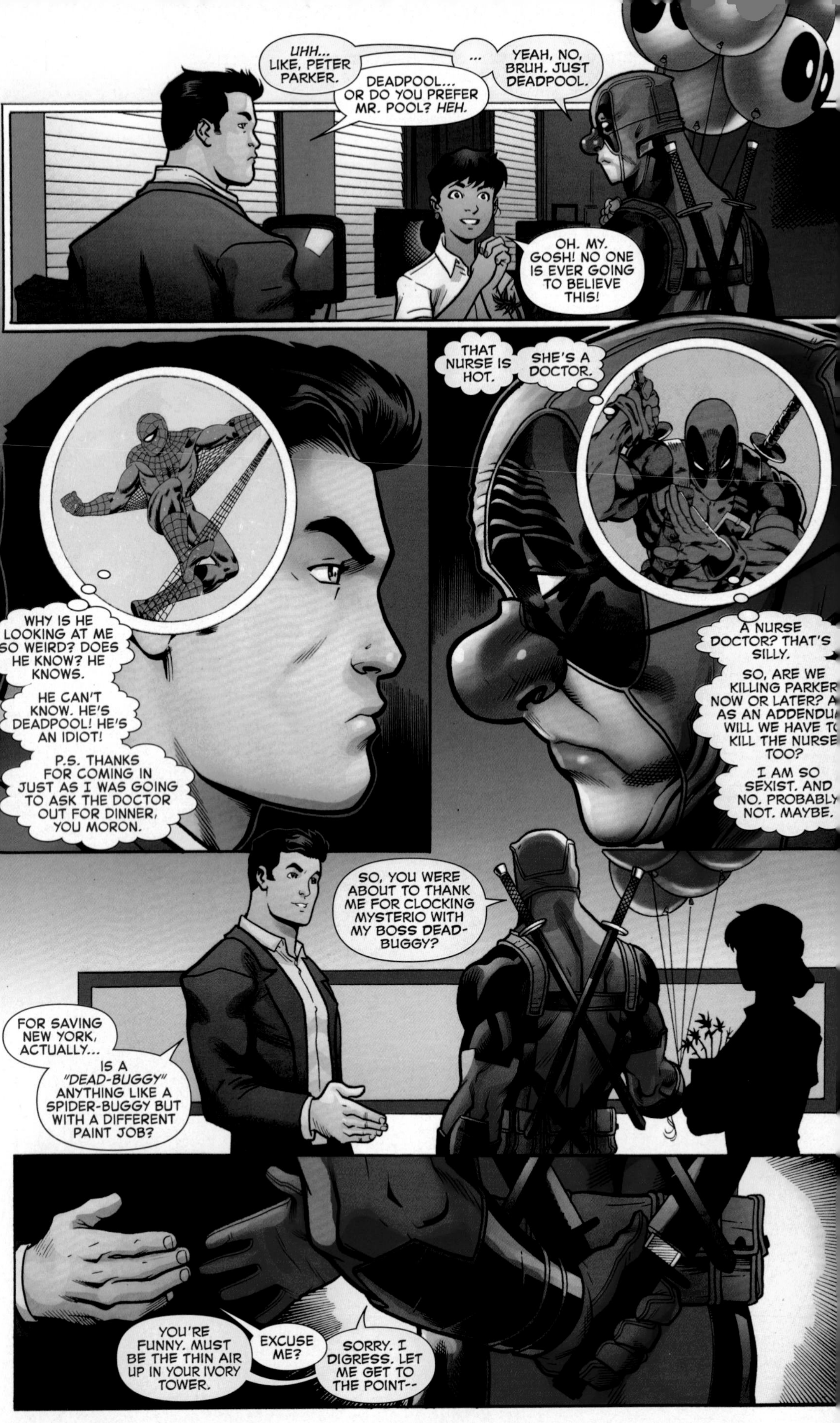
UHH... LIKE, PETER PARKER.
DEADPOOL... OR DO YOU PREFER MR. POOL? HEH.
...
YEAH, NO, BRUH. JUST DEADPOOL.
OH. MY. GOSH! NO ONE IS EVER GOING TO BELIEVE THIS!
THAT NURSE IS HOT.
SHE'S A DOCTOR.
WHY IS HE LOOKING AT ME SO WEIRD? DOES HE KNOW? HE KNOWS.
HE CAN'T KNOW. HE'S DEADPOOL! HE'S AN IDIOT!
P.S. THANKS FOR COMING IN JUST AS I WAS GOING TO ASK THE DOCTOR OUT FOR DINNER, YOU MORON.
A NURSE DOCTOR? THAT'S SILLY.
I AM SO SEXIST. AND NO. PROBABLY NOT. MAYBE.
SO, YOU WERE ABOUT TO THANK ME FOR CLOCKING MYSTERIO WITH MY BOSS DEAD-BUGGY?
FOR SAVING NEW YORK, ACTUALLY...
IS A "DEAD-BUGGY" ANYTHING LIKE A SPIDER-BUGGY BUT WITH A DIFFERENT PAINT JOB?
YOU'RE FUNNY. MUST BE THE THIN AIR UP IN YOUR IVORY TOWER.
EXCUSE ME?
SORRY. I DIGRESS. LET ME GET TO THE POINT--

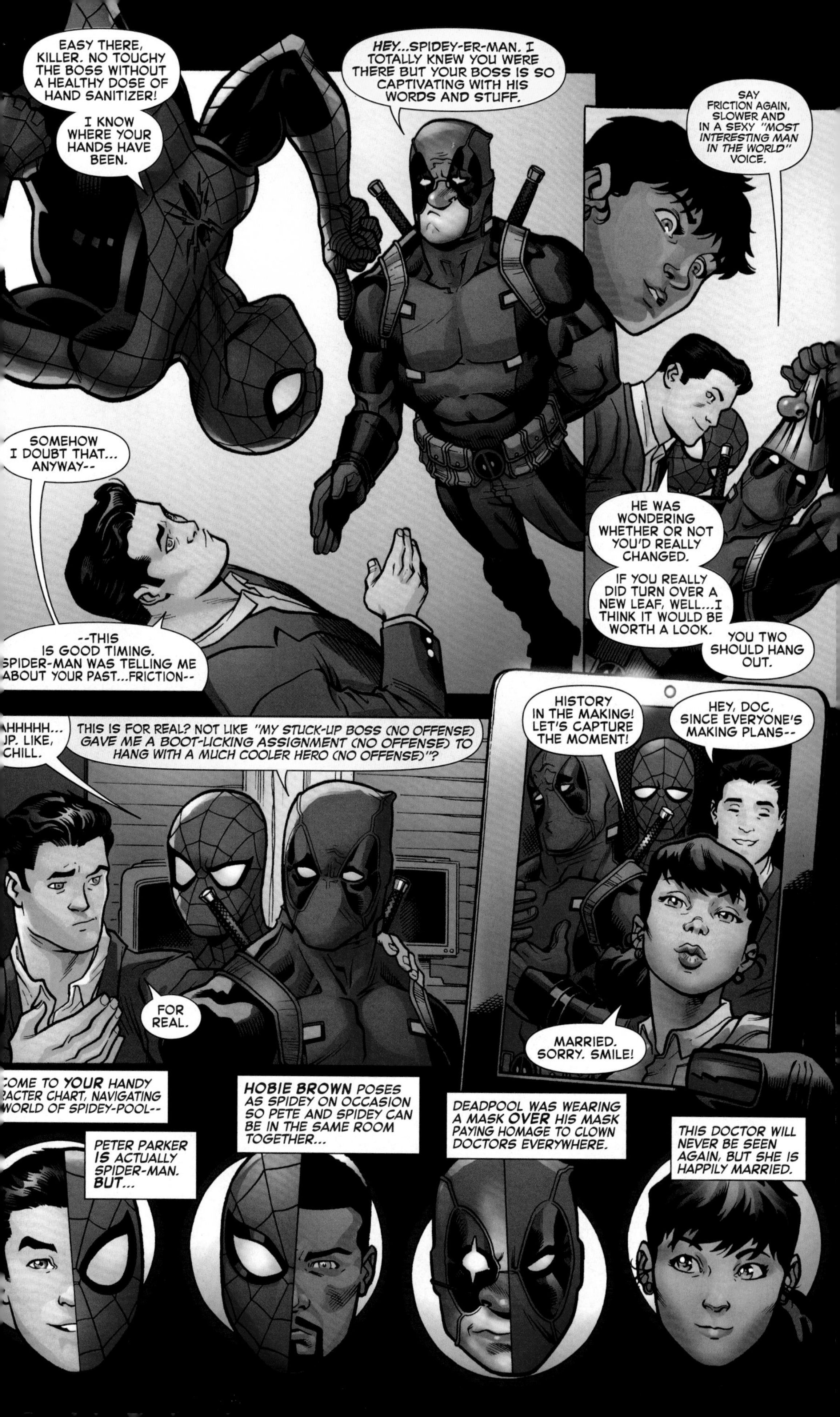

EASY THERE, KILLER. NO TOUCHY THE BOSS WITHOUT A HEALTHY DOSE OF HAND SANITIZER!
I KNOW WHERE YOUR HANDS HAVE BEEN.
HEY...SPIDEY-ER-MAN. I TOTALLY KNEW YOU WERE THERE BUT YOUR BOSS IS SO CAPTIVATING WITH HIS WORDS AND STUFF.
SOMEHOW I DOUBT THAT... ANYWAY--
--THIS IS GOOD TIMING. SPIDER-MAN WAS TELLING ME ABOUT YOUR PAST...FRICTION--
SAY FRICTION AGAIN, SLOWER AND IN A SEXY "MOST INTERESTING MAN IN THE WORLD" VOICE.
HE WAS WONDERING WHETHER OR NOT YOU'D REALLY CHANGED.
IF YOU REALLY DID TURN OVER A NEW LEAF, WELL...I THINK IT WOULD BE WORTH A LOOK.
YOU TWO SHOULD HANG OUT.
AHHHHH... UP. LIKE, CHILL.
THIS IS FOR REAL? NOT LIKE "MY STUCK-UP BOSS (NO OFFENSE) GAVE ME A BOOT-LICKING ASSIGNMENT (NO OFFENSE) TO HANG WITH A MUCH COOLER HERO (NO OFFENSE)"?
FOR REAL.
HISTORY IN THE MAKING! LET'S CAPTURE THE MOMENT!
HEY, DOC, SINCE EVERYONE'S MAKING PLANS--
MARRIED. SORRY. SMILE!
COME TO YOUR HANDY RACTER CHART, NAVIGATING WORLD OF SPIDEY-POOL--
PETER PARKER IS ACTUALLY SPIDER-MAN. BUT...
HOBIE BROWN POSES AS SPIDEY ON OCCASION SO PETE AND SPIDEY CAN BE IN THE SAME ROOM TOGETHER...
DEADPOOL WAS WEARING A MASK OVER HIS MASK PAYING HOMAGE TO CLOWN DOCTORS EVERYWHERE.
THIS DOCTOR WILL NEVER BE SEEN AGAIN, BUT SHE IS HAPPILY MARRIED.

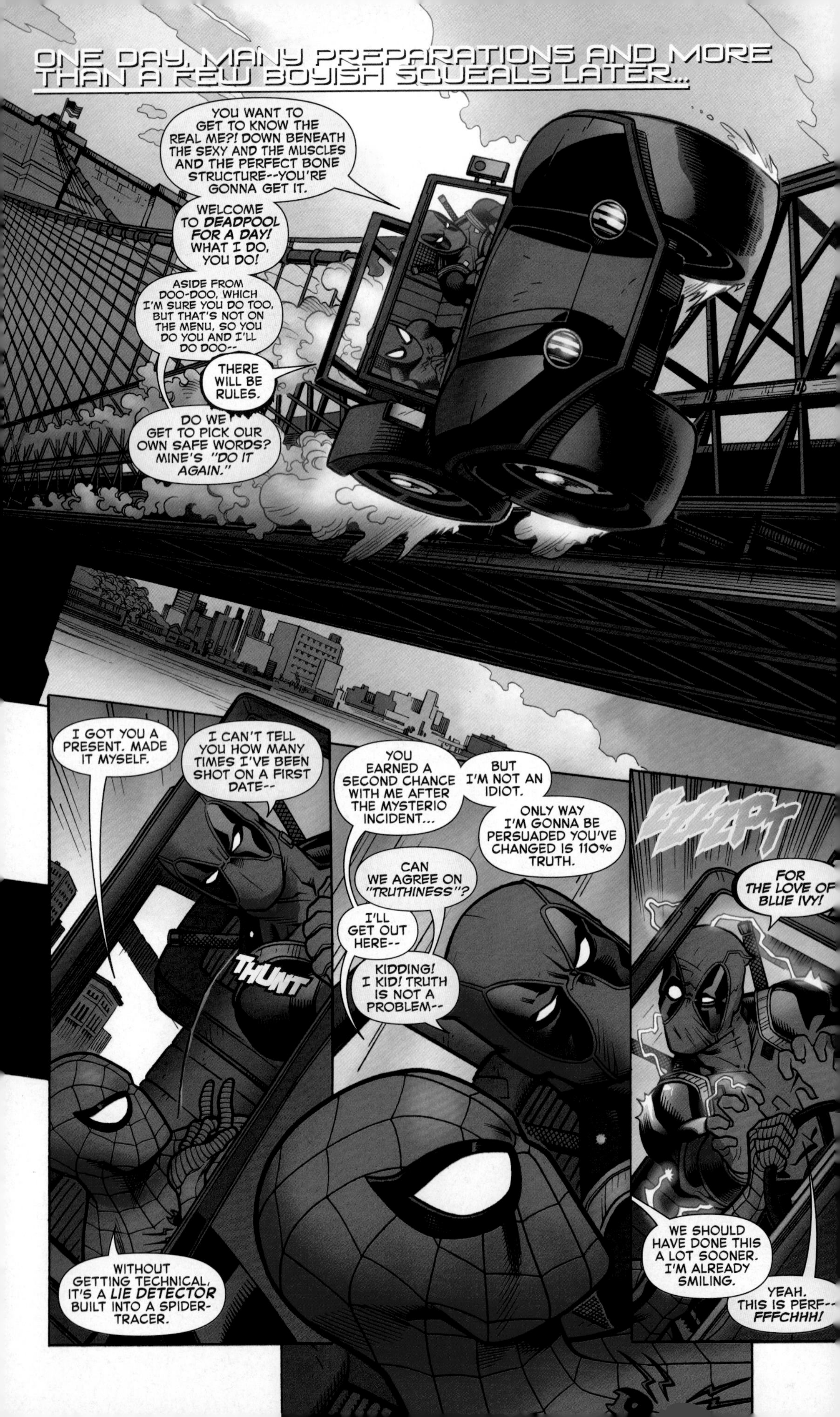
ONE DAY, MANY PREPARATIONS AND MORE THAN A FEW BOYISH SQUEALS LATER...
YOU WANT TO GET TO KNOW THE REAL ME?! DOWN BENEATH THE SEXY AND THE MUSCLES AND THE PERFECT BONE STRUCTURE--YOU'RE GONNA GET IT.
WELCOME TO DEADPOOL FOR A DAY! WHAT I DO, YOU DO!
ASIDE FROM DOO-DOO, WHICH I'M SURE YOU DO TOO, BUT THAT'S NOT ON THE MENU, SO YOU DO YOU AND I'LL DO DOO--
THERE WILL BE RULES.
DO WE GET TO PICK OUR OWN SAFE WORDS? MINE'S "DO IT AGAIN."
I GOT YOU A PRESENT. MADE IT MYSELF.
I CAN'T TELL YOU HOW MANY TIMES I'VE BEEN SHOT ON A FIRST DATE--
THUNT
WITHOUT GETTING TECHNICAL, IT'S A LIE DETECTOR BUILT INTO A SPIDER-TRACER.
YOU EARNED A SECOND CHANCE WITH ME AFTER THE MYSTERIO INCIDENT...
BUT I'M NOT AN IDIOT.
ONLY WAY I'M GONNA BE PERSUADED YOU'VE CHANGED IS 110% TRUTH.
CAN WE AGREE ON "TRUTHINESS"?
I'LL GET OUT HERE--
KIDDING! I KID! TRUTH IS NOT A PROBLEM--
ZZZZAPT
FOR THE LOVE OF BLUE IVY!
WE SHOULD HAVE DONE THIS A LOT SOONER. I'M ALREADY SMILING.
YEAH. THIS IS PERF--FFFCHHH!

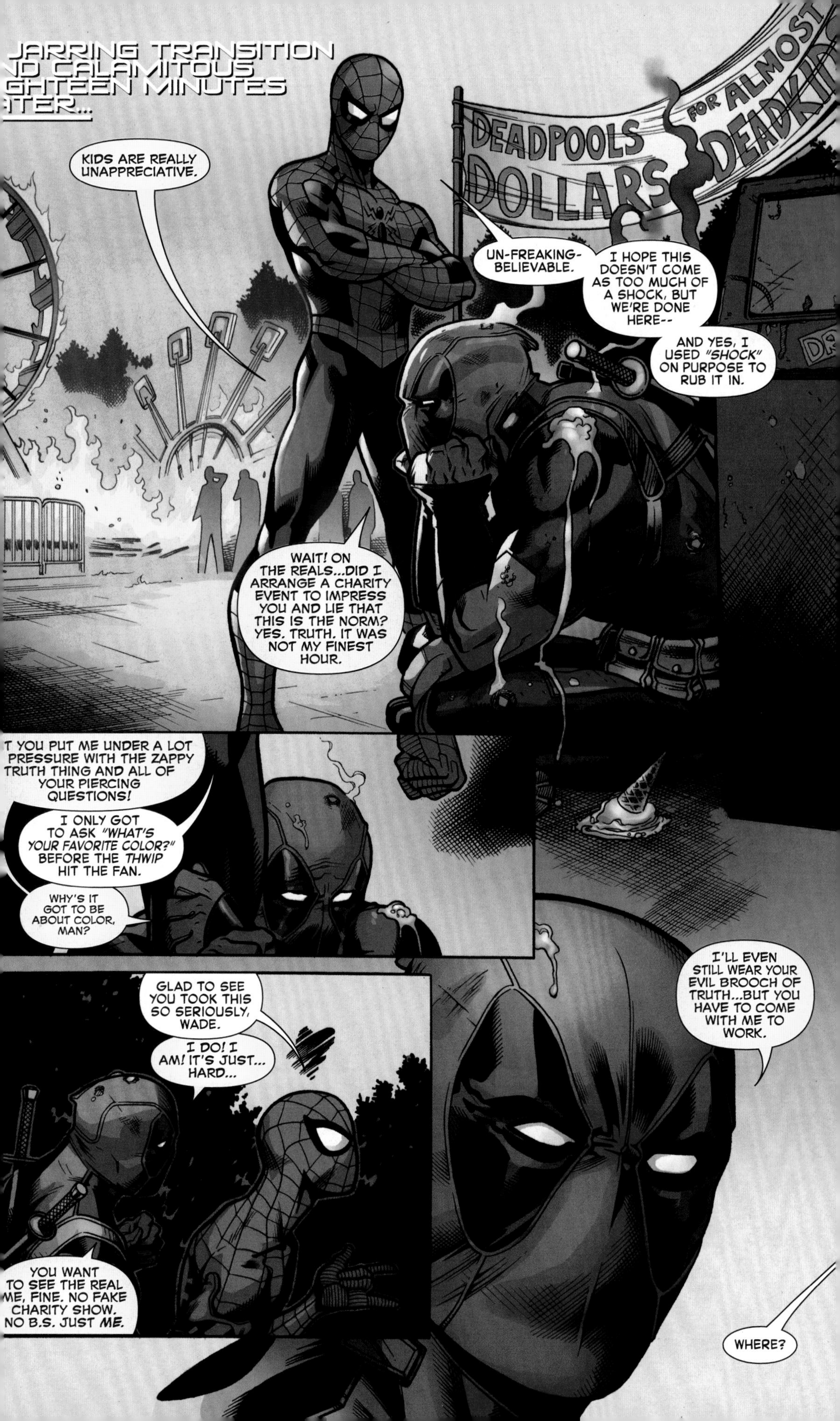
JARRING TRANSITION
ND CALAMITOUS
GHTEEN MINUTES
ATER...
KIDS ARE REALLY UNAPPRECIATIVE.
DEADPOOLS DOLLARS FOR ALMOST DEADKID
UN-FREAKING-BELIEVABLE.
I HOPE THIS DOESN'T COME AS TOO MUCH OF A SHOCK, BUT WE'RE DONE HERE--
AND YES, I USED "SHOCK" ON PURPOSE TO RUB IT IN.
WAIT! ON THE REALS...DID I ARRANGE A CHARITY EVENT TO IMPRESS YOU AND LIE THAT THIS IS THE NORM? YES. TRUTH. IT WAS NOT MY FINEST HOUR.
T YOU PUT ME UNDER A LOT PRESSURE WITH THE ZAPPY TRUTH THING AND ALL OF YOUR PIERCING QUESTIONS!
I ONLY GOT TO ASK "WHAT'S YOUR FAVORITE COLOR?" BEFORE THE THWIP HIT THE FAN.
WHY'S IT GOT TO BE ABOUT COLOR, MAN?
GLAD TO SEE YOU TOOK THIS SO SERIOUSLY, WADE.
I DO! I AM! IT'S JUST... HARD...
YOU WANT TO SEE THE REAL ME, FINE. NO FAKE CHARITY SHOW. NO B.S. JUST ME.
I'LL EVEN STILL WEAR YOUR EVIL BROOCH OF TRUTH...BUT YOU HAVE TO COME WITH ME TO WORK.
WHERE?

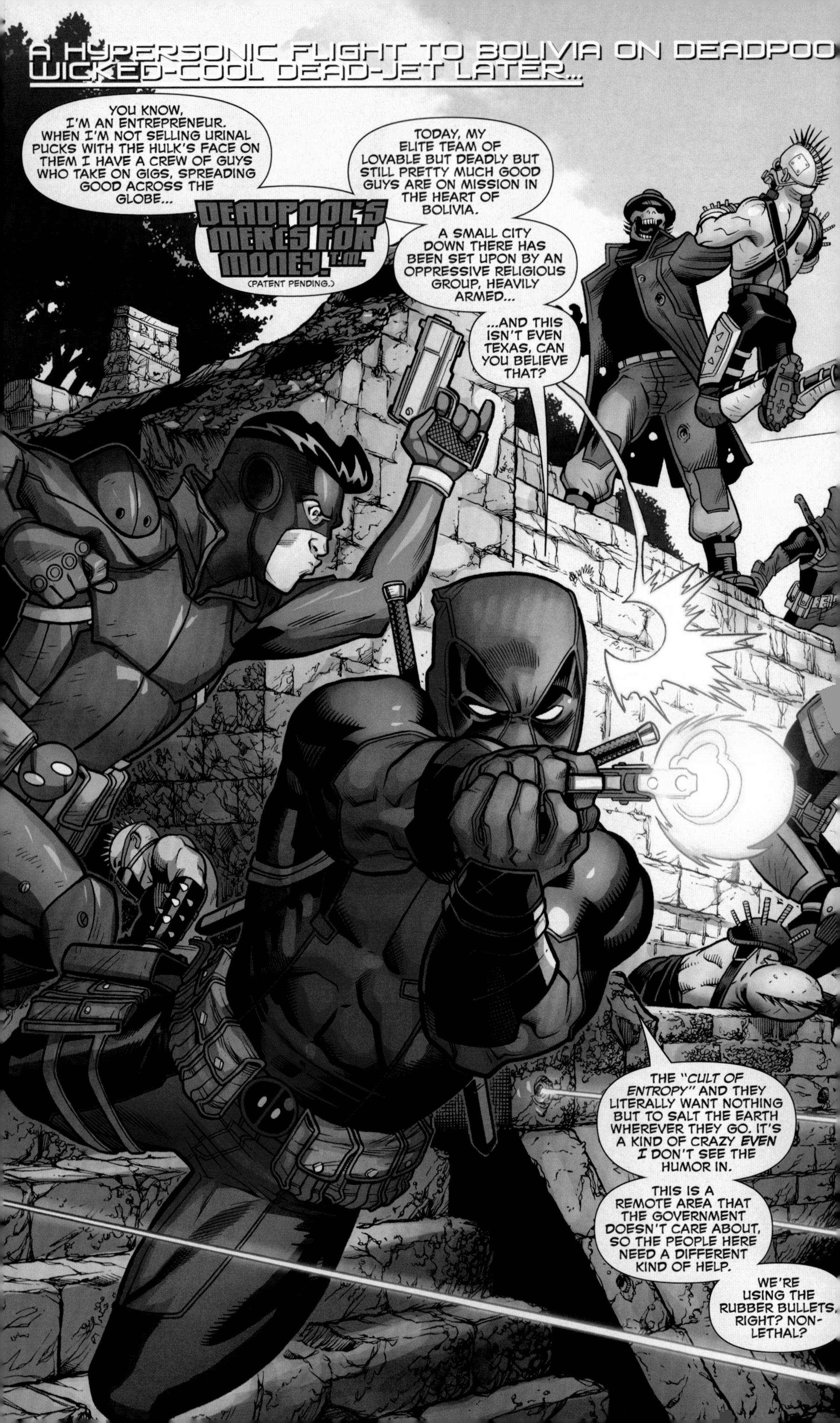
A HYPERSONIC FLIGHT TO BOLIVIA ON DEADPOO WICKED-COOL DEAD-JET LATER...
YOU KNOW, I'M AN ENTREPRENEUR. WHEN I'M NOT SELLING URINAL PUCKS WITH THE HULK'S FACE ON THEM I HAVE A CREW OF GUYS WHO TAKE ON GIGS, SPREADING GOOD ACROSS THE GLOBE...
DEADPOOL'S MERCS FOR MONEY. T.M.
(PATENT PENDING.)
TODAY, MY ELITE TEAM OF LOVABLE BUT DEADLY BUT STILL PRETTY MUCH GOOD GUYS ARE ON MISSION IN THE HEART OF BOLIVIA.
A SMALL CITY DOWN THERE HAS BEEN SET UPON BY AN OPPRESSIVE RELIGIOUS GROUP, HEAVILY ARMED...
...AND THIS ISN'T EVEN TEXAS, CAN YOU BELIEVE THAT?
THE "CULT OF ENTROPY" AND THEY LITERALLY WANT NOTHING BUT TO SALT THE EARTH WHEREVER THEY GO. IT'S A KIND OF CRAZY EVEN I DON'T SEE THE HUMOR IN.
THIS IS A REMOTE AREA THAT THE GOVERNMENT DOESN'T CARE ABOUT, SO THE PEOPLE HERE NEED A DIFFERENT KIND OF HELP.
WE'RE USING THE RUBBER BULLETS, RIGHT? NON-LETHAL?

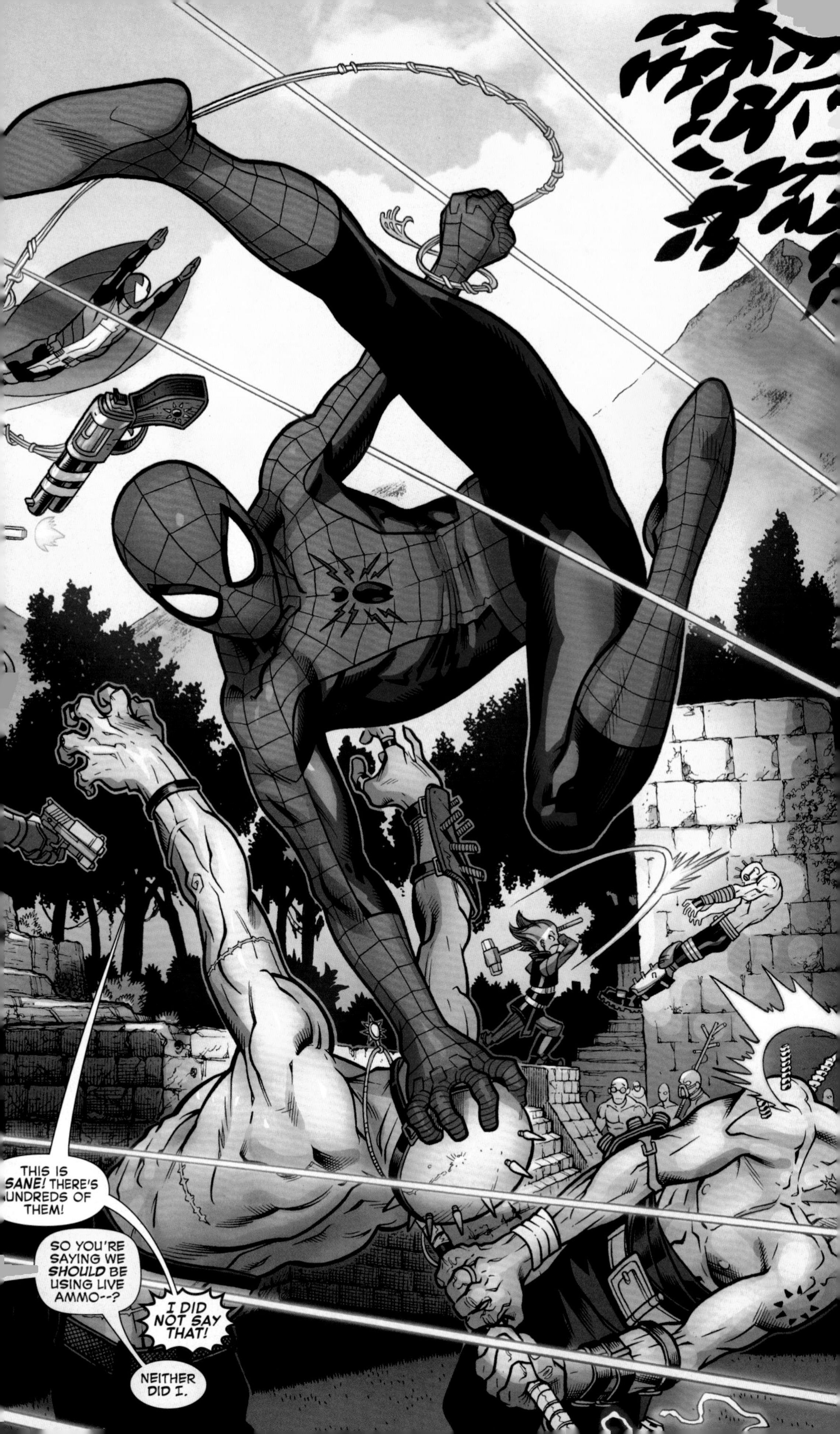
THIS IS
SANE! THERE'S
UNDREDS OF
THEM!
SO YOU'RE SAYING WE SHOULD BE USING LIVE AMMO--?
I DID NOT SAY THAT!
NEITHER DID I.

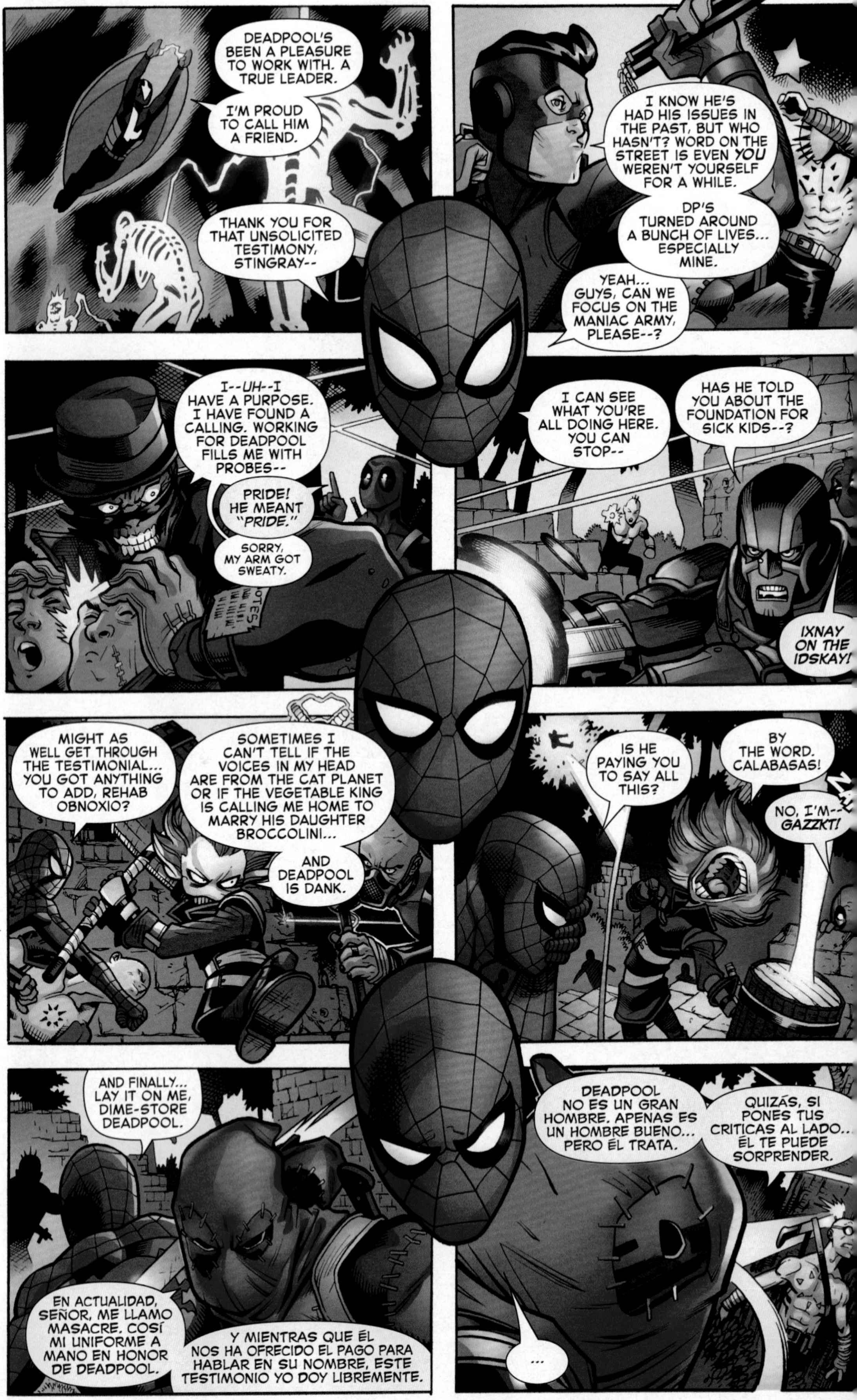
DEADPOOL'S BEEN A PLEASURE TO WORK WITH. A TRUE LEADER.
I'M PROUD TO CALL HIM A FRIEND.
THANK YOU FOR THAT UNSOLICITED TESTIMONY, STINGRAY--
I KNOW HE'S HAD HIS ISSUES IN THE PAST, BUT WHO HASN'T? WORD ON THE STREET IS EVEN YOU WEREN'T YOURSELF FOR A WHILE.
DP'S TURNED AROUND A BUNCH OF LIVES... ESPECIALLY MINE.
YEAH... GUYS, CAN WE FOCUS ON THE MANIAC ARMY, PLEASE--?
I--UH--I HAVE A PURPOSE. I HAVE FOUND A CALLING. WORKING FOR DEADPOOL FILLS ME WITH PROBES--
PRIDE! HE MEANT "PRIDE."
SORRY, MY ARM GOT SWEATY.
NOTES
I CAN SEE WHAT YOU'RE ALL DOING HERE. YOU CAN STOP--
HAS HE TOLD YOU ABOUT THE FOUNDATION FOR SICK KIDS--?
IXNAY ON THE IDSKAY!
MIGHT AS WELL GET THROUGH THE TESTIMONIAL... YOU GOT ANYTHING TO ADD, REHAB OBNOXIO?
SOMETIMES I CAN'T TELL IF THE VOICES IN MY HEAD ARE FROM THE CAT PLANET OR IF THE VEGETABLE KING IS CALLING ME HOME TO MARRY HIS DAUGHTER BROCCOLINI...
AND DEADPOOL IS DANK.
IS HE PAYING YOU TO SAY ALL THIS?
BY THE WORD. CALABASAS!
NO, I'M--GAZZKT!
AND FINALLY... LAY IT ON ME, DIME-STORE DEADPOOL.
EN ACTUALIDAD, SEÑOR, ME LLAMO MASACRE. COSÍ MI UNIFORME A MANO EN HONOR DE DEADPOOL.
Y MIENTRAS QUE ÉL NOS HA OFRECIDO EL PAGO PARA HABLAR EN SU NOMBRE, ESTE TESTIMONIO YO DOY LIBREMENTE.
DEADPOOL NO ES UN GRAN HOMBRE. APENAS ES UN HOMBRE BUENO... PERO ÉL TRATA.
QUIZÁS, SI PONES TUS CRITICAS AL LADO... ÉL TE PUEDE SORPRENDER.
...

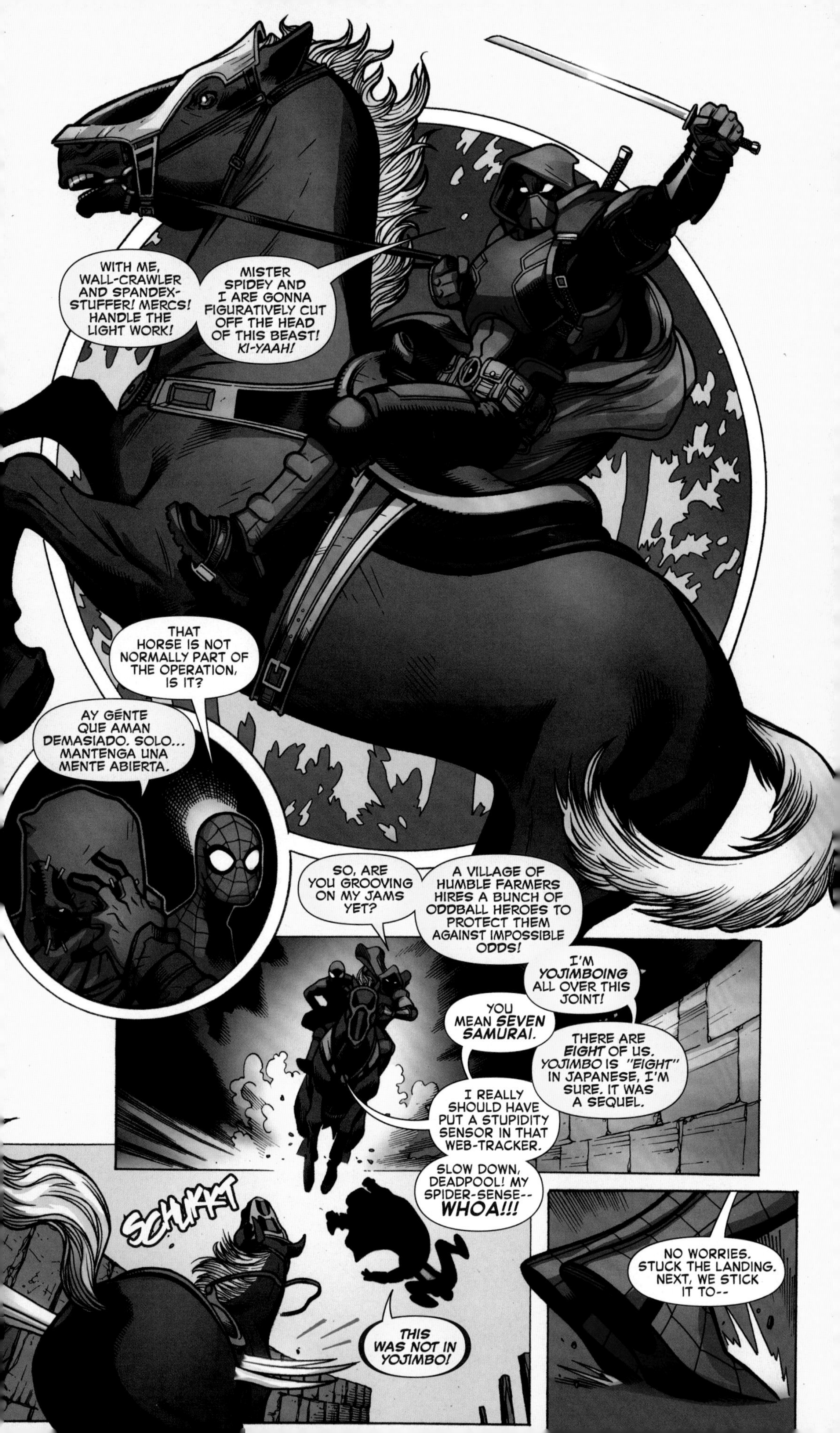
WITH ME, WALL-CRAWLER AND SPANDEX-STUFFER! MERCS! HANDLE THE LIGHT WORK!
MISTER SPIDEY AND I ARE GONNA FIGURATIVELY CUT OFF THE HEAD OF THIS BEAST! KI-YAAH!
THAT HORSE IS NOT NORMALLY PART OF THE OPERATION, IS IT?
AY GÉNTE QUE AMAN DEMASIADO. SOLO... MANTENGA UNA MENTE ABIERTA.
SO, ARE YOU GROOVING ON MY JAMS YET?
A VILLAGE OF HUMBLE FARMERS HIRES A BUNCH OF ODDBALL HEROES TO PROTECT THEM AGAINST IMPOSSIBLE ODDS!
I'M YOJIMBOING ALL OVER THIS JOINT!
YOU MEAN SEVEN SAMURAI.
THERE ARE EIGHT OF US. YOJIMBO IS "EIGHT" IN JAPANESE, I'M SURE. IT WAS A SEQUEL.
I REALLY SHOULD HAVE PUT A STUPIDITY SENSOR IN THAT WEB-TRACKER.
SLOW DOWN, DEADPOOL! MY SPIDER-SENSE-- WHOA!!!
SCHKKT
THIS WAS NOT IN YOJIMBO!
NO WORRIES. STUCK THE LANDING. NEXT, WE STICK IT TO--

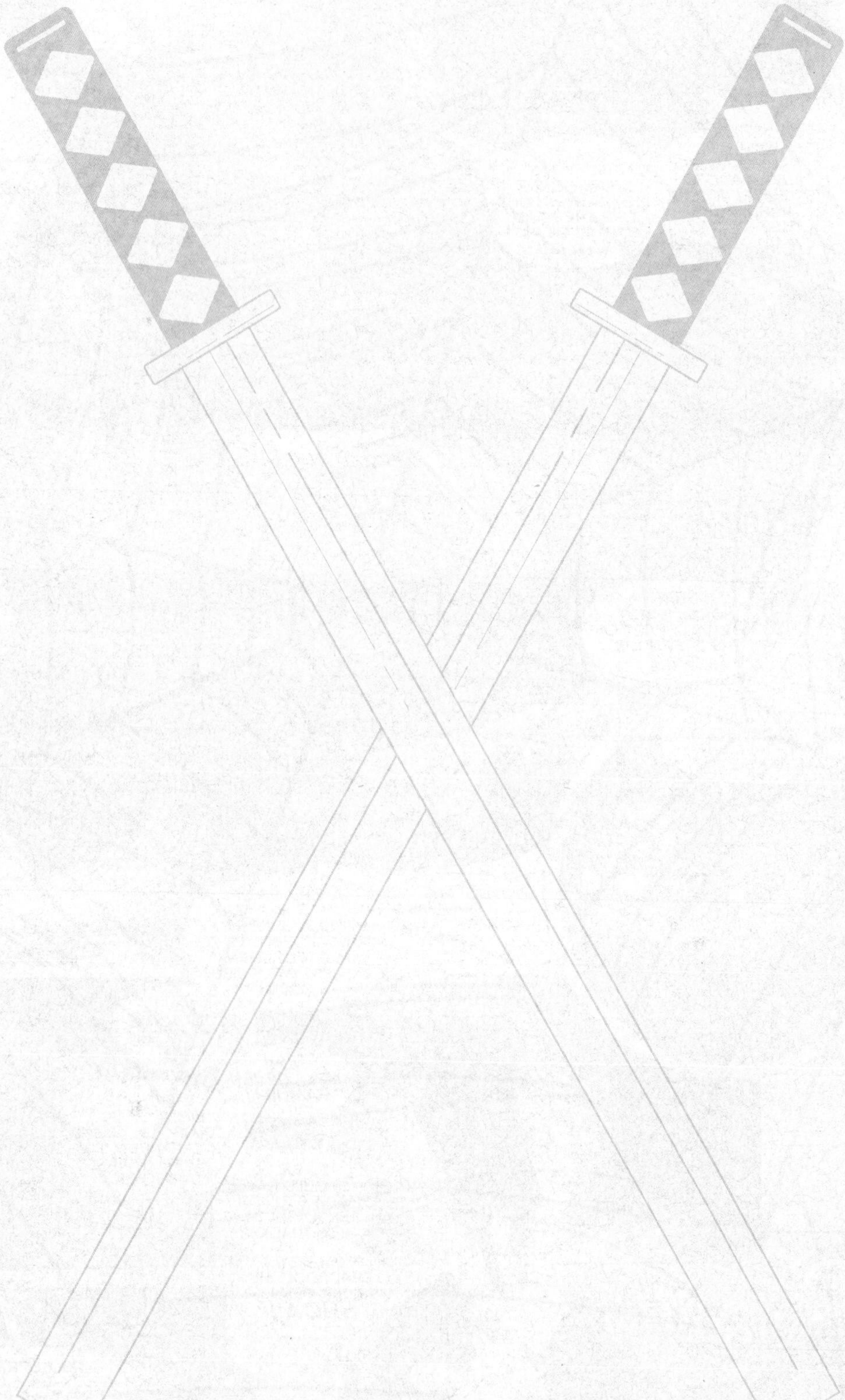

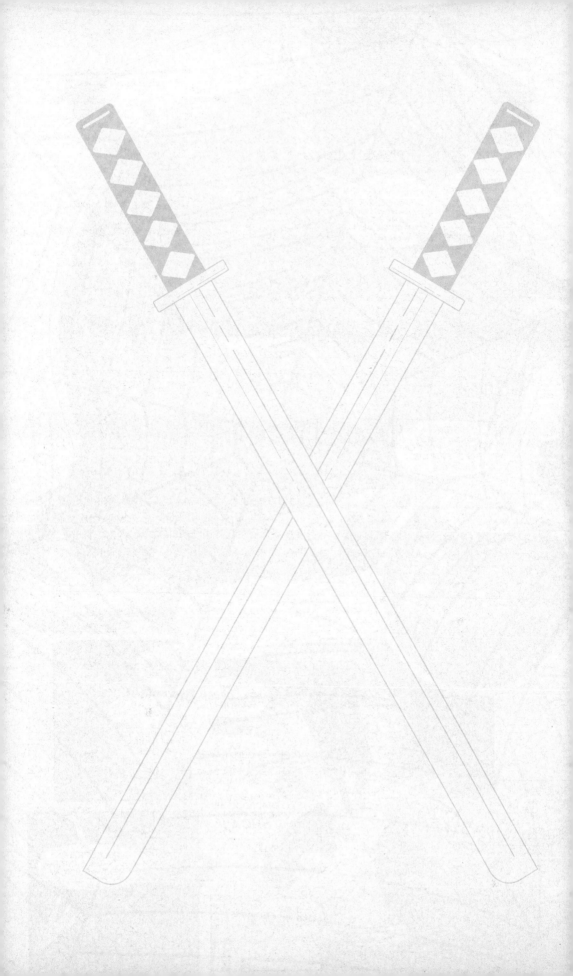

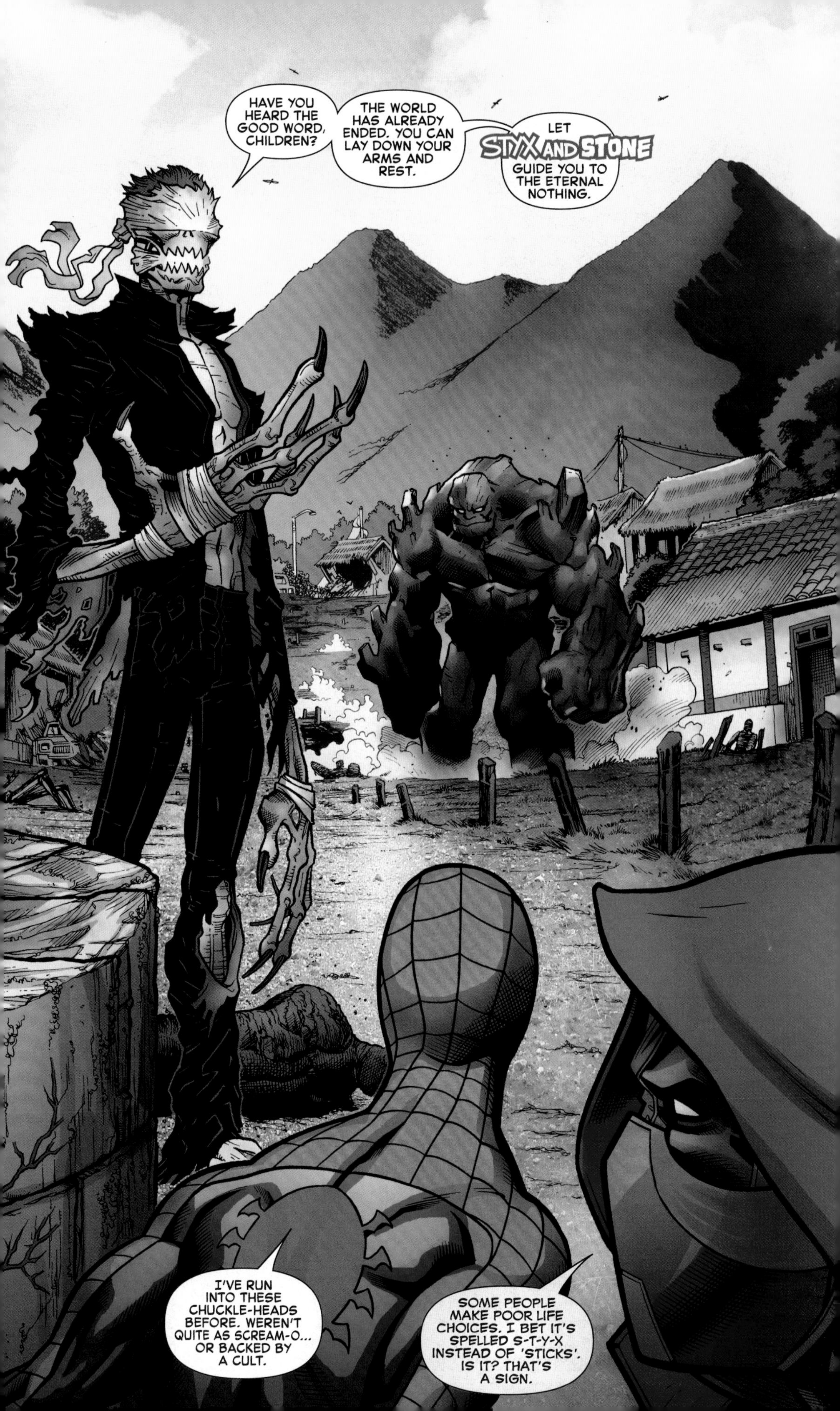
HAVE YOU HEARD THE GOOD WORD, CHILDREN?
THE WORLD HAS ALREADY ENDED. YOU CAN LAY DOWN YOUR ARMS AND REST.
LET STYX AND STONE GUIDE YOU TO THE ETERNAL NOTHING.
I'VE RUN INTO THESE CHUCKLE-HEADS BEFORE. WEREN'T QUITE AS SCREAM-O... OR BACKED BY A CULT.
SOME PEOPLE MAKE POOR LIFE CHOICES. I BET IT'S SPELLED S-T-Y-X INSTEAD OF 'STICKS'. IS IT? THAT'S A SIGN.

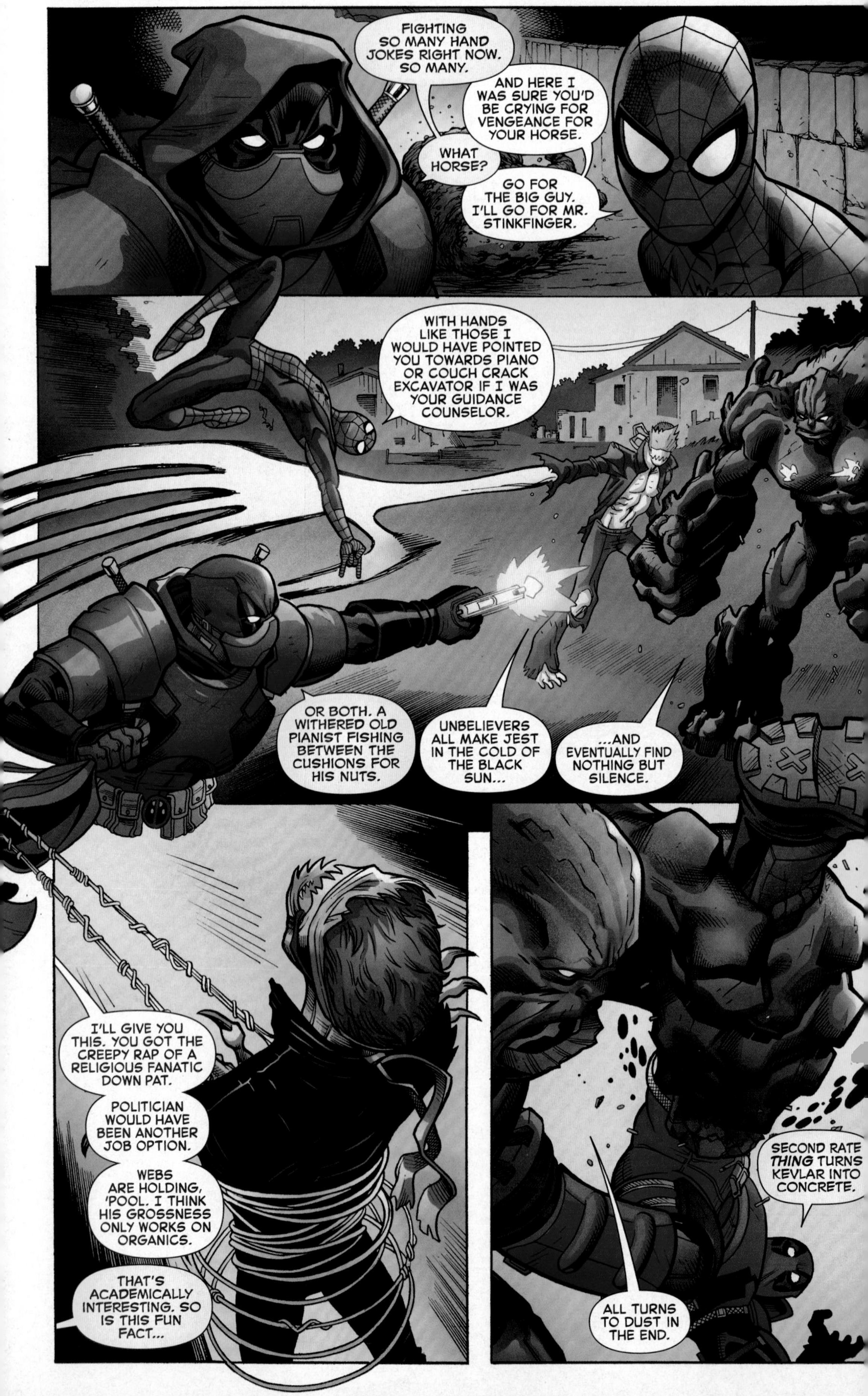
FIGHTING SO MANY HAND JOKES RIGHT NOW. SO MANY.
AND HERE I WAS SURE YOU'D BE CRYING FOR VENGEANCE FOR YOUR HORSE.
WHAT HORSE?
GO FOR THE BIG GUY. I'LL GO FOR MR. STINKFINGER.
WITH HANDS LIKE THOSE I WOULD HAVE POINTED YOU TOWARDS PIANO OR COUCH CRACK EXCAVATOR IF I WAS YOUR GUIDANCE COUNSELOR.
OR BOTH. A WITHERED OLD PIANIST FISHING BETWEEN THE CUSHIONS FOR HIS NUTS.
UNBELIEVERS ALL MAKE JEST IN THE COLD OF THE BLACK SUN...
...AND EVENTUALLY FIND NOTHING BUT SILENCE.
I'LL GIVE YOU THIS. YOU GOT THE CREEPY RAP OF A RELIGIOUS FANATIC DOWN PAT.
POLITICIAN WOULD HAVE BEEN ANOTHER JOB OPTION.
WEBS ARE HOLDING, 'POOL. I THINK HIS GROSSNESS ONLY WORKS ON ORGANICS.
THAT'S ACADEMICALLY INTERESTING. SO IS THIS FUN FACT...
SECOND RATE *THING* TURNS KEVLAR INTO CONCRETE.
ALL TURNS TO DUST IN THE END.

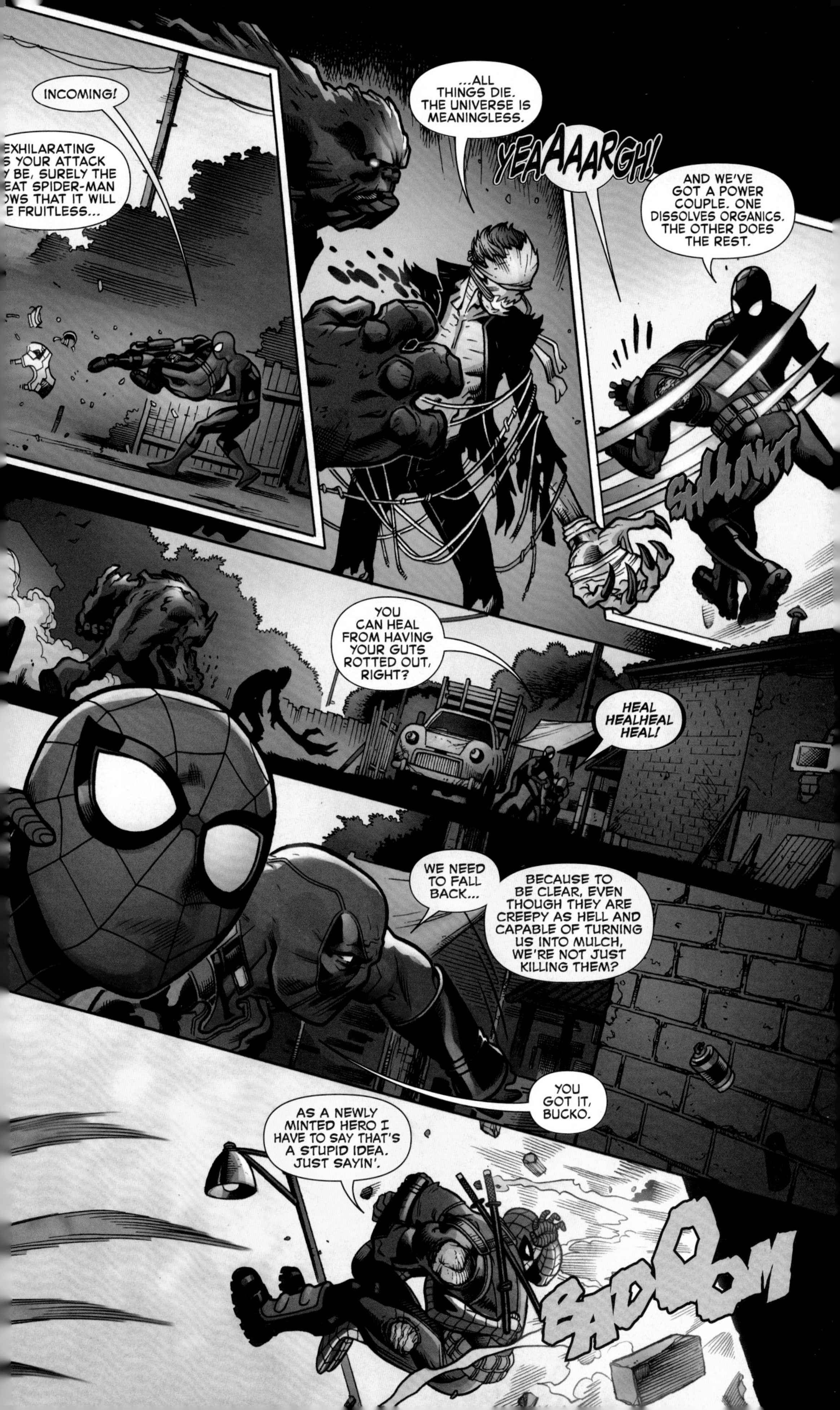

INCOMING!
EXHILARATING
S YOUR ATTACK
Y BE, SURELY THE
EAT SPIDER-MAN
OWS THAT IT WILL
E FRUITLESS...
...ALL THINGS DIE. THE UNIVERSE IS MEANINGLESS.
YEAAAARGH!
AND WE'VE GOT A POWER COUPLE. ONE DISSOLVES ORGANICS. THE OTHER DOES THE REST.
SHHUNKT
YOU CAN HEAL FROM HAVING YOUR GUTS ROTTED OUT, RIGHT?
HEAL HEALHEAL HEAL!
WE NEED TO FALL BACK...
BECAUSE TO BE CLEAR, EVEN THOUGH THEY ARE CREEPY AS HELL AND CAPABLE OF TURNING US INTO MULCH, WE'RE NOT JUST KILLING THEM?
YOU GOT IT, BUCKO.
AS A NEWLY MINTED HERO I HAVE TO SAY THAT'S A STUPID IDEA. JUST SAYIN'.
BADOOOM

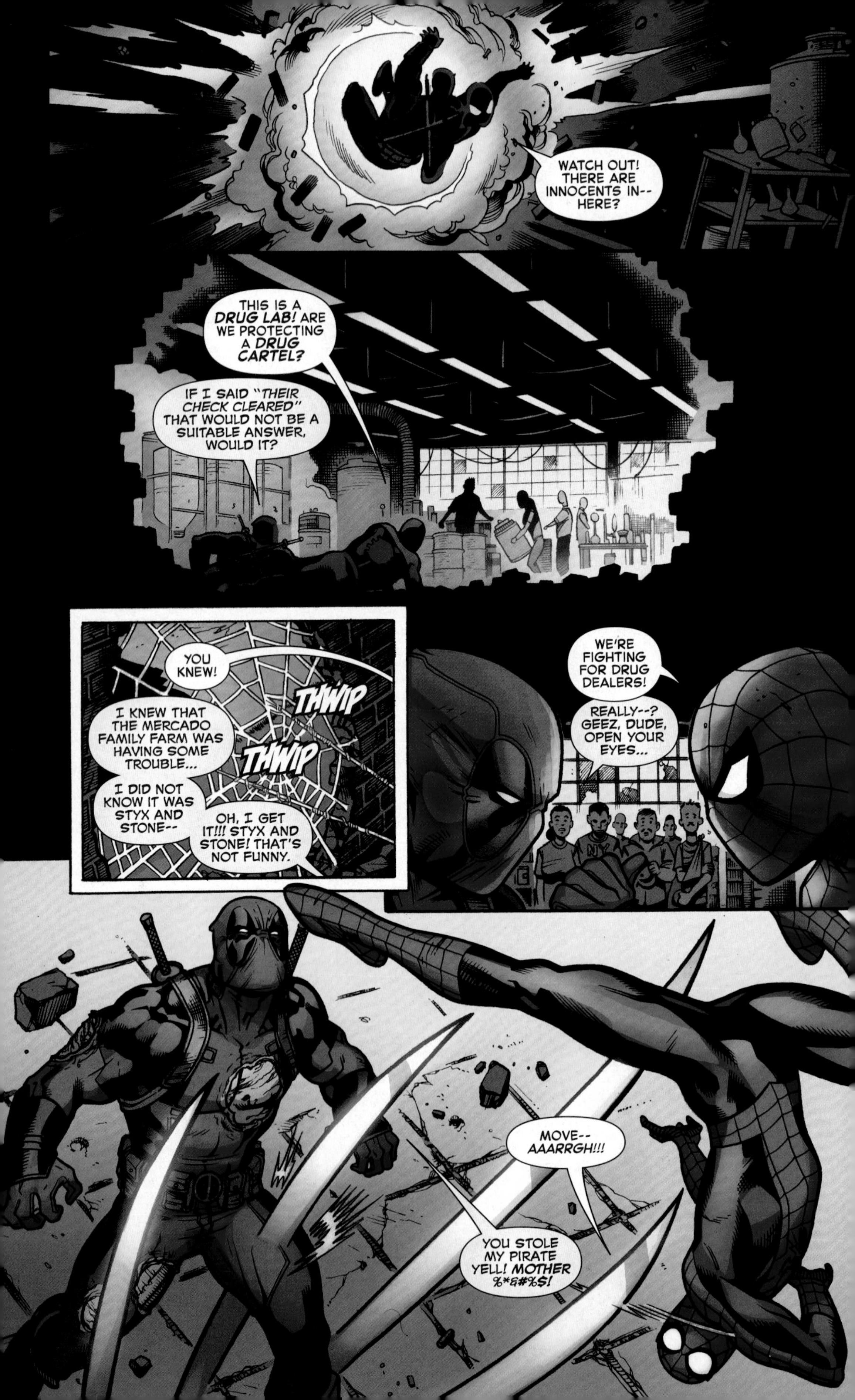
WATCH OUT! THERE ARE INNOCENTS IN-- HERE?
THIS IS A DRUG LAB! ARE WE PROTECTING A DRUG CARTEL?
IF I SAID "THEIR CHECK CLEARED" THAT WOULD NOT BE A SUITABLE ANSWER, WOULD IT?
YOU KNEW!
THWIP
I KNEW THAT THE MERCADO FAMILY FARM WAS HAVING SOME TROUBLE...
THWIP
I DID NOT KNOW IT WAS STYX AND STONE--
OH, I GET IT!!! STYX AND STONE! THAT'S NOT FUNNY.
WE'RE FIGHTING FOR DRUG DEALERS!
REALLY--? GEEZ, DUDE, OPEN YOUR EYES...
MOVE-- AAARRGH!!!
YOU STOLE MY PIRATE YELL! MOTHER %*&#%$!

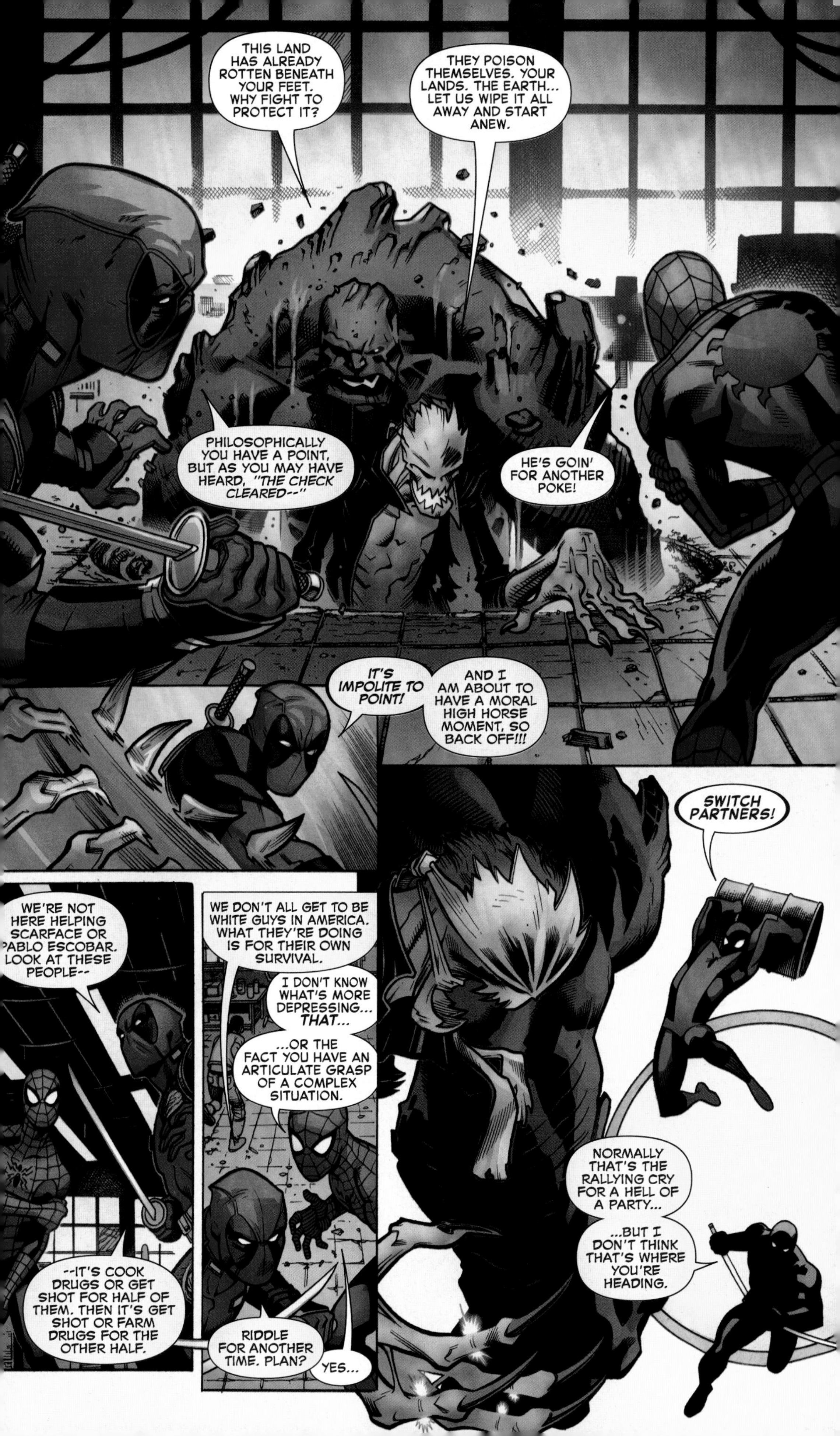
THIS LAND HAS ALREADY ROTTEN BENEATH YOUR FEET. WHY FIGHT TO PROTECT IT?
THEY POISON THEMSELVES. YOUR LANDS. THE EARTH... LET US WIPE IT ALL AWAY AND START ANEW.
PHILOSOPHICALLY YOU HAVE A POINT, BUT AS YOU MAY HAVE HEARD, "THE CHECK CLEARED--"
HE'S GOIN' FOR ANOTHER POKE!
IT'S IMPOLITE TO POINT!
AND I AM ABOUT TO HAVE A MORAL HIGH HORSE MOMENT, SO BACK OFF!!!
SWITCH PARTNERS!
WE'RE NOT HERE HELPING SCARFACE OR PABLO ESCOBAR. LOOK AT THESE PEOPLE--
--IT'S COOK DRUGS OR GET SHOT FOR HALF OF THEM. THEN IT'S GET SHOT OR FARM DRUGS FOR THE OTHER HALF.
WE DON'T ALL GET TO BE WHITE GUYS IN AMERICA. WHAT THEY'RE DOING IS FOR THEIR OWN SURVIVAL.
I DON'T KNOW WHAT'S MORE DEPRESSING... THAT...
...OR THE FACT YOU HAVE AN ARTICULATE GRASP OF A COMPLEX SITUATION.
RIDDLE FOR ANOTHER TIME. PLAN?
YES...
NORMALLY THAT'S THE RALLYING CRY FOR A HELL OF A PARTY...
...BUT I DON'T THINK THAT'S WHERE YOU'RE HEADING.

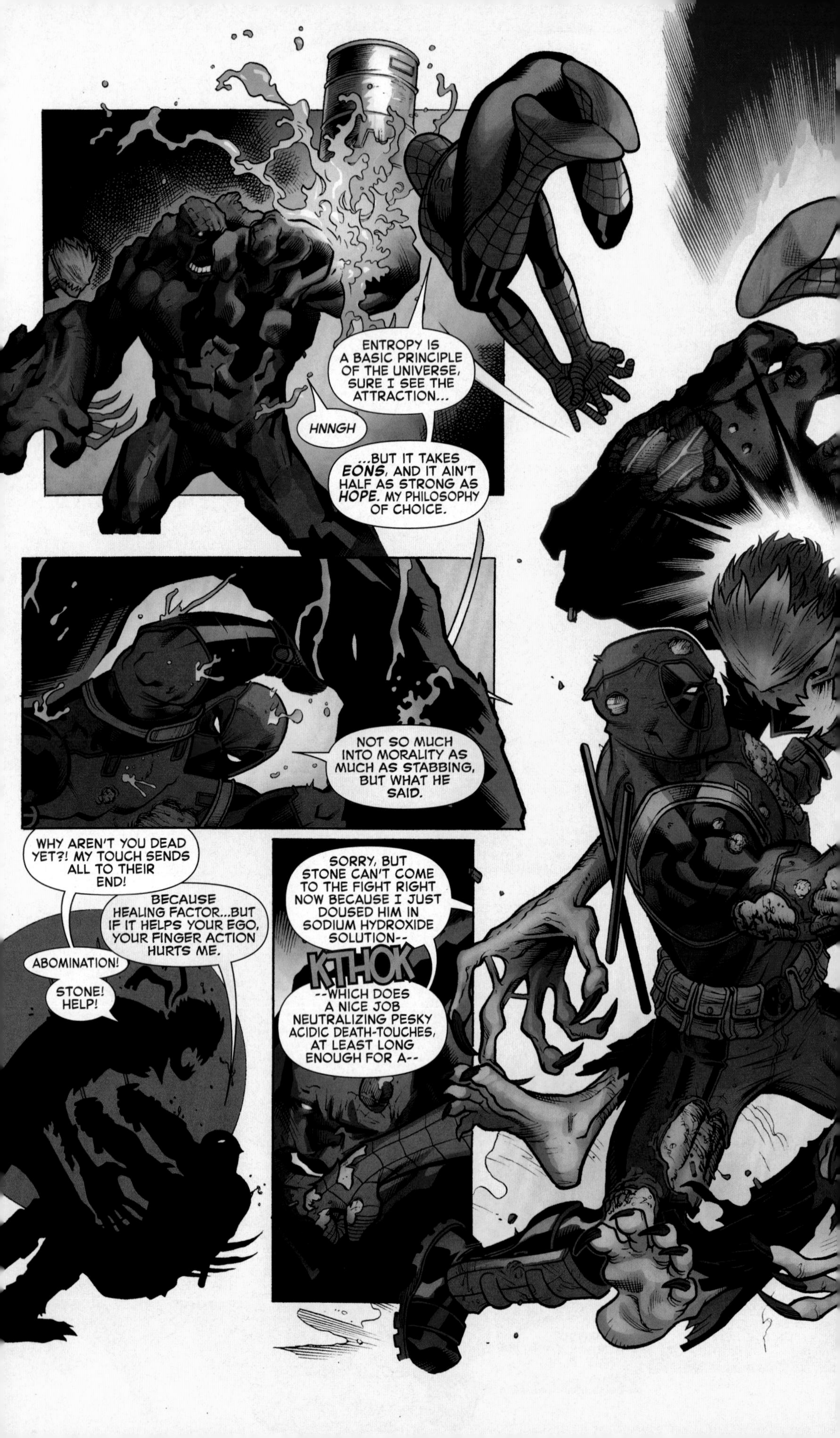
ENTROPY IS A BASIC PRINCIPLE OF THE UNIVERSE, SURE I SEE THE ATTRACTION...
HNNGH
...BUT IT TAKES EONS, AND IT AIN'T HALF AS STRONG AS HOPE. MY PHILOSOPHY OF CHOICE.
NOT SO MUCH INTO MORALITY AS MUCH AS STABBING, BUT WHAT HE SAID.
WHY AREN'T YOU DEAD YET?! MY TOUCH SENDS ALL TO THEIR END!
BECAUSE HEALING FACTOR...BUT IF IT HELPS YOUR EGO, YOUR FINGER ACTION HURTS ME.
ABOMINATION!
STONE! HELP!
SORRY, BUT STONE CAN'T COME TO THE FIGHT RIGHT NOW BECAUSE I JUST DOUSED HIM IN SODIUM HYDROXIDE SOLUTION--
K-THOK
--WHICH DOES A NICE JOB NEUTRALIZING PESKY ACIDIC DEATH-TOUCHES, AT LEAST LONG ENOUGH FOR A--

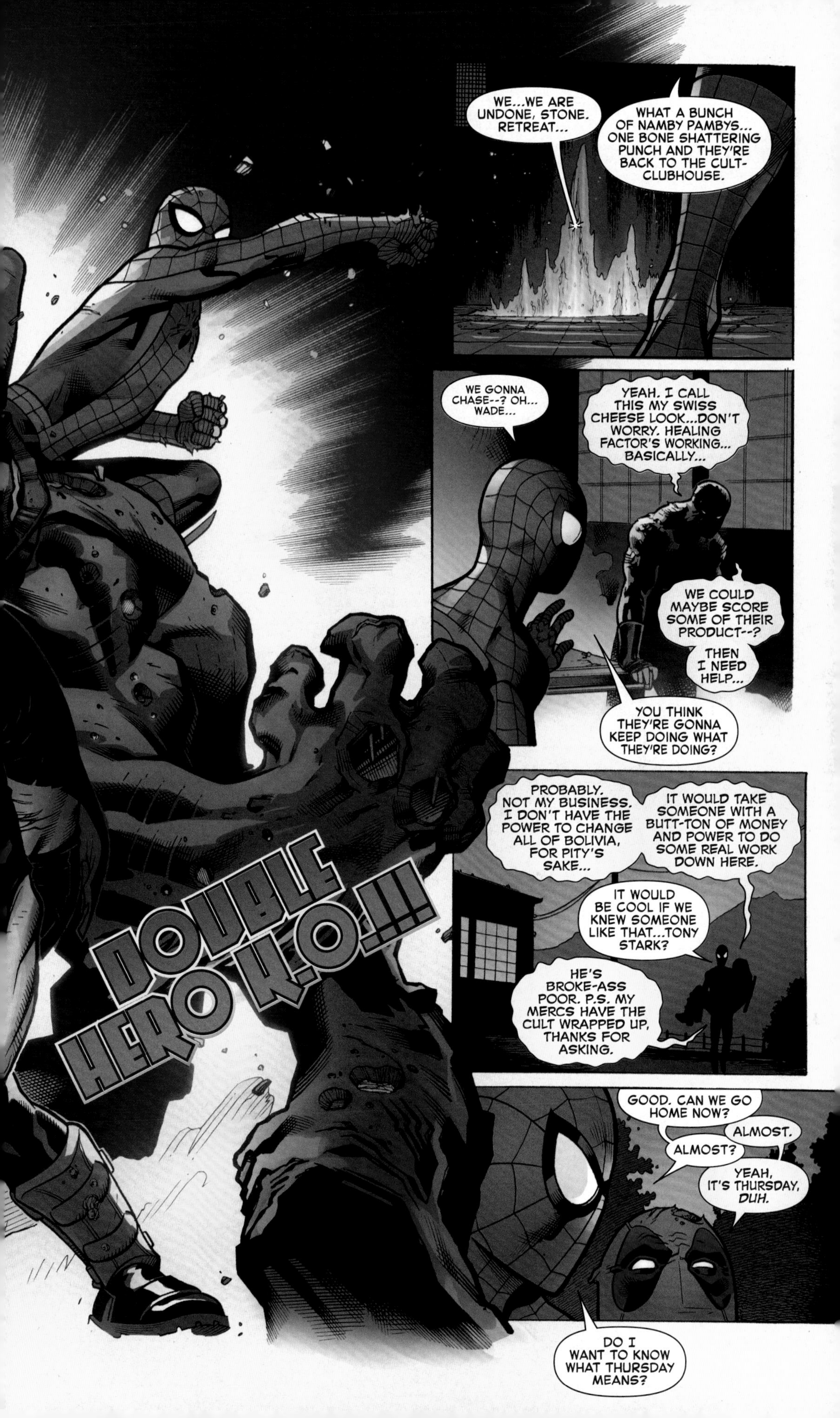
DOUBLE HERO K.O.!!!
WE...WE ARE UNDONE, STONE. RETREAT...
WHAT A BUNCH OF NAMBY PAMBYS... ONE BONE SHATTERING PUNCH AND THEY'RE BACK TO THE CULT-CLUBHOUSE.
WE GONNA CHASE--? OH... WADE...
YEAH. I CALL THIS MY SWISS CHEESE LOOK...DON'T WORRY. HEALING FACTOR'S WORKING... BASICALLY...
WE COULD MAYBE SCORE SOME OF THEIR PRODUCT--?
THEN I NEED HELP...
YOU THINK THEY'RE GONNA KEEP DOING WHAT THEY'RE DOING?
PROBABLY. NOT MY BUSINESS. I DON'T HAVE THE POWER TO CHANGE ALL OF BOLIVIA, FOR PITY'S SAKE...
IT WOULD TAKE SOMEONE WITH A BUTT-TON OF MONEY AND POWER TO DO SOME REAL WORK DOWN HERE.
IT WOULD BE COOL IF WE KNEW SOMEONE LIKE THAT...TONY STARK?
HE'S BROKE-ASS POOR. P.S. MY MERCS HAVE THE CULT WRAPPED UP, THANKS FOR ASKING.
GOOD. CAN WE GO HOME NOW?
ALMOST.
ALMOST?
YEAH, IT'S THURSDAY, *DUH.*
DO I WANT TO KNOW WHAT THURSDAY MEANS?

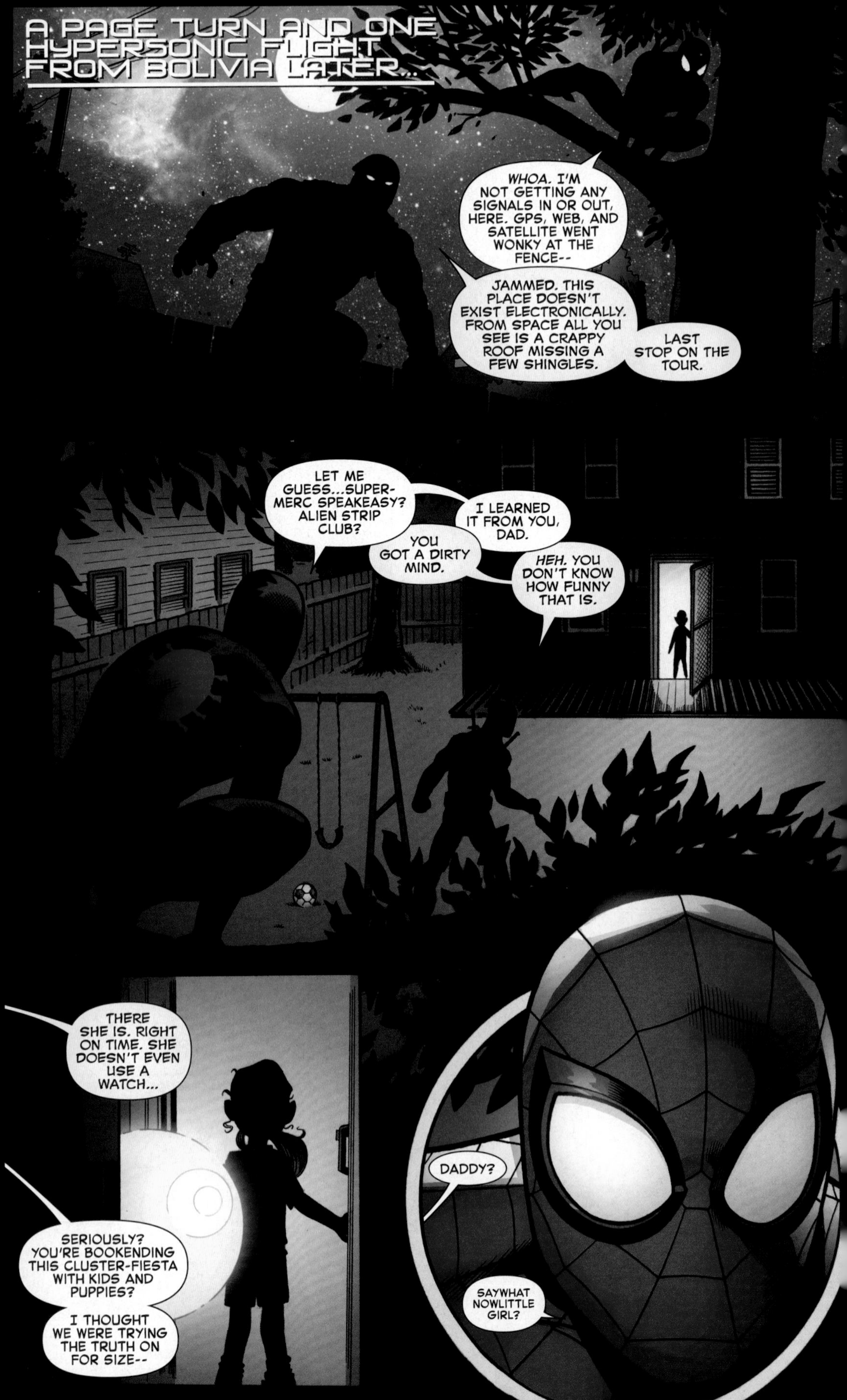
A PAGE TURN AND ONE HYPERSONIC FLIGHT FROM BOLIVIA LATER...
WHOA. I'M NOT GETTING ANY SIGNALS IN OR OUT, HERE. GPS, WEB, AND SATELLITE WENT WONKY AT THE FENCE--
JAMMED. THIS PLACE DOESN'T EXIST ELECTRONICALLY. FROM SPACE ALL YOU SEE IS A CRAPPY ROOF MISSING A FEW SHINGLES.
LAST STOP ON THE TOUR.
LET ME GUESS...SUPER-MERC SPEAKEASY? ALIEN STRIP CLUB?
YOU GOT A DIRTY MIND.
I LEARNED IT FROM YOU, DAD.
HEH. YOU DON'T KNOW HOW FUNNY THAT IS.
THERE SHE IS. RIGHT ON TIME. SHE DOESN'T EVEN USE A WATCH...
SERIOUSLY? YOU'RE BOOKENDING THIS CLUSTER-FIESTA WITH KIDS AND PUPPIES?
I THOUGHT WE WERE TRYING THE TRUTH ON FOR SIZE--
DADDY?
SAYWHAT NOWLITTLE GIRL?

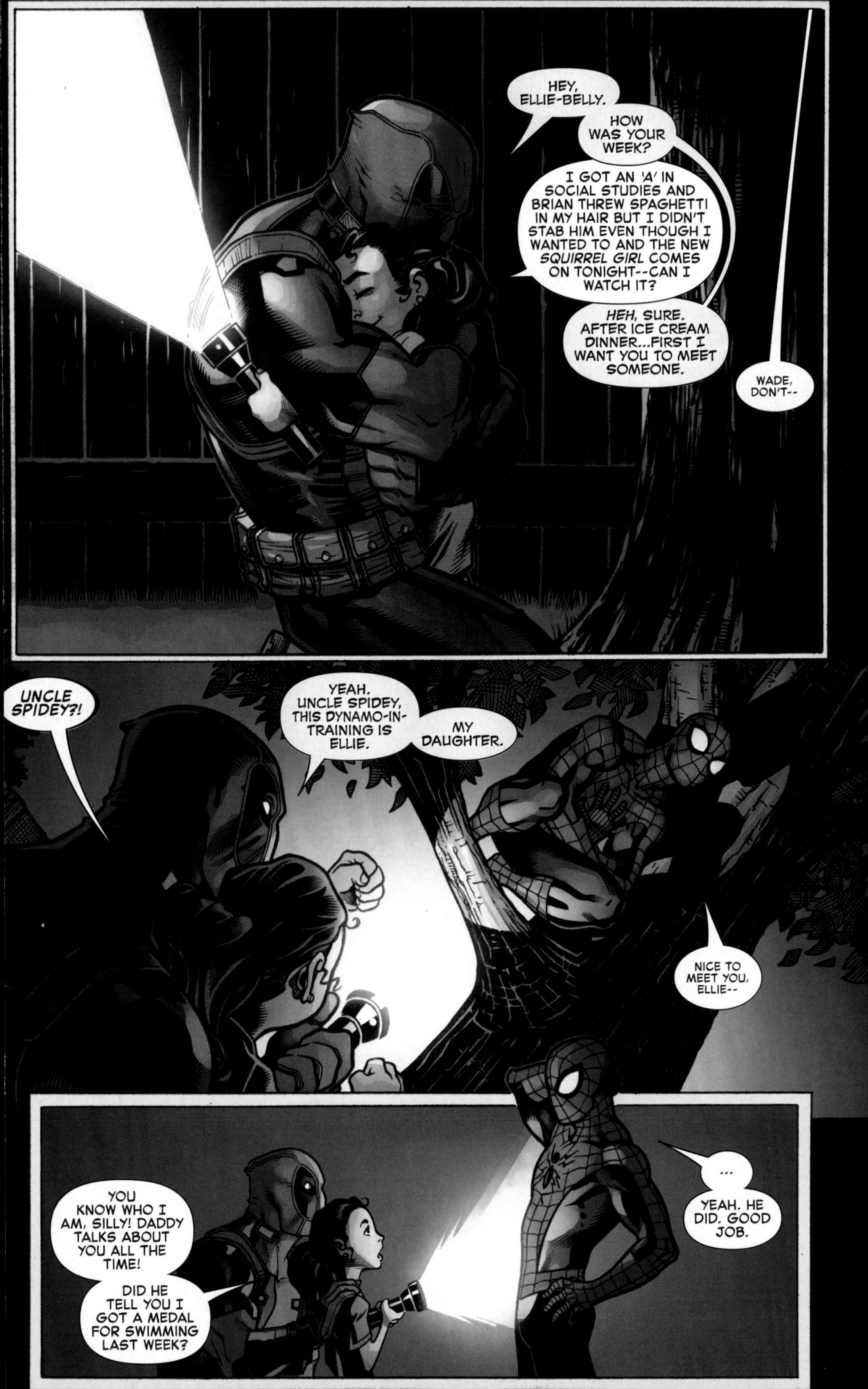

HEY, ELLIE-BELLY.
HOW WAS YOUR WEEK?
I GOT AN 'A' IN SOCIAL STUDIES AND BRIAN THREW SPAGHETTI IN MY HAIR BUT I DIDN'T STAB HIM EVEN THOUGH I WANTED TO AND THE NEW *SQUIRREL GIRL* COMES ON TONIGHT--CAN I WATCH IT?
HEH, SURE. AFTER ICE CREAM DINNER...FIRST I WANT YOU TO MEET SOMEONE.
WADE, DON'T--
UNCLE SPIDEY?!
YEAH. UNCLE SPIDEY, THIS DYNAMO-IN-TRAINING IS ELLIE.
MY DAUGHTER.
NICE TO MEET YOU, ELLIE--
YOU KNOW WHO I AM, SILLY! DADDY TALKS ABOUT YOU ALL THE TIME!
DID HE TELL YOU I GOT A MEDAL FOR SWIMMING LAST WEEK?
...
YEAH. HE DID. GOOD JOB.

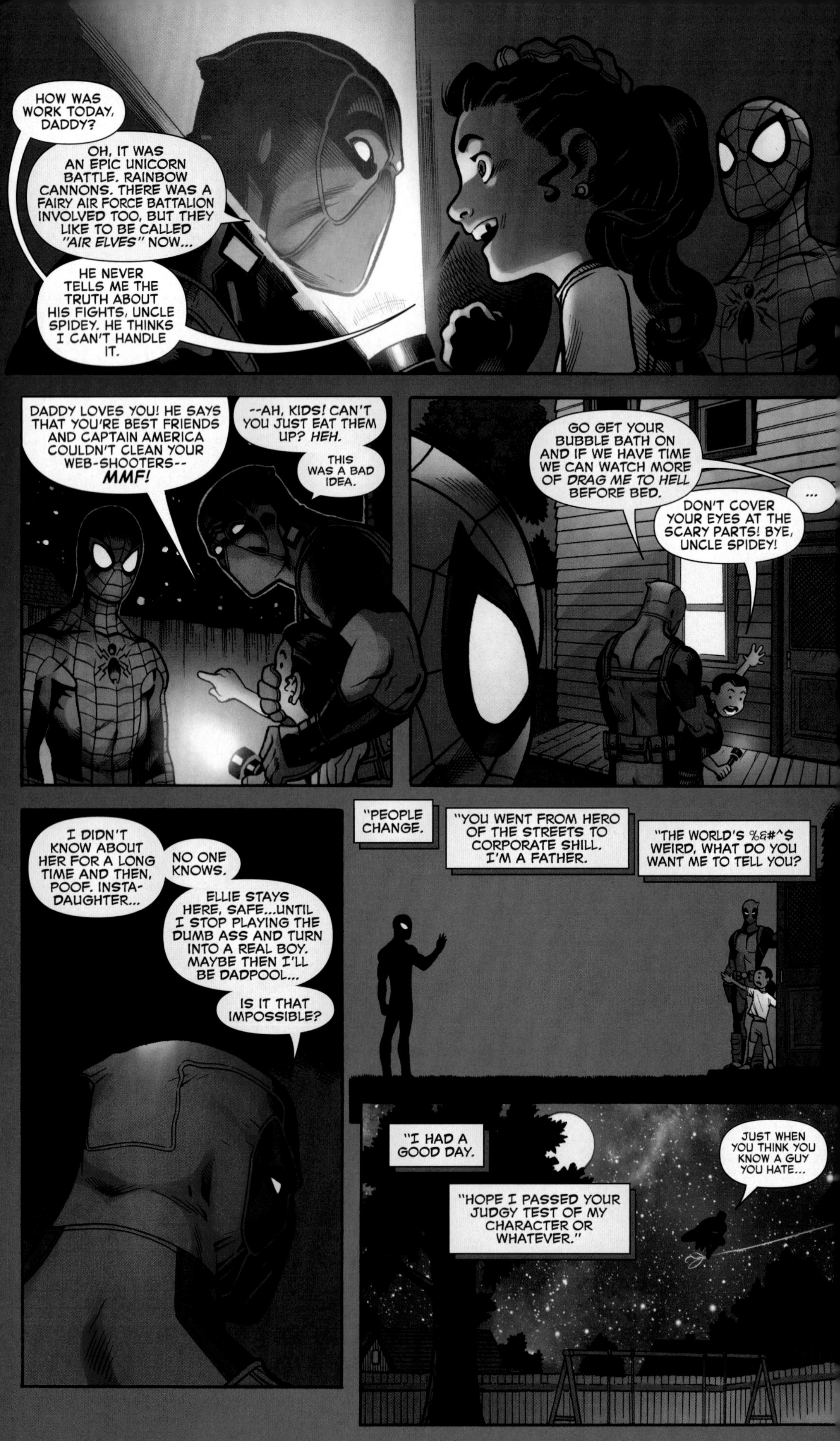
HOW WAS WORK TODAY, DADDY?
OH, IT WAS AN EPIC UNICORN BATTLE. RAINBOW CANNONS. THERE WAS A FAIRY AIR FORCE BATTALION INVOLVED TOO, BUT THEY LIKE TO BE CALLED *"AIR ELVES"* NOW...
HE NEVER TELLS ME THE TRUTH ABOUT HIS FIGHTS, UNCLE SPIDEY. HE THINKS I CAN'T HANDLE IT.
DADDY LOVES YOU! HE SAYS THAT YOU'RE BEST FRIENDS AND CAPTAIN AMERICA COULDN'T CLEAN YOUR WEB-SHOOTERS-- ***MMF!***
--AH, *KIDS!* CAN'T YOU JUST EAT THEM UP? *HEH.*
THIS WAS A BAD IDEA.
GO GET YOUR BUBBLE BATH ON AND IF WE HAVE TIME WE CAN WATCH MORE OF *DRAG ME TO HELL* BEFORE BED.
...
DON'T COVER YOUR EYES AT THE SCARY PARTS! BYE, UNCLE SPIDEY!
I DIDN'T KNOW ABOUT HER FOR A LONG TIME AND THEN, POOF. INSTA-DAUGHTER...
NO ONE KNOWS.
ELLIE STAYS HERE, SAFE...UNTIL I STOP PLAYING THE DUMB ASS AND TURN INTO A REAL BOY. MAYBE THEN I'LL BE DADPOOL...
IS IT THAT IMPOSSIBLE?
"PEOPLE CHANGE.
"YOU WENT FROM HERO OF THE STREETS TO CORPORATE SHILL. I'M A FATHER.
"THE WORLD'S %&#^$ WEIRD, WHAT DO YOU WANT ME TO TELL YOU?
"I HAD A GOOD DAY.
"HOPE I PASSED YOUR JUDGY TEST OF MY CHARACTER OR WHATEVER."
JUST WHEN YOU THINK YOU KNOW A GUY YOU HATE...

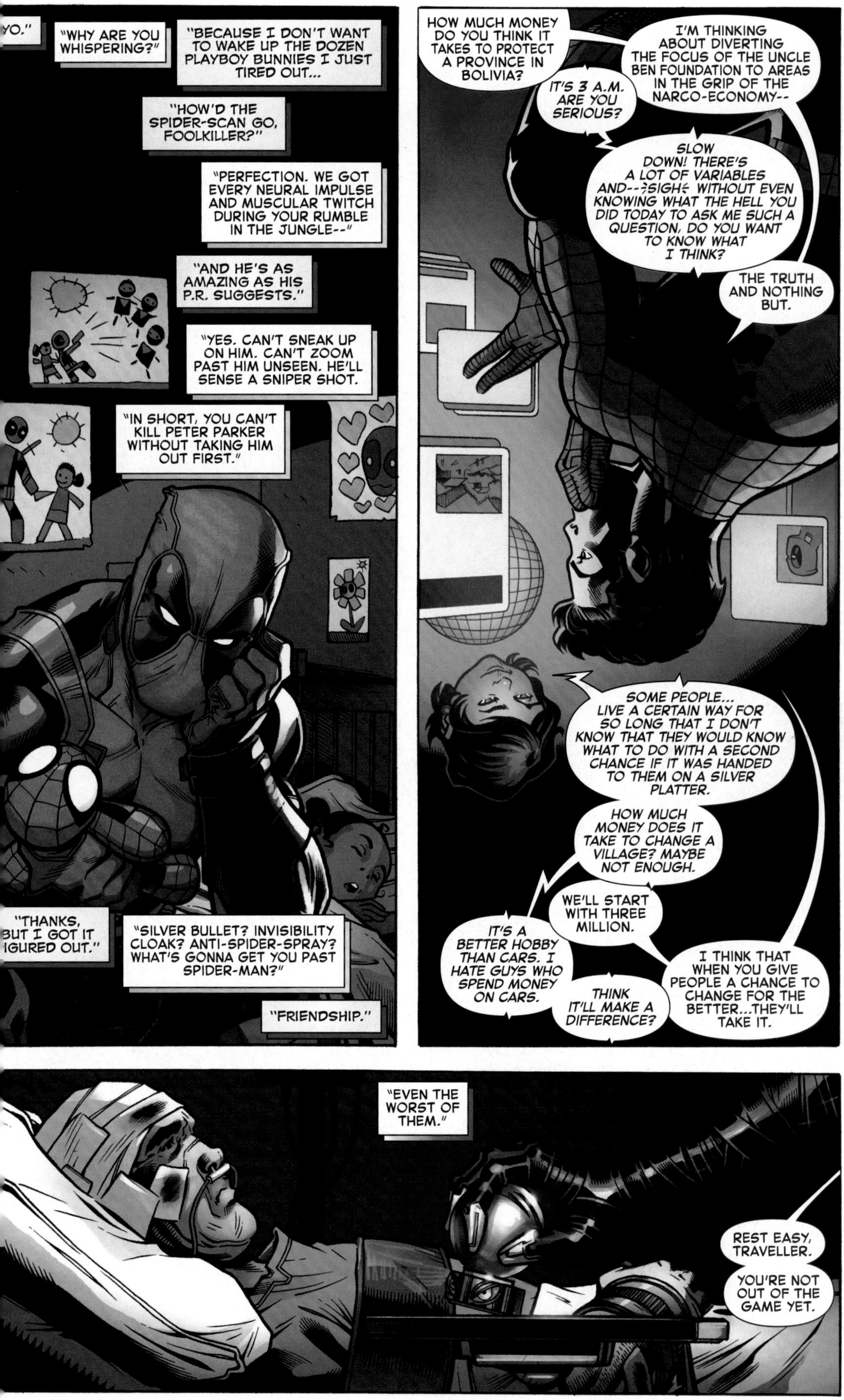
YO."
"WHY ARE YOU WHISPERING?"
"BECAUSE I DON'T WANT TO WAKE UP THE DOZEN PLAYBOY BUNNIES I JUST TIRED OUT...
"HOW'D THE SPIDER-SCAN GO, FOOLKILLER?"
"PERFECTION. WE GOT EVERY NEURAL IMPULSE AND MUSCULAR TWITCH DURING YOUR RUMBLE IN THE JUNGLE--"
"AND HE'S AS AMAZING AS HIS P.R. SUGGESTS."
"YES. CAN'T SNEAK UP ON HIM. CAN'T ZOOM PAST HIM UNSEEN. HE'LL SENSE A SNIPER SHOT.
"IN SHORT, YOU CAN'T KILL PETER PARKER WITHOUT TAKING HIM OUT FIRST."
"THANKS, BUT I GOT IT IGURED OUT."
"SILVER BULLET? INVISIBILITY CLOAK? ANTI-SPIDER-SPRAY? WHAT'S GONNA GET YOU PAST SPIDER-MAN?"
"FRIENDSHIP."
HOW MUCH MONEY DO YOU THINK IT TAKES TO PROTECT A PROVINCE IN BOLIVIA?
IT'S 3 A.M. ARE YOU SERIOUS?
I'M THINKING ABOUT DIVERTING THE FOCUS OF THE UNCLE BEN FOUNDATION TO AREAS IN THE GRIP OF THE NARCO-ECONOMY--
SLOW DOWN! THERE'S A LOT OF VARIABLES AND--›SIGH‹ WITHOUT EVEN KNOWING WHAT THE HELL YOU DID TODAY TO ASK ME SUCH A QUESTION, DO YOU WANT TO KNOW WHAT I THINK?
THE TRUTH AND NOTHING BUT.
SOME PEOPLE... LIVE A CERTAIN WAY FOR SO LONG THAT I DON'T KNOW THAT THEY WOULD KNOW WHAT TO DO WITH A SECOND CHANCE IF IT WAS HANDED TO THEM ON A SILVER PLATTER.
HOW MUCH MONEY DOES IT TAKE TO CHANGE A VILLAGE? MAYBE NOT ENOUGH.
WE'LL START WITH THREE MILLION.
IT'S A BETTER HOBBY THAN CARS. I HATE GUYS WHO SPEND MONEY ON CARS.
THINK IT'LL MAKE A DIFFERENCE?
I THINK THAT WHEN YOU GIVE PEOPLE A CHANCE TO CHANGE FOR THE BETTER...THEY'LL TAKE IT.
"EVEN THE WORST OF THEM."
REST EASY, TRAVELLER.
YOU'RE NOT OUT OF THE GAME YET.

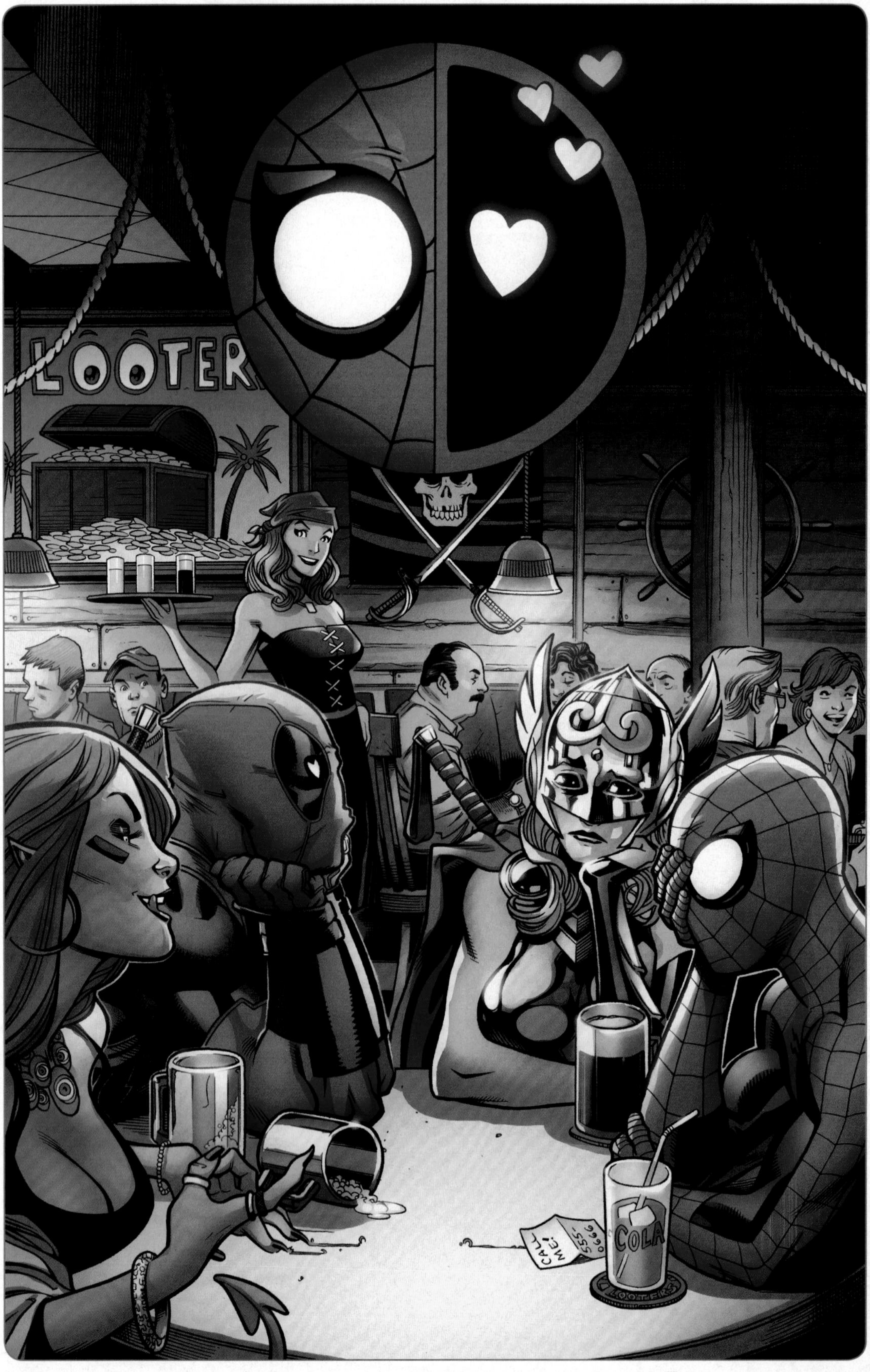
LOOTER
CALL ME!
555-0666
COLA
LOOTERS

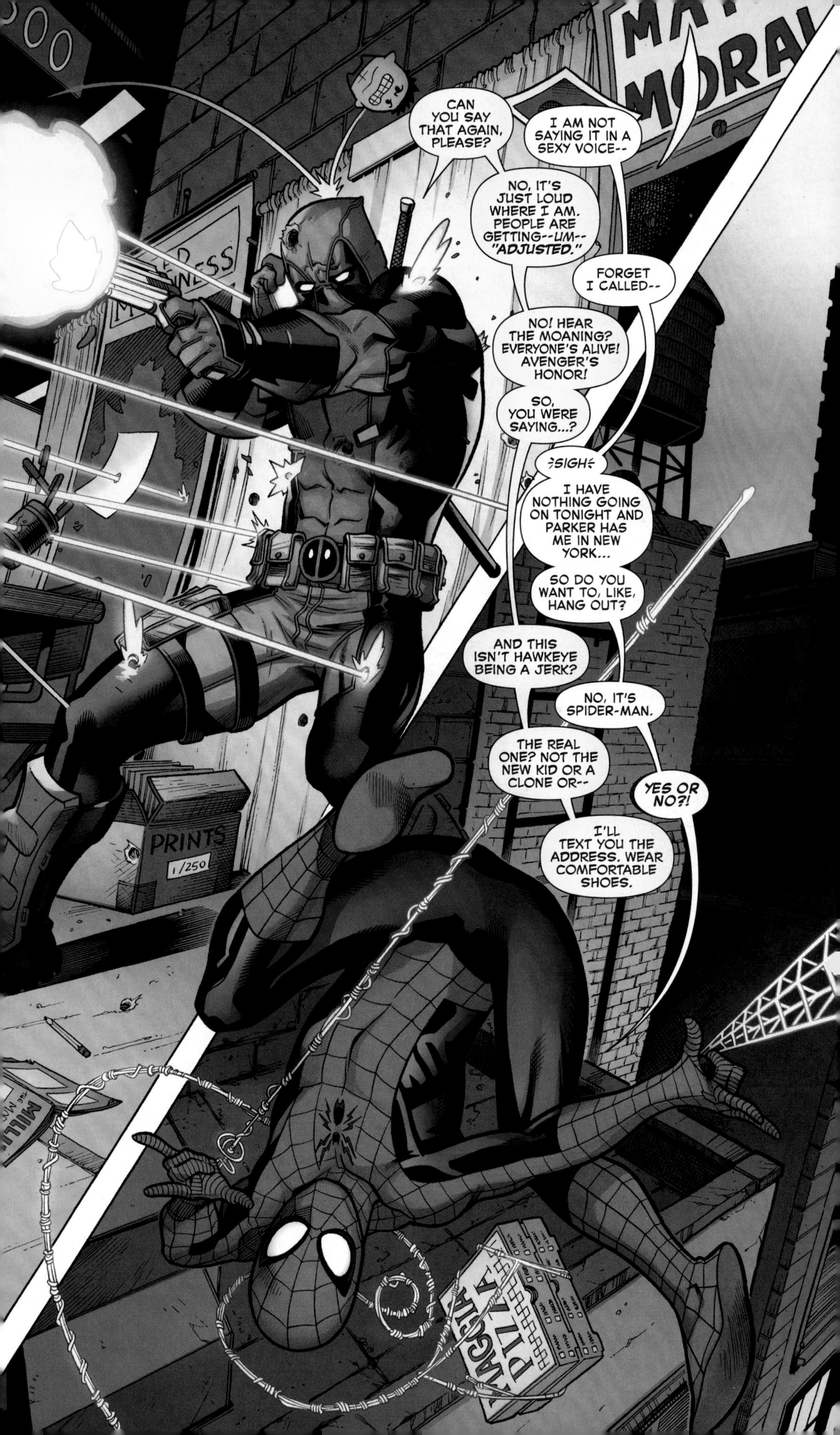

CAN YOU SAY THAT AGAIN, PLEASE?
I AM NOT SAYING IT IN A SEXY VOICE--
NO, IT'S JUST LOUD WHERE I AM. PEOPLE ARE GETTING--UM-- "ADJUSTED."
FORGET I CALLED--
NO! HEAR THE MOANING? EVERYONE'S ALIVE! AVENGER'S HONOR!
SO, YOU WERE SAYING...?
SIGH
I HAVE NOTHING GOING ON TONIGHT AND PARKER HAS ME IN NEW YORK...
SO DO YOU WANT TO, LIKE, HANG OUT?
AND THIS ISN'T HAWKEYE BEING A JERK?
NO, IT'S SPIDER-MAN.
THE REAL ONE? NOT THE NEW KID OR A CLONE OR--
YES OR NO?!
I'LL TEXT YOU THE ADDRESS. WEAR COMFORTABLE SHOES.
PRINTS
1/250

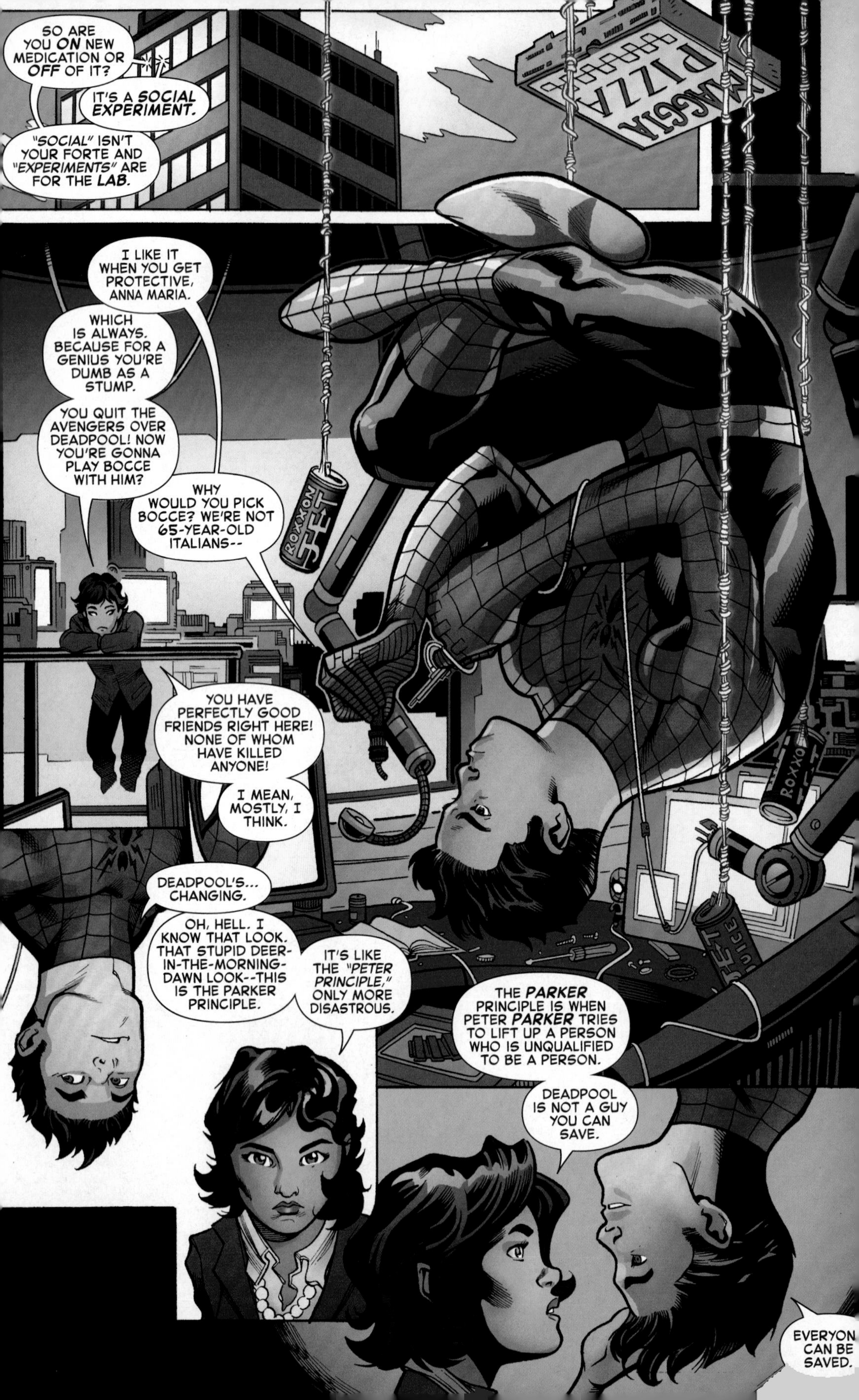
SO ARE YOU ON NEW MEDICATION OR OFF OF IT?
IT'S A SOCIAL EXPERIMENT.
"SOCIAL" ISN'T YOUR FORTE AND "EXPERIMENTS" ARE FOR THE LAB.
MAGGIA PIZZA
I LIKE IT WHEN YOU GET PROTECTIVE, ANNA MARIA.
WHICH IS ALWAYS. BECAUSE FOR A GENIUS YOU'RE DUMB AS A STUMP.
YOU QUIT THE AVENGERS OVER DEADPOOL! NOW YOU'RE GONNA PLAY BOCCE WITH HIM?
WHY WOULD YOU PICK BOCCE? WE'RE NOT 65-YEAR-OLD ITALIANS--
ROXXON JET
YOU HAVE PERFECTLY GOOD FRIENDS RIGHT HERE! NONE OF WHOM HAVE KILLED ANYONE!
I MEAN, MOSTLY, I THINK.
DEADPOOL'S... CHANGING.
OH, HELL. I KNOW THAT LOOK. THAT STUPID DEER-IN-THE-MORNING-DAWN LOOK--THIS IS THE PARKER PRINCIPLE.
IT'S LIKE THE "PETER PRINCIPLE," ONLY MORE DISASTROUS.
THE PARKER PRINCIPLE IS WHEN PETER PARKER TRIES TO LIFT UP A PERSON WHO IS UNQUALIFIED TO BE A PERSON.
DEADPOOL IS NOT A GUY YOU CAN SAVE.
EVERYON CAN BE SAVED.

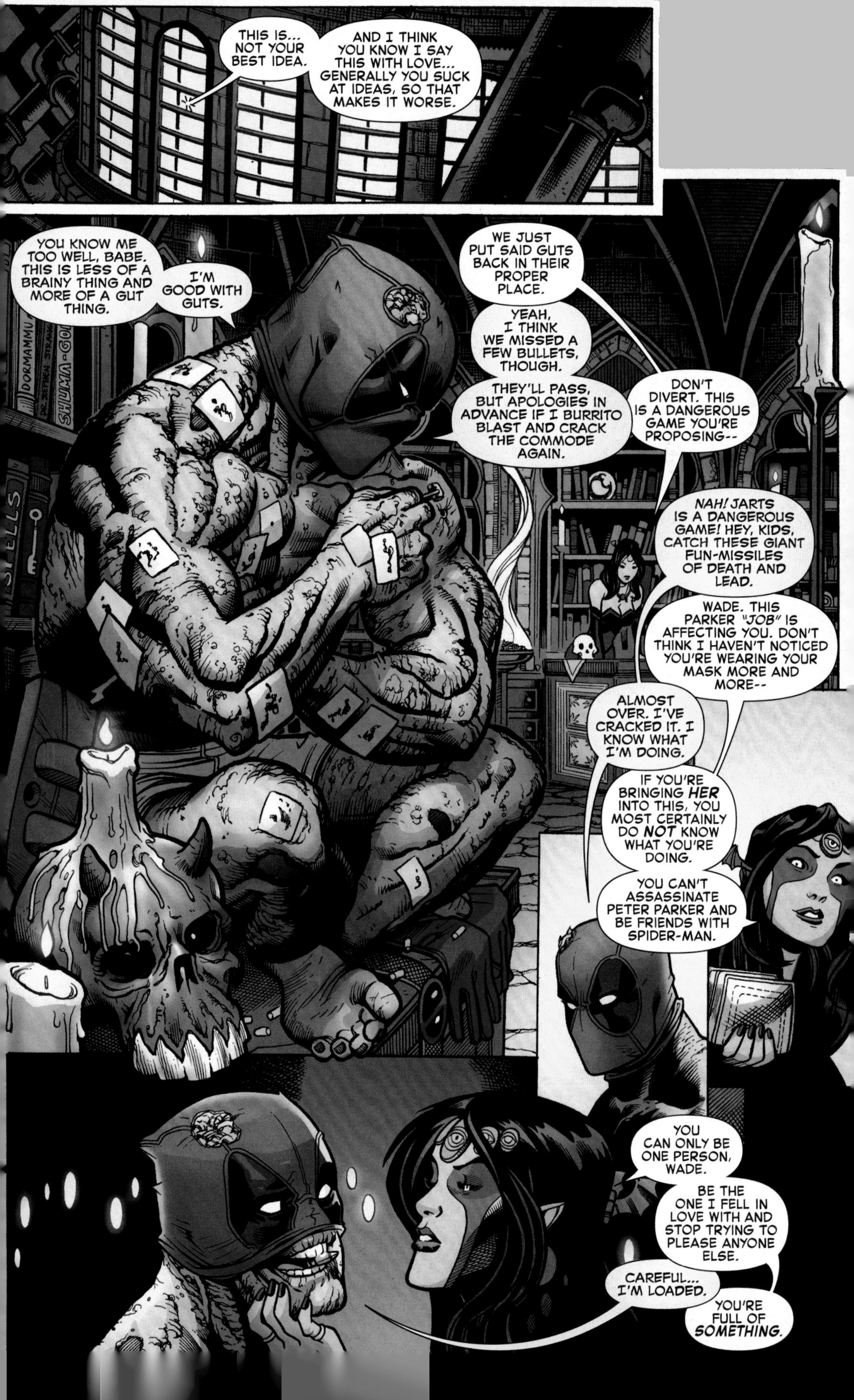

THIS IS... NOT YOUR BEST IDEA.
AND I THINK YOU KNOW I SAY THIS WITH LOVE... GENERALLY YOU SUCK AT IDEAS, SO THAT MAKES IT WORSE.
YOU KNOW ME TOO WELL, BABE. THIS IS LESS OF A BRAINY THING AND MORE OF A GUT THING.
I'M GOOD WITH GUTS.
WE JUST PUT SAID GUTS BACK IN THEIR PROPER PLACE.
YEAH, I THINK WE MISSED A FEW BULLETS, THOUGH.
THEY'LL PASS, BUT APOLOGIES IN ADVANCE IF I BURRITO BLAST AND CRACK THE COMMODE AGAIN.
DON'T DIVERT. THIS IS A DANGEROUS GAME YOU'RE PROPOSING--
NAH! JARTS IS A DANGEROUS GAME! HEY, KIDS, CATCH THESE GIANT FUN-MISSILES OF DEATH AND LEAD.
WADE. THIS PARKER "JOB" IS AFFECTING YOU. DON'T THINK I HAVEN'T NOTICED YOU'RE WEARING YOUR MASK MORE AND MORE--
ALMOST OVER. I'VE CRACKED IT. I KNOW WHAT I'M DOING.
IF YOU'RE BRINGING HER INTO THIS, YOU MOST CERTAINLY DO NOT KNOW WHAT YOU'RE DOING.
YOU CAN'T ASSASSINATE PETER PARKER AND BE FRIENDS WITH SPIDER-MAN.
YOU CAN ONLY BE ONE PERSON, WADE.
BE THE ONE I FELL IN LOVE WITH AND STOP TRYING TO PLEASE ANYONE ELSE.
CAREFUL... I'M LOADED.
YOU'RE FULL OF SOMETHING.

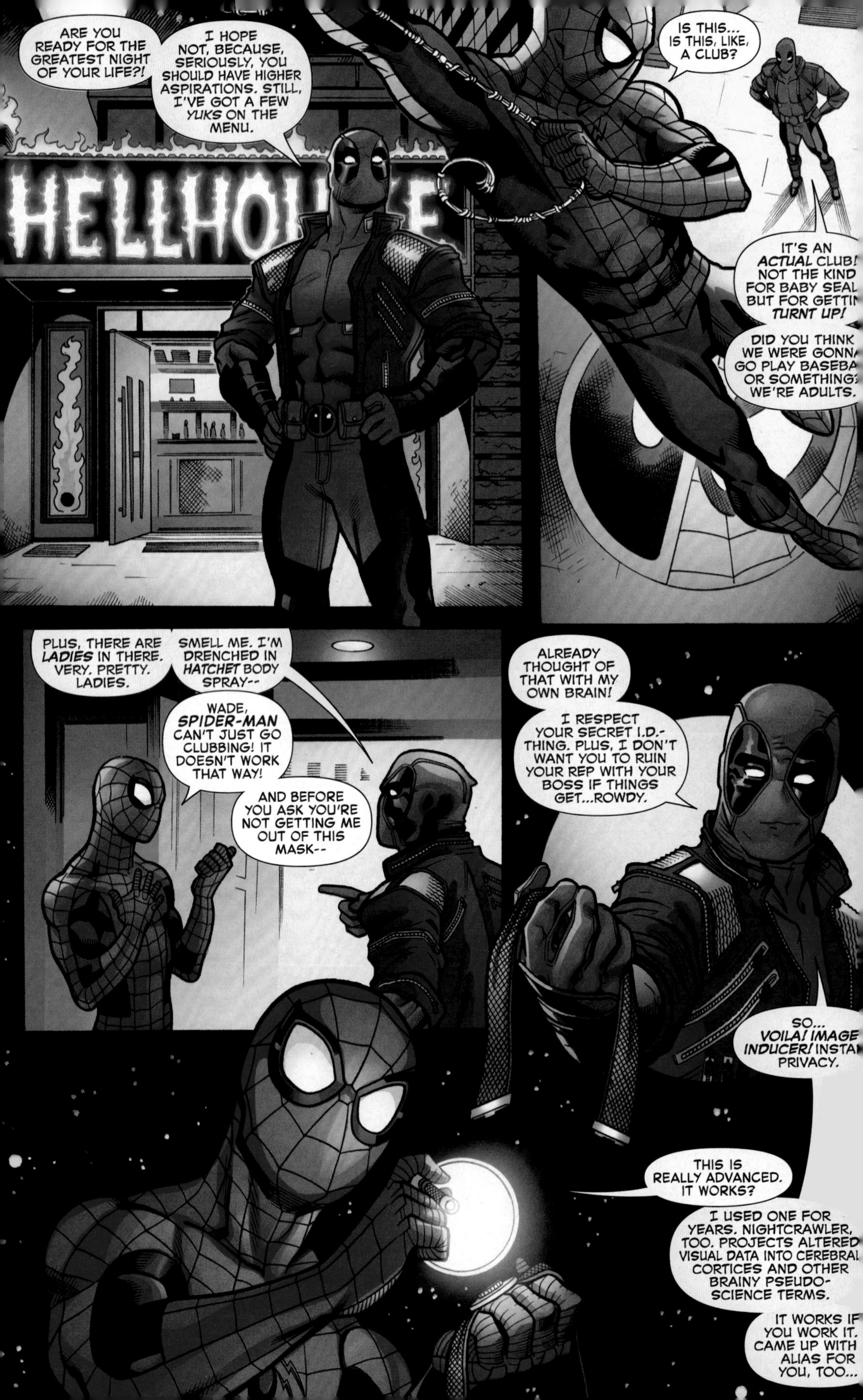
ARE YOU READY FOR THE GREATEST NIGHT OF YOUR LIFE?!
I HOPE NOT, BECAUSE, SERIOUSLY, YOU SHOULD HAVE HIGHER ASPIRATIONS. STILL, I'VE GOT A FEW *YUKS* ON THE MENU.
HELLHOU
IS THIS... IS THIS, LIKE, A CLUB?
IT'S AN *ACTUAL* CLUB! NOT THE KIND FOR BABY SEAL BUT FOR GETTI *TURNT UP!*
DID YOU THINK WE WERE GONN GO PLAY BASEBA OR SOMETHING WE'RE ADULTS.
PLUS, THERE ARE *LADIES* IN THERE. VERY. PRETTY. LADIES.
SMELL ME. I'M DRENCHED IN *HATCHET* BODY SPRAY--
WADE, *SPIDER-MAN* CAN'T JUST GO CLUBBING! IT DOESN'T WORK THAT WAY!
AND BEFORE YOU ASK YOU'RE NOT GETTING ME OUT OF THIS MASK--
ALREADY THOUGHT OF THAT WITH MY OWN BRAIN!
I RESPECT YOUR SECRET I.D.-THING. PLUS, I DON'T WANT YOU TO RUIN YOUR REP WITH YOUR BOSS IF THINGS GET...ROWDY.
SO... *VOILA! IMAGE INDUCER!* INSTA PRIVACY.
THIS IS REALLY ADVANCED. IT WORKS?
I USED ONE FOR YEARS. NIGHTCRAWLER, TOO. PROJECTS ALTERED VISUAL DATA INTO CEREBRA CORTICES AND OTHER BRAINY PSEUDO-SCIENCE TERMS.
IT WORKS IF YOU WORK IT. CAME UP WITH ALIAS FOR YOU, TOO...

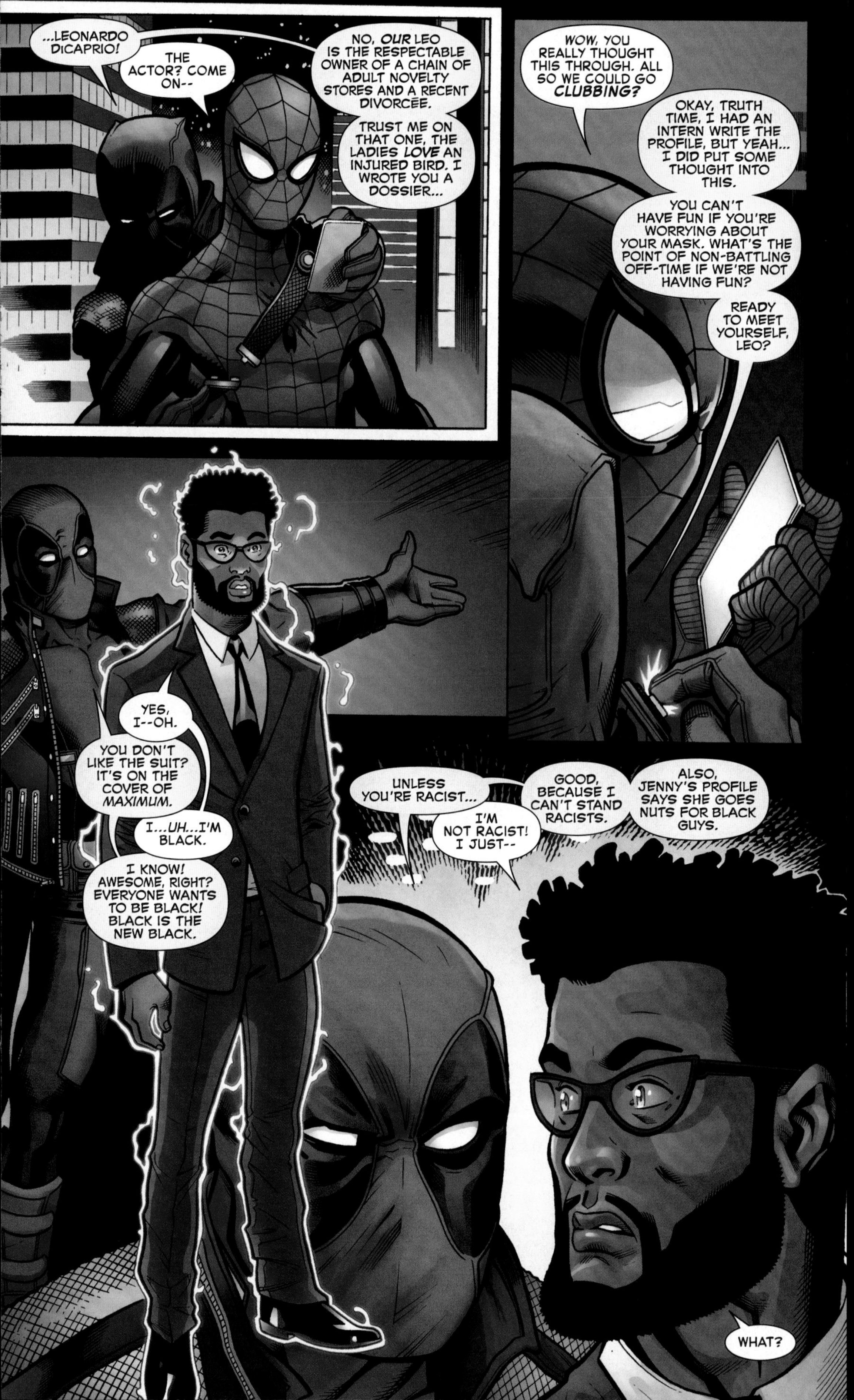

...LEONARDO DICAPRIO!
THE ACTOR? COME ON--
NO, OUR LEO IS THE RESPECTABLE OWNER OF A CHAIN OF ADULT NOVELTY STORES AND A RECENT DIVORCÉE.
TRUST ME ON THAT ONE, THE LADIES LOVE AN INJURED BIRD. I WROTE YOU A DOSSIER...
WOW, YOU REALLY THOUGHT THIS THROUGH. ALL SO WE COULD GO CLUBBING?
OKAY, TRUTH TIME, I HAD AN INTERN WRITE THE PROFILE, BUT YEAH... I DID PUT SOME THOUGHT INTO THIS.
YOU CAN'T HAVE FUN IF YOU'RE WORRYING ABOUT YOUR MASK. WHAT'S THE POINT OF NON-BATTLING OFF-TIME IF WE'RE NOT HAVING FUN?
READY TO MEET YOURSELF, LEO?
YES, I--OH.
YOU DON'T LIKE THE SUIT? IT'S ON THE COVER OF MAXIMUM.
I...UH...I'M BLACK.
I KNOW! AWESOME, RIGHT? EVERYONE WANTS TO BE BLACK! BLACK IS THE NEW BLACK.
UNLESS YOU'RE RACIST...
I'M NOT RACIST! I JUST--
GOOD, BECAUSE I CAN'T STAND RACISTS.
ALSO, JENNY'S PROFILE SAYS SHE GOES NUTS FOR BLACK GUYS.
WHAT?

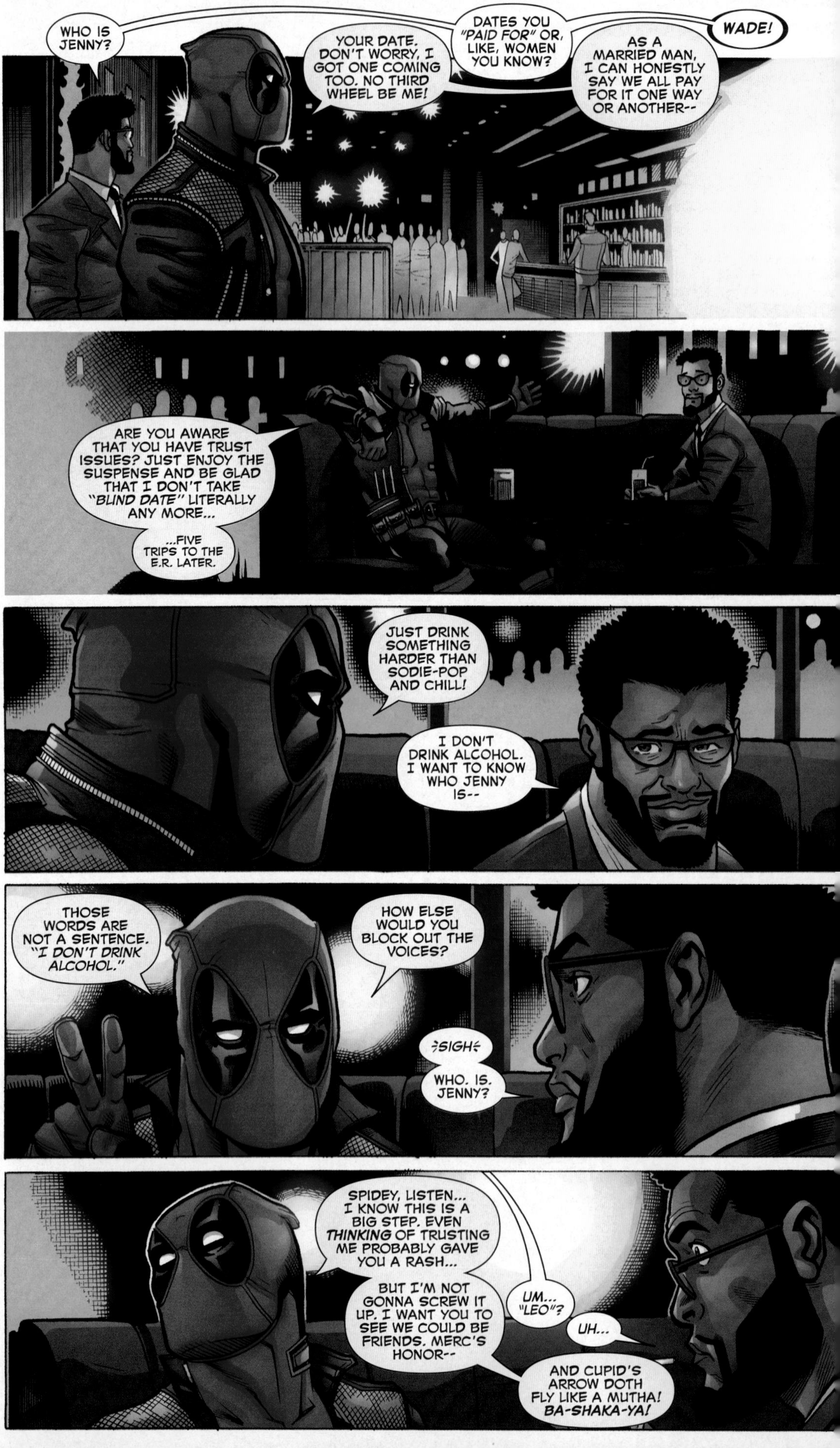
WHO IS JENNY?
YOUR DATE. DON'T WORRY, I GOT ONE COMING TOO. NO THIRD WHEEL BE ME!
DATES YOU "PAID FOR" OR, LIKE, WOMEN YOU KNOW?
WADE!
AS A MARRIED MAN, I CAN HONESTLY SAY WE ALL PAY FOR IT ONE WAY OR ANOTHER--
ARE YOU AWARE THAT YOU HAVE TRUST ISSUES? JUST ENJOY THE SUSPENSE AND BE GLAD THAT I DON'T TAKE "BLIND DATE" LITERALLY ANY MORE...
...FIVE TRIPS TO THE E.R. LATER.
JUST DRINK SOMETHING HARDER THAN SODIE-POP AND CHILL!
I DON'T DRINK ALCOHOL. I WANT TO KNOW WHO JENNY IS--
THOSE WORDS ARE NOT A SENTENCE. "I DON'T DRINK ALCOHOL."
HOW ELSE WOULD YOU BLOCK OUT THE VOICES?
⊰SIGH⊱
WHO. IS. JENNY?
SPIDEY, LISTEN... I KNOW THIS IS A BIG STEP. EVEN THINKING OF TRUSTING ME PROBABLY GAVE YOU A RASH...
BUT I'M NOT GONNA SCREW IT UP. I WANT YOU TO SEE WE COULD BE FRIENDS. MERC'S HONOR--
UM... "LEO"?
UH...
AND CUPID'S ARROW DOTH FLY LIKE A MUTHA! BA-SHAKA-YA!

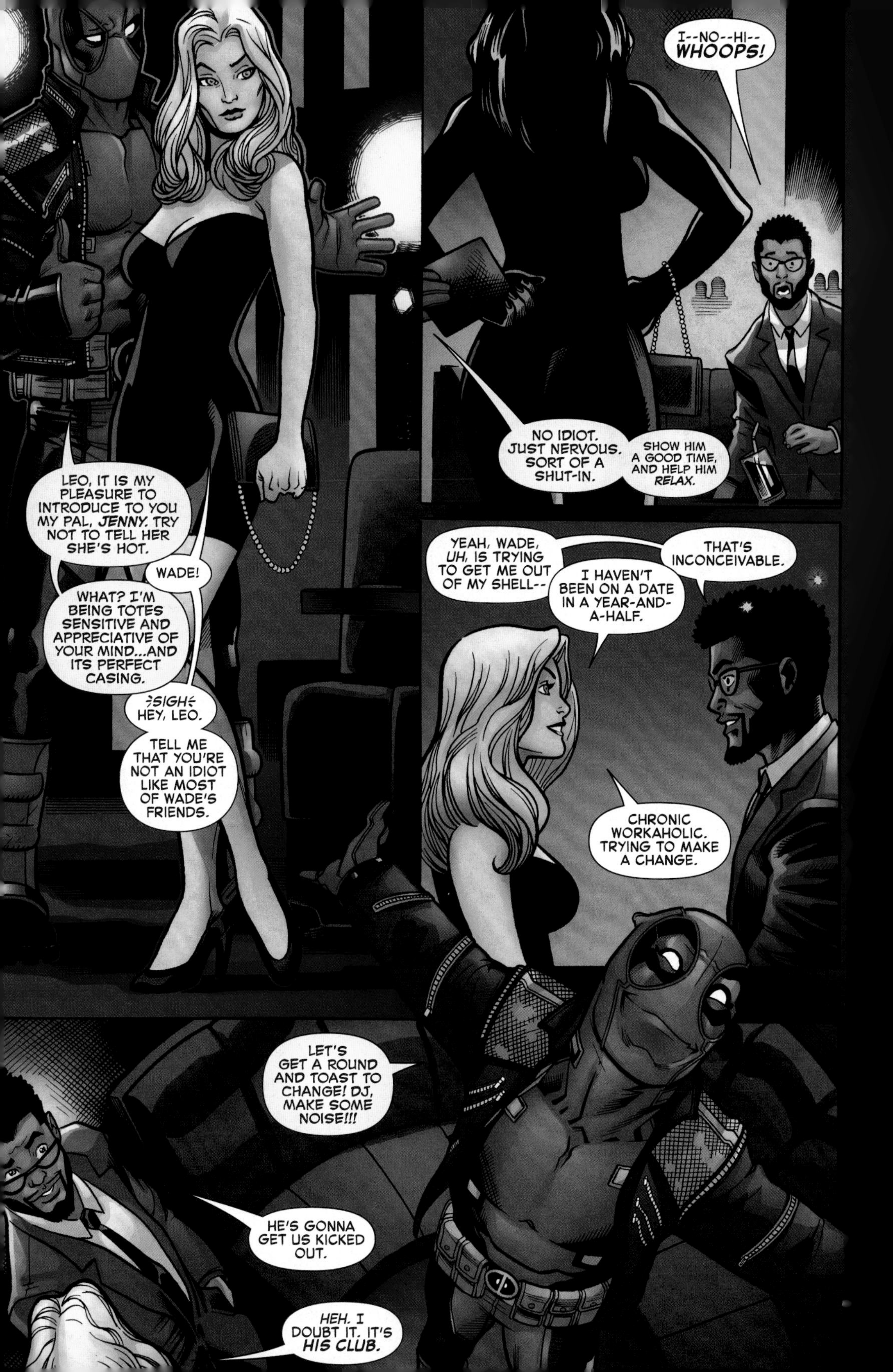
LEO, IT IS MY PLEASURE TO INTRODUCE TO YOU MY PAL, JENNY. TRY NOT TO TELL HER SHE'S HOT.
WADE!
WHAT? I'M BEING TOTES SENSITIVE AND APPRECIATIVE OF YOUR MIND...AND ITS PERFECT CASING.
SIGH
HEY, LEO.
TELL ME THAT YOU'RE NOT AN IDIOT LIKE MOST OF WADE'S FRIENDS.
I--NO--HI--
WHOOPS!
NO IDIOT. JUST NERVOUS. SORT OF A SHUT-IN.
SHOW HIM A GOOD TIME, AND HELP HIM RELAX.
YEAH, WADE, UH, IS TRYING TO GET ME OUT OF MY SHELL--
I HAVEN'T BEEN ON A DATE IN A YEAR-AND-A-HALF.
THAT'S INCONCEIVABLE.
CHRONIC WORKAHOLIC. TRYING TO MAKE A CHANGE.
LET'S GET A ROUND AND TOAST TO CHANGE! DJ, MAKE SOME NOISE!!!
HE'S GONNA GET US KICKED OUT.
HEH. I DOUBT IT. IT'S HIS CLUB.

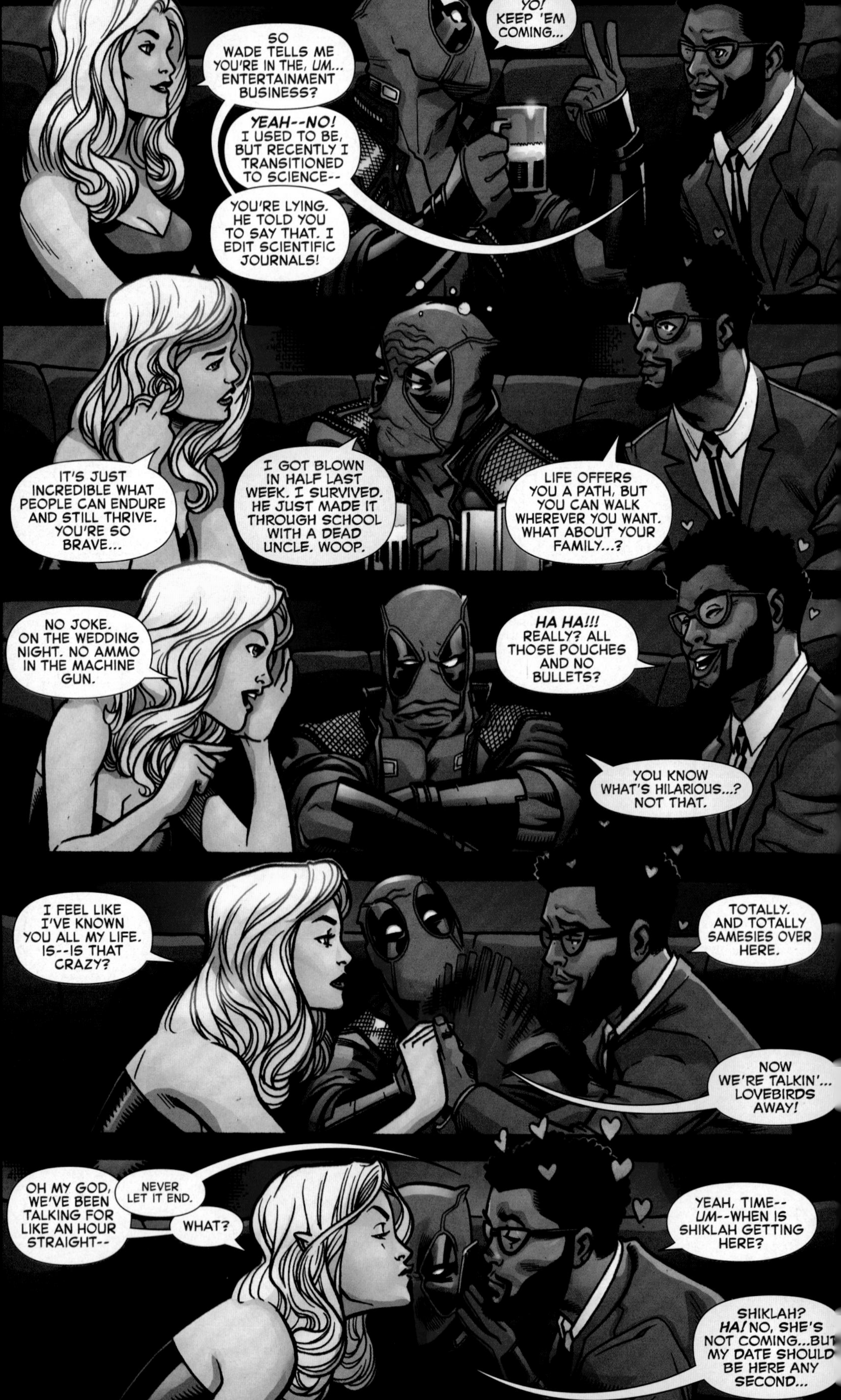
SO WADE TELLS ME YOU'RE IN THE, UM... ENTERTAINMENT BUSINESS?
YO! KEEP 'EM COMING...
YEAH--NO! I USED TO BE, BUT RECENTLY I TRANSITIONED TO SCIENCE--
YOU'RE LYING. HE TOLD YOU TO SAY THAT. I EDIT SCIENTIFIC JOURNALS!
IT'S JUST INCREDIBLE WHAT PEOPLE CAN ENDURE AND STILL THRIVE. YOU'RE SO BRAVE...
I GOT BLOWN IN HALF LAST WEEK. I SURVIVED. HE JUST MADE IT THROUGH SCHOOL WITH A DEAD UNCLE. WOOP.
LIFE OFFERS YOU A PATH, BUT YOU CAN WALK WHEREVER YOU WANT. WHAT ABOUT YOUR FAMILY...?
NO JOKE. ON THE WEDDING NIGHT. NO AMMO IN THE MACHINE GUN.
HA HA!!! REALLY? ALL THOSE POUCHES AND NO BULLETS?
YOU KNOW WHAT'S HILARIOUS...? NOT THAT.
I FEEL LIKE I'VE KNOWN YOU ALL MY LIFE. IS--IS THAT CRAZY?
TOTALLY. AND TOTALLY SAMESIES OVER HERE.
NOW WE'RE TALKIN'... LOVEBIRDS AWAY!
OH MY GOD, WE'VE BEEN TALKING FOR LIKE AN HOUR STRAIGHT--
NEVER LET IT END.
WHAT?
YEAH, TIME-- UM--WHEN IS SHIKLAH GETTING HERE?
SHIKLAH? HA! NO, SHE'S NOT COMING...BUT MY DATE SHOULD BE HERE ANY SECOND...

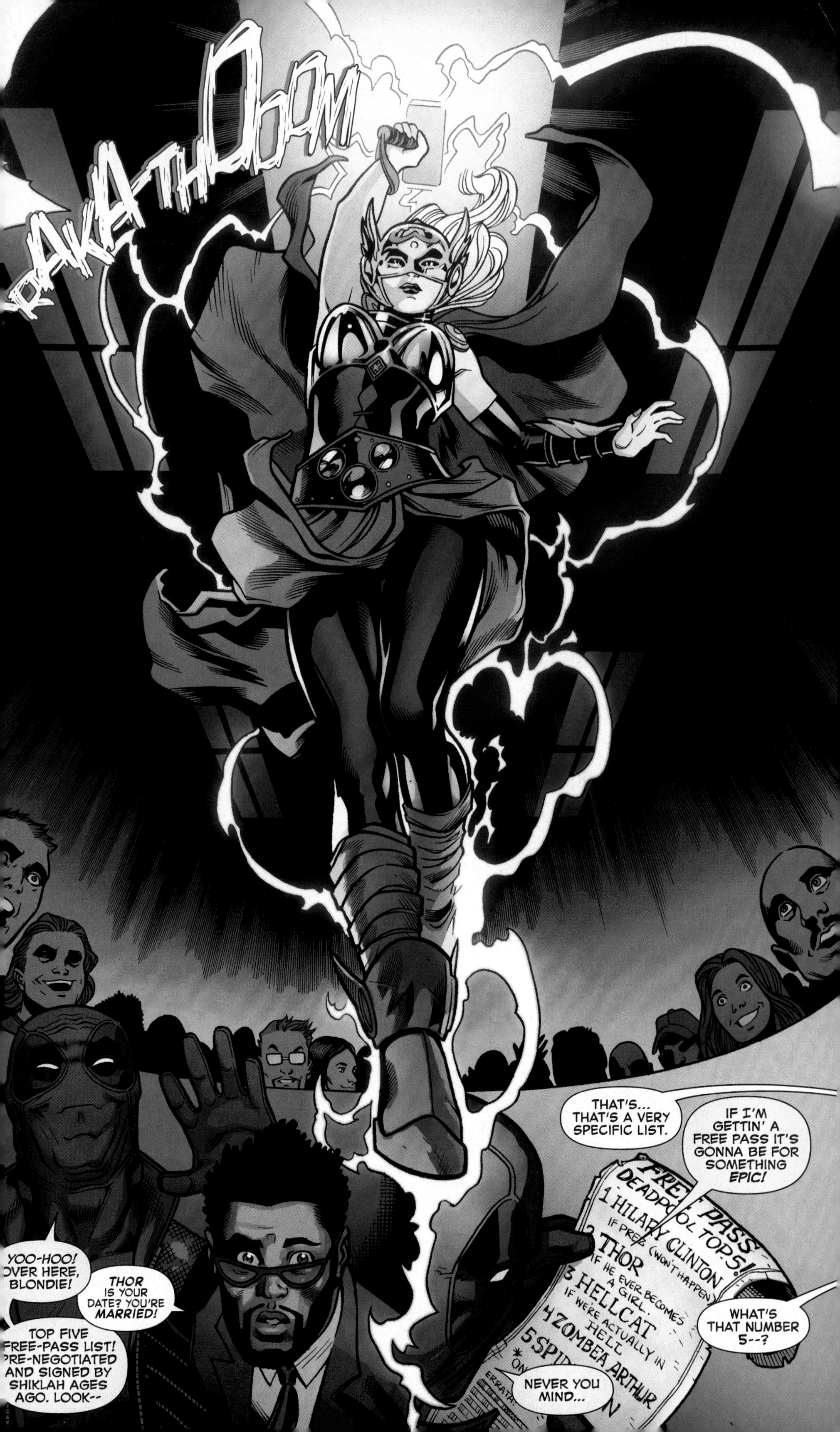
RAKA-THOOOM
THAT'S... THAT'S A VERY SPECIFIC LIST.
IF I'M GETTIN' A FREE PASS IT'S GONNA BE FOR SOMETHING *EPIC!*
FREE PASS! DEADPOOL TOPS!
1 HILARY CLINTON IF PREZ (WON'T HAPPEN)
2 THOR IF HE EVER BECOMES A GIRL.
3 HELLCAT IF WERE ACTUALLY IN HELL
4 ZOMBEA ARTHUR
5 SPID
* ON
ERRATA:
WHAT'S THAT NUMBER 5--?
NEVER YOU MIND...
YOO-HOO! VER HERE, BLONDIE!
THOR IS YOUR DATE? YOU'RE *MARRIED!*
TOP FIVE FREE-PASS LIST! RE-NEGOTIATED AND SIGNED BY SHIKLAH AGES AGO. LOOK--

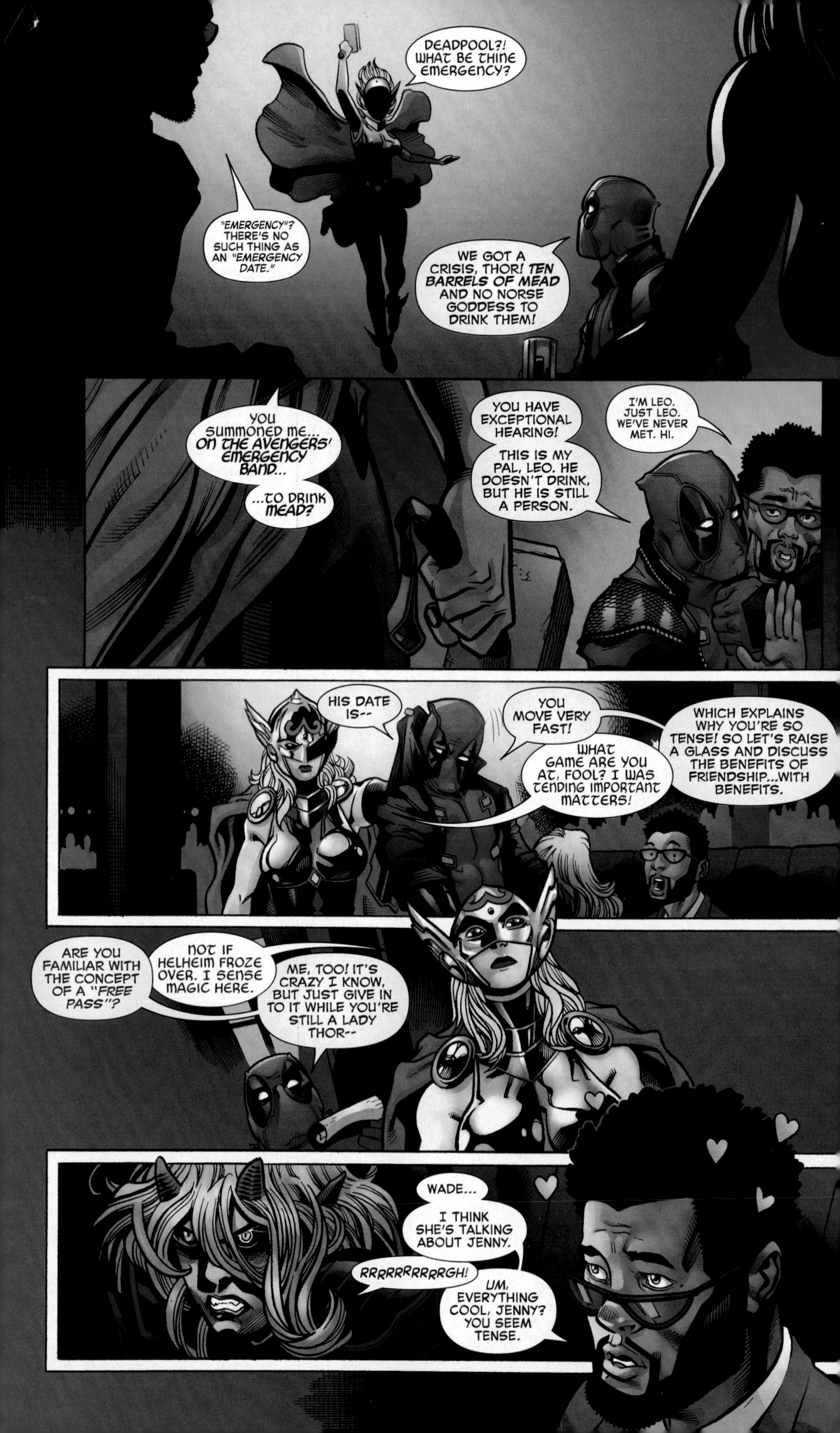
DEADPOOL?! WHAT BE THINE EMERGENCY?
"EMERGENCY"? THERE'S NO SUCH THING AS AN "EMERGENCY DATE."
WE GOT A CRISIS, THOR! TEN BARRELS OF MEAD AND NO NORSE GODDESS TO DRINK THEM!
YOU SUMMONED ME... ON THE AVENGERS' EMERGENCY BAND...
...TO DRINK MEAD?
YOU HAVE EXCEPTIONAL HEARING!
THIS IS MY PAL, LEO. HE DOESN'T DRINK, BUT HE IS STILL A PERSON.
I'M LEO. JUST LEO. WE'VE NEVER MET. HI.
HIS DATE IS--
YOU MOVE VERY FAST!
WHAT GAME ARE YOU AT, FOOL? I WAS TENDING IMPORTANT MATTERS!
WHICH EXPLAINS WHY YOU'RE SO TENSE! SO LET'S RAISE A GLASS AND DISCUSS THE BENEFITS OF FRIENDSHIP...WITH BENEFITS.
ARE YOU FAMILIAR WITH THE CONCEPT OF A "FREE PASS"?
NOT IF HELHEIM FROZE OVER. I SENSE MAGIC HERE.
ME, TOO! IT'S CRAZY I KNOW, BUT JUST GIVE IN TO IT WHILE YOU'RE STILL A LADY THOR--
WADE...
I THINK SHE'S TALKING ABOUT JENNY.
RRRRRRRRRRGH!
UM, EVERYTHING COOL, JENNY? YOU SEEM TENSE.

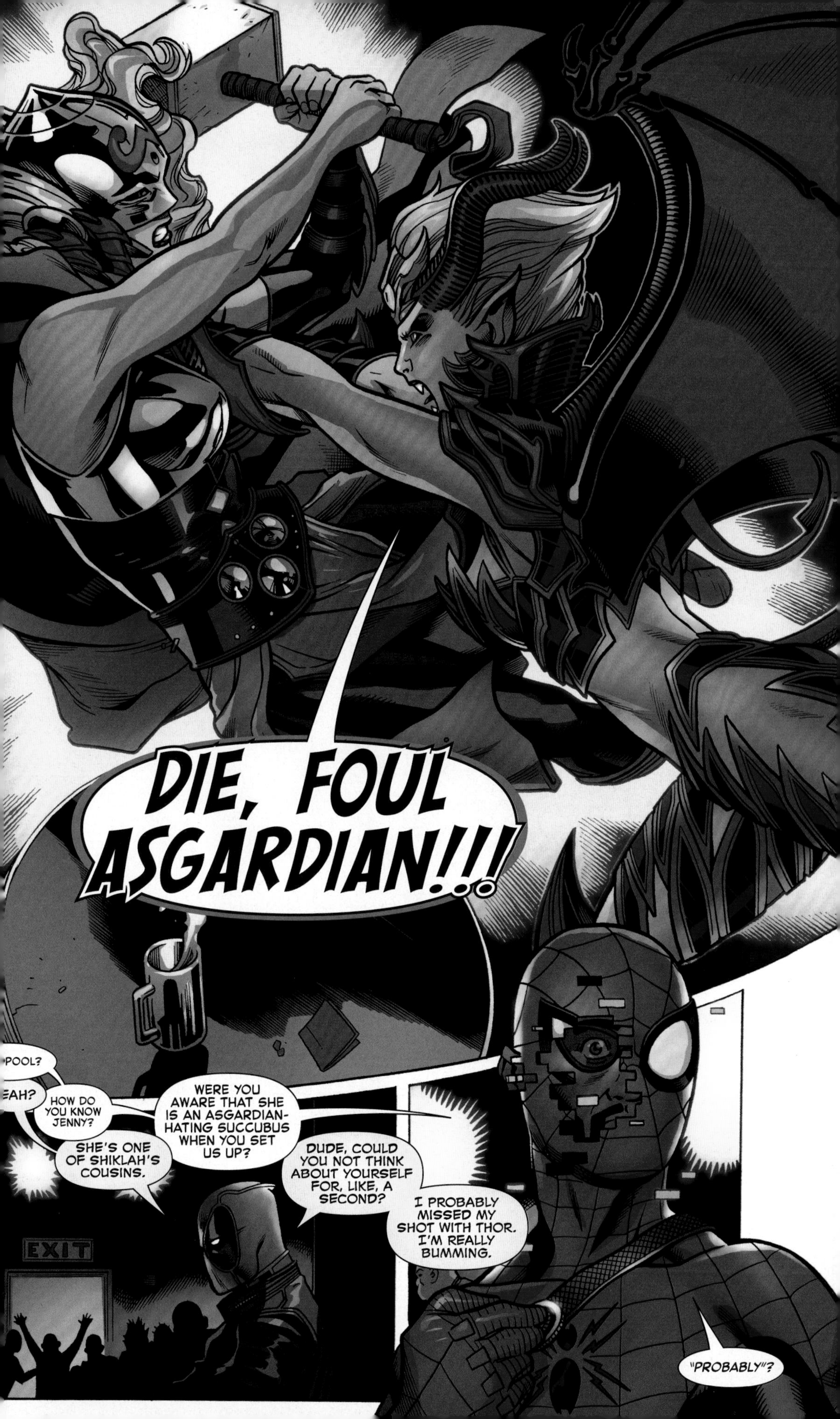
DIE, FOUL ASGARDIAN!!!
POOL?
EAH?
HOW DO YOU KNOW JENNY?
SHE'S ONE OF SHIKLAH'S COUSINS.
WERE YOU AWARE THAT SHE IS AN ASGARDIAN-HATING SUCCUBUS WHEN YOU SET US UP?
DUDE, COULD YOU NOT THINK ABOUT YOURSELF FOR, LIKE, A SECOND?
I PROBABLY MISSED MY SHOT WITH THOR. I'M REALLY BUMMING.
"PROBABLY"?
EXIT

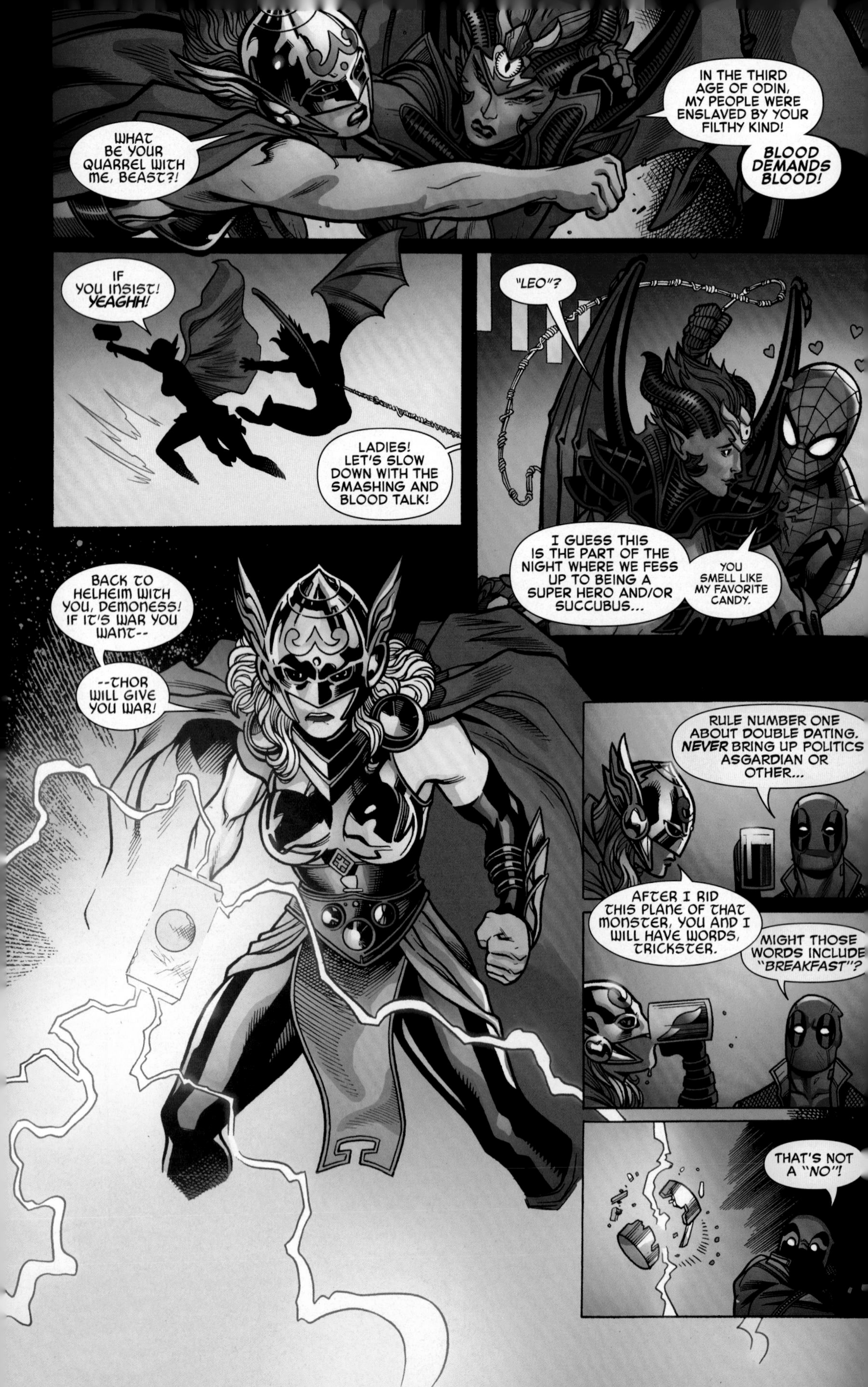
WHAT BE YOUR QUARREL WITH ME, BEAST?!
IN THE THIRD AGE OF ODIN, MY PEOPLE WERE ENSLAVED BY YOUR FILTHY KIND!
BLOOD DEMANDS BLOOD!
IF YOU INSIST! YEAGHH!
LADIES! LET'S SLOW DOWN WITH THE SMASHING AND BLOOD TALK!
"LEO"?
I GUESS THIS IS THE PART OF THE NIGHT WHERE WE FESS UP TO BEING A SUPER HERO AND/OR SUCCUBUS...
YOU SMELL LIKE MY FAVORITE CANDY.
BACK TO HELHEIM WITH YOU, DEMONESS! IF IT'S WAR YOU WANT--
--THOR WILL GIVE YOU WAR!
RULE NUMBER ONE ABOUT DOUBLE DATING. NEVER BRING UP POLITICS ASGARDIAN OR OTHER...
AFTER I RID THIS PLANE OF THAT MONSTER, YOU AND I WILL HAVE WORDS, TRICKSTER.
MIGHT THOSE WORDS INCLUDE "BREAKFAST"?
THAT'S NOT A "NO"!

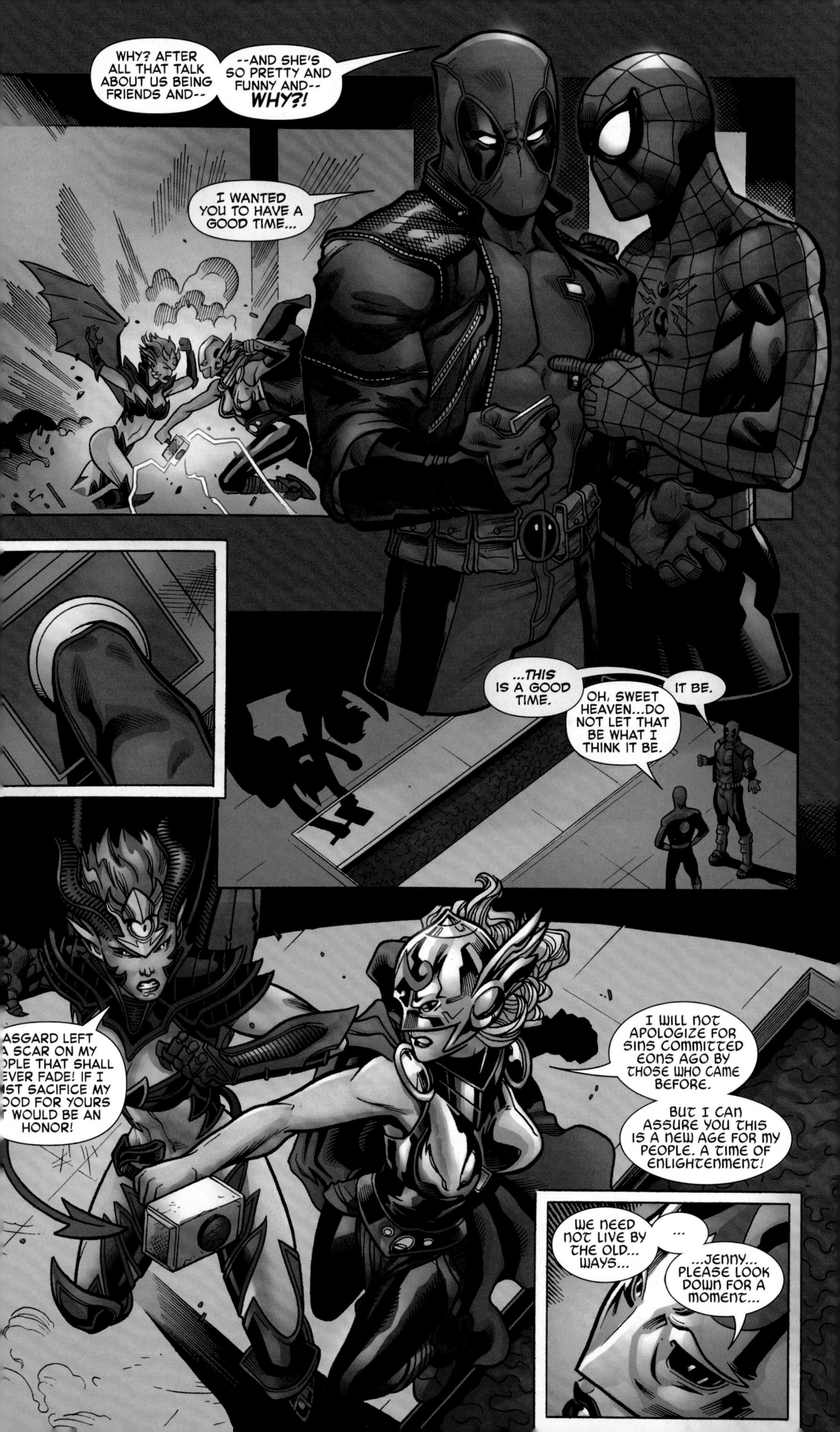
WHY? AFTER ALL THAT TALK ABOUT US BEING FRIENDS AND--
--AND SHE'S SO PRETTY AND FUNNY AND-- WHY?!
I WANTED YOU TO HAVE A GOOD TIME...
...THIS IS A GOOD TIME.
OH, SWEET HEAVEN...DO NOT LET THAT BE WHAT I THINK IT BE.
IT BE.
ASGARD LEFT A SCAR ON MY OPLE THAT SHALL EVER FADE! IF I IST SACIFICE MY OOD FOR YOURS T WOULD BE AN HONOR!
I WILL NOT APOLOGIZE FOR SINS COMMITTED EONS AGO BY THOSE WHO CAME BEFORE.
BUT I CAN ASSURE YOU THIS IS A NEW AGE FOR MY PEOPLE. A TIME OF ENLIGHTENMENT!
WE NEED NOT LIVE BY THE OLD... WAYS...
...
...JENNY... PLEASE LOOK DOWN FOR A MOMENT...

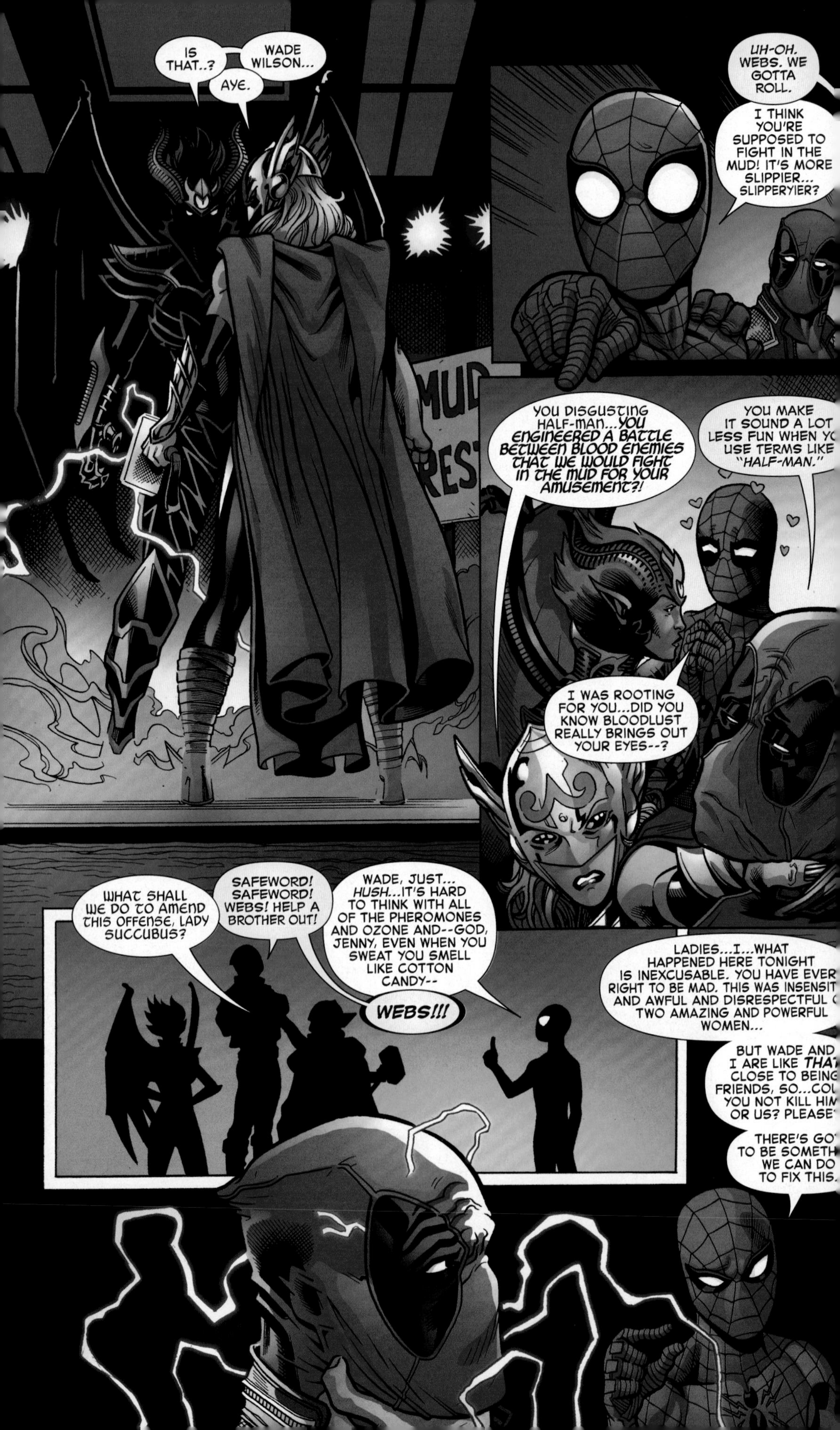
IS THAT..?
WADE WILSON...
AYE.
UH-OH. WEBS. WE GOTTA ROLL.
I THINK YOU'RE SUPPOSED TO FIGHT IN THE MUD! IT'S MORE SLIPPIER... SLIPPERYIER?
MUD
RES
YOU DISGUSTING HALF-MAN... YOU ENGINEERED A BATTLE BETWEEN BLOOD ENEMIES THAT WE WOULD FIGHT IN THE MUD FOR YOUR AMUSEMENT?!
YOU MAKE IT SOUND A LOT LESS FUN WHEN YO USE TERMS LIKE "HALF-MAN."
I WAS ROOTING FOR YOU...DID YOU KNOW BLOODLUST REALLY BRINGS OUT YOUR EYES--?
WHAT SHALL WE DO TO AMEND THIS OFFENSE, LADY SUCCUBUS?
SAFEWORD! SAFEWORD! WEBS! HELP A BROTHER OUT!
WADE, JUST... HUSH...IT'S HARD TO THINK WITH ALL OF THE PHEROMONES AND OZONE AND--GOD, JENNY, EVEN WHEN YOU SWEAT YOU SMELL LIKE COTTON CANDY--
WEBS!!!
LADIES...I...WHAT HAPPENED HERE TONIGHT IS INEXCUSABLE. YOU HAVE EVER RIGHT TO BE MAD. THIS WAS INSENSIT AND AWFUL AND DISRESPECTFUL TWO AMAZING AND POWERFUL WOMEN...
BUT WADE AND I ARE LIKE THA CLOSE TO BEING FRIENDS, SO...COU YOU NOT KILL HIM OR US? PLEASE
THERE'S GO TO BE SOMETH WE CAN DO TO FIX THIS.

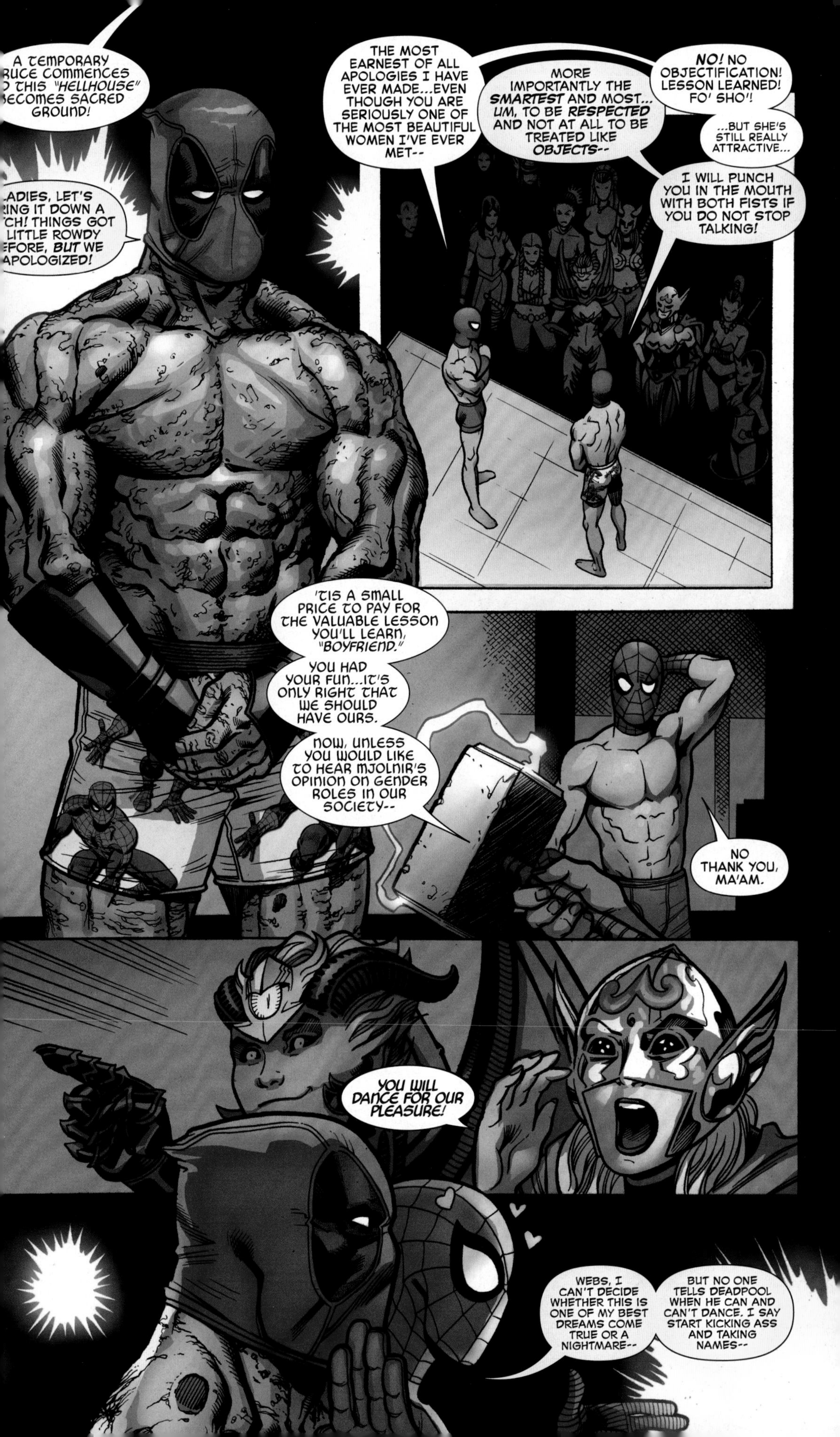
A TEMPORARY
RUCE COMMENCES
D THIS "HELLHOUSE"
BECOMES SACRED
GROUND!
LADIES, LET'S
RING IT DOWN A
TCH! THINGS GOT
LITTLE ROWDY
EFORE, BUT WE
APOLOGIZED!
THE MOST EARNEST OF ALL APOLOGIES I HAVE EVER MADE...EVEN THOUGH YOU ARE SERIOUSLY ONE OF THE MOST BEAUTIFUL WOMEN I'VE EVER MET--
MORE IMPORTANTLY THE SMARTEST AND MOST... UM, TO BE RESPECTED AND NOT AT ALL TO BE TREATED LIKE OBJECTS--
NO! NO OBJECTIFICATION! LESSON LEARNED! FO' SHO'!
...BUT SHE'S STILL REALLY ATTRACTIVE...
I WILL PUNCH YOU IN THE MOUTH WITH BOTH FISTS IF YOU DO NOT STOP TALKING!
'TIS A SMALL PRICE TO PAY FOR THE VALUABLE LESSON YOU'LL LEARN, "BOYFRIEND."
YOU HAD YOUR FUN...IT'S ONLY RIGHT THAT WE SHOULD HAVE OURS.
NOW, UNLESS YOU WOULD LIKE TO HEAR MJOLNIR'S OPINION ON GENDER ROLES IN OUR SOCIETY--
NO THANK YOU, MA'AM.
YOU WILL DANCE FOR OUR PLEASURE!
WEBS, I CAN'T DECIDE WHETHER THIS IS ONE OF MY BEST DREAMS COME TRUE OR A NIGHTMARE--
BUT NO ONE TELLS DEADPOOL WHEN HE CAN AND CAN'T DANCE. I SAY START KICKING ASS AND TAKING NAMES--

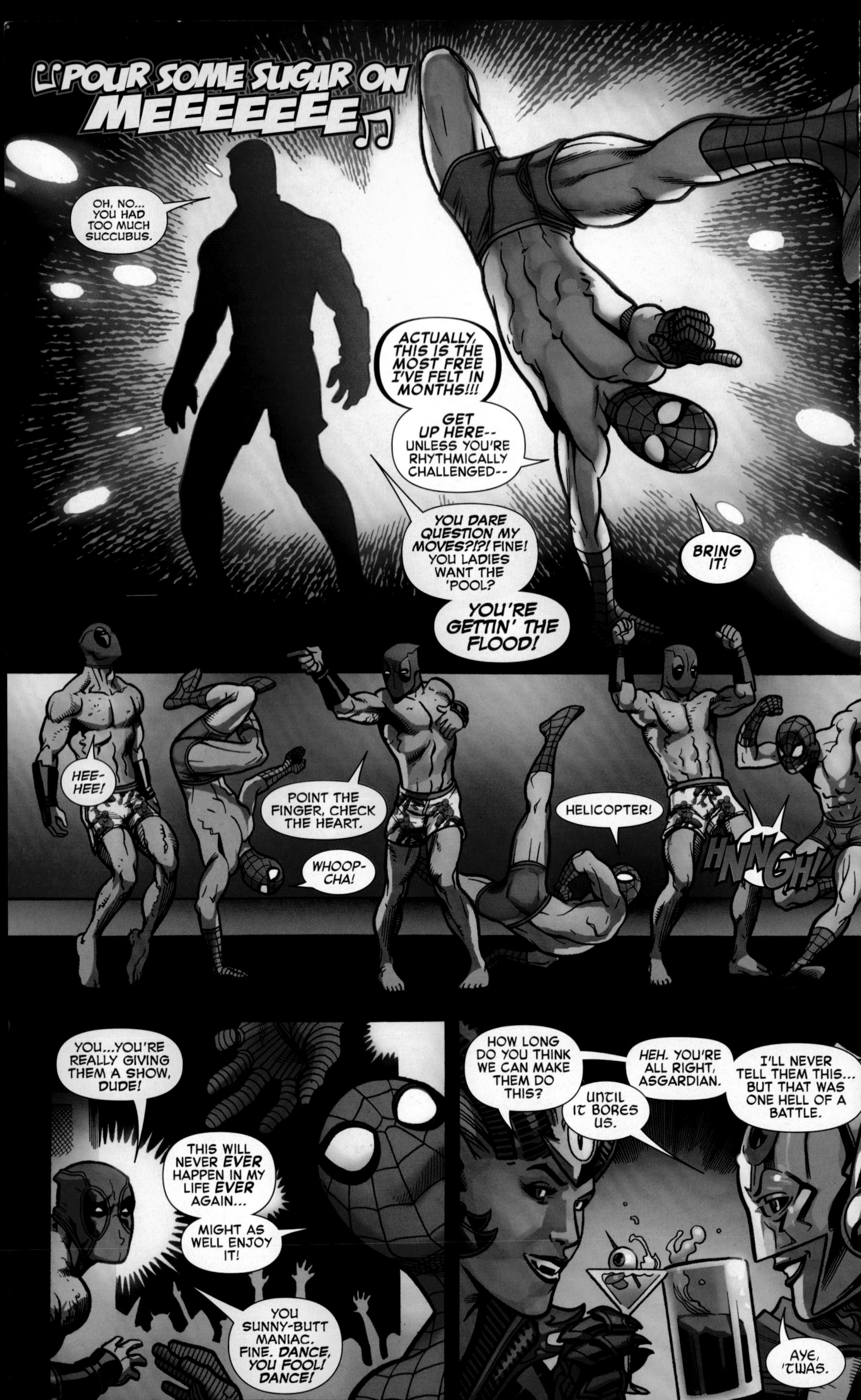

♫POUR SOME SUGAR ON MEEEEEEE♫
OH, NO... YOU HAD TOO MUCH SUCCUBUS.
ACTUALLY, THIS IS THE MOST FREE I'VE FELT IN MONTHS!!!
GET UP HERE-- UNLESS YOU'RE RHYTHMICALLY CHALLENGED--
YOU DARE QUESTION MY MOVES?!?! FINE! YOU LADIES WANT THE 'POOL?
YOU'RE GETTIN' THE FLOOD!
BRING IT!
HEE-HEE!
POINT THE FINGER, CHECK THE HEART.
WHOOP-CHA!
HELICOPTER!
HNNGH!
YOU...YOU'RE REALLY GIVING THEM A SHOW, DUDE!
THIS WILL NEVER EVER HAPPEN IN MY LIFE EVER AGAIN...
MIGHT AS WELL ENJOY IT!
YOU SUNNY-BUTT MANIAC. FINE. DANCE, YOU FOOL! DANCE!
HOW LONG DO YOU THINK WE CAN MAKE THEM DO THIS?
UNTIL IT BORES US.
HEH. YOU'RE ALL RIGHT, ASGARDIAN.
I'LL NEVER TELL THEM THIS... BUT THAT WAS ONE HELL OF A BATTLE.
AYE, 'TWAS.

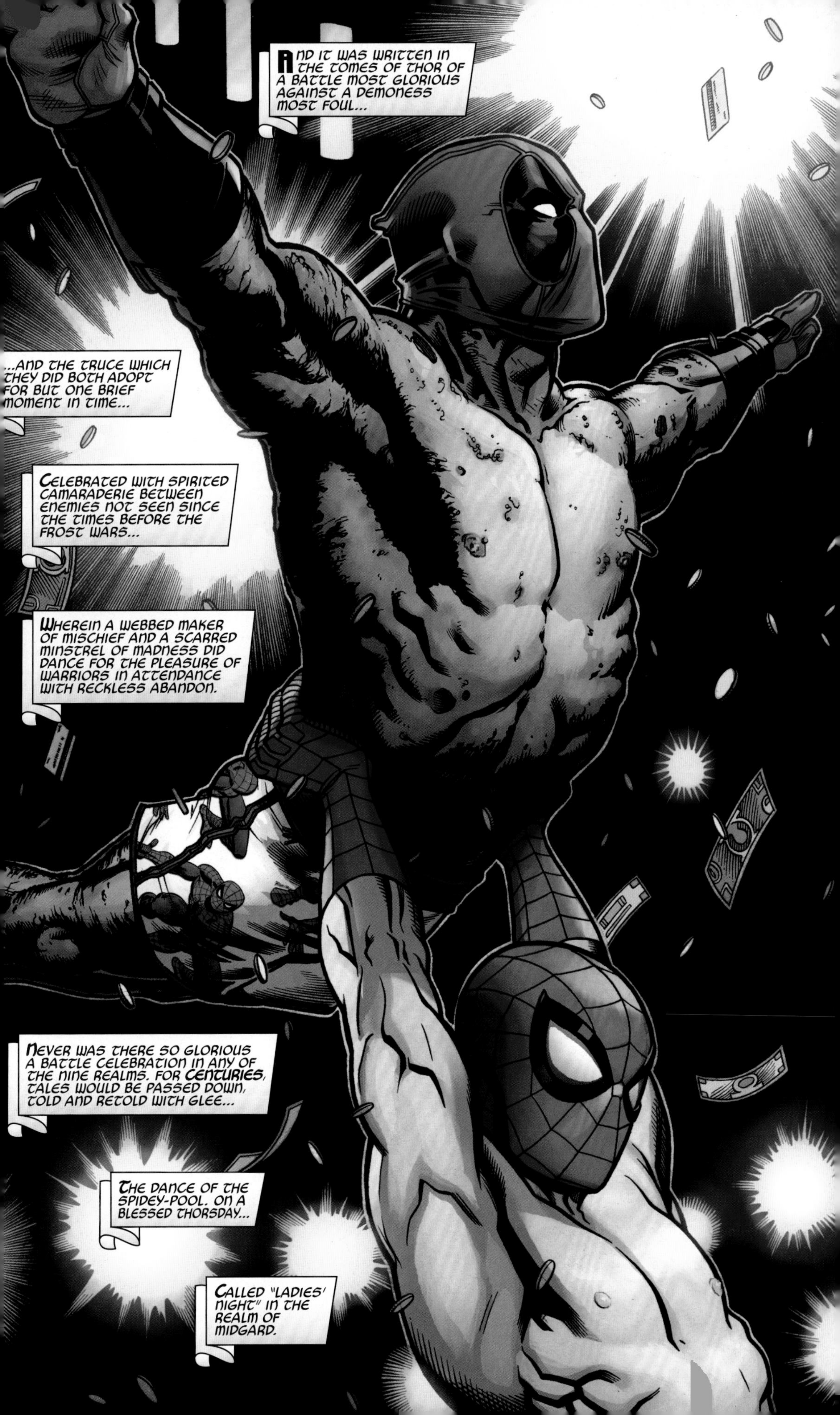
AND IT WAS WRITTEN IN THE TOMES OF THOR OF A BATTLE MOST GLORIOUS AGAINST A DEMONESS MOST FOUL...
...AND THE TRUCE WHICH THEY DID BOTH ADOPT FOR BUT ONE BRIEF MOMENT IN TIME...
CELEBRATED WITH SPIRITED CAMARADERIE BETWEEN ENEMIES NOT SEEN SINCE THE TIMES BEFORE THE FROST WARS...
WHEREIN A WEBBED MAKER OF MISCHIEF AND A SCARRED MINSTREL OF MADNESS DID DANCE FOR THE PLEASURE OF WARRIORS IN ATTENDANCE WITH RECKLESS ABANDON.
NEVER WAS THERE SO GLORIOUS A BATTLE CELEBRATION IN ANY OF THE NINE REALMS. FOR CENTURIES, TALES WOULD BE PASSED DOWN, TOLD AND RETOLD WITH GLEE...
THE DANCE OF THE SPIDEY-POOL. ON A BLESSED THORSDAY...
CALLED "LADIES' NIGHT" IN THE REALM OF MIDGARD.

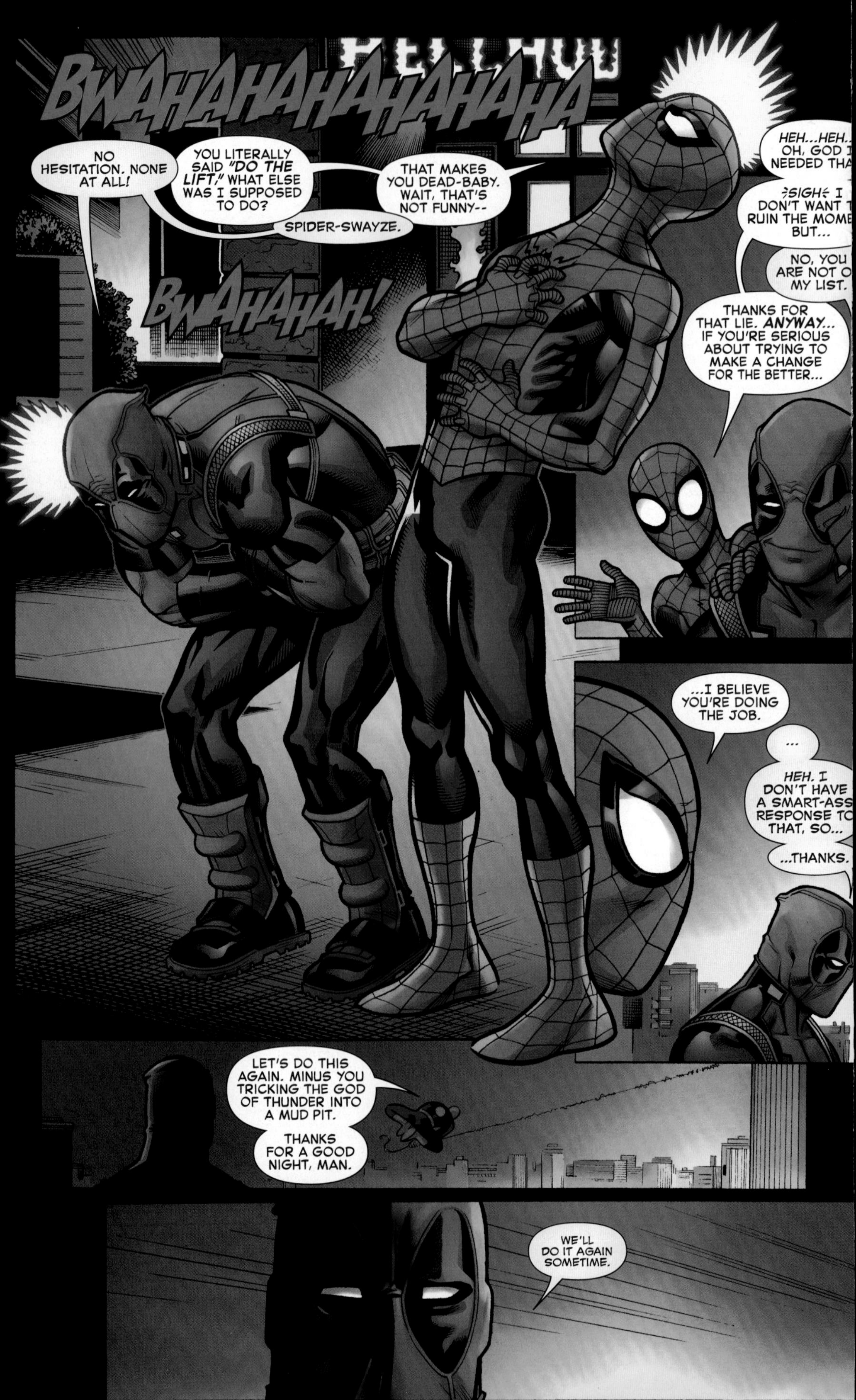
BWAHAHAHAHAHAHAHA
NO HESITATION. NONE AT ALL!
YOU LITERALLY SAID "DO THE LIFT," WHAT ELSE WAS I SUPPOSED TO DO?
SPIDER-SWAYZE.
THAT MAKES YOU DEAD-BABY. WAIT, THAT'S NOT FUNNY--
BWAHAHAH!
HEH...HEH... OH, GOD I NEEDED THA
SIGH I DON'T WANT T RUIN THE MOME BUT...
NO, YOU ARE NOT O MY LIST.
THANKS FOR THAT LIE. ANYWAY... IF YOU'RE SERIOUS ABOUT TRYING TO MAKE A CHANGE FOR THE BETTER...
...I BELIEVE YOU'RE DOING THE JOB.
...
HEH. I DON'T HAVE A SMART-ASS RESPONSE TO THAT, SO...
...THANKS.
LET'S DO THIS AGAIN. MINUS YOU TRICKING THE GOD OF THUNDER INTO A MUD PIT.
THANKS FOR A GOOD NIGHT, MAN.
WE'LL DO IT AGAIN SOMETIME.

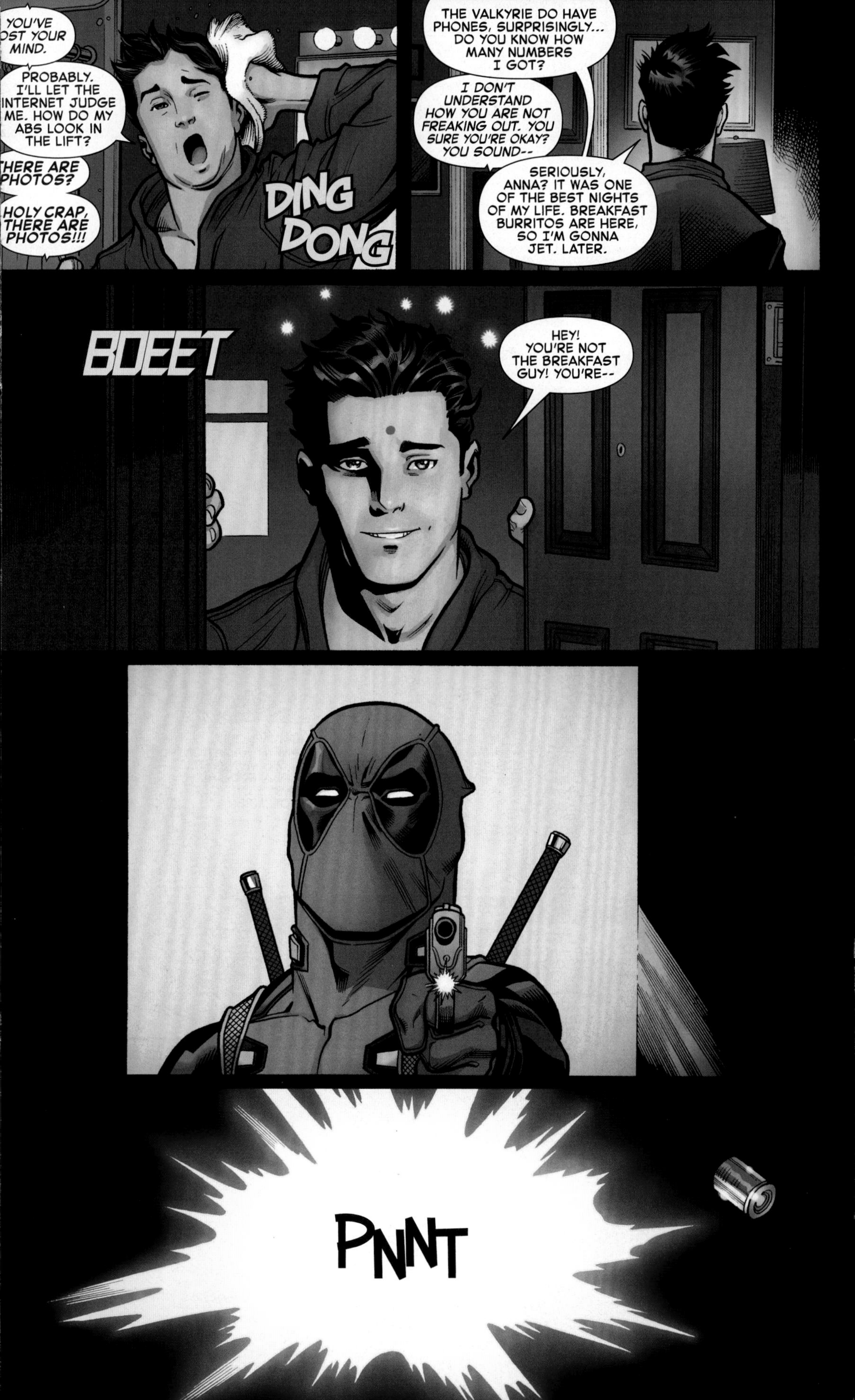
YOU'VE OST YOUR MIND.
PROBABLY. I'LL LET THE INTERNET JUDGE ME. HOW DO MY ABS LOOK IN THE LIFT?
HERE ARE PHOTOS?
HOLY CRAP, THERE ARE PHOTOS!!!
DING DONG
THE VALKYRIE DO HAVE PHONES, SURPRISINGLY... DO YOU KNOW HOW MANY NUMBERS I GOT?
I DON'T UNDERSTAND HOW YOU ARE NOT FREAKING OUT. YOU SURE YOU'RE OKAY? YOU SOUND--
SERIOUSLY, ANNA? IT WAS ONE OF THE BEST NIGHTS OF MY LIFE. BREAKFAST BURRITOS ARE HERE, SO I'M GONNA JET. LATER.
BDEET
HEY! YOU'RE NOT THE BREAKFAST GUY! YOU'RE--
PNNT

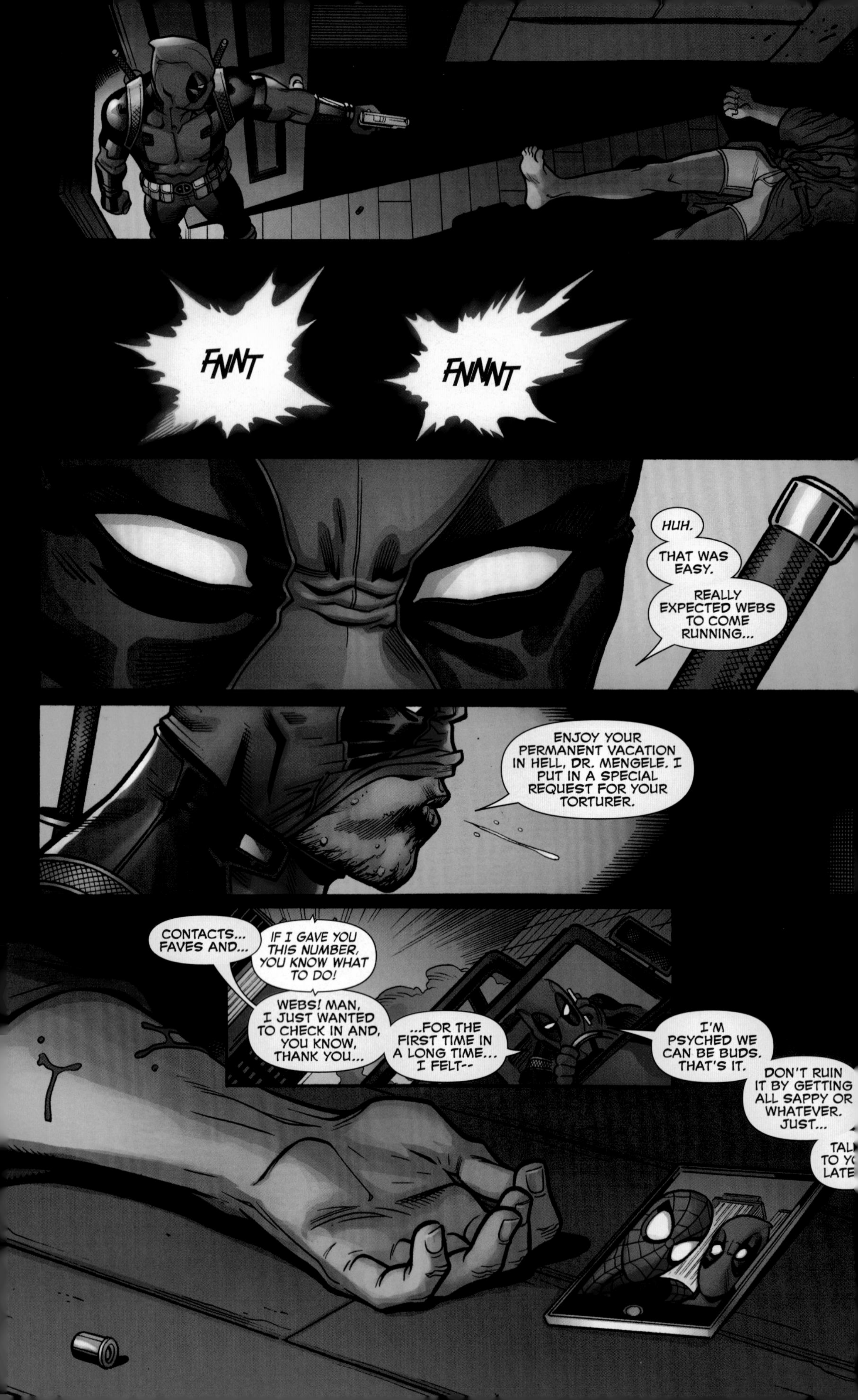
FNNT
FNNNT
HUH.
THAT WAS EASY.
REALLY EXPECTED WEBS TO COME RUNNING...
ENJOY YOUR PERMANENT VACATION IN HELL, DR. MENGELE. I PUT IN A SPECIAL REQUEST FOR YOUR TORTURER.
CONTACTS... FAVES AND...
IF I GAVE YOU THIS NUMBER, YOU KNOW WHAT TO DO!
WEBS! MAN, I JUST WANTED TO CHECK IN AND, YOU KNOW, THANK YOU...
...FOR THE FIRST TIME IN A LONG TIME... I FELT--
I'M PSYCHED WE CAN BE BUDS. THAT'S IT.
DON'T RUIN IT BY GETTING ALL SAPPY OR WHATEVER. JUST...

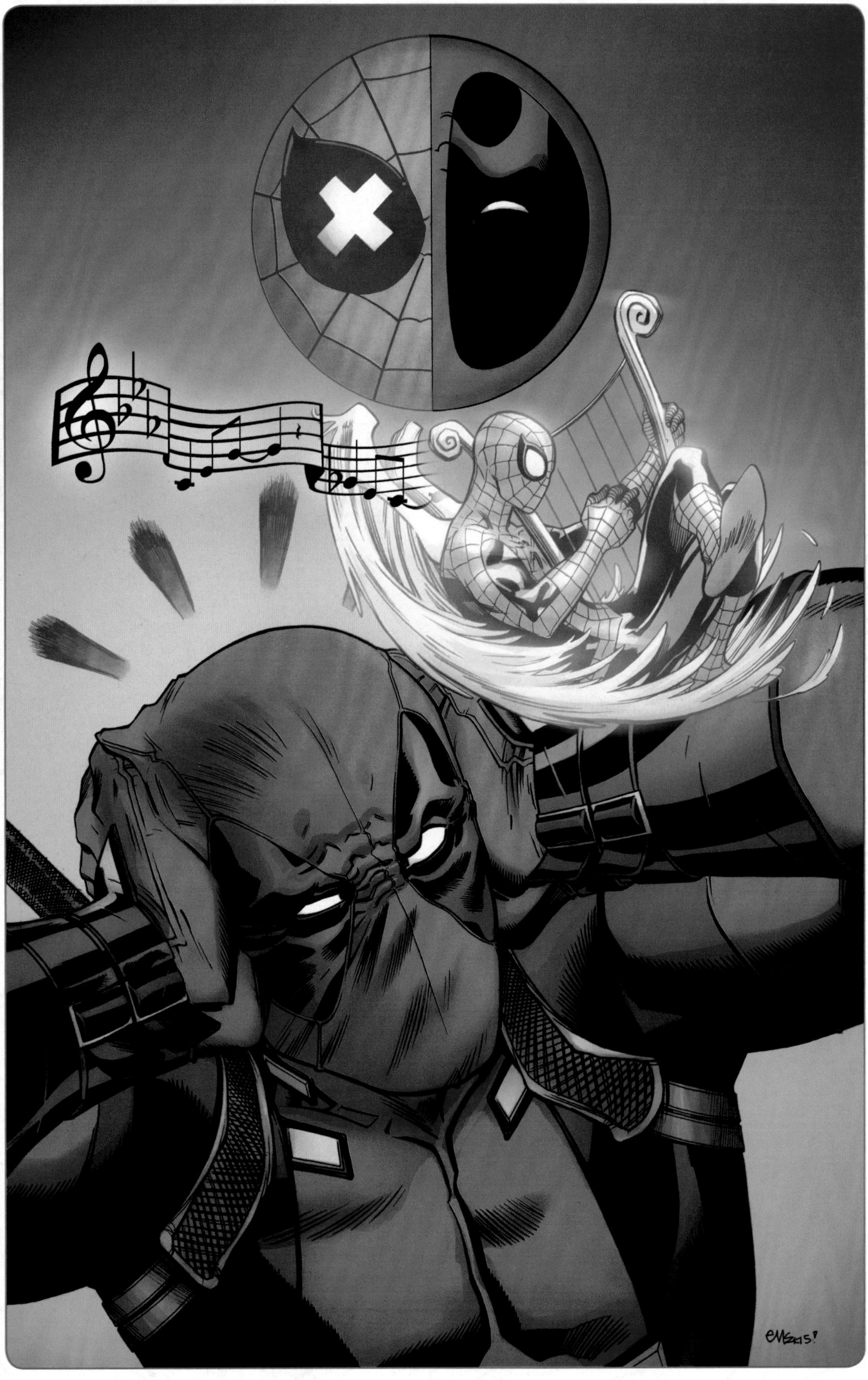

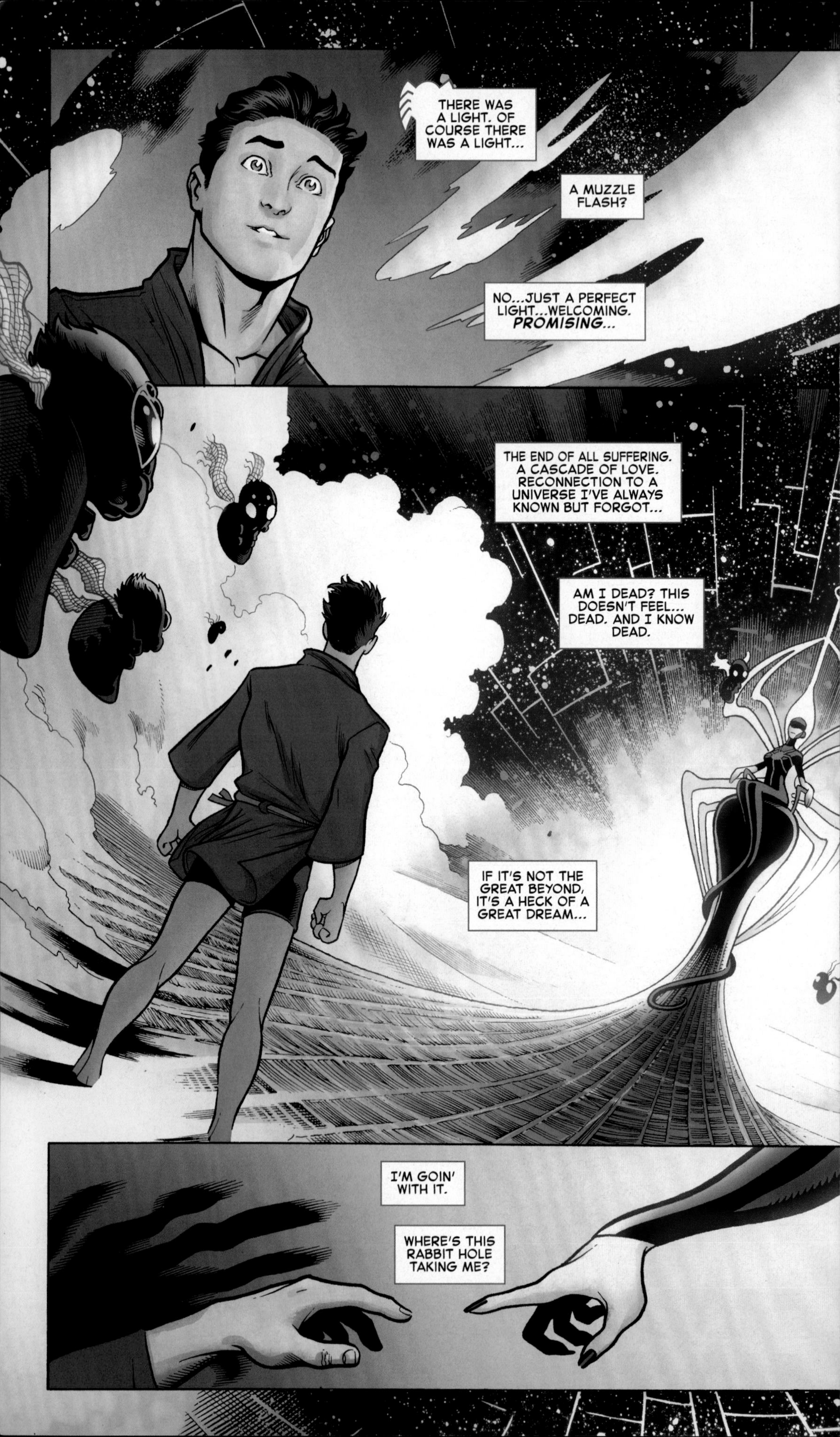
THERE WAS A LIGHT. OF COURSE THERE WAS A LIGHT...
A MUZZLE FLASH?
NO...JUST A PERFECT LIGHT...WELCOMING. *PROMISING*...
THE END OF ALL SUFFERING. A CASCADE OF LOVE. RECONNECTION TO A UNIVERSE I'VE ALWAYS KNOWN BUT FORGOT...
AM I DEAD? THIS DOESN'T FEEL... DEAD. AND I KNOW DEAD.
IF IT'S NOT THE GREAT BEYOND, IT'S A HECK OF A GREAT DREAM...
I'M GOIN' WITH IT.
WHERE'S THIS RABBIT HOLE TAKING ME?

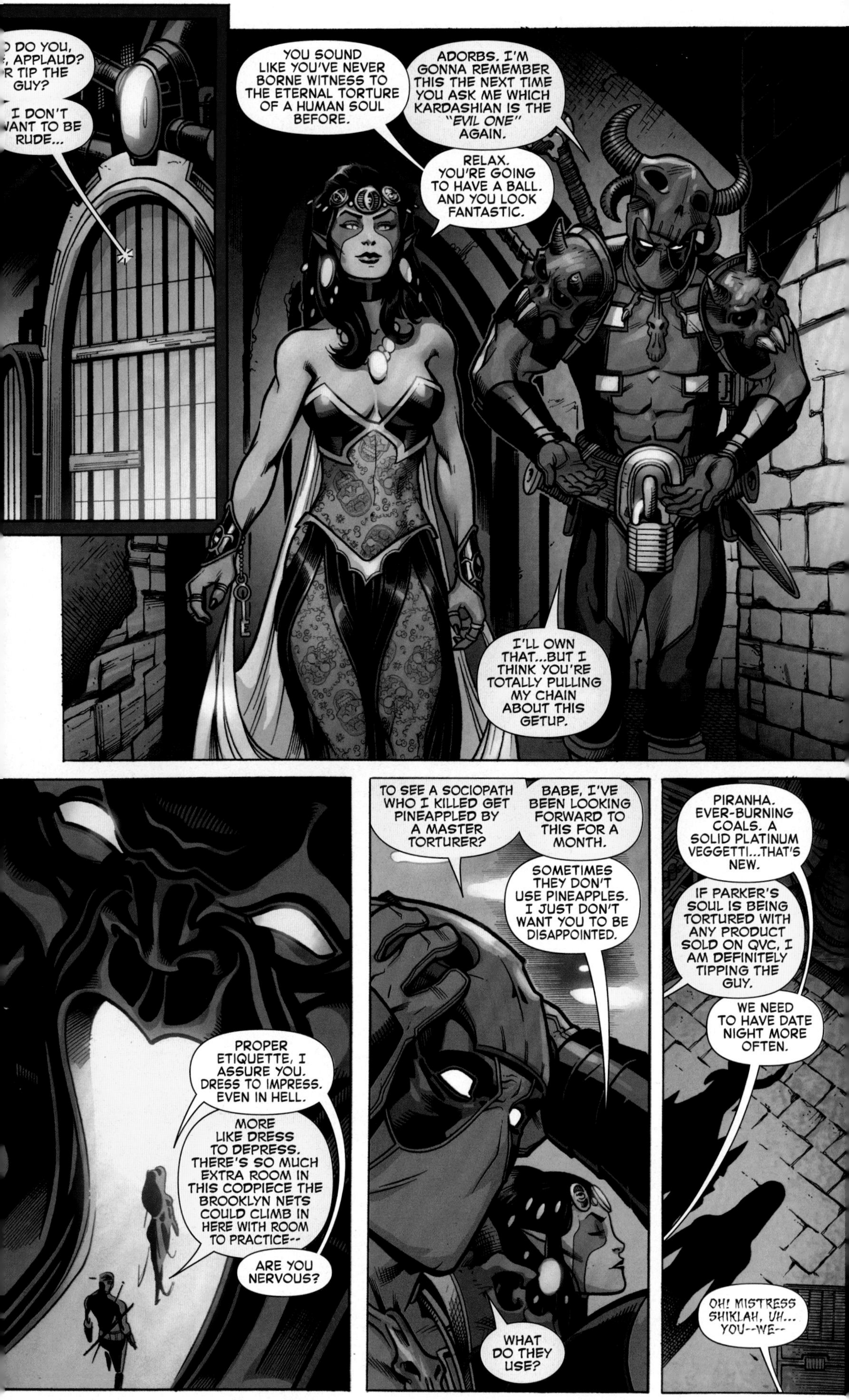

D DO YOU, , APPLAUD? R TIP THE GUY?
I DON'T WANT TO BE RUDE...
YOU SOUND LIKE YOU'VE NEVER BORNE WITNESS TO THE ETERNAL TORTURE OF A HUMAN SOUL BEFORE.
ADORBS. I'M GONNA REMEMBER THIS THE NEXT TIME YOU ASK ME WHICH KARDASHIAN IS THE "EVIL ONE" AGAIN.
RELAX. YOU'RE GOING TO HAVE A BALL. AND YOU LOOK FANTASTIC.
I'LL OWN THAT...BUT I THINK YOU'RE TOTALLY PULLING MY CHAIN ABOUT THIS GETUP.
PROPER ETIQUETTE, I ASSURE YOU. DRESS TO IMPRESS. EVEN IN HELL.
MORE LIKE DRESS TO DEPRESS. THERE'S SO MUCH EXTRA ROOM IN THIS CODPIECE THE BROOKLYN NETS COULD CLIMB IN HERE WITH ROOM TO PRACTICE--
ARE YOU NERVOUS?
TO SEE A SOCIOPATH WHO I KILLED GET PINEAPPLED BY A MASTER TORTURER?
BABE, I'VE BEEN LOOKING FORWARD TO THIS FOR A MONTH.
SOMETIMES THEY DON'T USE PINEAPPLES. I JUST DON'T WANT YOU TO BE DISAPPOINTED.
WHAT DO THEY USE?
PIRANHA. EVER-BURNING COALS. A SOLID PLATINUM VEGGETTI...THAT'S NEW.
IF PARKER'S SOUL IS BEING TORTURED WITH ANY PRODUCT SOLD ON QVC, I AM DEFINITELY TIPPING THE GUY.
WE NEED TO HAVE DATE NIGHT MORE OFTEN.
OH! MISTRESS SHIKLAH, UH... YOU--WE--

WHERE IN THE HELL, *LITERALLY,* IS THE SOUL OF PETER PARKER?!

UM, I...CHECKING... UM, ARE YOU CERTAIN THAT MISTER PARKER HAD A RESERVATION FOR TODAY--?

I MADE THE RESERVATION WHEN I PUT TWO SLUGS IN HIS BRAIN BOX, YOU HALF-BAKED HOT STUFF! WHERE IS HE?!

NO NEED TO BE RUDE, SIR...JUST BECAUSE WE'RE THE GRAND TORTURERS OF HELL DOESN'T MEAN WE DON'T HAVE FEELINGS.

PARKER INDUSTRIES.

MY FAVORITE ENGINEER! UP TOP!

YOU NEVER REMEMBER HIS NAME.

I KNOW, BUT IT'S GOOD FOR MORALE. WHAT IS IT, ANYWAY?

PETER. HE'S PETER SCIOLI.

WELL, YOU KNOW ME, ANNA MARIA...I STINK WITH NAMES...

...BUT I'M GREAT WIT[H] FACES.

LET'S G[O] MAKE SO[ME] SCIENCE[...]

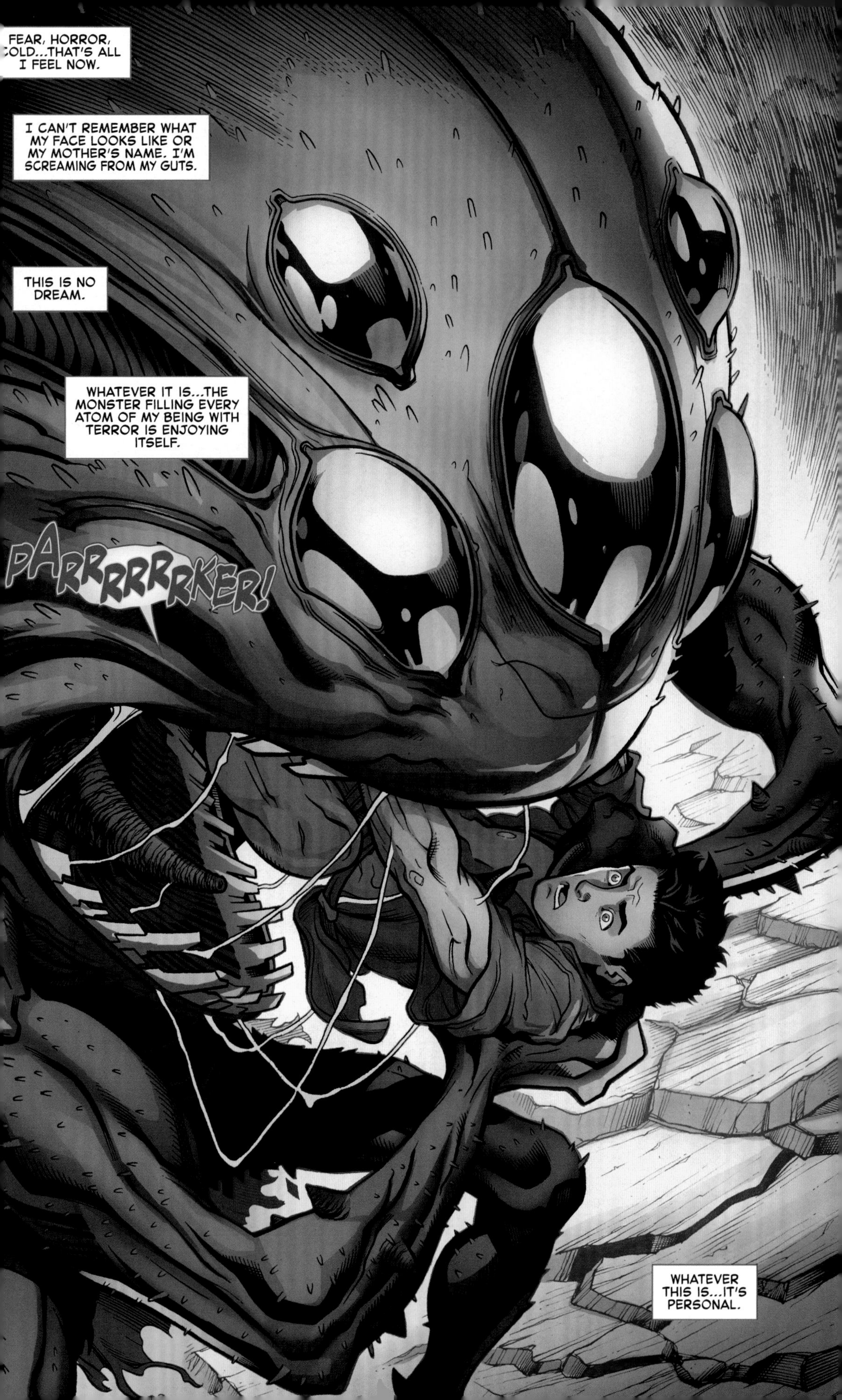

FEAR, HORROR, COLD...THAT'S ALL I FEEL NOW.
I CAN'T REMEMBER WHAT MY FACE LOOKS LIKE OR MY MOTHER'S NAME. I'M SCREAMING FROM MY GUTS.
THIS IS NO DREAM.
WHATEVER IT IS...THE MONSTER FILLING EVERY ATOM OF MY BEING WITH TERROR IS ENJOYING ITSELF.
PARRRRRRRKER!
WHATEVER THIS IS...IT'S PERSONAL.

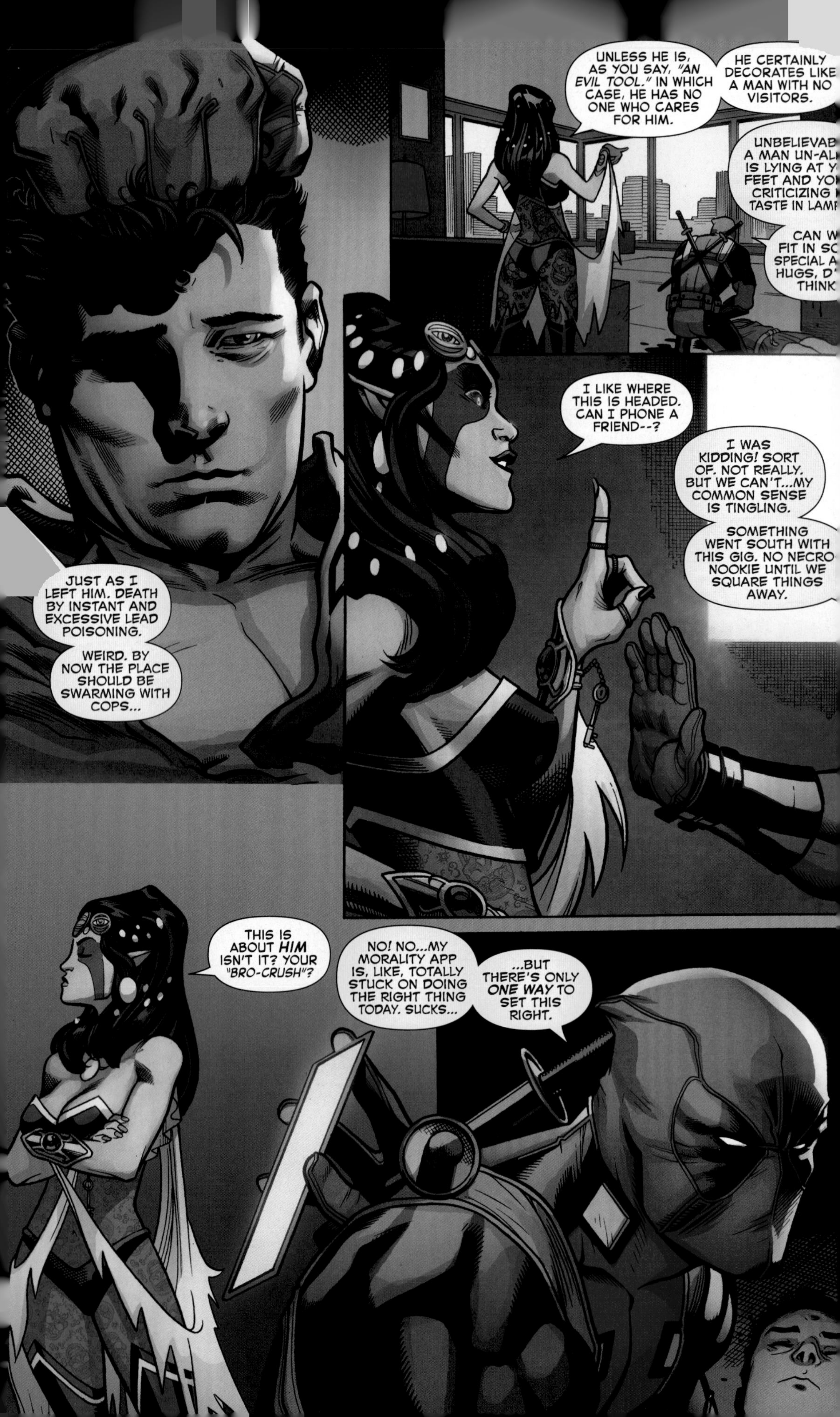

JUST AS I LEFT HIM. DEATH BY INSTANT AND EXCESSIVE LEAD POISONING.
WEIRD. BY NOW THE PLACE SHOULD BE SWARMING WITH COPS...
UNLESS HE IS, AS YOU SAY, "AN EVIL TOOL." IN WHICH CASE, HE HAS NO ONE WHO CARES FOR HIM.
HE CERTAINLY DECORATES LIKE A MAN WITH NO VISITORS.
UNBELIEVAB A MAN UN-AL IS LYING AT Y FEET AND YO CRITICIZING TASTE IN LAMP
CAN W FIT IN SC SPECIAL A HUGS, D' THINK
I LIKE WHERE THIS IS HEADED. CAN I PHONE A FRIEND--?
I WAS KIDDING! SORT OF. NOT REALLY. BUT WE CAN'T...MY COMMON SENSE IS TINGLING.
SOMETHING WENT SOUTH WITH THIS GIG. NO NECRO NOOKIE UNTIL WE SQUARE THINGS AWAY.
THIS IS ABOUT HIM ISN'T IT? YOUR "BRO-CRUSH"?
NO! NO...MY MORALITY APP IS, LIKE, TOTALLY STUCK ON DOING THE RIGHT THING TODAY. SUCKS...
...BUT THERE'S ONLY ONE WAY TO SET THIS RIGHT.

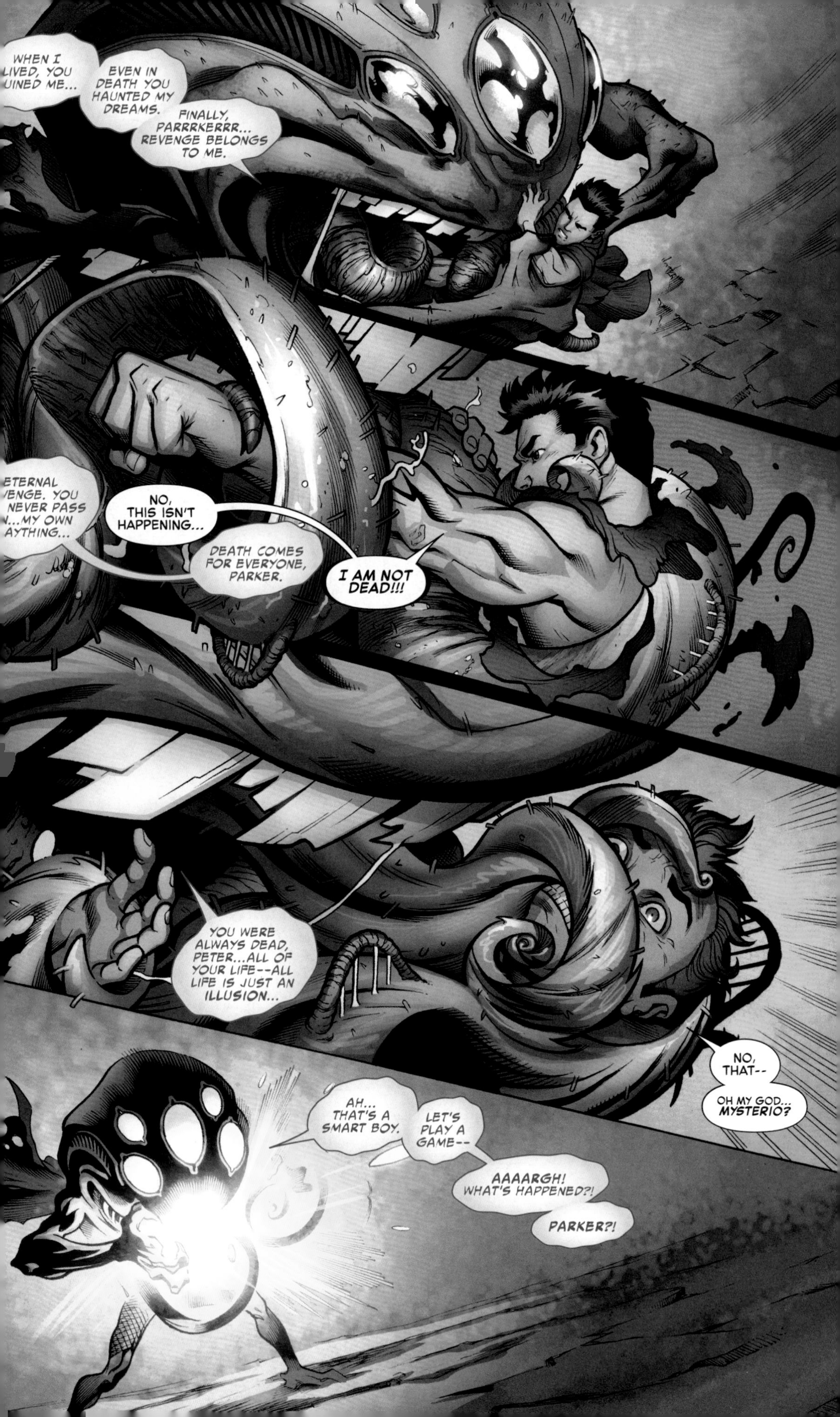

WHEN I LIVED, YOU UINED ME...
EVEN IN DEATH YOU HAUNTED MY DREAMS.
FINALLY, PARRRKERRR... REVENGE BELONGS TO ME.
ETERNAL VENGE. YOU NEVER PASS N...MY OWN AYTHING...
NO, THIS ISN'T HAPPENING...
DEATH COMES FOR EVERYONE, PARKER.
I AM NOT DEAD!!!
YOU WERE ALWAYS DEAD, PETER...ALL OF YOUR LIFE--ALL LIFE IS JUST AN ILLUSION...
NO, THAT--
OH MY GOD... MYSTERIO?
AH... THAT'S A SMART BOY.
LET'S PLAY A GAME--
AAAARGH! WHAT'S HAPPENED?!
PARKER?!

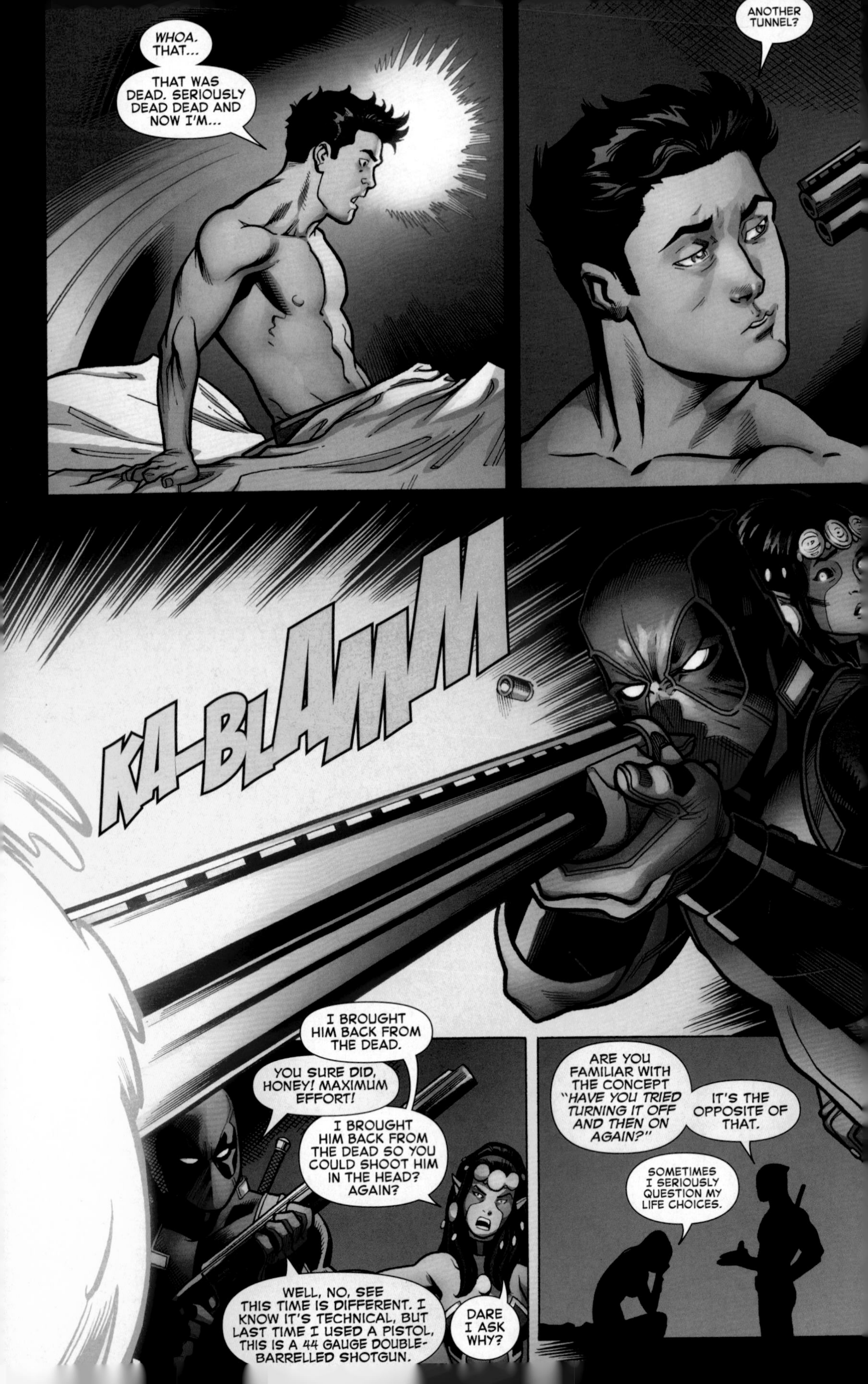
WHOA. THAT...
THAT WAS DEAD. SERIOUSLY DEAD DEAD AND NOW I'M...
ANOTHER TUNNEL?
KA-BLAMM
I BROUGHT HIM BACK FROM THE DEAD.
YOU SURE DID, HONEY! MAXIMUM EFFORT!
I BROUGHT HIM BACK FROM THE DEAD SO YOU COULD SHOOT HIM IN THE HEAD? AGAIN?
WELL, NO, SEE THIS TIME IS DIFFERENT. I KNOW IT'S TECHNICAL, BUT LAST TIME I USED A PISTOL, THIS IS A 44 GAUGE DOUBLE-BARRELLED SHOTGUN.
DARE I ASK WHY?
ARE YOU FAMILIAR WITH THE CONCEPT "HAVE YOU TRIED TURNING IT OFF AND THEN ON AGAIN?"
IT'S THE OPPOSITE OF THAT.
SOMETIMES I SERIOUSLY QUESTION MY LIFE CHOICES.

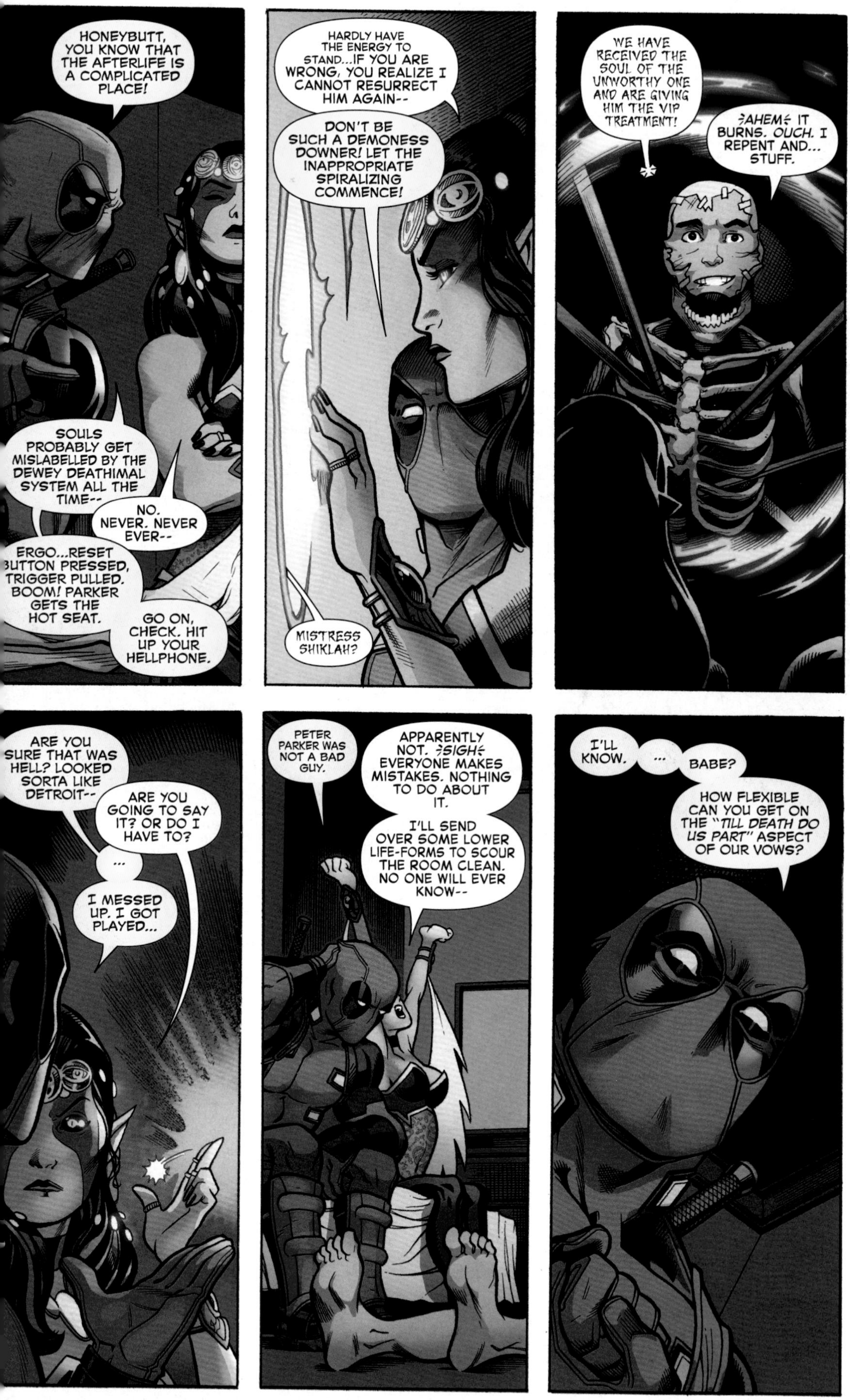
HONEYBUTT, YOU KNOW THAT THE AFTERLIFE IS A COMPLICATED PLACE!
SOULS PROBABLY GET MISLABELLED BY THE DEWEY DEATHIMAL SYSTEM ALL THE TIME--
NO. NEVER. NEVER EVER--
ERGO...RESET BUTTON PRESSED, TRIGGER PULLED. BOOM! PARKER GETS THE HOT SEAT.
GO ON, CHECK. HIT UP YOUR HELLPHONE.
HARDLY HAVE THE ENERGY TO STAND...IF YOU ARE WRONG, YOU REALIZE I CANNOT RESURRECT HIM AGAIN--
DON'T BE SUCH A DEMONESS DOWNER! LET THE INAPPROPRIATE SPIRALIZING COMMENCE!
MISTRESS SHIKLAH?
WE HAVE RECEIVED THE SOUL OF THE UNWORTHY ONE AND ARE GIVING HIM THE VIP TREATMENT!
AHEM IT BURNS. OUCH. I REPENT AND... STUFF.
ARE YOU SURE THAT WAS HELL? LOOKED SORTA LIKE DETROIT--
ARE YOU GOING TO SAY IT? OR DO I HAVE TO?
...
I MESSED UP. I GOT PLAYED...
PETER PARKER WAS NOT A BAD GUY.
APPARENTLY NOT. SIGH EVERYONE MAKES MISTAKES. NOTHING TO DO ABOUT IT.
I'LL SEND OVER SOME LOWER LIFE-FORMS TO SCOUR THE ROOM CLEAN. NO ONE WILL EVER KNOW--
I'LL KNOW.
...
BABE?
HOW FLEXIBLE CAN YOU GET ON THE "TILL DEATH DO US PART" ASPECT OF OUR VOWS?

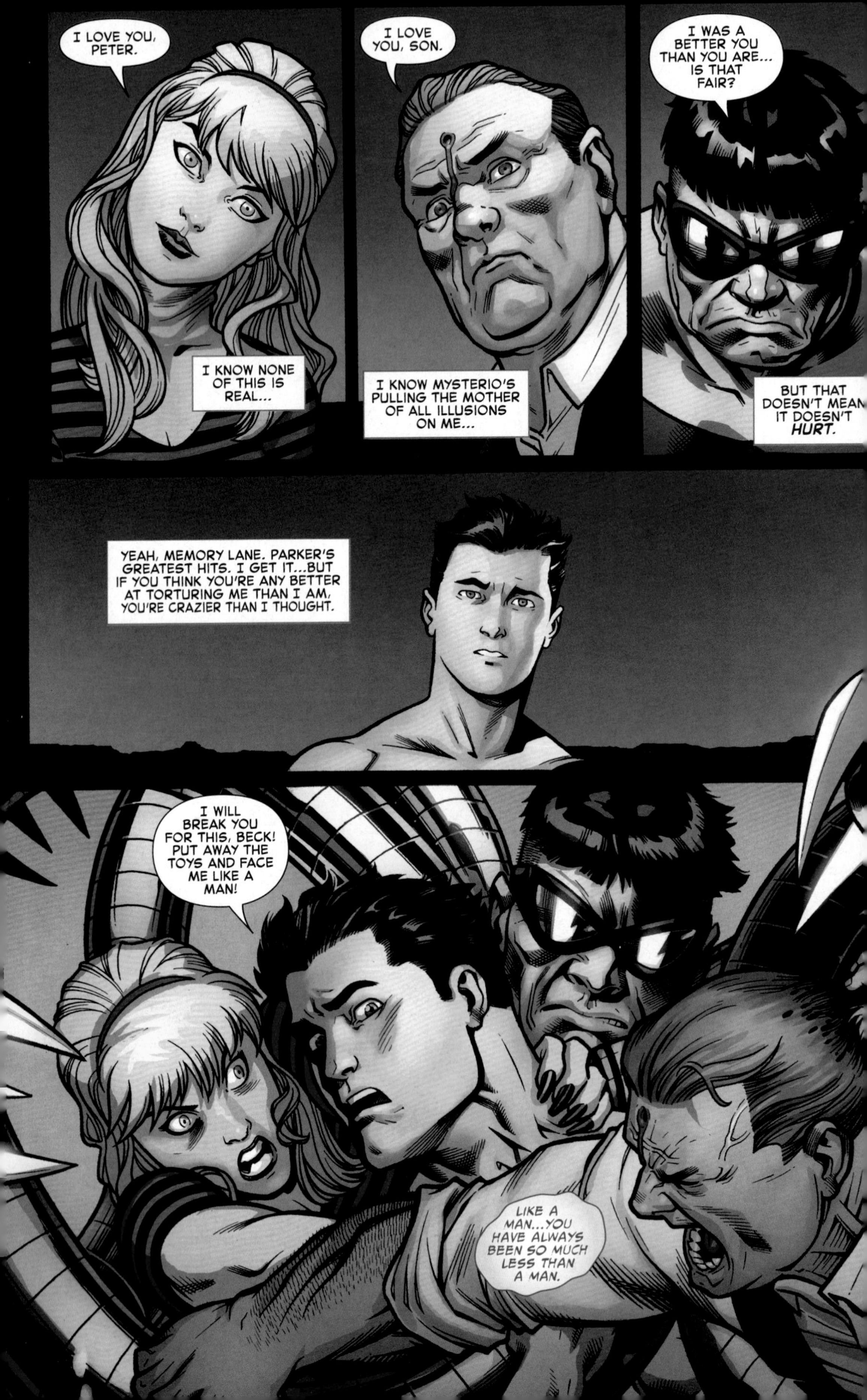
I LOVE YOU, PETER.
I KNOW NONE OF THIS IS REAL...
I LOVE YOU, SON.
I KNOW MYSTERIO'S PULLING THE MOTHER OF ALL ILLUSIONS ON ME...
I WAS A BETTER YOU THAN YOU ARE... IS THAT FAIR?
BUT THAT DOESN'T MEAN IT DOESN'T HURT.
YEAH, MEMORY LANE. PARKER'S GREATEST HITS. I GET IT...BUT IF YOU THINK YOU'RE ANY BETTER AT TORTURING ME THAN I AM, YOU'RE CRAZIER THAN I THOUGHT.
I WILL BREAK YOU FOR THIS, BECK! PUT AWAY THE TOYS AND FACE ME LIKE A MAN!
LIKE A MAN...YOU HAVE ALWAYS BEEN SO MUCH LESS THAN A MAN.

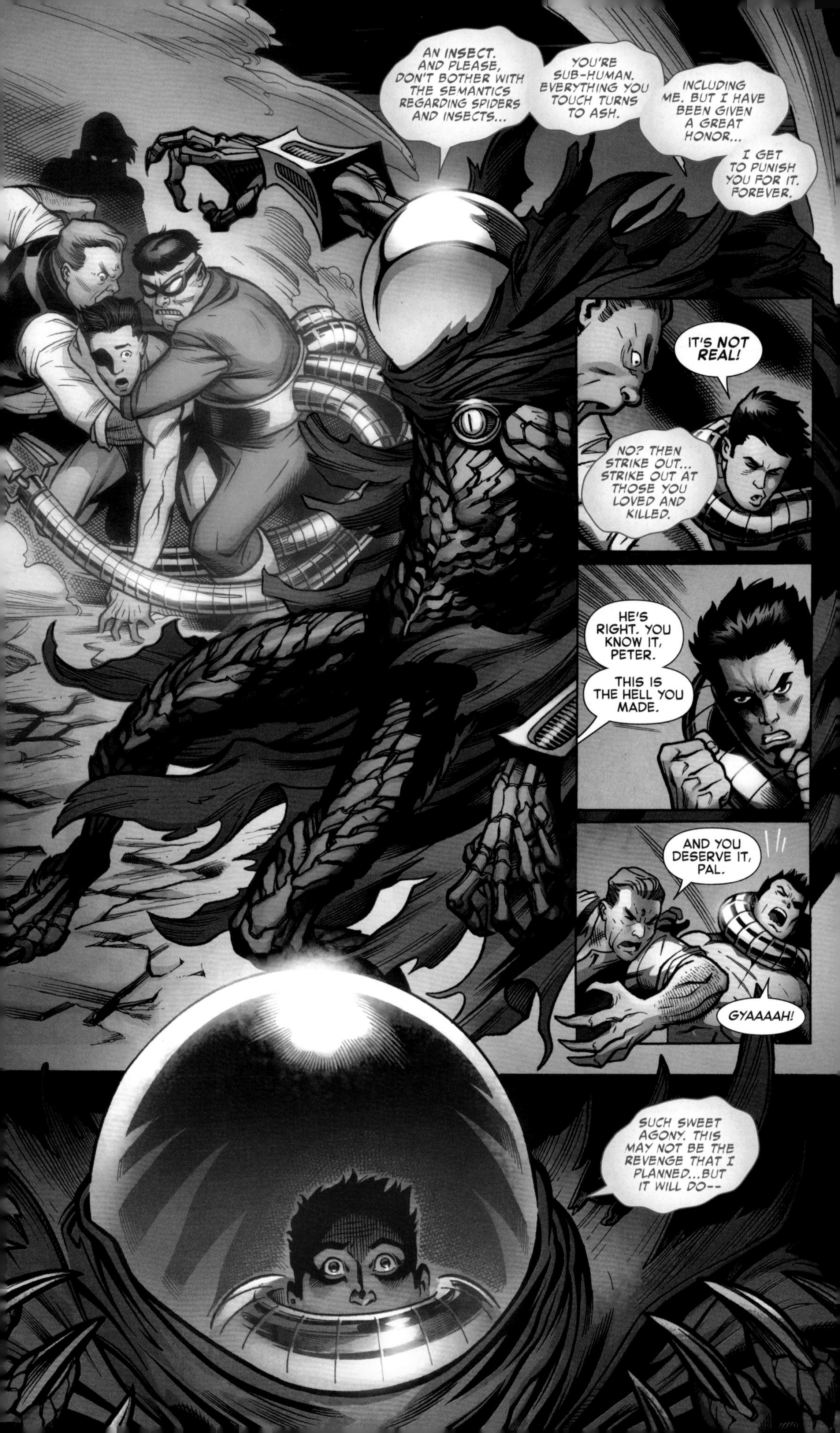
AN INSECT. AND PLEASE, DON'T BOTHER WITH THE SEMANTICS REGARDING SPIDERS AND INSECTS...
YOU'RE SUB-HUMAN. EVERYTHING YOU TOUCH TURNS TO ASH.
INCLUDING ME. BUT I HAVE BEEN GIVEN A GREAT HONOR...
I GET TO PUNISH YOU FOR IT. FOREVER.
IT'S NOT REAL!
NO? THEN STRIKE OUT... STRIKE OUT AT THOSE YOU LOVED AND KILLED.
HE'S RIGHT. YOU KNOW IT, PETER.
THIS IS THE HELL YOU MADE.
AND YOU DESERVE IT, PAL.
GYAAAAH!
SUCH SWEET AGONY. THIS MAY NOT BE THE REVENGE THAT I PLANNED...BUT IT WILL DO--

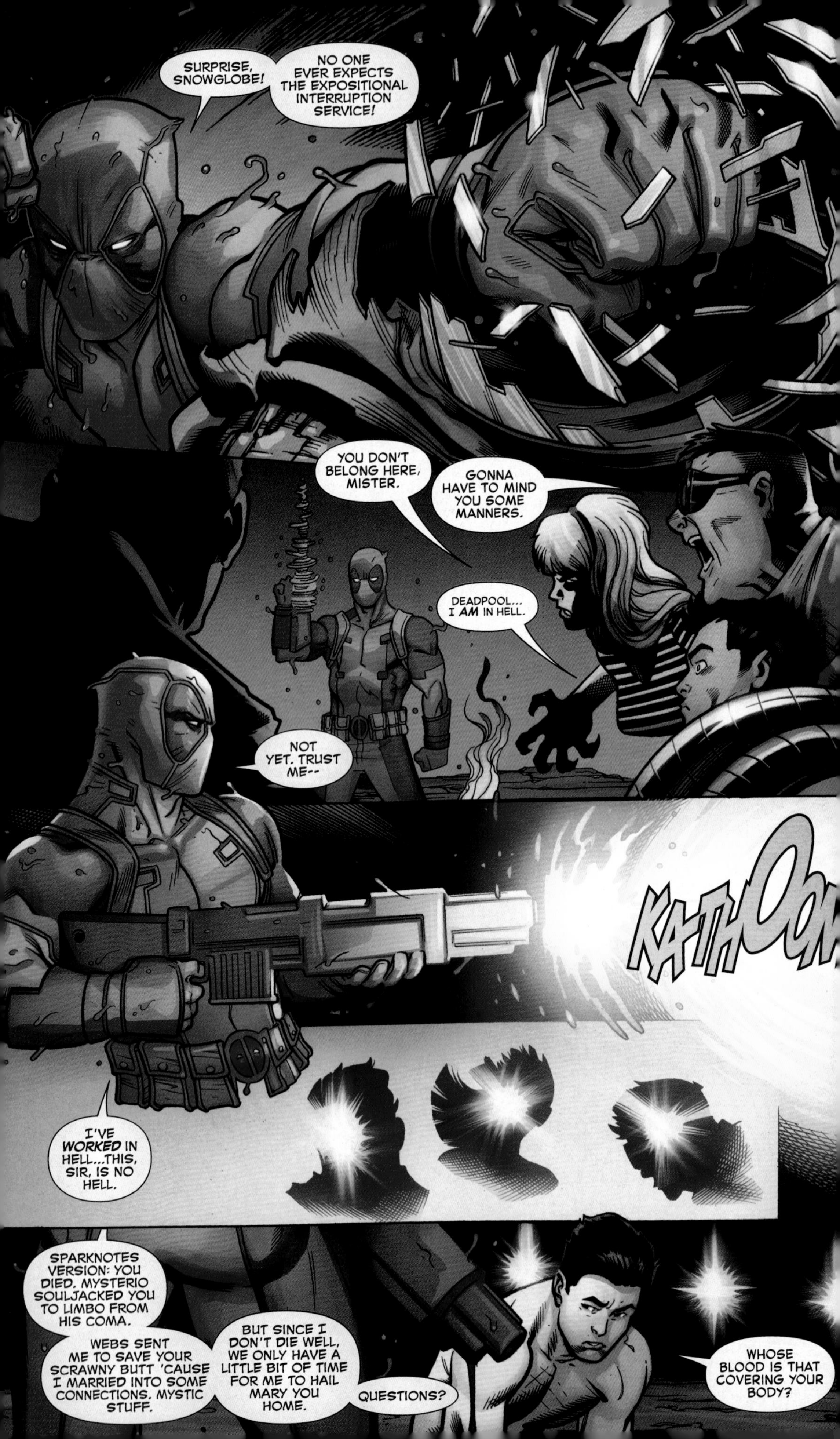
SURPRISE, SNOWGLOBE!
NO ONE EVER EXPECTS THE EXPOSITIONAL INTERRUPTION SERVICE!
YOU DON'T BELONG HERE, MISTER.
GONNA HAVE TO MIND YOU SOME MANNERS.
DEADPOOL... I AM IN HELL.
NOT YET. TRUST ME--
KA-THOOM
I'VE WORKED IN HELL...THIS, SIR, IS NO HELL.
SPARKNOTES VERSION: YOU DIED. MYSTERIO SOULJACKED YOU TO LIMBO FROM HIS COMA.
WEBS SENT ME TO SAVE YOUR SCRAWNY BUTT 'CAUSE I MARRIED INTO SOME CONNECTIONS. MYSTIC STUFF.
BUT SINCE I DON'T DIE WELL, WE ONLY HAVE A LITTLE BIT OF TIME FOR ME TO HAIL MARY YOU HOME.
QUESTIONS?
WHOSE BLOOD IS THAT COVERING YOUR BODY?

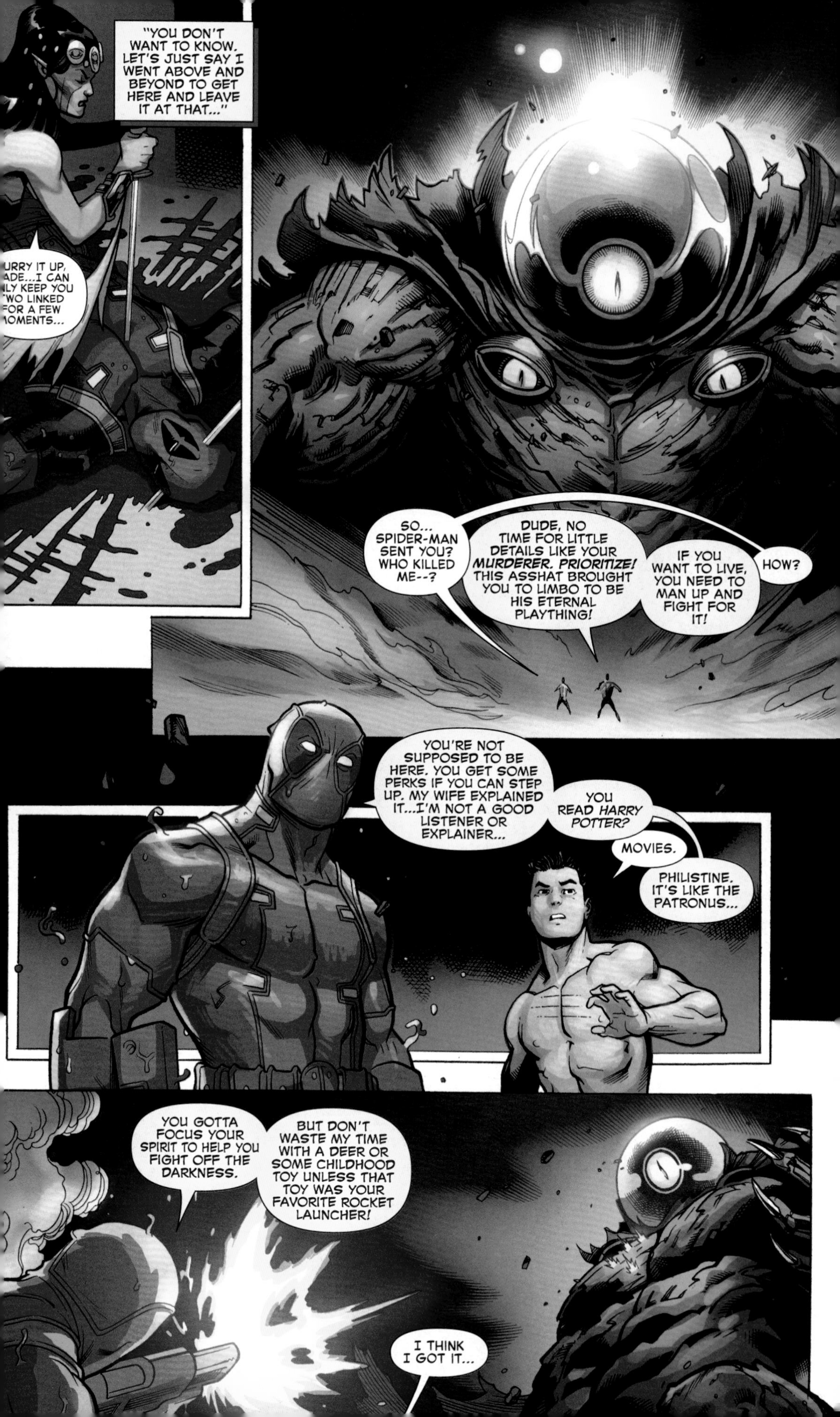
"YOU DON'T WANT TO KNOW. LET'S JUST SAY I WENT ABOVE AND BEYOND TO GET HERE AND LEAVE IT AT THAT..."
URRY IT UP, ADE...I CAN LY KEEP YOU WO LINKED FOR A FEW MOMENTS...
SO... SPIDER-MAN SENT YOU? WHO KILLED ME--?
DUDE, NO TIME FOR LITTLE DETAILS LIKE YOUR MURDERER. PRIORITIZE! THIS ASSHAT BROUGHT YOU TO LIMBO TO BE HIS ETERNAL PLAYTHING!
IF YOU WANT TO LIVE, YOU NEED TO MAN UP AND FIGHT FOR IT!
HOW?
YOU'RE NOT SUPPOSED TO BE HERE. YOU GET SOME PERKS IF YOU CAN STEP UP. MY WIFE EXPLAINED IT...I'M NOT A GOOD LISTENER OR EXPLAINER...
YOU READ HARRY POTTER?
MOVIES.
PHILISTINE. IT'S LIKE THE PATRONUS...
YOU GOTTA FOCUS YOUR SPIRIT TO HELP YOU FIGHT OFF THE DARKNESS.
BUT DON'T WASTE MY TIME WITH A DEER OR SOME CHILDHOOD TOY UNLESS THAT TOY WAS YOUR FAVORITE ROCKET LAUNCHER!
I THINK I GOT IT...

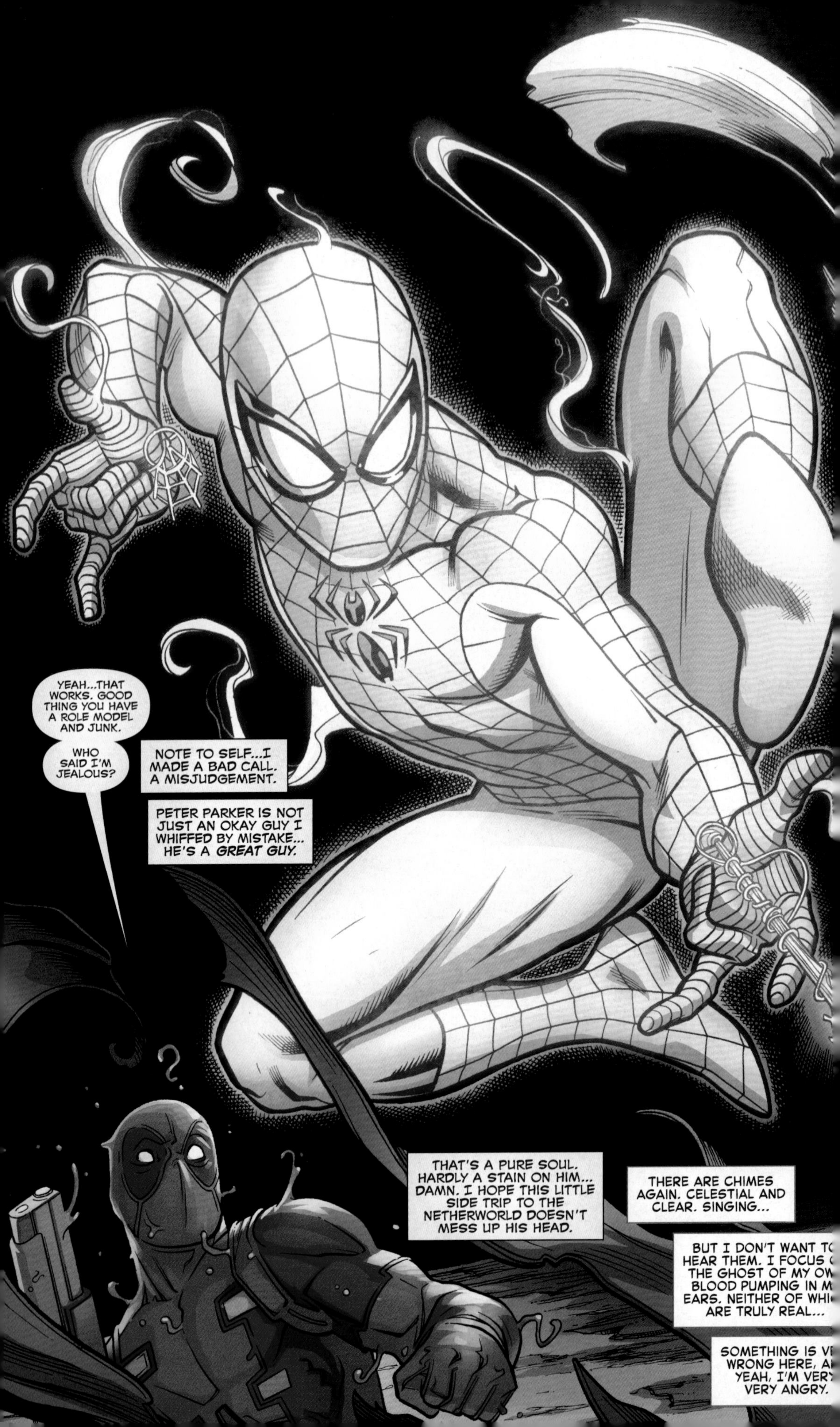

YEAH...THAT WORKS. GOOD THING YOU HAVE A ROLE MODEL AND JUNK.
WHO SAID I'M JEALOUS?
NOTE TO SELF...I MADE A BAD CALL. A MISJUDGEMENT.
PETER PARKER IS NOT JUST AN OKAY GUY I WHIFFED BY MISTAKE... HE'S A *GREAT GUY.*
?
THAT'S A PURE SOUL. HARDLY A STAIN ON HIM... DAMN. I HOPE THIS LITTLE SIDE TRIP TO THE NETHERWORLD DOESN'T MESS UP HIS HEAD.
THERE ARE CHIMES AGAIN. CELESTIAL AND CLEAR. SINGING...
BUT I DON'T WANT T HEAR THEM. I FOCUS THE GHOST OF MY OW BLOOD PUMPING IN M EARS. NEITHER OF WHI ARE TRULY REAL...
SOMETHING IS V WRONG HERE, A YEAH, I'M VERY VERY ANGRY.

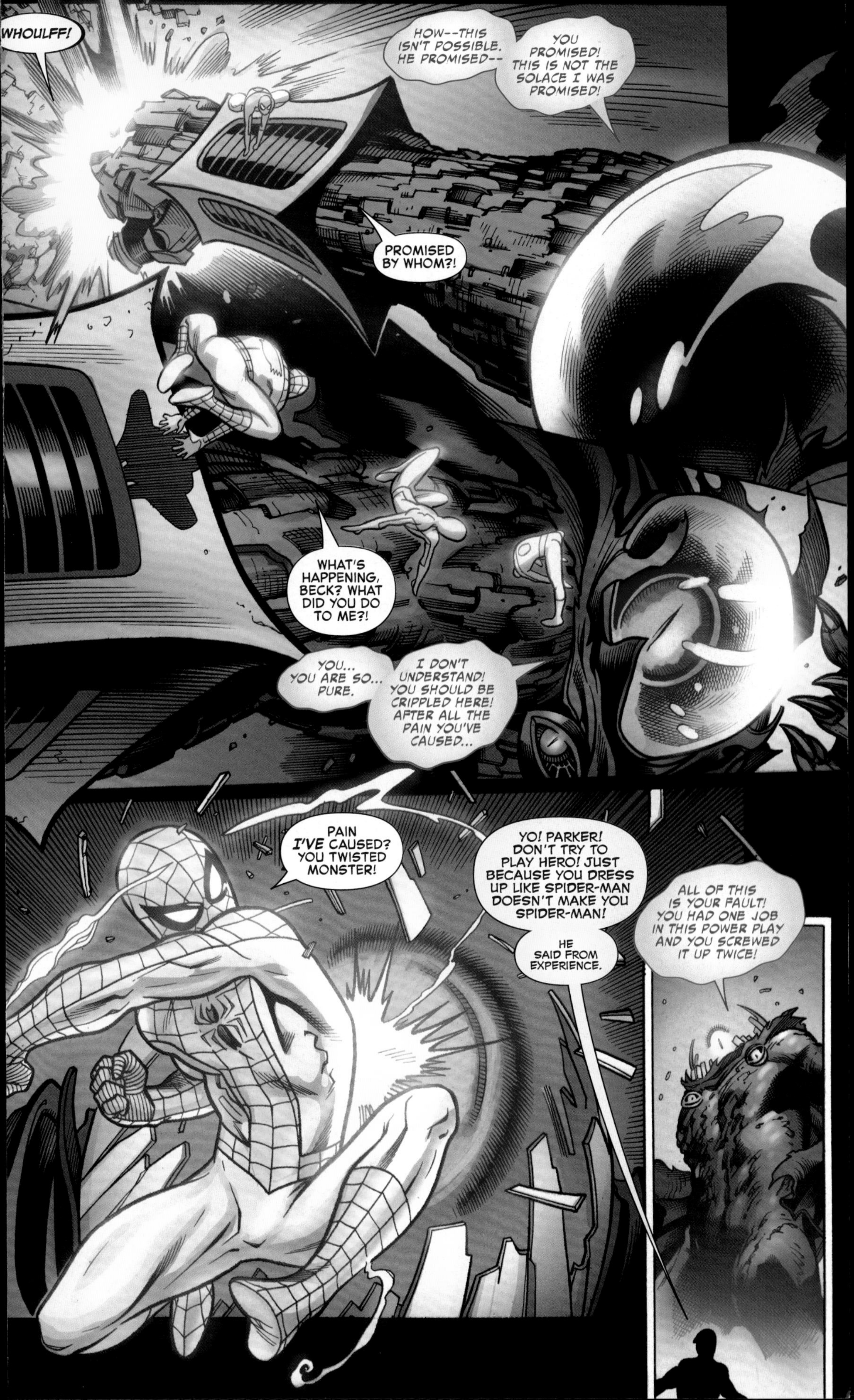
WHOULFF!
HOW--THIS ISN'T POSSIBLE. HE PROMISED--
YOU PROMISED! THIS IS NOT THE SOLACE I WAS PROMISED!
PROMISED BY WHOM?!
WHAT'S HAPPENING, BECK? WHAT DID YOU DO TO ME?!
YOU... YOU ARE SO... PURE.
I DON'T UNDERSTAND! YOU SHOULD BE CRIPPLED HERE! AFTER ALL THE PAIN YOU'VE CAUSED...
PAIN I'VE CAUSED? YOU TWISTED MONSTER!
YO! PARKER! DON'T TRY TO PLAY HERO! JUST BECAUSE YOU DRESS UP LIKE SPIDER-MAN DOESN'T MAKE YOU SPIDER-MAN!
HE SAID FROM EXPERIENCE.
ALL OF THIS IS YOUR FAULT! YOU HAD ONE JOB IN THIS POWER PLAY AND YOU SCREWED IT UP TWICE!

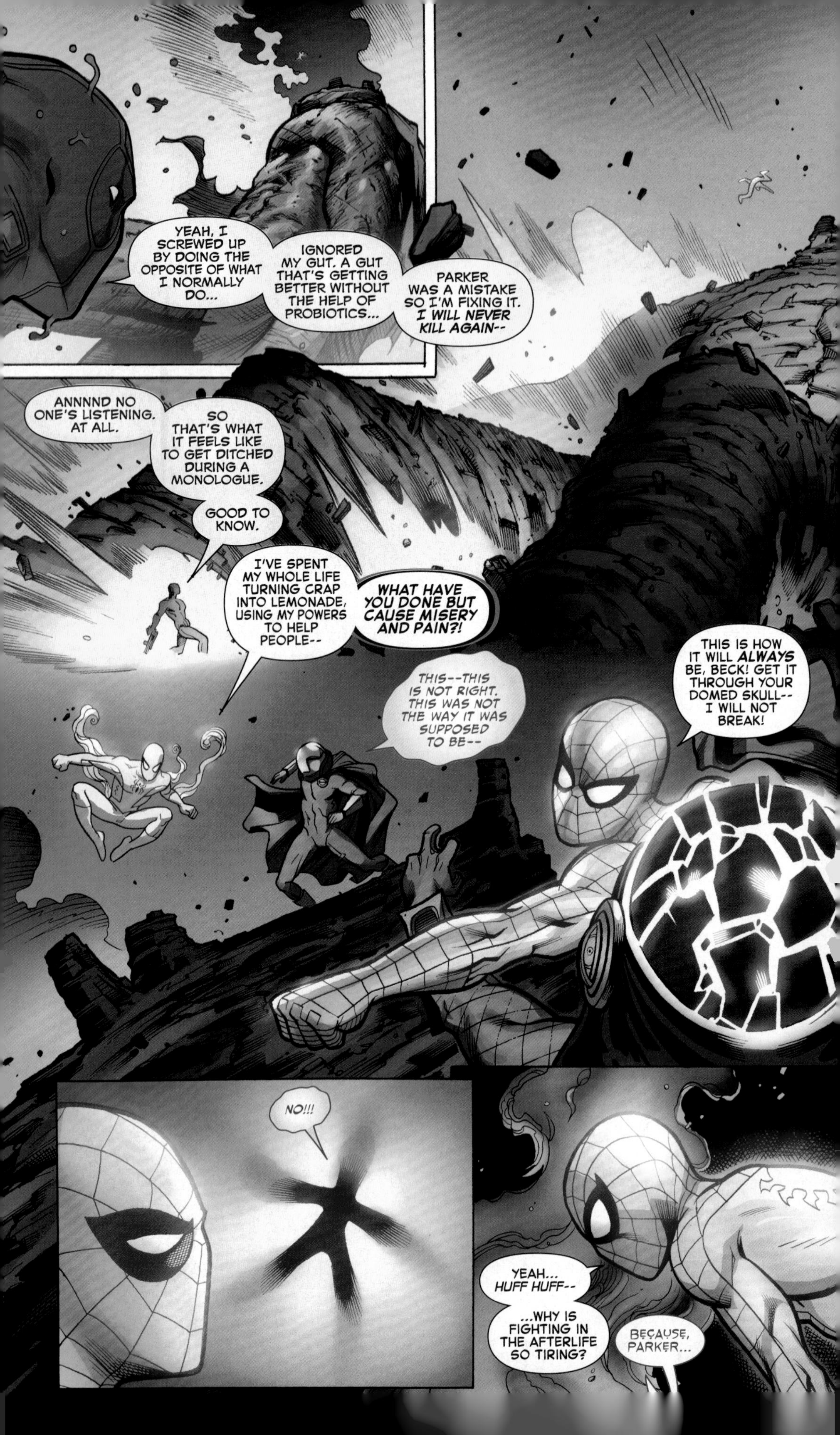
YEAH, I SCREWED UP BY DOING THE OPPOSITE OF WHAT I NORMALLY DO...
IGNORED MY GUT. A GUT THAT'S GETTING BETTER WITHOUT THE HELP OF PROBIOTICS...
PARKER WAS A MISTAKE SO I'M FIXING IT. I WILL NEVER KILL AGAIN--
ANNNND NO ONE'S LISTENING. AT ALL.
SO THAT'S WHAT IT FEELS LIKE TO GET DITCHED DURING A MONOLOGUE.
GOOD TO KNOW.
I'VE SPENT MY WHOLE LIFE TURNING CRAP INTO LEMONADE, USING MY POWERS TO HELP PEOPLE--
WHAT HAVE YOU DONE BUT CAUSE MISERY AND PAIN?!
THIS--THIS IS NOT RIGHT. THIS WAS NOT THE WAY IT WAS SUPPOSED TO BE--
THIS IS HOW IT WILL ALWAYS BE, BECK! GET IT THROUGH YOUR DOMED SKULL-- I WILL NOT BREAK!
NO!!!
YEAH... HUFF HUFF--
...WHY IS FIGHTING IN THE AFTERLIFE SO TIRING?
BECAUSE, PARKER...

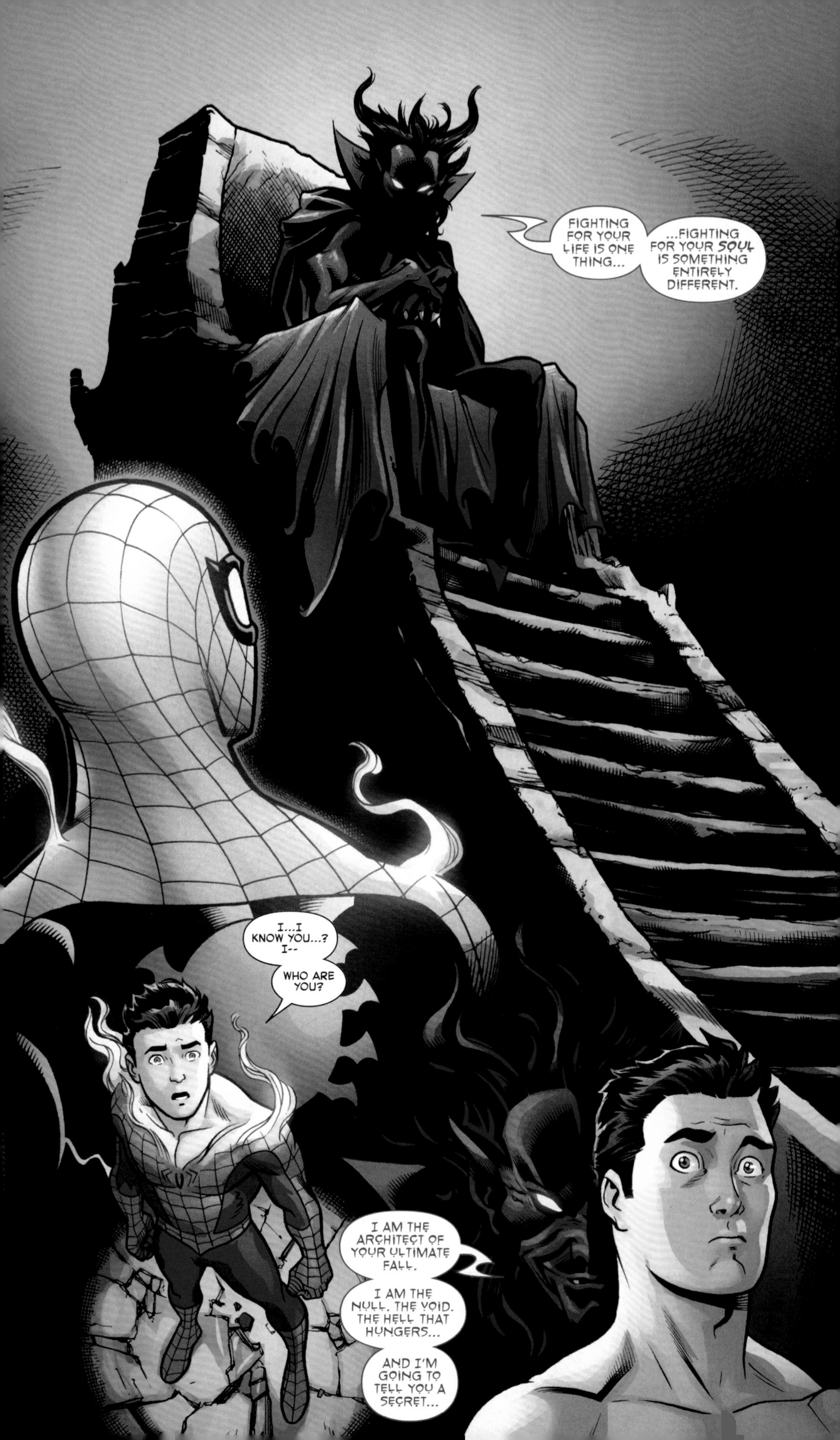
FIGHTING FOR YOUR LIFE IS ONE THING...
...FIGHTING FOR YOUR SOUL IS SOMETHING ENTIRELY DIFFERENT.
I...I KNOW YOU...? I--
WHO ARE YOU?
I AM THE ARCHITECT OF YOUR ULTIMATE FALL.
I AM THE NULL. THE VOID. THE HELL THAT HUNGERS...
AND I'M GOING TO TELL YOU A SECRET...

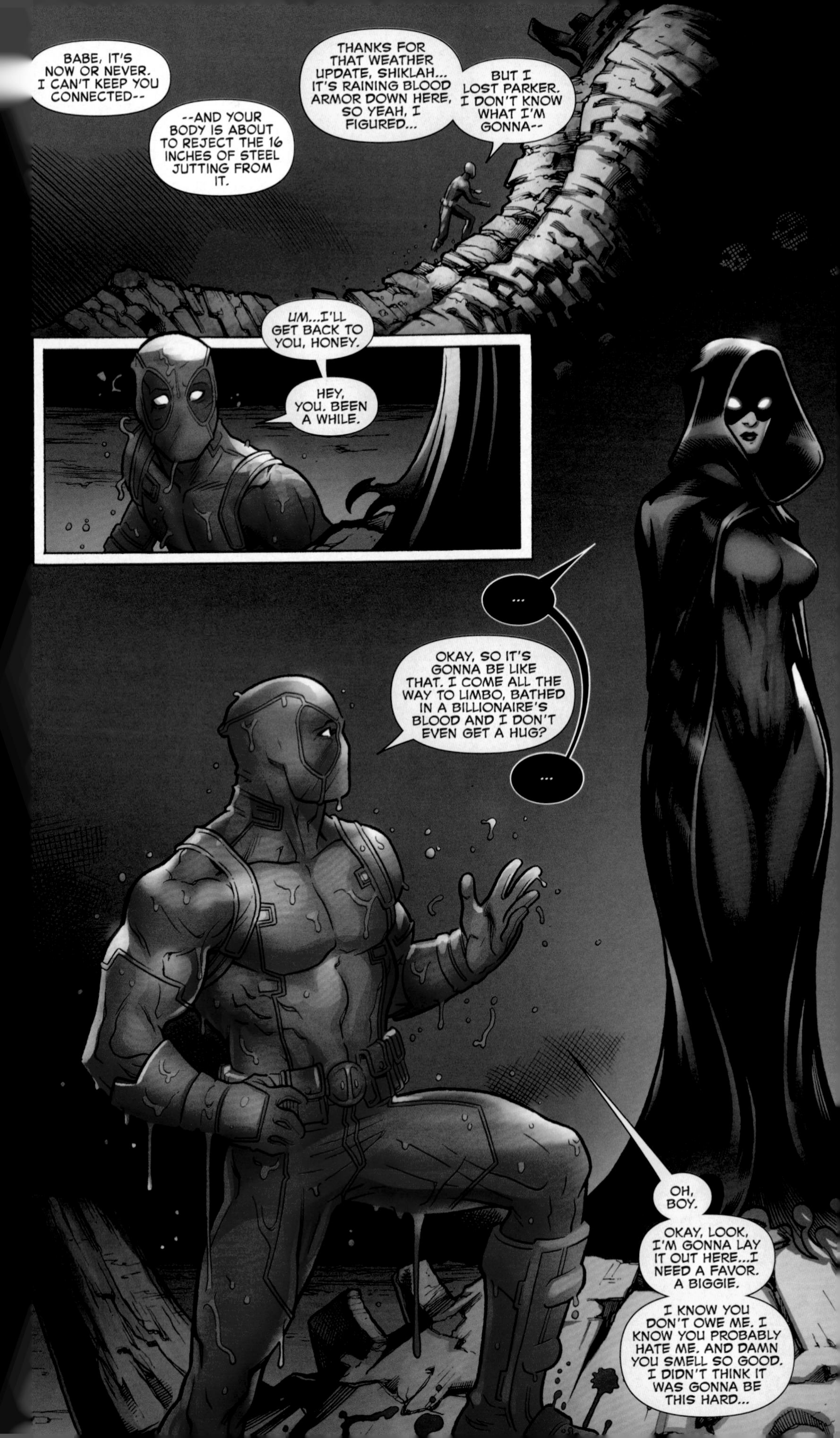
BABE, IT'S NOW OR NEVER. I CAN'T KEEP YOU CONNECTED--
--AND YOUR BODY IS ABOUT TO REJECT THE 16 INCHES OF STEEL JUTTING FROM IT.
THANKS FOR THAT WEATHER UPDATE, SHIKLAH... IT'S RAINING BLOOD ARMOR DOWN HERE, SO YEAH, I FIGURED...
BUT I LOST PARKER. I DON'T KNOW WHAT I'M GONNA--
UM...I'LL GET BACK TO YOU, HONEY.
HEY, YOU. BEEN A WHILE.
...
OKAY, SO IT'S GONNA BE LIKE THAT. I COME ALL THE WAY TO LIMBO, BATHED IN A BILLIONAIRE'S BLOOD AND I DON'T EVEN GET A HUG?
...
OH, BOY.
OKAY, LOOK, I'M GONNA LAY IT OUT HERE...I NEED A FAVOR. A BIGGIE.
I KNOW YOU DON'T OWE ME. I KNOW YOU PROBABLY HATE ME. AND DAMN YOU SMELL SO GOOD. I DIDN'T THINK IT WAS GONNA BE THIS HARD...

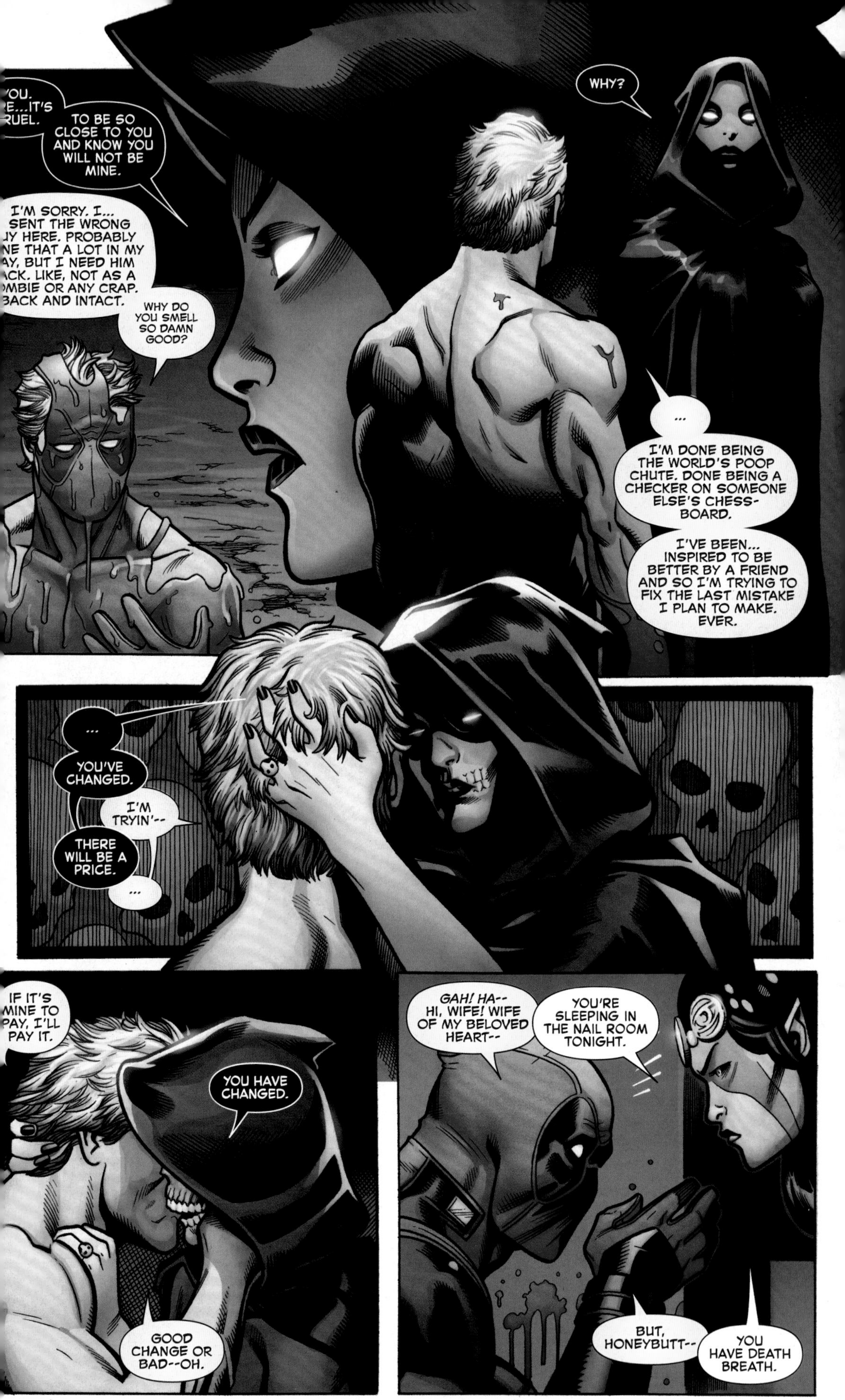

'OU.
E...IT'S
RUEL.
TO BE SO CLOSE TO YOU AND KNOW YOU WILL NOT BE MINE.
I'M SORRY. I... SENT THE WRONG
JY HERE. PROBABLY
NE THAT A LOT IN MY
AY, BUT I NEED HIM
ACK. LIKE, NOT AS A
MBIE OR ANY CRAP.
BACK AND INTACT.
WHY DO YOU SMELL SO DAMN GOOD?
WHY?
...
I'M DONE BEING THE WORLD'S POOP CHUTE. DONE BEING A CHECKER ON SOMEONE ELSE'S CHESS-BOARD.
I'VE BEEN... INSPIRED TO BE BETTER BY A FRIEND AND SO I'M TRYING TO FIX THE LAST MISTAKE I PLAN TO MAKE. EVER.
...
YOU'VE CHANGED.
I'M TRYIN'--
THERE WILL BE A PRICE.
...
IF IT'S
MINE TO
PAY, I'LL
PAY IT.
YOU HAVE CHANGED.
GOOD CHANGE OR BAD--OH.
GAH! HA-- HI, WIFE! WIFE OF MY BELOVED HEART--
YOU'RE SLEEPING IN THE NAIL ROOM TONIGHT.
BUT, HONEYBUTT--
YOU HAVE DEATH BREATH.

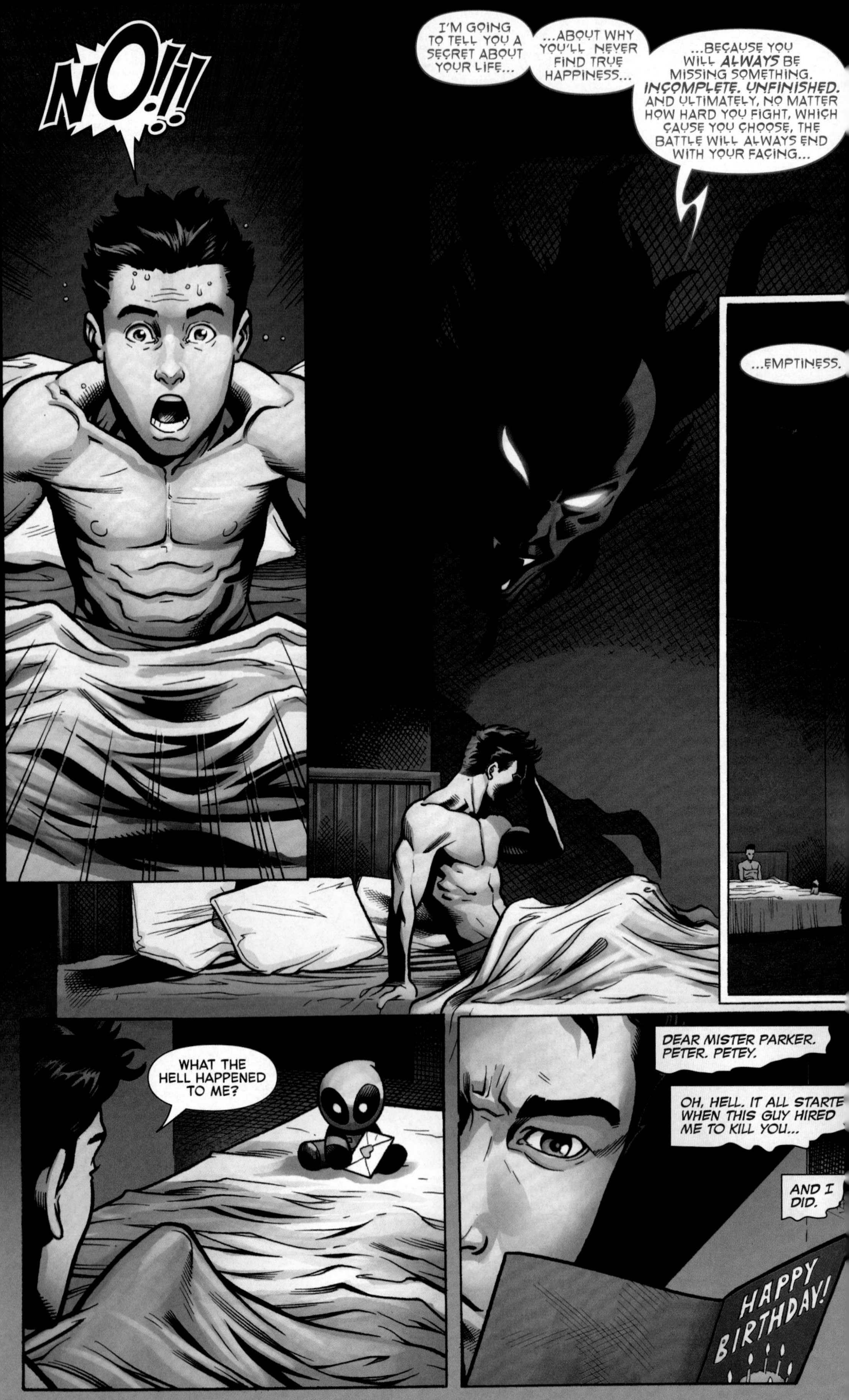
NO!!!
I'M GOING TO TELL YOU A SECRET ABOUT YOUR LIFE...
...ABOUT WHY YOU'LL NEVER FIND TRUE HAPPINESS...
...BECAUSE YOU WILL ALWAYS BE MISSING SOMETHING. INCOMPLETE. UNFINISHED. AND ULTIMATELY, NO MATTER HOW HARD YOU FIGHT, WHICH CAUSE YOU CHOOSE, THE BATTLE WILL ALWAYS END WITH YOUR FACING...
...EMPTINESS.
WHAT THE HELL HAPPENED TO ME?
DEAR MISTER PARKER. PETER. PETEY.
OH, HELL. IT ALL STARTE WHEN THIS GUY HIRED ME TO KILL YOU...
AND I DID.
HAPPY BIRTHDAY!

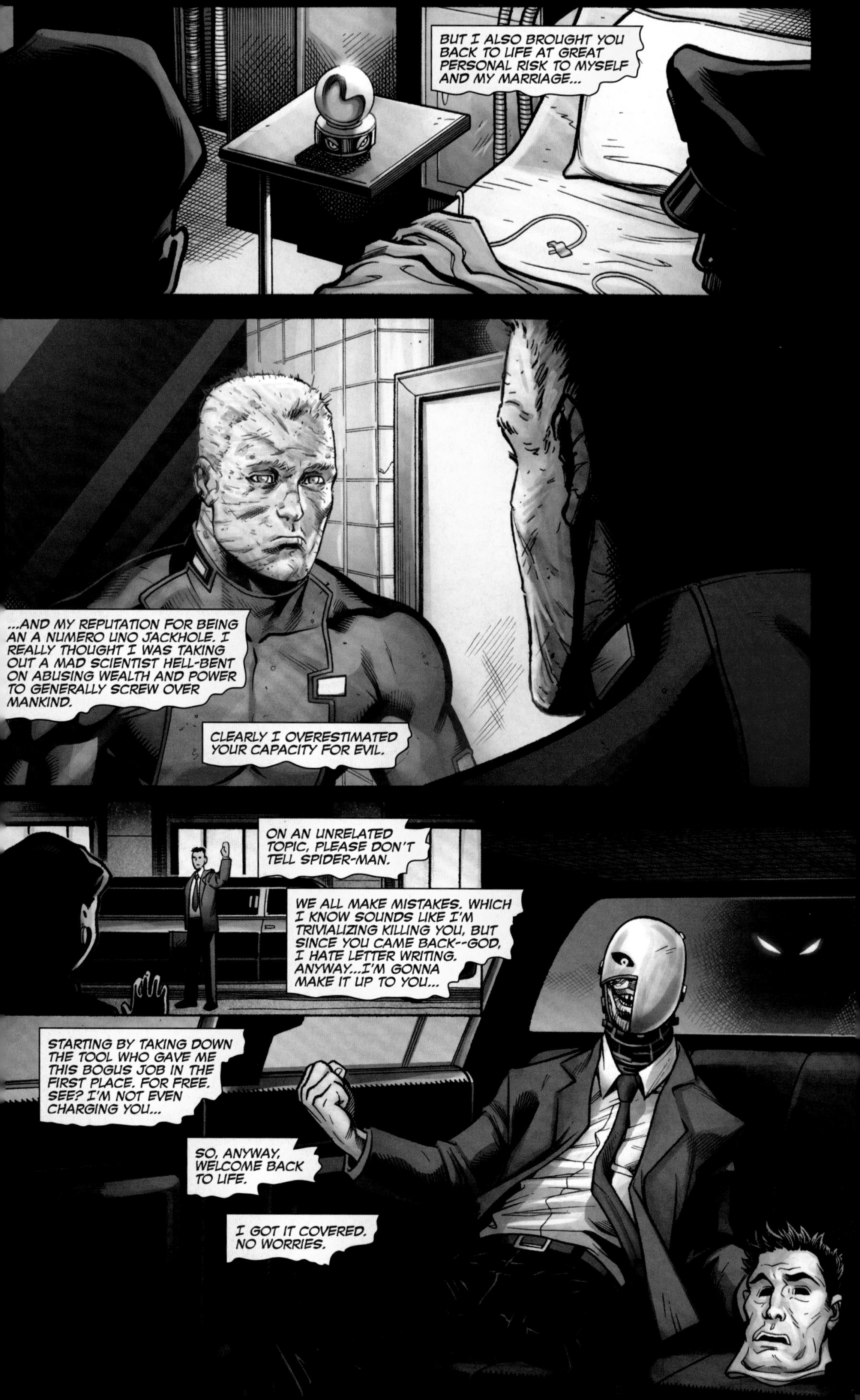

BUT I ALSO BROUGHT YOU BACK TO LIFE AT GREAT PERSONAL RISK TO MYSELF AND MY MARRIAGE...
...AND MY REPUTATION FOR BEING AN A NUMERO UNO JACKHOLE. I REALLY THOUGHT I WAS TAKING OUT A MAD SCIENTIST HELL-BENT ON ABUSING WEALTH AND POWER TO GENERALLY SCREW OVER MANKIND.
CLEARLY I OVERESTIMATED YOUR CAPACITY FOR EVIL.
ON AN UNRELATED TOPIC, PLEASE DON'T TELL SPIDER-MAN.
WE ALL MAKE MISTAKES. WHICH I KNOW SOUNDS LIKE I'M TRIVIALIZING KILLING YOU, BUT SINCE YOU CAME BACK--GOD, I HATE LETTER WRITING. ANYWAY...I'M GONNA MAKE IT UP TO YOU...
STARTING BY TAKING DOWN THE TOOL WHO GAVE ME THIS BOGUS JOB IN THE FIRST PLACE. FOR FREE. SEE? I'M NOT EVEN CHARGING YOU...
SO, ANYWAY, WELCOME BACK TO LIFE.
I GOT IT COVERED. NO WORRIES.

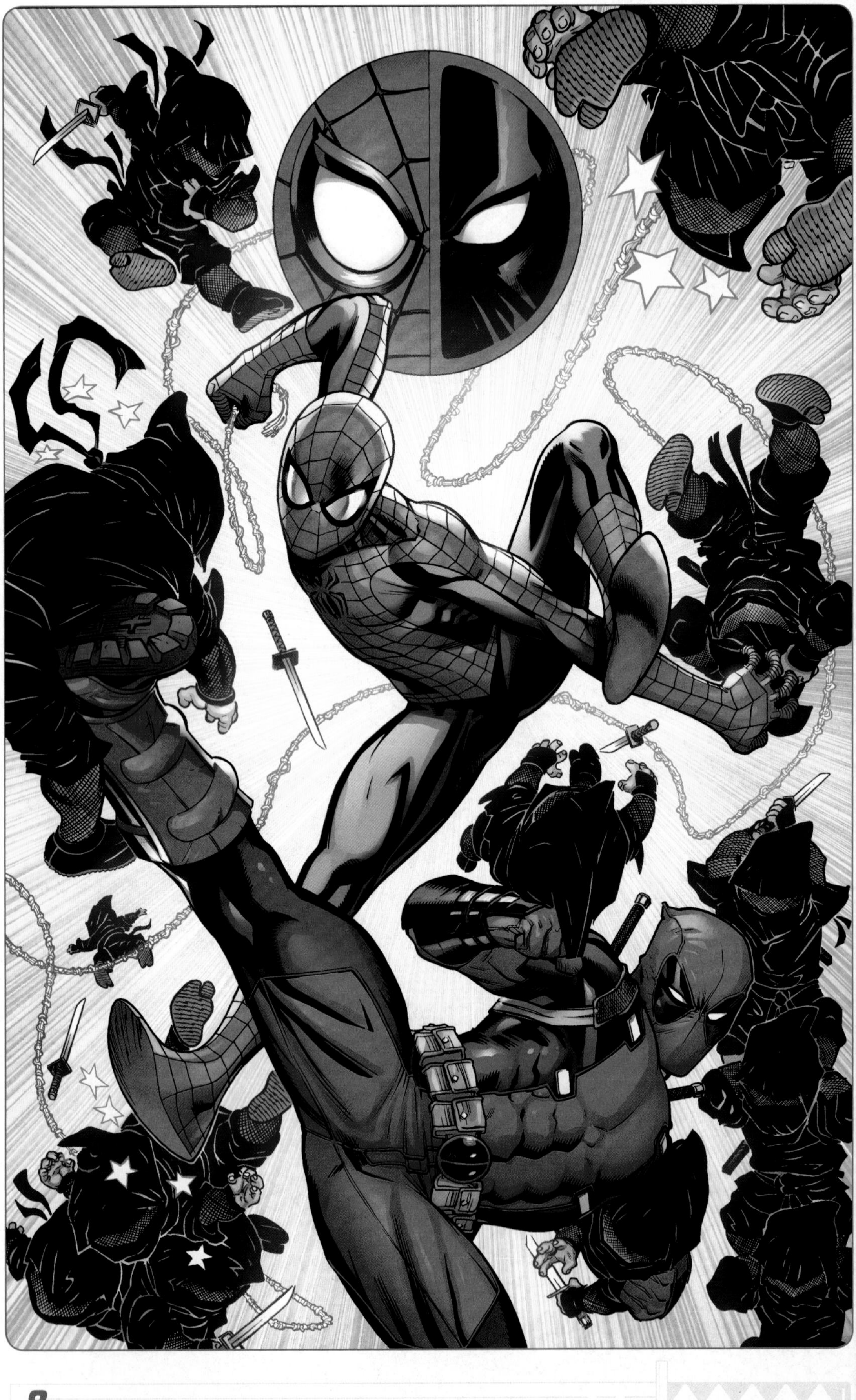

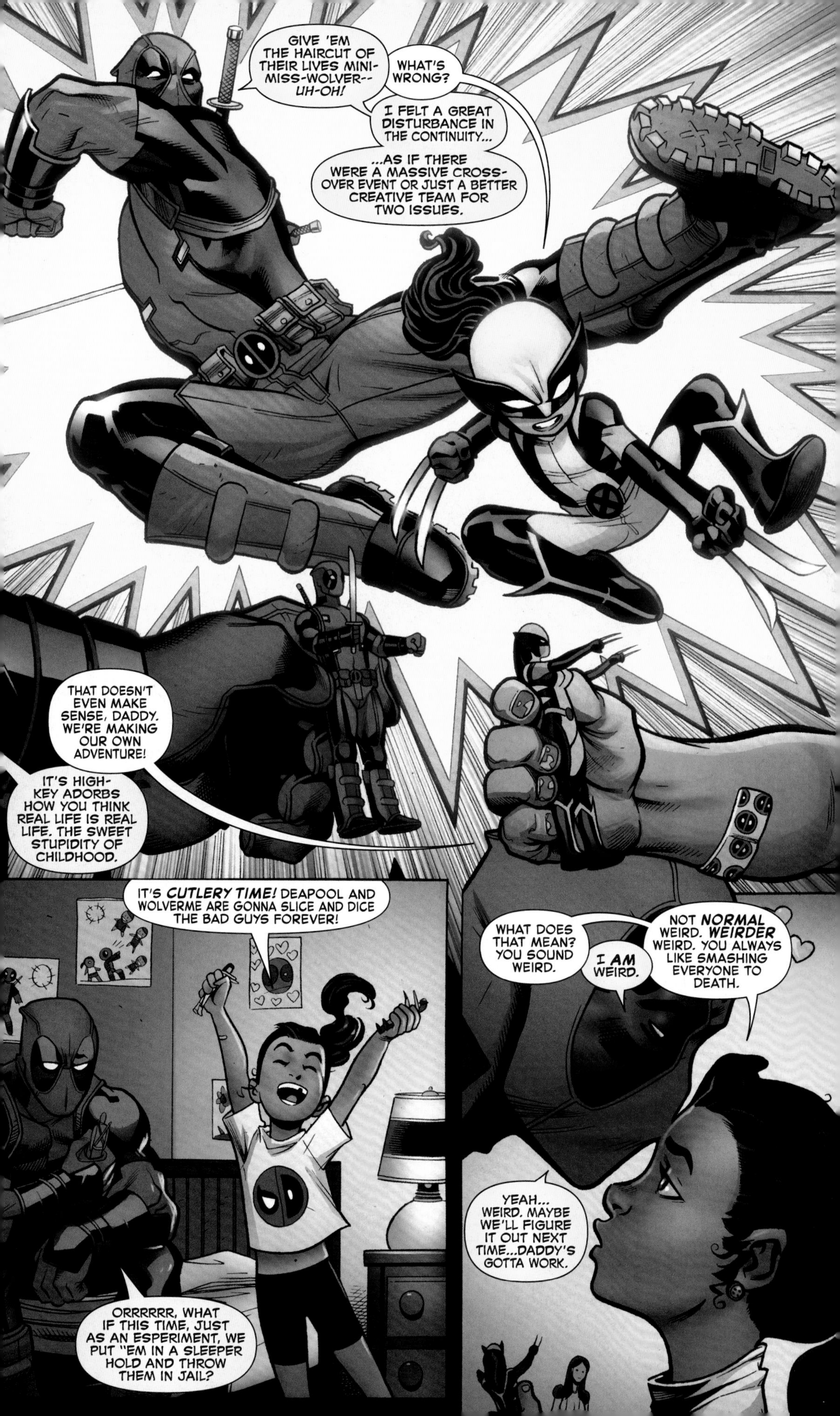
GIVE 'EM THE HAIRCUT OF THEIR LIVES MINI-MISS-WOLVER-- UH-OH!
WHAT'S WRONG?
I FELT A GREAT DISTURBANCE IN THE CONTINUITY...
...AS IF THERE WERE A MASSIVE CROSS-OVER EVENT OR JUST A BETTER CREATIVE TEAM FOR TWO ISSUES.
THAT DOESN'T EVEN MAKE SENSE, DADDY. WE'RE MAKING OUR OWN ADVENTURE!
IT'S HIGH-KEY ADORBS HOW YOU THINK REAL LIFE IS REAL LIFE. THE SWEET STUPIDITY OF CHILDHOOD.
IT'S *CUTLERY TIME!* DEAPOOL AND WOLVERME ARE GONNA SLICE AND DICE THE BAD GUYS FOREVER!
ORRRRRR, WHAT IF THIS TIME, JUST AS AN ESPERIMENT, WE PUT "EM IN A SLEEPER HOLD AND THROW THEM IN JAIL?
WHAT DOES THAT MEAN? YOU SOUND WEIRD.
I AM WEIRD.
NOT *NORMAL* WEIRD. *WEIRDER* WEIRD. YOU ALWAYS LIKE SMASHING EVERYONE TO DEATH.
YEAH... WEIRD. MAYBE WE'LL FIGURE IT OUT NEXT TIME...DADDY'S GOTTA WORK.

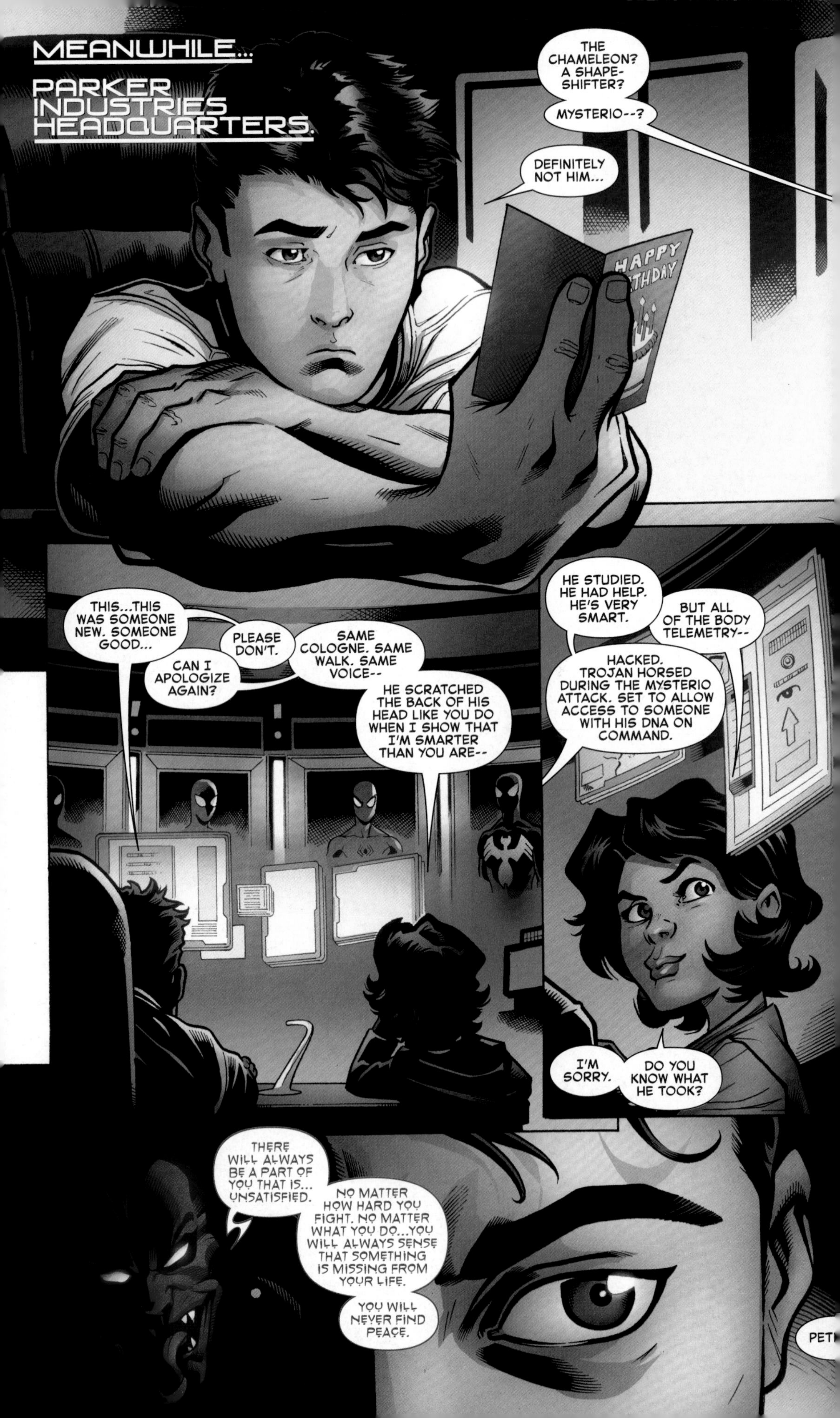
MEANWHILE...
PARKER INDUSTRIES HEADQUARTERS.
THE CHAMELEON? A SHAPE-SHIFTER?
MYSTERIO--?
DEFINITELY NOT HIM...
HAPPY
THIS...THIS WAS SOMEONE NEW. SOMEONE GOOD...
PLEASE DON'T.
CAN I APOLOGIZE AGAIN?
SAME COLOGNE. SAME WALK. SAME VOICE--
HE SCRATCHED THE BACK OF HIS HEAD LIKE YOU DO WHEN I SHOW THAT I'M SMARTER THAN YOU ARE--
HE STUDIED. HE HAD HELP. HE'S VERY SMART.
BUT ALL OF THE BODY TELEMETRY--
HACKED. TROJAN HORSED DURING THE MYSTERIO ATTACK. SET TO ALLOW ACCESS TO SOMEONE WITH HIS DNA ON COMMAND.
I'M SORRY.
DO YOU KNOW WHAT HE TOOK?
THERE WILL ALWAYS BE A PART OF YOU THAT IS... UNSATISFIED.
NO MATTER HOW HARD YOU FIGHT. NO MATTER WHAT YOU DO...YOU WILL ALWAYS SENSE THAT SOMETHING IS MISSING FROM YOUR LIFE.
YOU WILL NEVER FIND PEACE.

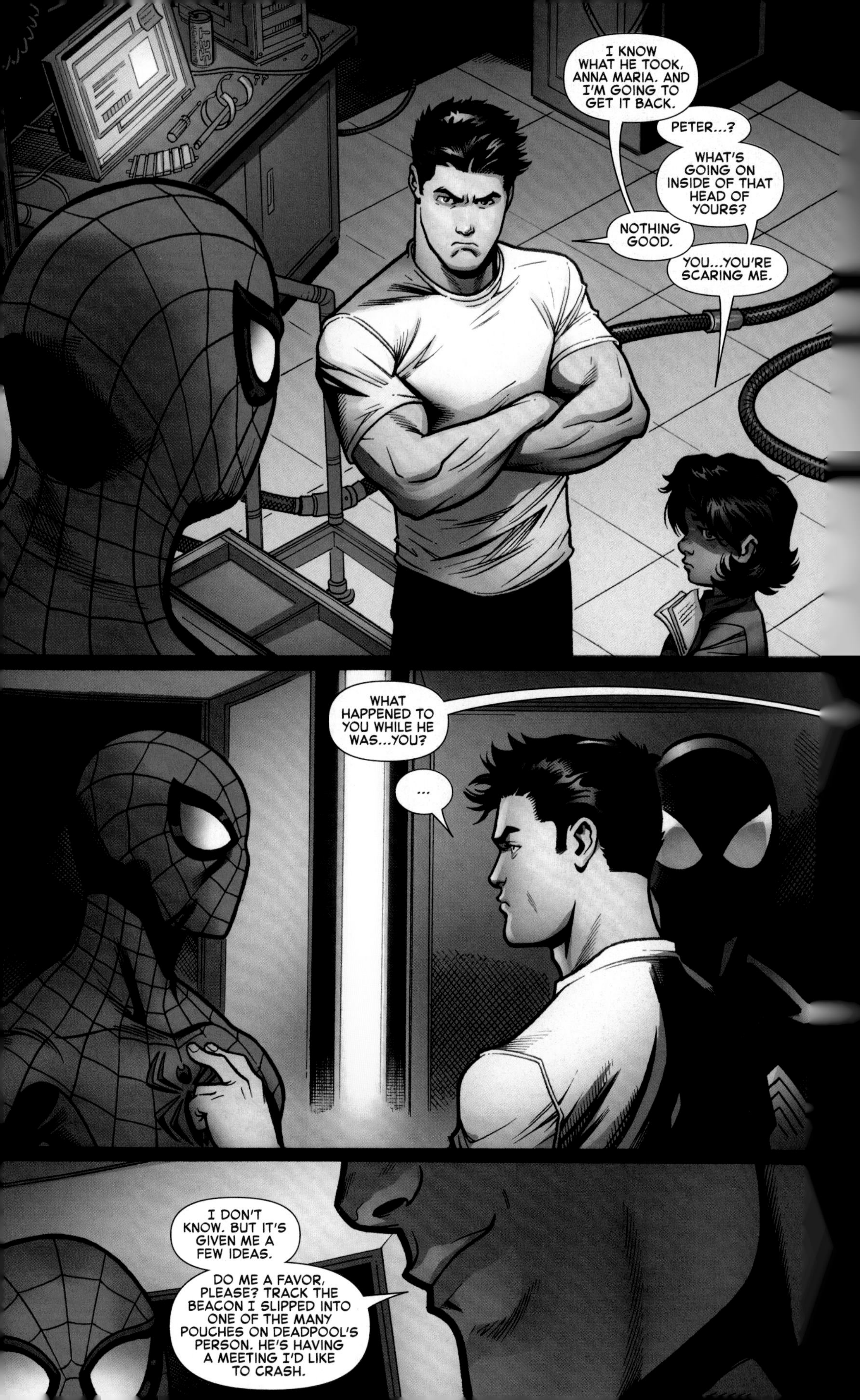
I KNOW WHAT HE TOOK, ANNA MARIA. AND I'M GOING TO GET IT BACK.
PETER...?
WHAT'S GOING ON INSIDE OF THAT HEAD OF YOURS?
NOTHING GOOD.
YOU...YOU'RE SCARING ME.
WHAT HAPPENED TO YOU WHILE HE WAS...YOU?
...
I DON'T KNOW. BUT IT'S GIVEN ME A FEW IDEAS.
DO ME A FAVOR, PLEASE? TRACK THE BEACON I SLIPPED INTO ONE OF THE MANY POUCHES ON DEADPOOL'S PERSON. HE'S HAVING A MEETING I'D LIKE TO CRASH.

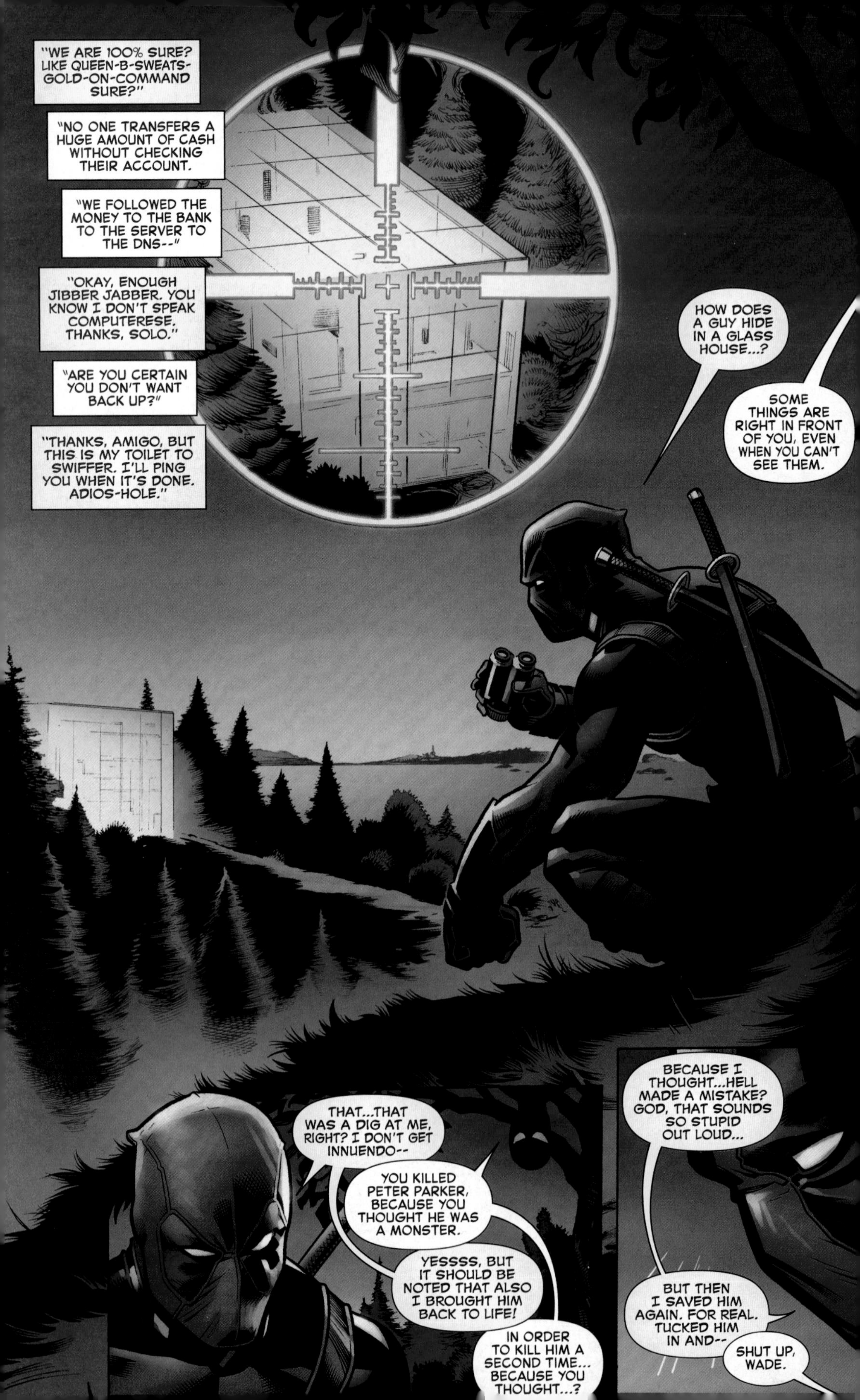
"WE ARE 100% SURE? LIKE QUEEN-B-SWEATS-GOLD-ON-COMMAND SURE?"
"NO ONE TRANSFERS A HUGE AMOUNT OF CASH WITHOUT CHECKING THEIR ACCOUNT.
"WE FOLLOWED THE MONEY TO THE BANK TO THE SERVER TO THE DNS--"
"OKAY, ENOUGH JIBBER JABBER. YOU KNOW I DON'T SPEAK COMPUTERESE. THANKS, SOLO."
"ARE YOU CERTAIN YOU DON'T WANT BACK UP?"
"THANKS, AMIGO, BUT THIS IS MY TOILET TO SWIFFER. I'LL PING YOU WHEN IT'S DONE. ADIOS-HOLE."
HOW DOES A GUY HIDE IN A GLASS HOUSE...?
SOME THINGS ARE RIGHT IN FRONT OF YOU, EVEN WHEN YOU CAN'T SEE THEM.
THAT...THAT WAS A DIG AT ME, RIGHT? I DON'T GET INNUENDO--
YOU KILLED PETER PARKER, BECAUSE YOU THOUGHT HE WAS A MONSTER.
YESSSS, BUT IT SHOULD BE NOTED THAT ALSO I BROUGHT HIM BACK TO LIFE!
IN ORDER TO KILL HIM A SECOND TIME... BECAUSE YOU THOUGHT...?
BECAUSE I THOUGHT...HELL MADE A MISTAKE? GOD, THAT SOUNDS SO STUPID OUT LOUD...
BUT THEN I SAVED HIM AGAIN. FOR REAL. TUCKED HIM IN AND--
SHUT UP, WADE.

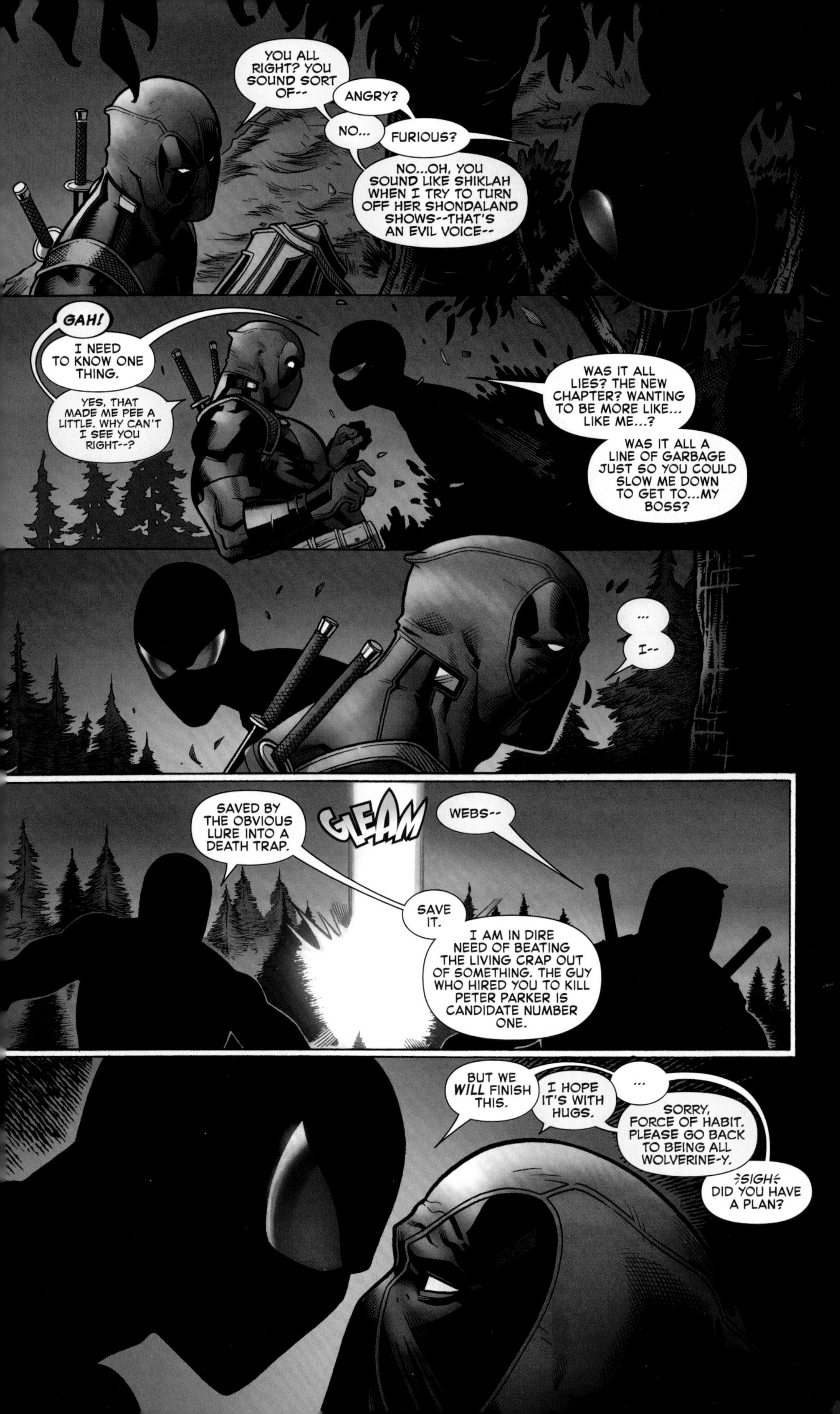
YOU ALL RIGHT? YOU SOUND SORT OF--
ANGRY?
NO...
FURIOUS?
NO...OH, YOU SOUND LIKE SHIKLAH WHEN I TRY TO TURN OFF HER SHONDALAND SHOWS--THAT'S AN EVIL VOICE--
GAH!
I NEED TO KNOW ONE THING.
YES, THAT MADE ME PEE A LITTLE. WHY CAN'T I SEE YOU RIGHT--?
WAS IT ALL LIES? THE NEW CHAPTER? WANTING TO BE MORE LIKE... LIKE ME...?
WAS IT ALL A LINE OF GARBAGE JUST SO YOU COULD SLOW ME DOWN TO GET TO...MY BOSS?
...
I--
SAVED BY THE OBVIOUS LURE INTO A DEATH TRAP.
GLEAM
WEBS--
SAVE IT.
I AM IN DIRE NEED OF BEATING THE LIVING CRAP OUT OF SOMETHING. THE GUY WHO HIRED YOU TO KILL PETER PARKER IS CANDIDATE NUMBER ONE.
BUT WE WILL FINISH THIS.
I HOPE IT'S WITH HUGS.
...
SORRY, FORCE OF HABIT. PLEASE GO BACK TO BEING ALL WOLVERINE-Y.
SIGH
DID YOU HAVE A PLAN?

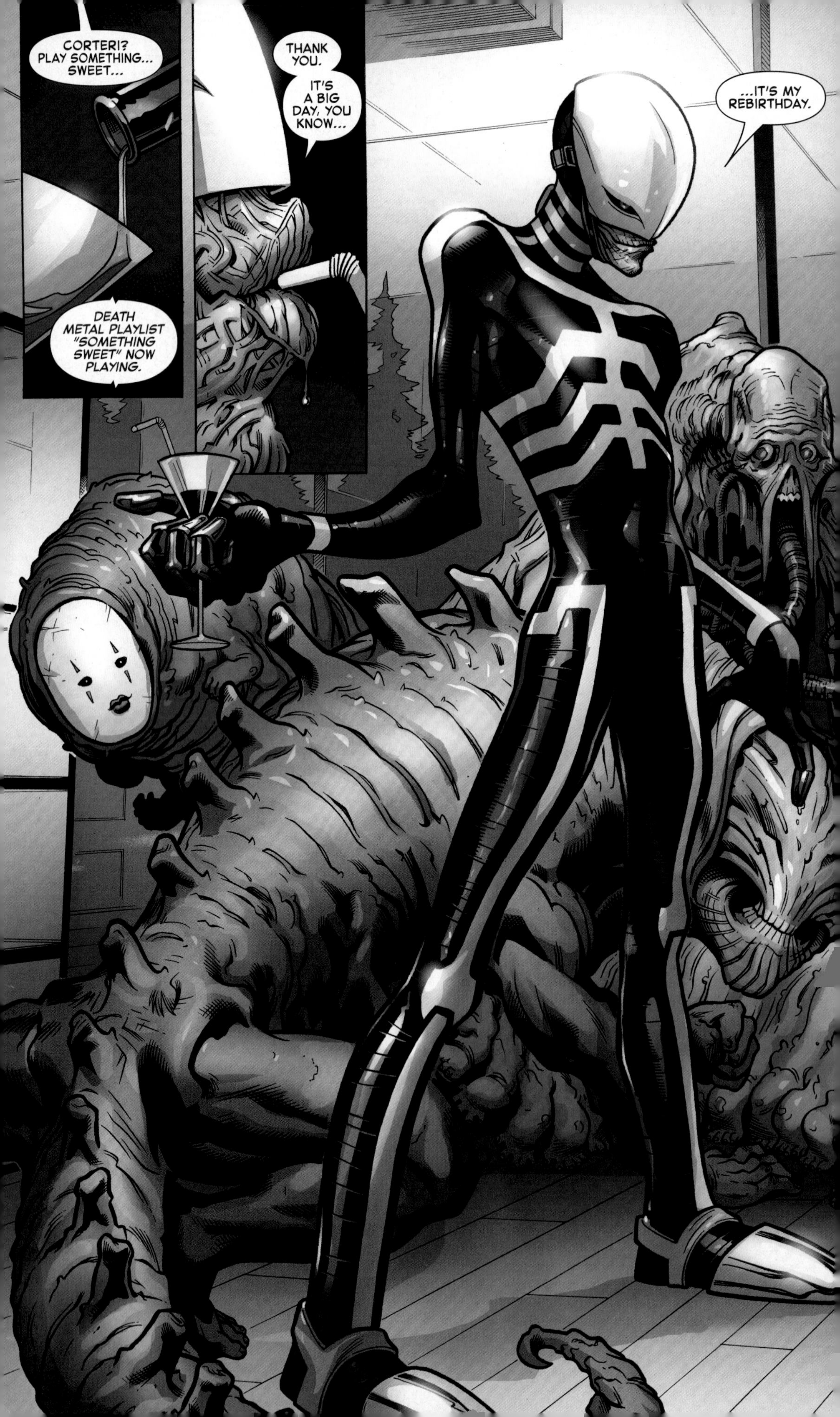
CORTERI? PLAY SOMETHING... SWEET...
DEATH METAL PLAYLIST "SOMETHING SWEET" NOW PLAYING.
THANK YOU.
IT'S A BIG DAY, YOU KNOW...
...IT'S MY REBIRTHDAY.

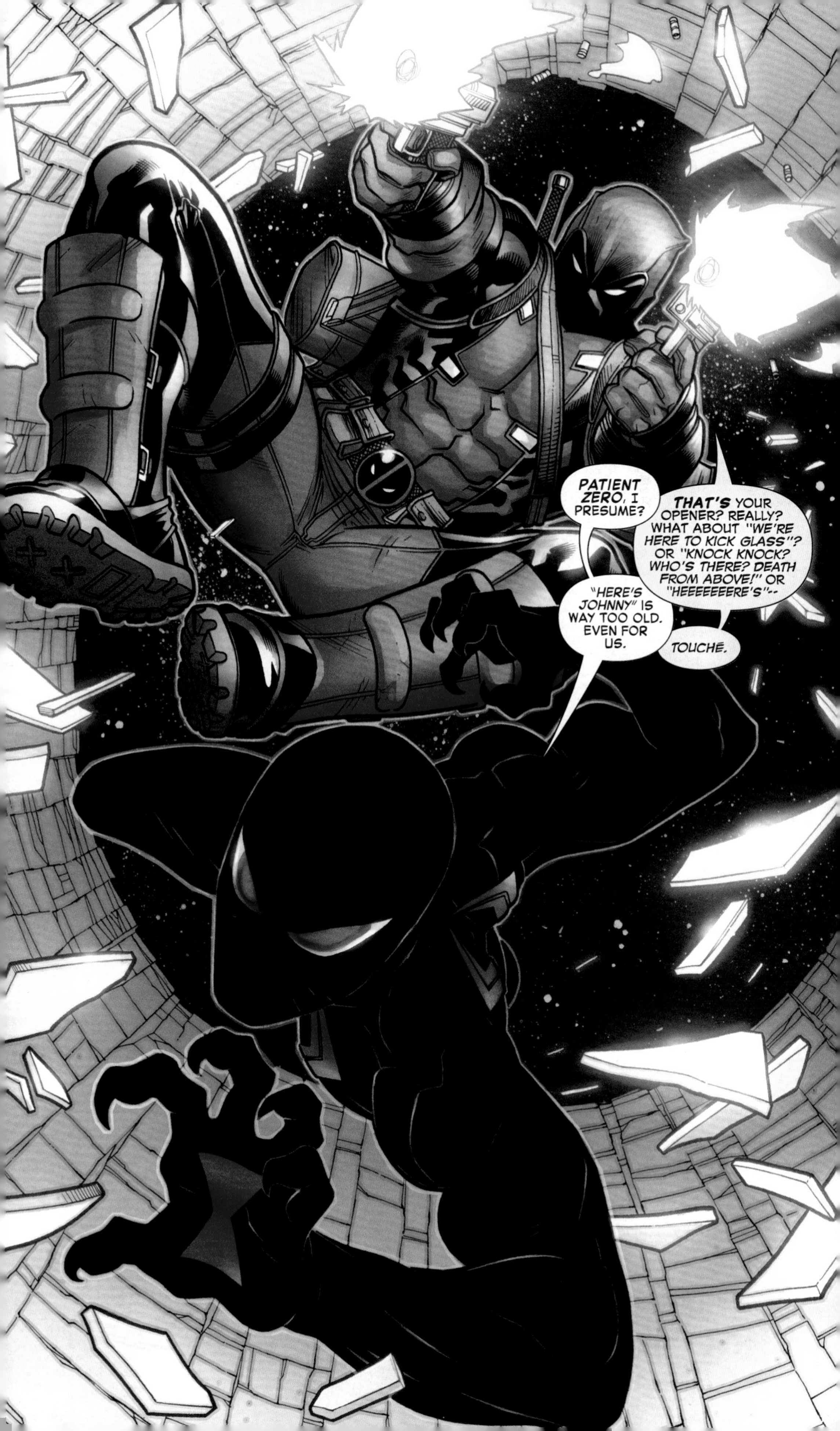
PATIENT ZERO, I PRESUME?
"HERE'S JOHNNY" IS WAY TOO OLD. EVEN FOR US.
THAT'S YOUR OPENER? REALLY? WHAT ABOUT "WE'RE HERE TO KICK GLASS"? OR "KNOCK KNOCK? WHO'S THERE? DEATH FROM ABOVE!" OR "HEEEEEEERE'S"--
TOUCHÉ.

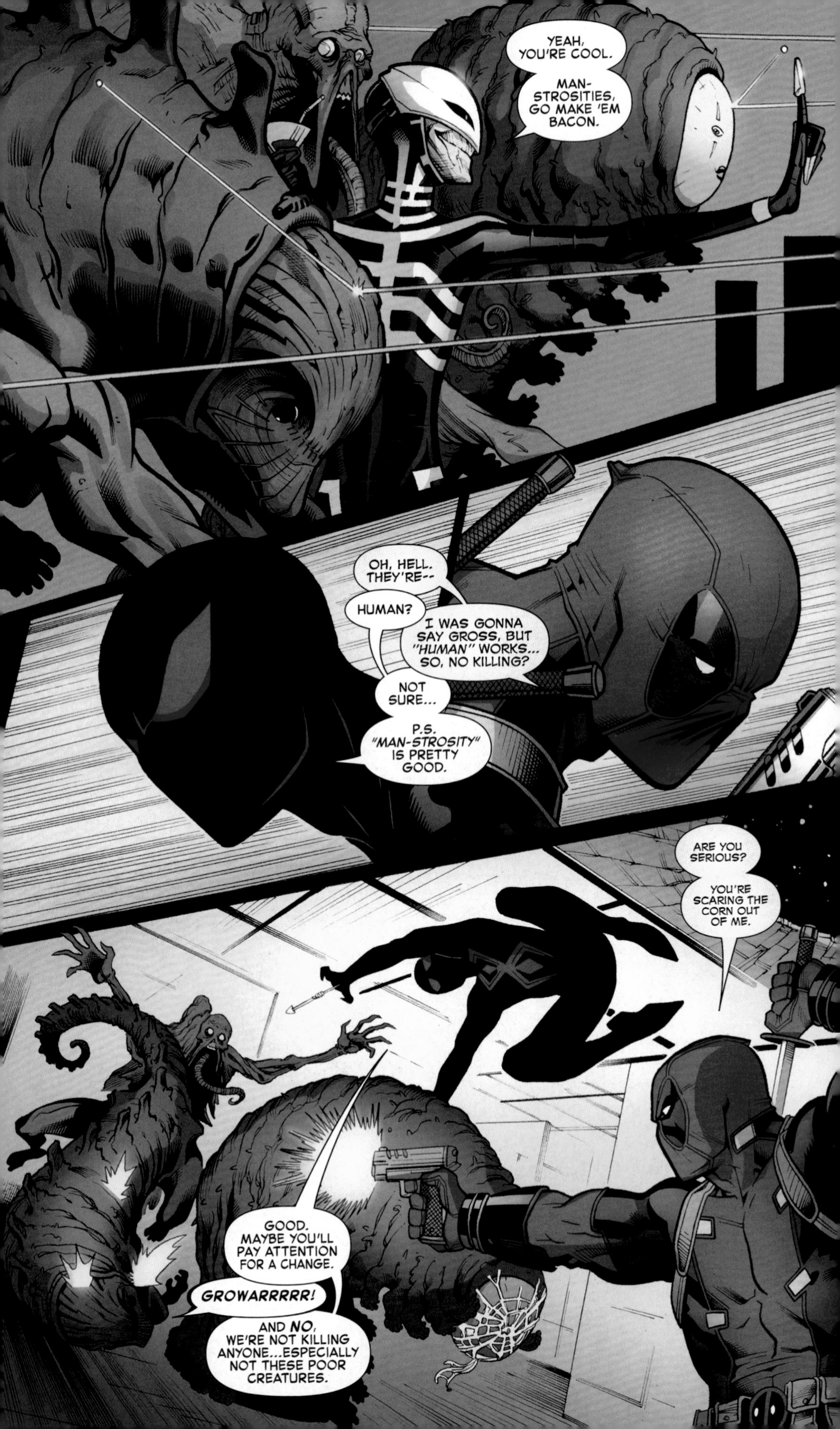
YEAH, YOU'RE COOL.
MAN-STROSITIES, GO MAKE 'EM BACON.
OH, HELL. THEY'RE--
HUMAN?
I WAS GONNA SAY GROSS, BUT "HUMAN" WORKS... SO, NO KILLING?
NOT SURE...
P.S. "MAN-STROSITY" IS PRETTY GOOD.
ARE YOU SERIOUS?
YOU'RE SCARING THE CORN OUT OF ME.
GOOD. MAYBE YOU'LL PAY ATTENTION FOR A CHANGE.
GROWARRRRR!
AND NO, WE'RE NOT KILLING ANYONE...ESPECIALLY NOT THESE POOR CREATURES.

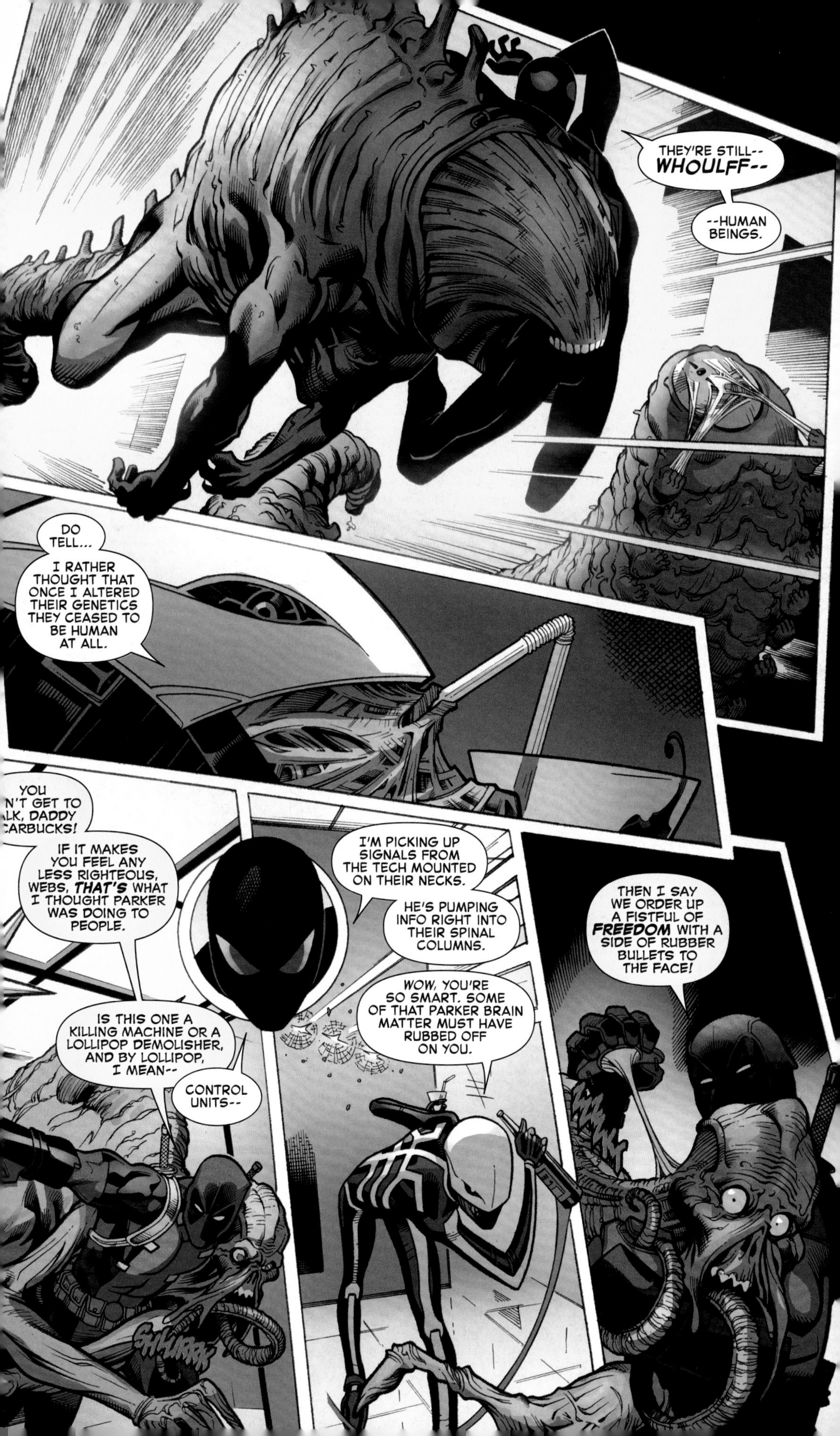

THEY'RE STILL-- WHOULFF--
--HUMAN BEINGS.
DO TELL...
I RATHER THOUGHT THAT ONCE I ALTERED THEIR GENETICS THEY CEASED TO BE HUMAN AT ALL.
YOU N'T GET TO LK, DADDY CARBUCKS!
IF IT MAKES YOU FEEL ANY LESS RIGHTEOUS, WEBS, THAT'S WHAT I THOUGHT PARKER WAS DOING TO PEOPLE.
IS THIS ONE A KILLING MACHINE OR A LOLLIPOP DEMOLISHER, AND BY LOLLIPOP, I MEAN--
CONTROL UNITS--
I'M PICKING UP SIGNALS FROM THE TECH MOUNTED ON THEIR NECKS.
HE'S PUMPING INFO RIGHT INTO THEIR SPINAL COLUMNS.
WOW, YOU'RE SO SMART. SOME OF THAT PARKER BRAIN MATTER MUST HAVE RUBBED OFF ON YOU.
THEN I SAY WE ORDER UP A FISTFUL OF FREEDOM WITH A SIDE OF RUBBER BULLETS TO THE FACE!
SHURRK

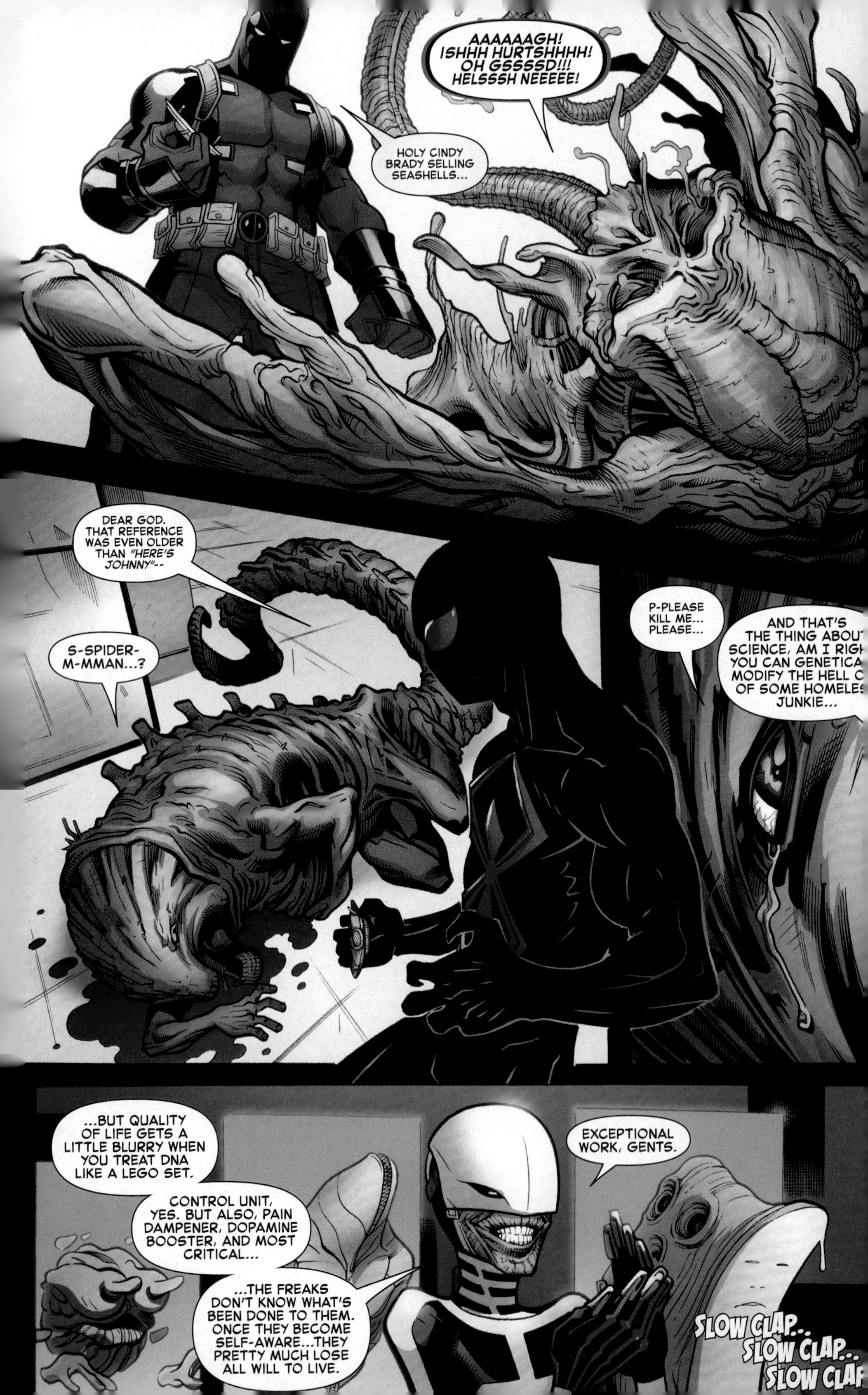

AAAAAAGH! ISHHH HURTSHHHH! OH GSSSSD!!! HELSSSH NEEEEE!
HOLY CINDY BRADY SELLING SEASHELLS...
DEAR GOD. THAT REFERENCE WAS EVEN OLDER THAN "HERE'S JOHNNY"--
S-SPIDER-M-MMAN...?
P-PLEASE KILL ME... PLEASE...
AND THAT'S THE THING ABOUT SCIENCE, AM I RIGH YOU CAN GENETICA MODIFY THE HELL C OF SOME HOMELES JUNKIE...
...BUT QUALITY OF LIFE GETS A LITTLE BLURRY WHEN YOU TREAT DNA LIKE A LEGO SET.
CONTROL UNIT, YES. BUT ALSO, PAIN DAMPENER, DOPAMINE BOOSTER, AND MOST CRITICAL...
...THE FREAKS DON'T KNOW WHAT'S BEEN DONE TO THEM. ONCE THEY BECOME SELF-AWARE...THEY PRETTY MUCH LOSE ALL WILL TO LIVE.
EXCEPTIONAL WORK, GENTS.
SLOW CLAP... SLOW CLAP... SLOW CLAP

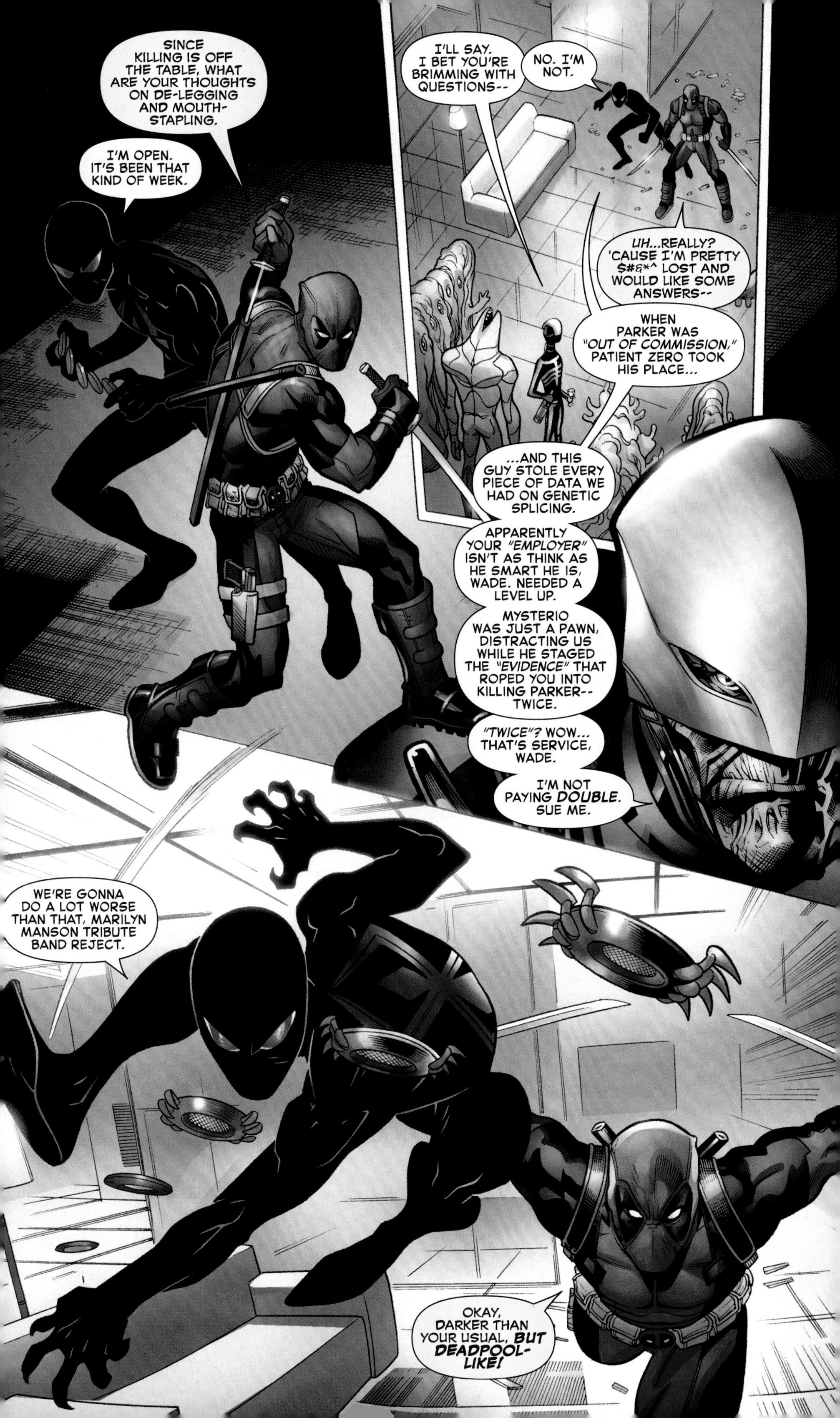
SINCE KILLING IS OFF THE TABLE, WHAT ARE YOUR THOUGHTS ON DE-LEGGING AND MOUTH-STAPLING.
I'M OPEN. IT'S BEEN THAT KIND OF WEEK.
I'LL SAY. I BET YOU'RE BRIMMING WITH QUESTIONS--
NO. I'M NOT.
UH...REALLY? 'CAUSE I'M PRETTY $#&*^ LOST AND WOULD LIKE SOME ANSWERS--
WHEN PARKER WAS "OUT OF COMMISSION," PATIENT ZERO TOOK HIS PLACE...
...AND THIS GUY STOLE EVERY PIECE OF DATA WE HAD ON GENETIC SPLICING.
APPARENTLY YOUR "EMPLOYER" ISN'T AS THINK AS HE SMART HE IS, WADE. NEEDED A LEVEL UP.
MYSTERIO WAS JUST A PAWN, DISTRACTING US WHILE HE STAGED THE "EVIDENCE" THAT ROPED YOU INTO KILLING PARKER--TWICE.
"TWICE"? WOW... THAT'S SERVICE, WADE.
I'M NOT PAYING DOUBLE. SUE ME.
WE'RE GONNA DO A LOT WORSE THAN THAT, MARILYN MANSON TRIBUTE BAND REJECT.
OKAY, DARKER THAN YOUR USUAL, BUT DEADPOOL-LIKE!

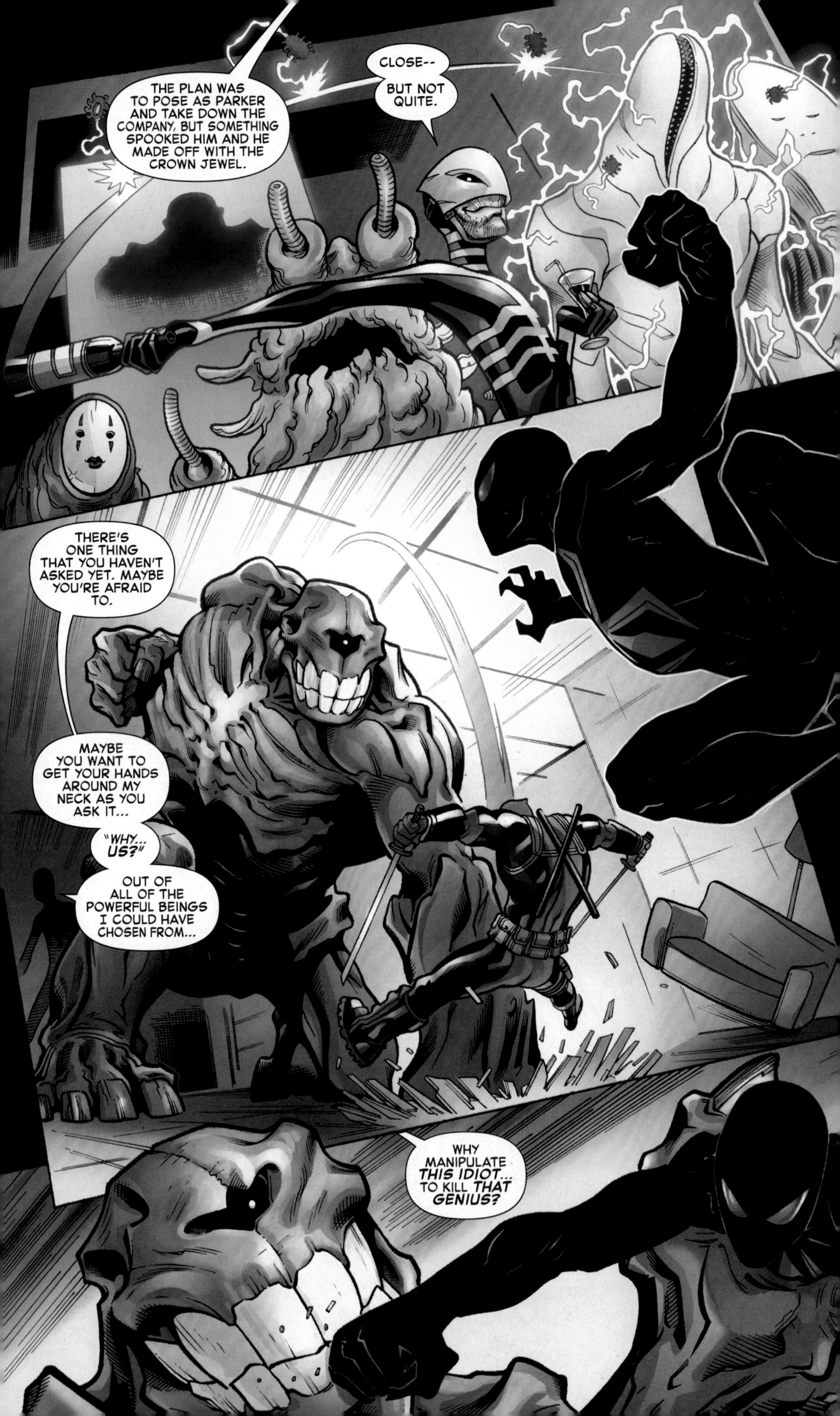
THE PLAN WAS TO POSE AS PARKER AND TAKE DOWN THE COMPANY, BUT SOMETHING SPOOKED HIM AND HE MADE OFF WITH THE CROWN JEWEL.
CLOSE--
BUT NOT QUITE.
THERE'S ONE THING THAT YOU HAVEN'T ASKED YET. MAYBE YOU'RE AFRAID TO.
MAYBE YOU WANT TO GET YOUR HANDS AROUND MY NECK AS YOU ASK IT...
"WHY... US?"
OUT OF ALL OF THE POWERFUL BEINGS I COULD HAVE CHOSEN FROM...
WHY MANIPULATE THIS IDIOT... TO KILL THAT GENIUS?

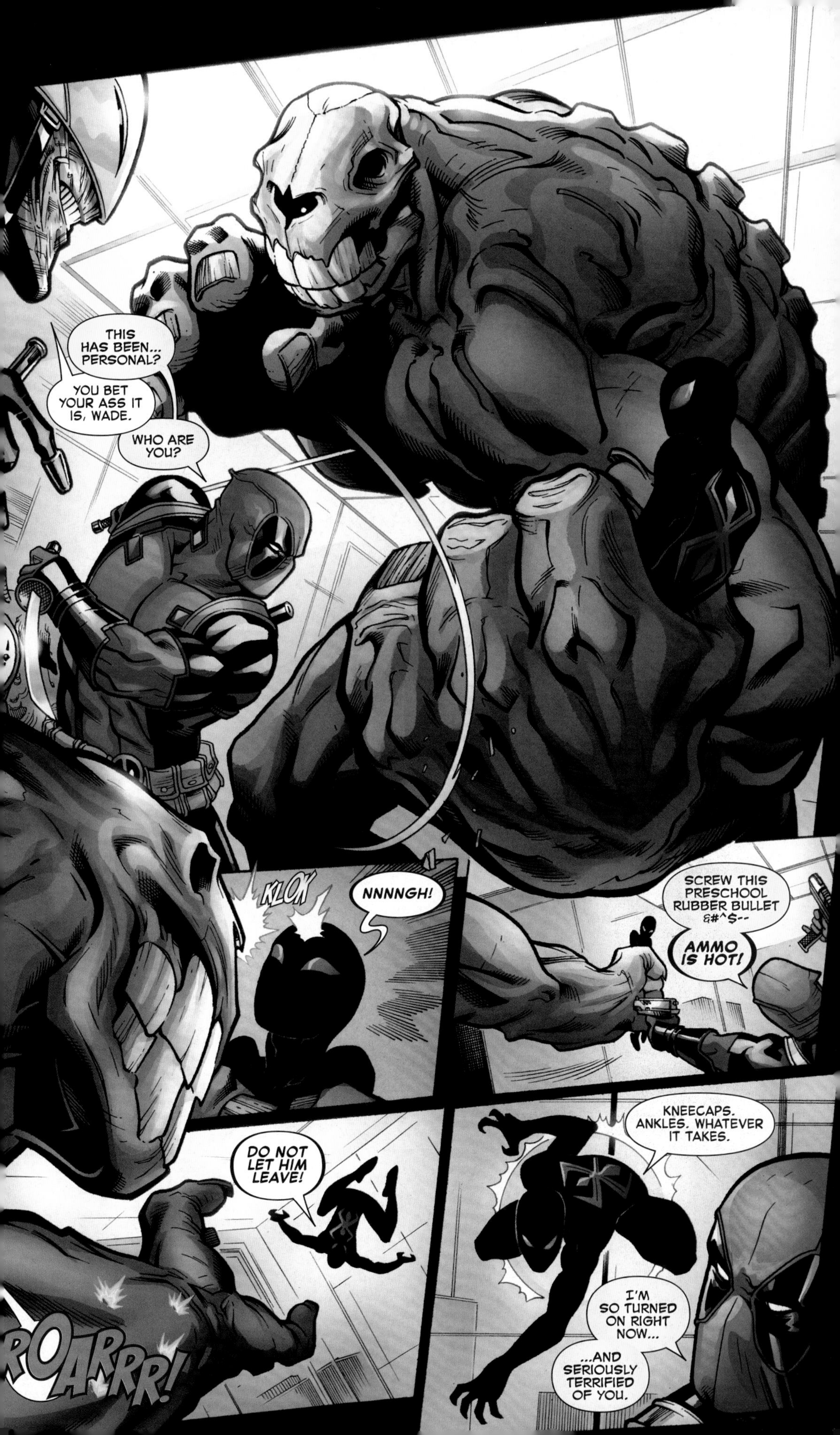
THIS HAS BEEN... PERSONAL?
YOU BET YOUR ASS IT IS, WADE.
WHO ARE YOU?
KLOK
NNNNGH!
SCREW THIS PRESCHOOL RUBBER BULLET &#^$--
AMMO IS HOT!
DO NOT LET HIM LEAVE!
ROARRR!
KNEECAPS. ANKLES. WHATEVER IT TAKES.
I'M SO TURNED ON RIGHT NOW...
...AND SERIOUSLY TERRIFIED OF YOU.

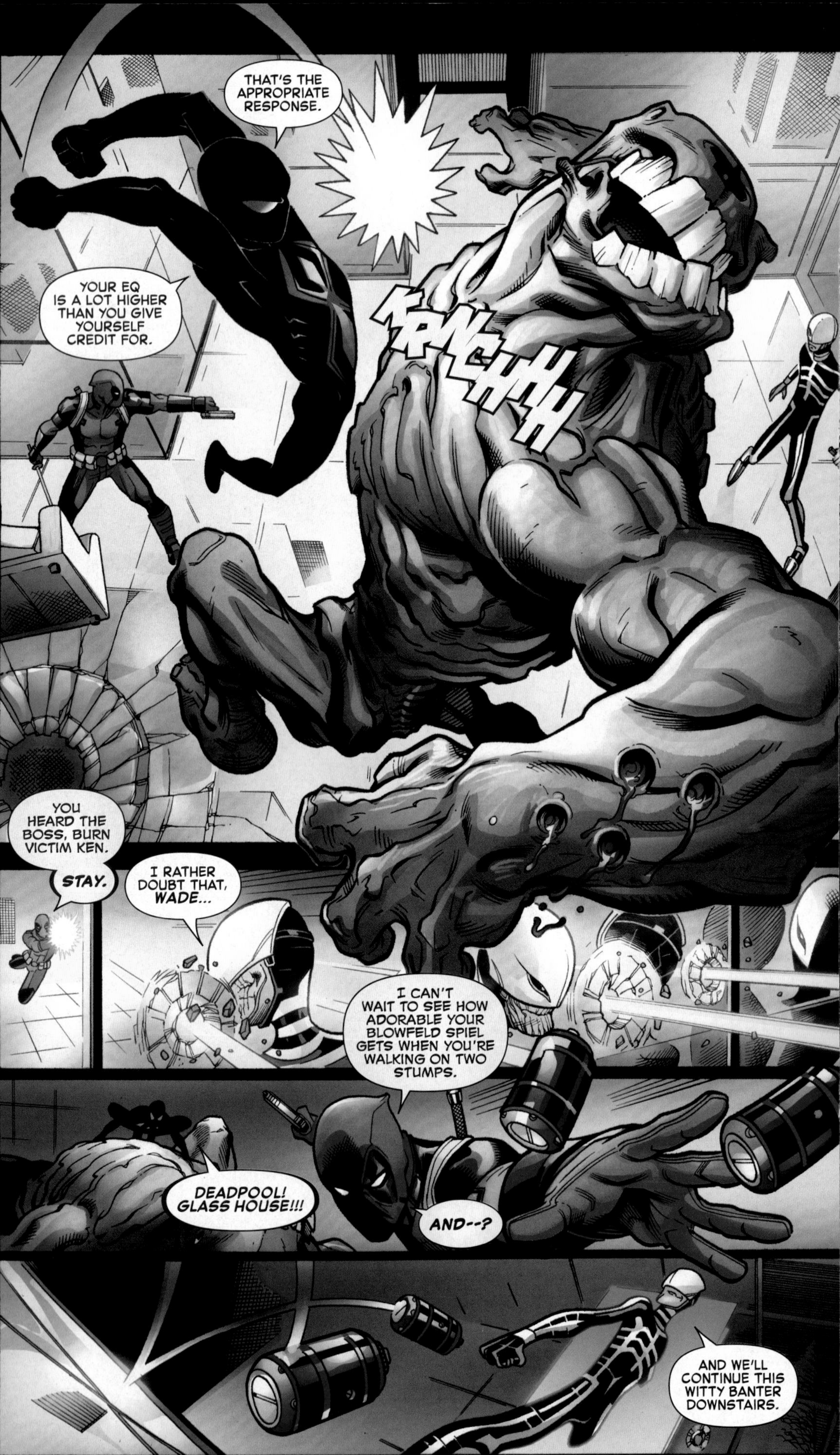

THAT'S THE APPROPRIATE RESPONSE.
YOUR EQ IS A LOT HIGHER THAN YOU GIVE YOURSELF CREDIT FOR.
KRNCHHH
YOU HEARD THE BOSS, BURN VICTIM KEN.
STAY.
I RATHER DOUBT THAT, WADE...
I CAN'T WAIT TO SEE HOW ADORABLE YOUR BLOWFELD SPIEL GETS WHEN YOU'RE WALKING ON TWO STUMPS.
DEADPOOL! GLASS HOUSE!!!
AND--?
AND WE'LL CONTINUE THIS WITTY BANTER DOWNSTAIRS.

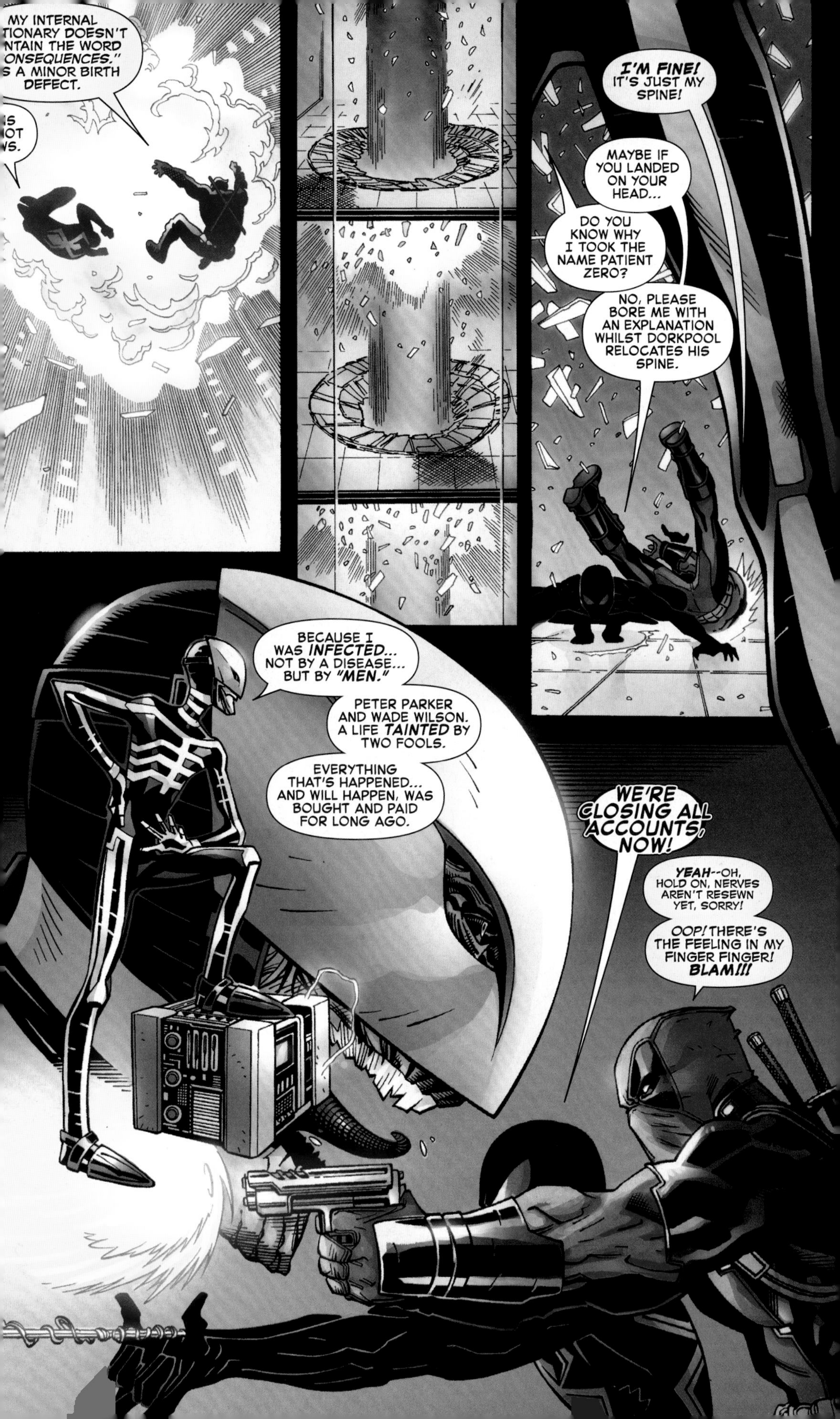

MY INTERNAL
TIONARY DOESN'T
NTAIN THE WORD
ONSEQUENCES."
S A MINOR BIRTH
DEFECT.
I'M FINE! IT'S JUST MY SPINE!
MAYBE IF YOU LANDED ON YOUR HEAD...
DO YOU KNOW WHY I TOOK THE NAME PATIENT ZERO?
NO, PLEASE BORE ME WITH AN EXPLANATION WHILST DORKPOOL RELOCATES HIS SPINE.
BECAUSE I WAS INFECTED... NOT BY A DISEASE... BUT BY "MEN."
PETER PARKER AND WADE WILSON. A LIFE TAINTED BY TWO FOOLS.
EVERYTHING THAT'S HAPPENED... AND WILL HAPPEN, WAS BOUGHT AND PAID FOR LONG AGO.
WE'RE CLOSING ALL ACCOUNTS, NOW!
YEAH--OH, HOLD ON, NERVES AREN'T RESEWN YET, SORRY!
OOP! THERE'S THE FEELING IN MY FINGER FINGER! BLAM!!!

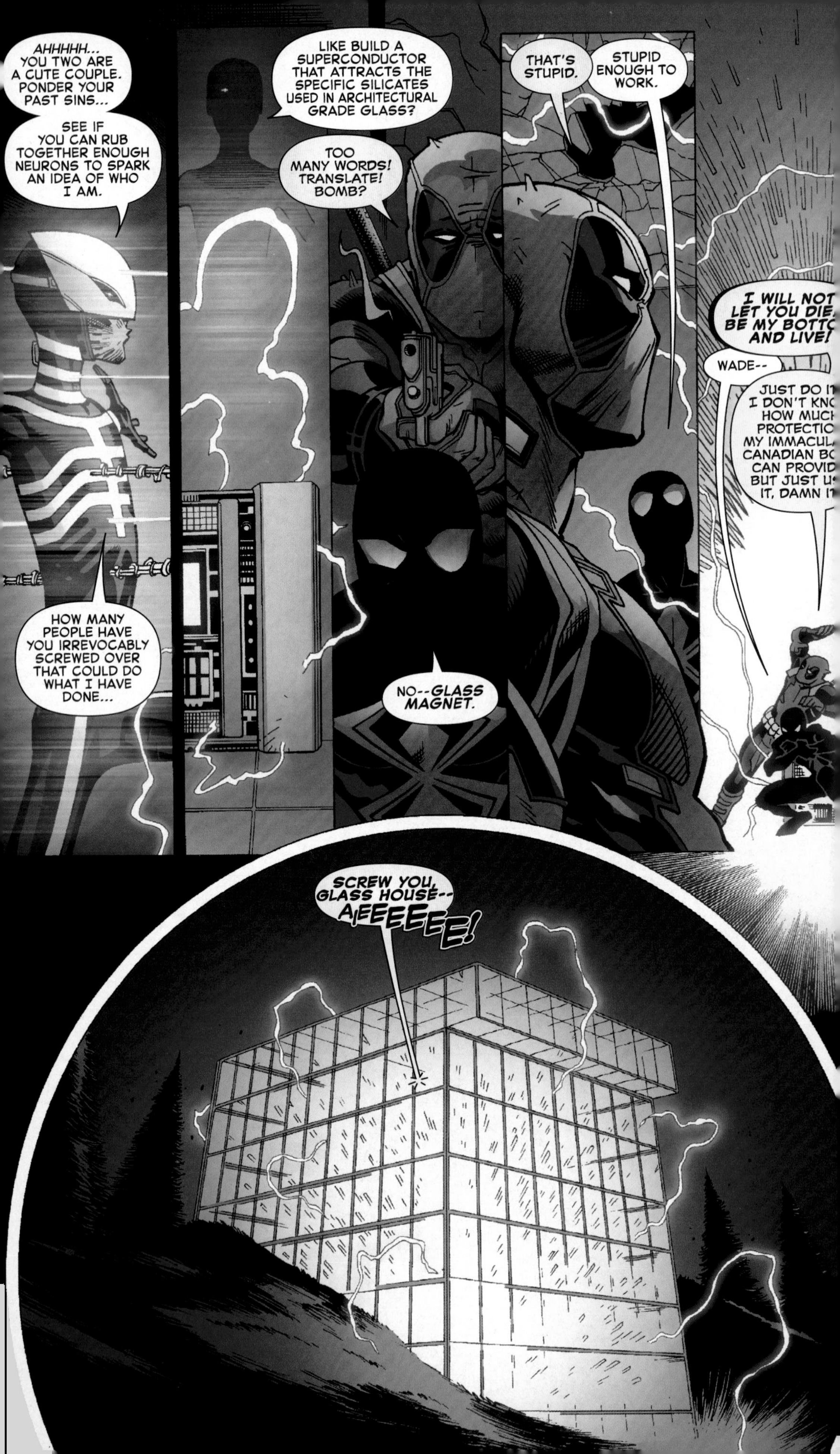

AHHHHH... YOU TWO ARE A CUTE COUPLE. PONDER YOUR PAST SINS...
SEE IF YOU CAN RUB TOGETHER ENOUGH NEURONS TO SPARK AN IDEA OF WHO I AM.
HOW MANY PEOPLE HAVE YOU IRREVOCABLY SCREWED OVER THAT COULD DO WHAT I HAVE DONE...
LIKE BUILD A SUPERCONDUCTOR THAT ATTRACTS THE SPECIFIC SILICATES USED IN ARCHITECTURAL GRADE GLASS?
TOO MANY WORDS! TRANSLATE! BOMB?
NO--GLASS MAGNET.
THAT'S STUPID.
STUPID ENOUGH TO WORK.
WADE--
SCREW YOU, GLASS HOUSE-- AEEEEEE!

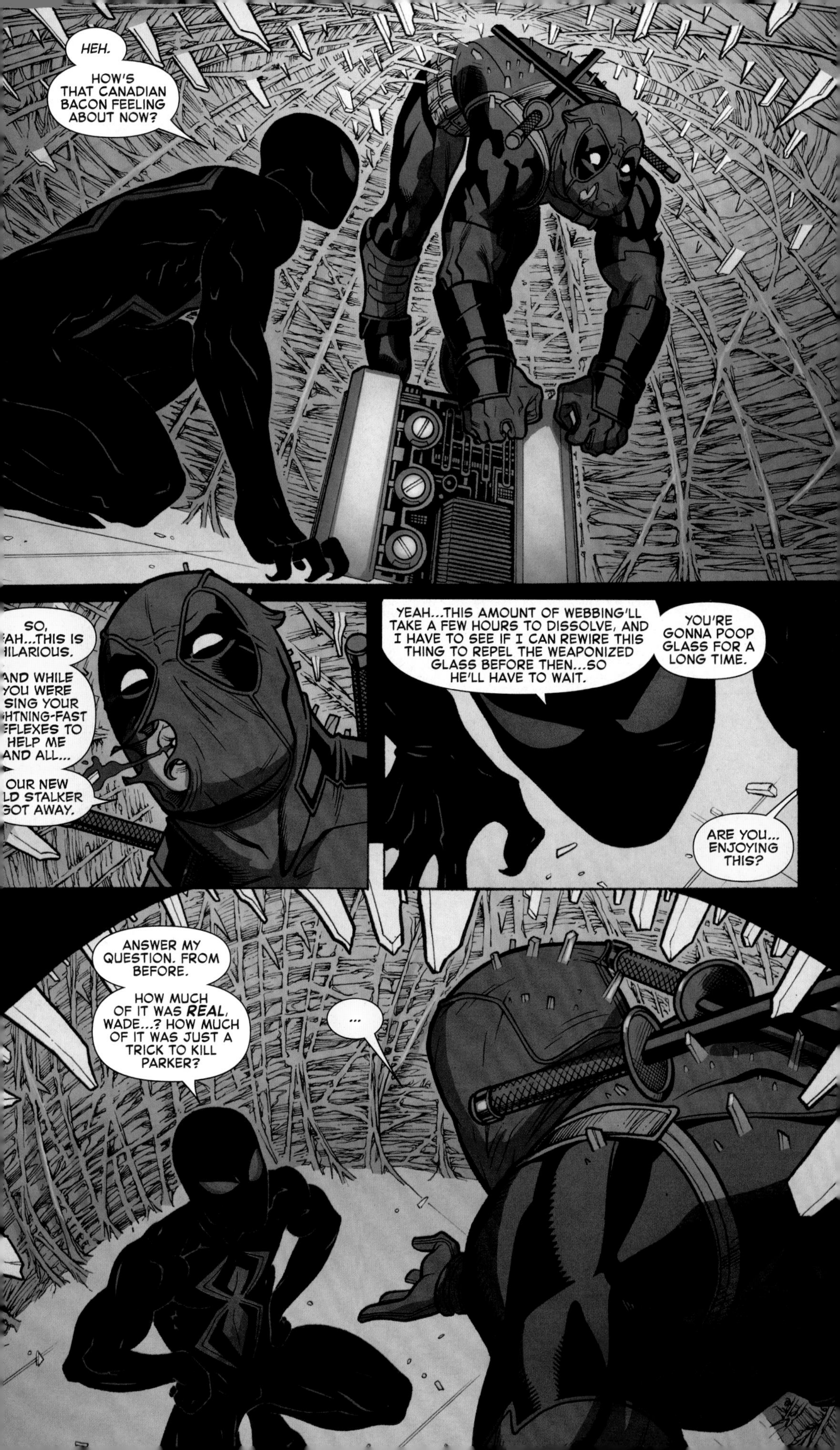
HEH.
HOW'S THAT CANADIAN BACON FEELING ABOUT NOW?
SO, EAH...THIS IS HILARIOUS.
AND WHILE YOU WERE SING YOUR GHTNING-FAST EFLEXES TO HELP ME AND ALL...
OUR NEW LD STALKER GOT AWAY.
YEAH...THIS AMOUNT OF WEBBING'LL TAKE A FEW HOURS TO DISSOLVE, AND I HAVE TO SEE IF I CAN REWIRE THIS THING TO REPEL THE WEAPONIZED GLASS BEFORE THEN...SO HE'LL HAVE TO WAIT.
YOU'RE GONNA POOP GLASS FOR A LONG TIME.
ARE YOU... ENJOYING THIS?
ANSWER MY QUESTION. FROM BEFORE.
HOW MUCH OF IT WAS *REAL*, WADE...? HOW MUCH OF IT WAS JUST A TRICK TO KILL PARKER?
...

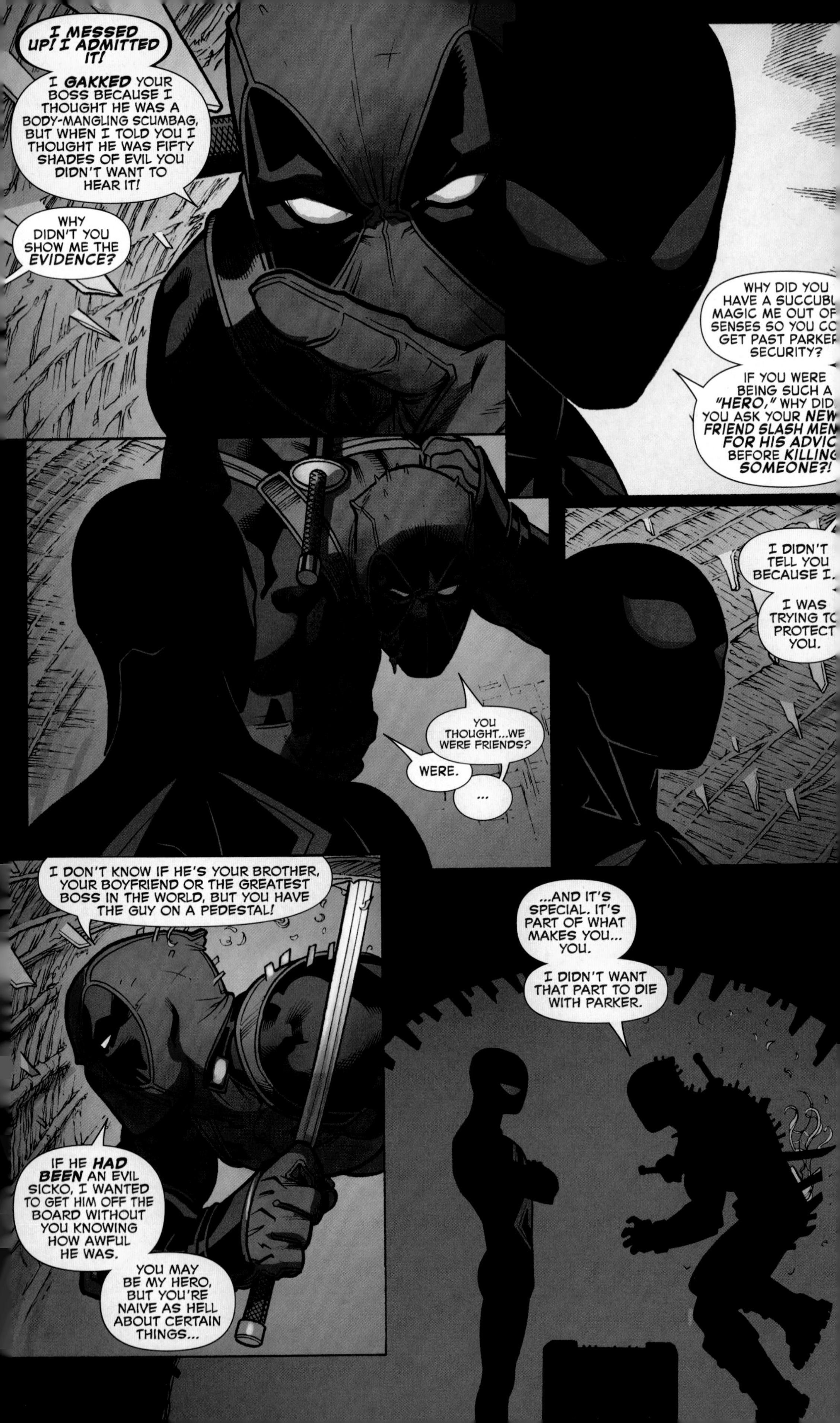
I MESSED UP! I ADMITTED IT!
I GAKKED YOUR BOSS BECAUSE I THOUGHT HE WAS A BODY-MANGLING SCUMBAG, BUT WHEN I TOLD YOU I THOUGHT HE WAS FIFTY SHADES OF EVIL YOU DIDN'T WANT TO HEAR IT!
WHY DIDN'T YOU SHOW ME THE EVIDENCE?
WHY DID YOU HAVE A SUCCUBI MAGIC ME OUT OF SENSES SO YOU CO GET PAST PARKER SECURITY?
IF YOU WERE BEING SUCH A "HERO," WHY DID YOU ASK YOUR NEW FRIEND SLASH MEN FOR HIS ADVIC BEFORE KILLING SOMEONE?!
I DIDN'T TELL YOU BECAUSE I...
I WAS TRYING TO PROTECT YOU.
YOU THOUGHT...WE WERE FRIENDS?
WERE.
...
I DON'T KNOW IF HE'S YOUR BROTHER, YOUR BOYFRIEND OR THE GREATEST BOSS IN THE WORLD, BUT YOU HAVE THE GUY ON A PEDESTAL!
IF HE HAD BEEN AN EVIL SICKO, I WANTED TO GET HIM OFF THE BOARD WITHOUT YOU KNOWING HOW AWFUL HE WAS.
YOU MAY BE MY HERO, BUT YOU'RE NAIVE AS HELL ABOUT CERTAIN THINGS...
...AND IT'S SPECIAL. IT'S PART OF WHAT MAKES YOU... YOU.
I DIDN'T WANT THAT PART TO DIE WITH PARKER.

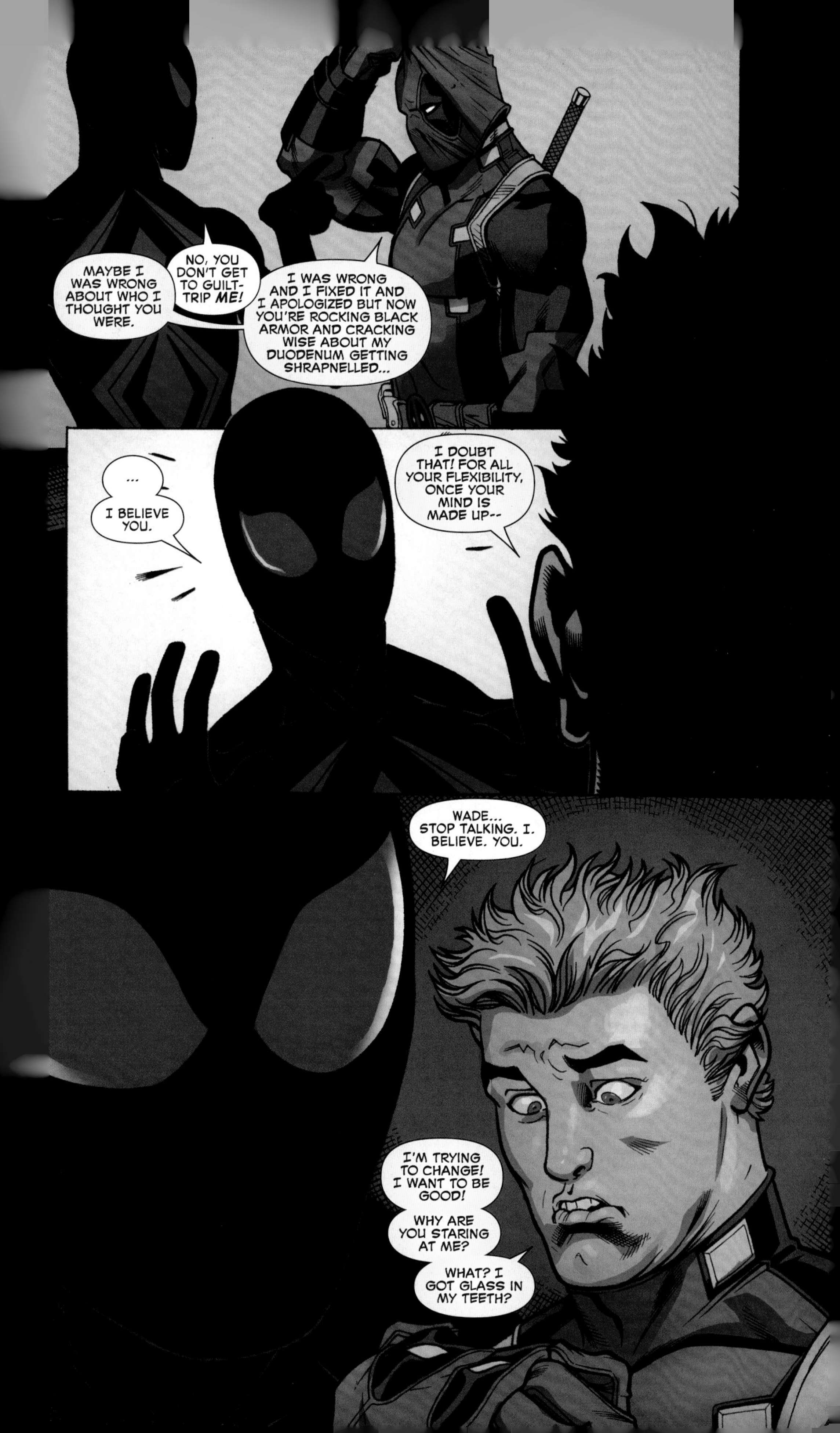
MAYBE I WAS WRONG ABOUT WHO I THOUGHT YOU WERE.
NO, YOU DON'T GET TO GUILT-TRIP ME!
I WAS WRONG AND I FIXED IT AND I APOLOGIZED BUT NOW YOU'RE ROCKING BLACK ARMOR AND CRACKING WISE ABOUT MY DUODENUM GETTING SHRAPNELLED...
...
I BELIEVE YOU.
I DOUBT THAT! FOR ALL YOUR FLEXIBILITY, ONCE YOUR MIND IS MADE UP--
WADE... STOP TALKING. I. BELIEVE. YOU.
I'M TRYING TO CHANGE! I WANT TO BE GOOD!
WHY ARE YOU STARING AT ME?
WHAT? I GOT GLASS IN MY TEETH?

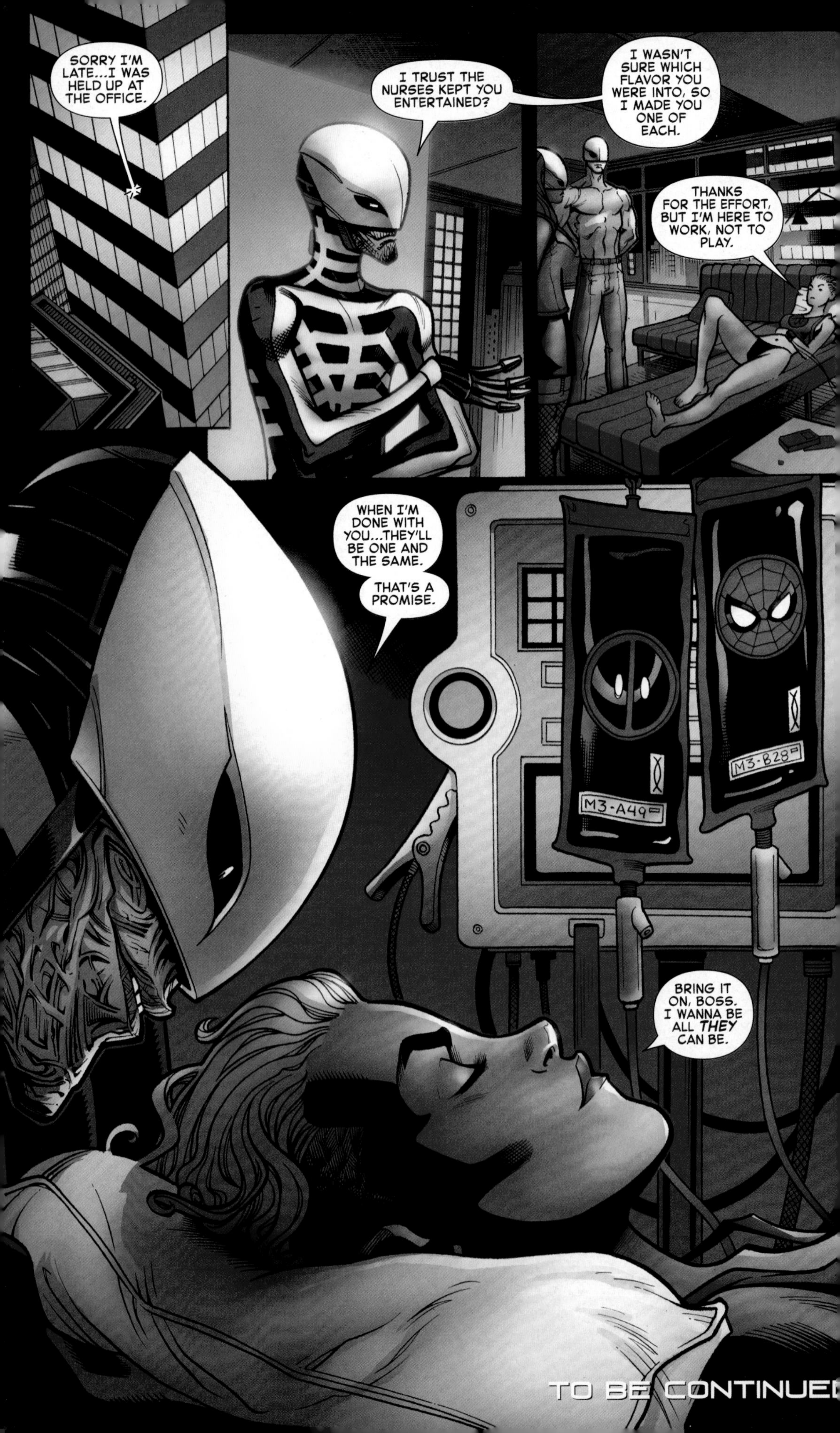

SORRY I'M LATE...I WAS HELD UP AT THE OFFICE.
I TRUST THE NURSES KEPT YOU ENTERTAINED?
I WASN'T SURE WHICH FLAVOR YOU WERE INTO, SO I MADE YOU ONE OF EACH.
THANKS FOR THE EFFORT, BUT I'M HERE TO WORK, NOT TO PLAY.
WHEN I'M DONE WITH YOU...THEY'LL BE ONE AND THE SAME.
THAT'S A PROMISE.
M3-A49
M3-B28
BRING IT ON, BOSS. I WANNA BE ALL *THEY* CAN BE.
TO BE CONTINUED

MC SPIDER
&
D-POOL
PAID & FULL

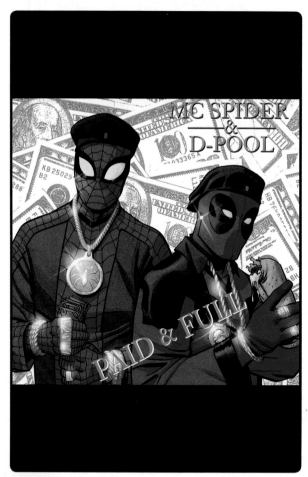

1 HIP-HOP VARIANT BY
DAVE JOHNSON

HOW DID THIS HAPPEN?
OHH! MINT CONDTION!
SUPER POSEABLE
DEADPOOL
LEGENDS
SPIDER-MAN

1 TOY VARIANT BY
ALEX KROPINAK

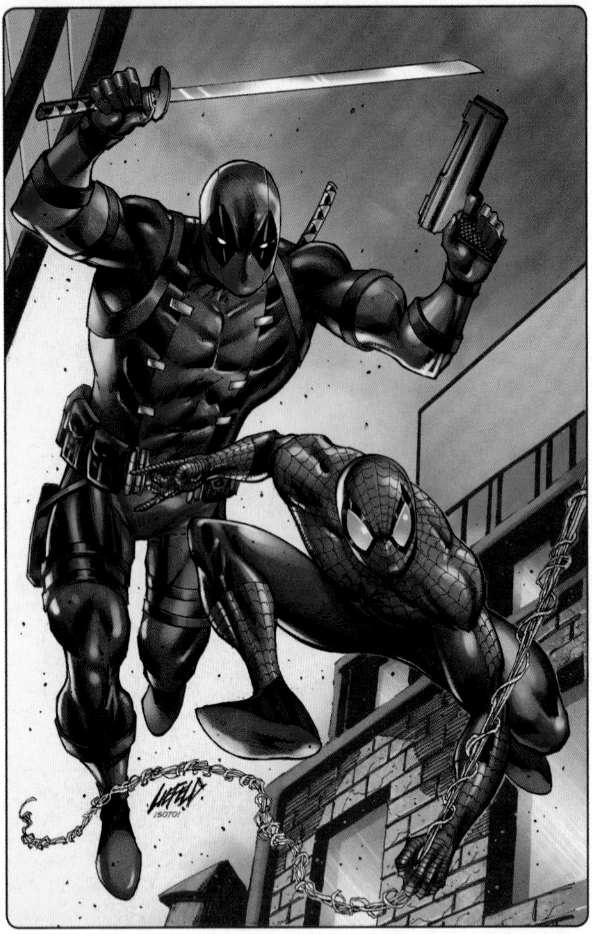

1 VARIANT BY
ROB LIEFELD & CHRIS SOTOMAYOR

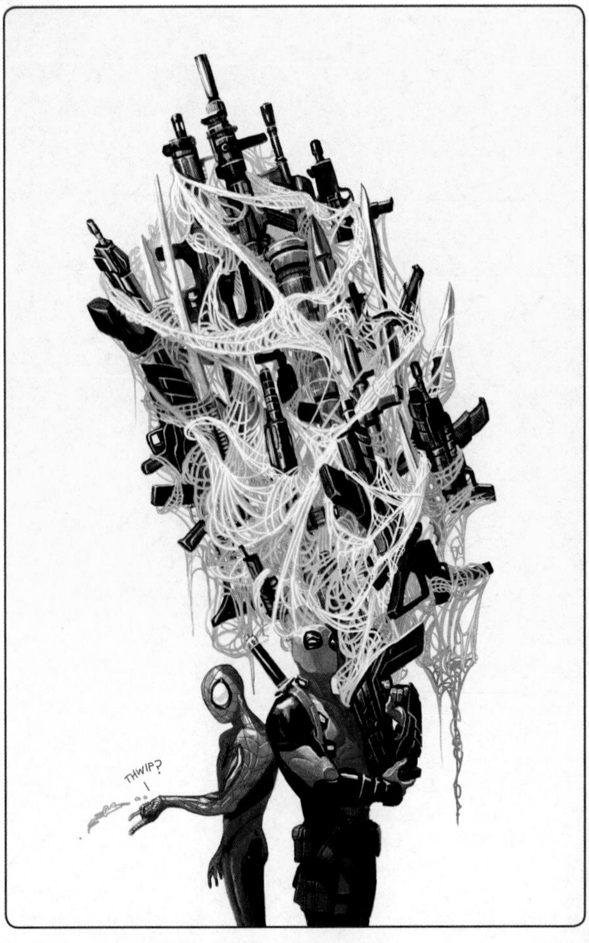
THWIP?

1 VARIANT BY
MIKE DEL MUNDO

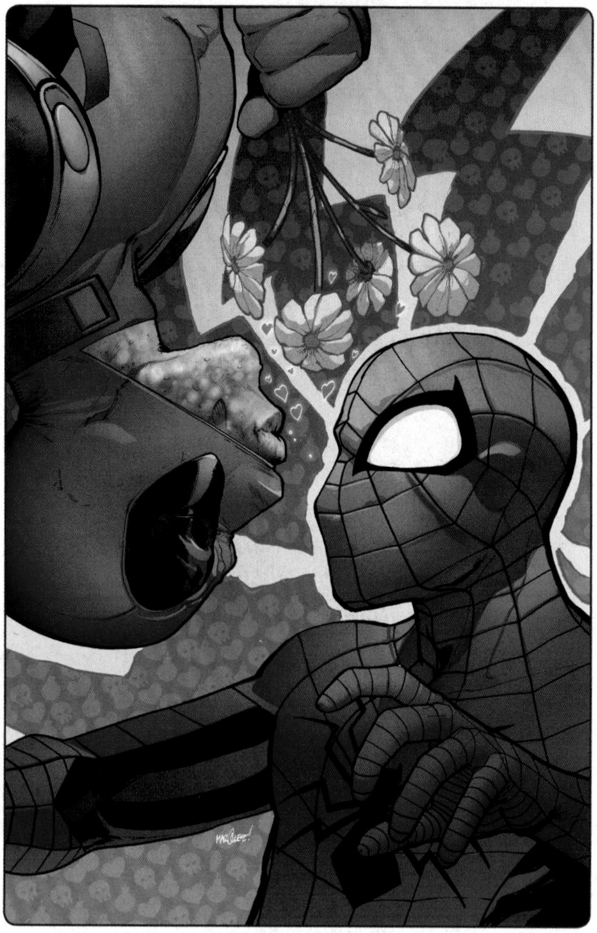

2 VARIANT BY
DAVID MARQUEZ & MARTE GRACIA

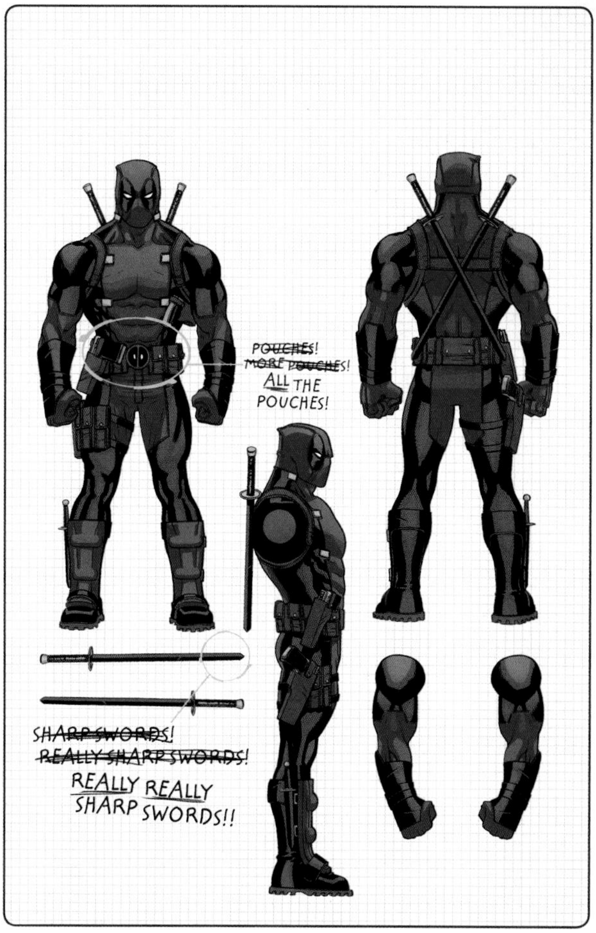
POUCHES!
MORE POUCHES!
ALL THE
POUCHES!
SHARP SWORDS!
REALLY SHARP SWORDS!
REALLY REALLY
SHARP SWORDS!!

2 DESIGN VARIANT BY
ED McGUINNESS & ANDREW CROSSLEY

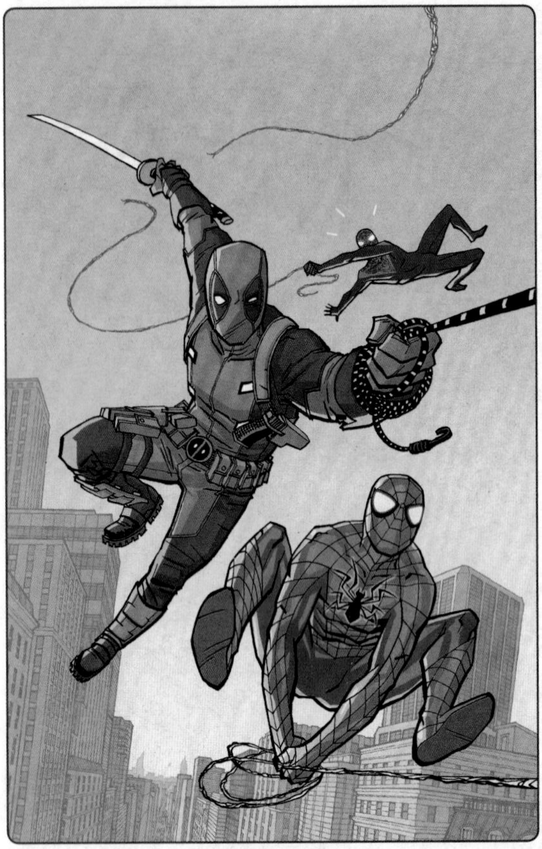

3 VARIANT BY
CLIFF CHIANG

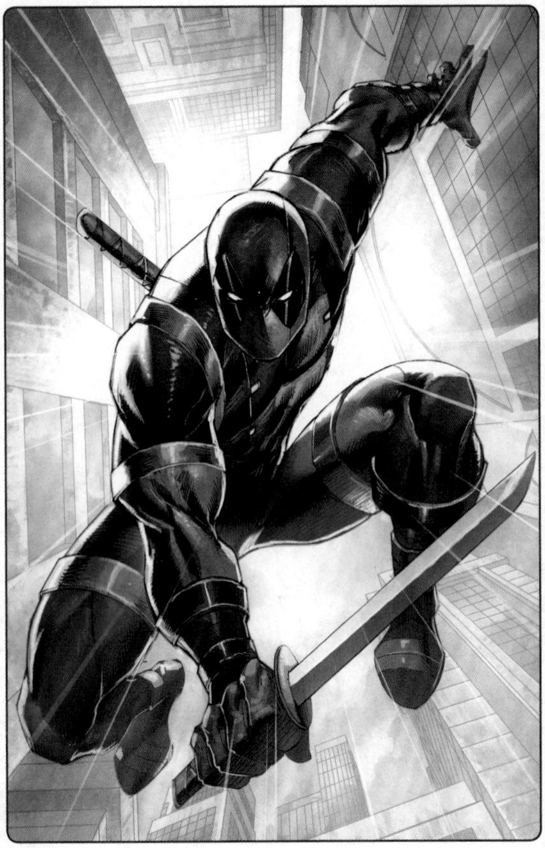

3 VARIANT BY
ROB LIEFELD

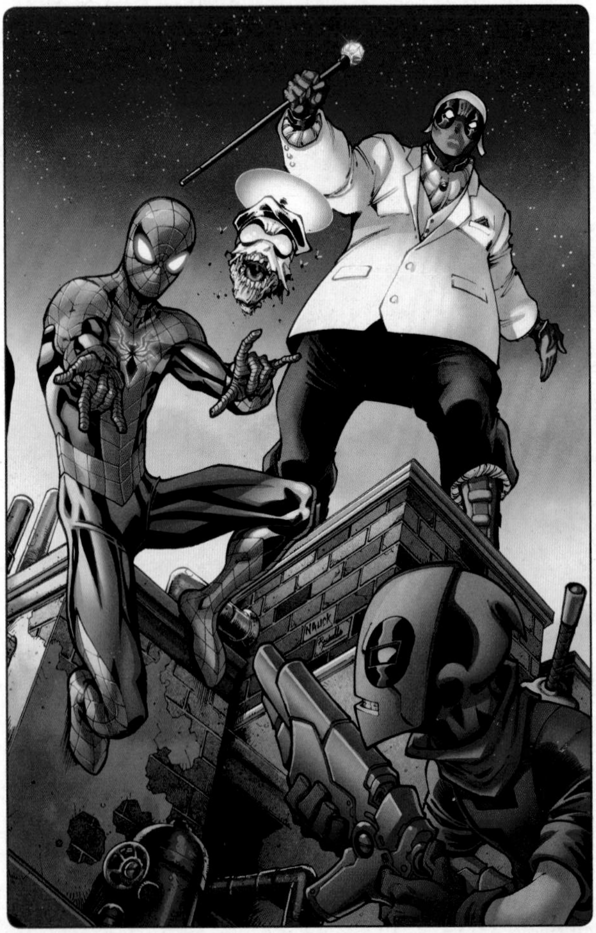

5 VARIANT BY
TODD NAUCK & RACHELLE ROSENBERG